Black Flag over Dixie

Edited by Gregory J. W. Urwin

BLACK FLAG
OVER DIXIE

Racial Atrocities and
Reprisals in the Civil War

Southern Illinois University Press

Carbondale

Library of Congress Cataloging-in-Publication Data
Black flag over Dixie : racial atrocities and reprisals in the Civil War /
edited by Gregory J. W. Urwin.
p. cm.
Includes bibliographic references and index.
1. United States—History—Civil War, 1861–1865—Participation, African American.
2. United States—History—Civil War, 1861–1865—Atrocities.
3. United States—Race relations.
4. African American soldiers—Crimes against—Southern States—History—19th century.
5. Racism—Southern States—History—19th century.
6. Massacres—Southern States—History—19th century.
7. Reprisals—History—19th century.
8. Southern States—Race relations. I. Urwin, Gregory J. W., 1955–
E540.N3 B595 2003
973.7'3—dc21
ISBN 0-8093-2546-2 (cloth : alk. paper)   2003010383
ISBN 0-8093-2678-7 (pbk. : alk. paper)

To Ronnie A. Nichols, my first sergeant in the reactivated 54th Massachusetts Volunteer Infantry, and to Boo Hodges, Mark Dolive, Phil Sample, Nathan Waggoner, and all my old "pards" in the Frontier Brigade

There are bonds of all sorts in this world of ours,
Fetters of friendship, and ties of flowers,
And true lover's knots I wean,
The boy and the girl are bound by a kiss,
But there's never a bond, old friend, like this,
We have drunk from the same canteen.
                    —Miles O'Reilly (Charles G. Halpine, 1829–1868),
                              "We've Drunk from the Same Canteen"

Contents

     Racial Atrocities and Reprisals in Civil War Arkansas / 132
            Gregory J. W. Urwin

8.   MASSACRE AT PLYMOUTH
     April 20, 1864 / 153
            Weymouth T. Jordan Jr. and Gerald W. Thomas

9.   THE BATTLE OF THE CRATER
     The Civil War's Worst Massacre / 203
            Bryce A. Suderow

10. SYMBOLS OF FREEDOM AND DEFEAT
     African American Soldiers, White Southerners, and the
     Christmas Insurrection Scare of 1865 / 210
            Chad L. Williams

11. "A VERY LONG SHADOW"
     Race, Atrocity, and the American Civil War / 231
            Mark Grimsley

     Select Bibliography / 247
     Contributors / 251
     Index / 253

Illustrations

Preface

This book traces its origins to the research I have done for nearly a decade on the Civil War west of the Mississippi River. The experiences of African American troops in Arkansas, Kansas, and Indian Territory represent some of the more dramatic and tragic episodes in the Civil War. It is time for historians to bring those stories out of the shadows and accord them the prominence they deserve in understanding the conflict that profoundly shaped modern America.

I received the inspiration and encouragement necessary to bring this project to fruition after I joined the history department at Temple University and became an associate director of Temple's Center for the Study of Force and Diplomacy (CENFAD). Over the past two years, the historians and political scientists associated with CENFAD have launched an exciting new initiative to define guidelines and processes that might help reduce the cost of war. Discussions regarding civilian immunity and casualty aversion have stimulated my thinking about the role race has played in making American wars more barbaric. I hope this book and the essays it contains will contribute to that dialogue. Whether they do or not, I am confident that the efforts of CENFAD will stimulate a broad reexamination of the ethics of modern warfare.

Black Flag over Dixie would have remained nothing more than a promising idea without the assistance of two of my superiors at Temple University. Morris J. Vogel, the former acting dean of the College of Liberal Arts, and Richard H. Immerman, the director of CENFAD and chair of Temple's history department, provided essential moral and material support when I needed it most. I am also indebted to Russell F. Weigley, Wilbert Jenkins, and graduate student Craig Stutman, three Temple colleagues who specialize in Civil War studies, for their feedback and encouragement. In addition, I wish to thank Mark Mattson, the director of Temple's Cartographic Laboratory, and graduate student Michelle A. Schmitt for the book's lovely map.

Other historians have contributed to this collection by deepening my understanding of African American troops during the Civil War. I would like to recognize the following: Dudley Taylor Cornish, formerly of Pittsburg

State University; Daniel E. Sutherland, University of Arkansas; Carl H. Moneyhon, University of Arkansas at Little Rock; William L. Shea, University of Arkansas at Monticello; Anne J. Bailey, Georgia College & State University; John T. Hubbell, formerly the director of Kent State University Press and editor of *Civil War History;* Arnold Schofield, Fort Scott National Historic Site; Ronnie A. Nichols, formerly the director of the Old State House Museum and now an independent scholar; Mark K. Christ, Arkansas Historic Preservation Project; and Frank Arey, Department of Arkansas Heritage.

Some of my deepest thanks must go to the technicians at the Instructional Support Center in Temple University's Gladfelter Hall. Without their assistance, I would have never learned how to scan the previously published articles that make up the bulk of this volume. Finally, I wish to thank the publishers of *Civil War History, Louisiana History, North Carolina Historical Review,* and *Southern Historian: A Journal of Southern History* for permission to reprint eight essays that appeared originally in their pages.

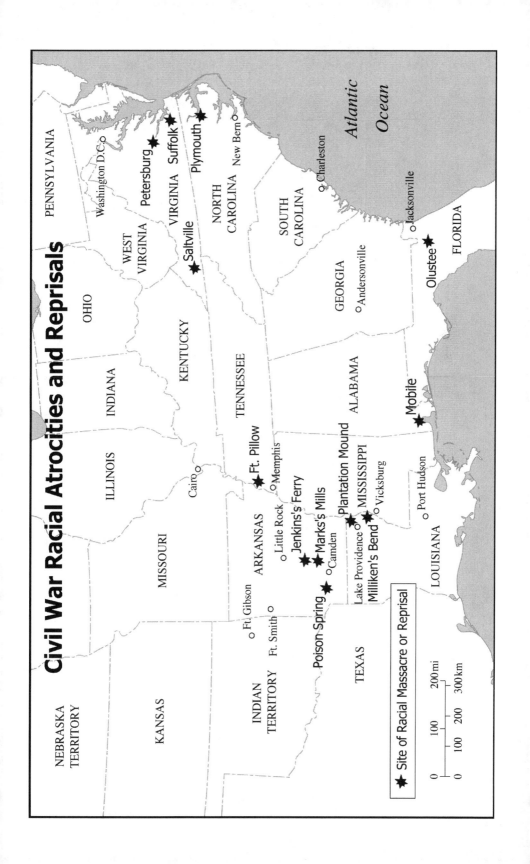

Civil War Racial Atrocities and Reprisals

★ Site of Racial Massacre or Reprisal

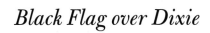

Black Flag over Dixie

Introduction
Warfare, Race, and the Civil War in American Memory

GREGORY J. W. URWIN

The Civil War ended more than 135 years ago, but it continues to tower above all competition as the most popular period in American history. It seems strange that anything as terrible and inhuman as a war can be described as popular—especially the conflict that destroyed more American lives and property than any other—but such is the case. In the last decade and a half, the mass media received two jarring reminders that public interest in the subject, which supposedly cooled after the centennial observances in the 1960s, pulsed stronger than ever. In 1988, James M. McPherson published *Battle Cry of Freedom,* a scholarly survey of the conflict that became a major best-seller. Two years later, filmmaker Ken Burns broke viewing records for the Public Broadcasting System with his eleven-hour documentary *The Civil War.*[1]

PBS and cable television networks have attempted to duplicate Ken Burns's success by producing dozens of Civil War documentaries. A musical titled *The Civil War* managed to make it to Broadway, and Hollywood has turned out an increasing number of feature films and miniseries devoted to the subject. For those Americans who still enjoy reading, the Civil War has never been more accessible. Commercial and university presses spew out a veritable mountain of Civil War books every year. Newsstands carry at least four glossy magazines catering to Civil War buffs. Several tour companies specialize in transporting enthusiasts to their favorite battlefields. Thanks to computer software companies, latter-day Lees and Grants can refight First and Second Bull Run, Shiloh, Antietam, Murfreesboro, Gettysburg, and Chickamauga without leaving the comfort of home.

The Civil War community draws much of its resilience from organization and camaraderie. Most serious buffs belong to Civil War round tables, a network of localized groups that meet monthly to hear presentations on their favorite subject. An estimated forty thousand fans desiring deeper immersion in the period have joined reenactment units. Lineal descendants of Civil

War soldiers are eligible for membership in such heritage organizations as the Sons of Union Veterans, Sons of Confederate Veterans, and United Daughters of the Confederacy. There are even historic preservation societies that raise funds to save battlefields and period structures from the ravages of modern development.

Two decades after the poet Walt Whitman nursed sick and wounded soldiers at a Union hospital in Washington, D.C., he wrote, "Future years will never know the seething hell ... of the Secession War; and it is best they should not—the real war will never get in the books."[2] Despite all the ink that has been spilled over the Civil War, Whitman is still right. This judgment is not intended as an indictment of Civil War scholarship. Unfortunately, much of the best work in the field goes unread by the greater portion of the Civil War community. This applies most of all to publications focusing on race— the war's central cause and the most convulsive issue to confront Americans as they patched together a sectional peace during Reconstruction.

Some may attribute the Civil War community's selective memory to the fact that military history enjoys wider appeal than social history, but that is just part of the story. This particular case of collective amnesia was deliberately nurtured by the men who lost the war as they schemed to cheat their black neighbors of the fruits of emancipation and Radical Reconstruction. "Civil War memory," explained historian Barbara A. Gannon,

> was crucial to Southerners' battle to ensure Northern acquiescence to their answer to the race question—black oppression. Propagandists of the "Lost Cause" wanted Northerners to remember a Civil War that had nothing to do with emancipation and the social and political rights of African Americans. The "War Between the States," the rubric of Southern apologists for this conflict, was waged by gallant white soldiers, all Americans who fought for their beliefs as African Americans stood idly by as "faithful slaves" uninterested in fighting for freedom and unable to appreciate political and civil equality.[3]

From the Gilded Age into the first half of the twentieth century, the United Confederate Veterans and their heirs in the Sons of Confederate Veterans (SCV) and United Daughters of the Confederacy (UDC) lobbied to ensure that only pro-Confederate history was taught in Southern schools. Educators who did not justify secession or who dared suggest that slavery had something to do with the Civil War ran the risk of censure, ostracism, and even termination. The UDC has abandoned such bullying for more genteel forms of ancestor worship, but the SCV continues to rail at the educational establishment. In 1984, Lynn J. Shaw, the SCV's "Commander-in-Chief," warned his compatriots about the "turncoats among us," including advocates of "minorityism, liberalism and anti-traditionalism" and "the son home from school, convinced he has found the 'truth' with the zeal to teach the family how wrong it has been all along."[4]

The SCV is no longer a dominant arbiter of Southern culture, but that does not prevent it from trying to impose its historical interpretations on others. During the fifteen years that I taught at the University of Central Arkansas, I drew the SCV's fire because my publications and classroom lectures did not satisfy neo-Confederate norms. Early in 1988, I published a guest editorial in the *Arkansas Gazette* advocating the erection of monuments honoring the black Southerners who fought for the Union. Within days, I received a letter from one of Lynn Shaw's successors as SCV commander-in-chief. Condemning my views, that gentleman declared, "You have betrayed your profession as a historian." He also charged that my discussing black involvement in the Civil War would "further racial division."[5]

The SCV's dissatisfaction escalated in 1993 after I persuaded the Arkansas Department of Parks and Tourism to change a roadside exhibit at Poison Springs Battlefield State Park because it justified the massacre of black Union troops. Over the next six years, my hate-mail folder grew fatter, and my superiors at the University of Central Arkansas received repeated demands that my professional conduct be investigated or that I be fired. Although one dean let himself be intimidated, UCA's senior administrators refused to compromise my academic freedom. The SCV got off its final salvo at me in late 1998, shortly before I left Arkansas to assume my current post at Temple University. I learned that I had been cited as a "heritage violator" by the SCV's official journal, *Confederate Veteran:* "Joe Miller of Arkansas reported that the Poison Springs Battlefield markers have been changed to be more anti-Confederate, and that the change was led by Dr. Gregory Urwin of the University of Central Arkansas, a Union re-enactor."[6]

After my move to Pennsylvania, I was surprised to discover that the desire for race-free Civil War history permeates the North almost as strongly as it does the South. The Civil War community prefers a sanitized picture of the most wrenching experience in American history. A vicious and bloody conflict is now fondly remembered as an ennobling experience. Combatants on both sides are depicted as self-sacrificing heroes who slaughtered each other in record numbers in the name of vague abstractions, such as states' rights. It was a brothers' war, devotees insist, as if the spectacle of kin killing kin and friend killing friend should make Americans proud. When the guns finally fell silent, the familiar story goes, no one held any grudges, and

America emerged from the fiery trial stronger and purer, with its white population united as one people. It all makes for a comforting national myth, one
consistent with the tenets of American exceptionalism.[7]

As historian David W. Blight put it:

> For Americans broadly, the Civil War has been a defining event upon which we have
> often imposed unity and continuity; as a culture, we have often preferred its music
> and pathos to its enduring challenges, the theme of reconciled conflict to resurgent,
> unresolved legacies. The greatest enthusiasts for Civil War history and memory often
> displace complicated consequences by endlessly focusing on the contest itself. We
> sometimes lift ourselves out of historical time, above the details, and render the war
> safe in a kind of national Passover offering as we view a photograph of the Blue and
> Gray veterans shaking hands across the stone walls at Gettysburg.[8]

Many of the middle-class white males who populate Civil War round
tables and reenactment groups prefer their history without African Americans in it. From personal observation, I would not accuse these people of
overt racism. In many ways, they are merely following the example set by the
conflict's veterans, whose growing fondness for reliving the adventures and
hardships of their youth turned them into America's first Civil War buffs.
One reason why Confederate veterans succeeded in establishing the myth
that they fought solely for Southern independence and not white supremacy
was that Union veterans decided that sectional reconciliation took prece-
dence over racial justice. The aging boys in blue celebrated their war as a
crusade to save the Union and ignored the fact that it also destroyed slavery.[9]

For most of today's buffs, the Civil War serves as escapist entertainment.
Acknowledging past racial problems reminds them of current squabbles, and
that strips the Civil War of its fun. Unfortunately, that also strips the Civil
War of its most valuable lessons—lessons that may well contain answers to
at least some of the questions that divide white and black Americans today.

This book attempts to highlight the central role that race played in the
Civil War by examining some of the most ugly incidents that stained its
battlefields. This knowledge, however unpleasant, is essential to understanding the nature of that conflict. As William W. Freehling, Singletary Professor of the Humanities at the University of Kentucky, recently put it, "In this
war, not two armies but two cultures confronted each other; and cultural
characteristics off the battlefield profoundly influenced the way blood was
spilled." Mark Grimsley of Ohio State University cut to the heart of the
matter when he observed, "Just as racism had helped to create the conflict,
it also played a part in shaping it."[10]

The essays that constitute this volume deal with a series of disturbing incidents, but the purpose here is something higher than mere sensationalism. These incidents are important because they reveal the values of the Confederacy and its people. Most serious Civil War historians agree that the War of Southern Independence was waged to preserve slavery. Apologists for the "Lost Cause" counter that the Confederacy did not stand for slavery, because the overwhelming majority of Rebel soldiers owned no slaves (which is tantamount to arguing that the Persian Gulf War of 1991 did not concern oil because most of the American soldiers engaged did not own gas stations). Neo-Confederates ignore the fact that numerous "Johnny Rebs" freely admitted they took up arms to keep blacks in bondage. On May 14, 1862, Capt. James C. Bates of the 9th Texas Cavalry wrote to his future wife from Corinth, Mississippi:

> I once thought that the mass of the northern people were ignorant of the true cause of this war. Ignorant of the fact that the subjugation of the South & the extinction of slavery was the prime object in view with Abe Lincoln & every other abolition leader in the north. But when so many public journals of the North boldly proclaim *the abolition of slavery* to be the object of this war, it is hard to believe that the most *credulous & stupid* even of the Northern masses could still be in ignorance. And if this be the motive for the war—and I have not a doubt of it, we can we *must* do nothing else but "conquer a peace" and teach *them* that we *have* no masters.[11]

Recognizing the Confederacy's attachment to slavery does not necessarily mean that Rebels were inhuman villains who took sadistic glee in keeping people of color in chains. John Singleton Mosby, the gifted Rebel guerrilla leader, frankly conceded, "The South went to war on account of Slavery." At the same time, he insisted, "People must be judged by the standard of their own age. If it was right to own slaves as property, it was right to fight for it.... A soldier fights for his country—right or wrong.... The South was my country."[12]

As the remarks of Bates and Mosby indicate, Confederates were typical Americans insofar as they resented outsiders telling them how to live. In addition to militant provincialism, however, Confederates found their motivation in the most dangerous of human emotions—fear.

Blacks were not the only Americans to pay a psychological price for slavery. Their masters and other Southern whites lived with a constant fear of slave revolt. The white South believed that people of African descent were inherently savage and had to remain enslaved to lead orderly and productive lives. Emancipation would allow them to turn on the master class, resulting in its extermination or theirs. When nonslaveholders resorted to force to defend slavery, they did not fight merely to preserve a socioeconomic system that benefited a privileged few. They believed they were fighting for self-preservation. In common with Captain Bates, they perceived the message of Northern abolitionists to be: "Let them (the Negroes) have their freedom if they can win it, *even though it be over the corpses of their masters and the ashes of their ruined homesteads.*"[13]

This mind-set explains why antebellum Southerners felt so threatened by the activities of the North's abolitionist minority. On October 25, 1856, the *Southern Shield,* a newspaper published in the Mississippi River cotton port of Helena, Arkansas, informed its readers: "We learn that there is great excitement in Union county, Arkansas, on account of the discovery of a plot among the Negroes to rise in rebellion. . . . Some of the Negroes say the rising was to take place the day of the Presidential election. The men all being from home that day, the plot was to murder the women and children first, and then attack the unarmed men at the polls." The newspaper concluded this chilling story with a caveat: "This all comes of the everlasting agitation of the slavery question by demagogues."[14]

For people schooled in such thinking, it was easy to construe the Emancipation Proclamation and the Lincoln administration's decision to raise black troops as deliberate calls for race war. "As strenuously and sternly as we have resisted all attempts to make this a black flag war [war of no quarter]," rumbled the *True Democrat* from Little Rock, Arkansas, "the enemy seems determined to drive us to it. They are organizing insurrections in South Carolina; they have sent a negro army into Florida; they are organizing black regiments in Tennessee . . . and now, they declare a war for extermination, not only of men, but of women and children."[15]

Certain that black Union soldiers were too barbarous to abide by the rules of civilized warfare, Confederates felt absolved of observing such rules themselves. Expecting to confront African savages among the Union hordes, many white Southerners—including educated and religious men—became savages themselves. As James Bates, now a major, informed his mother in September 1863: "Well, of Negroes and those who command them, we never have, and never will ask quarter. We have set a good many of them to stretching hemp & will take pleasure in 'setting up' in the same business all others we catch." In October 1864, Thomas Morris Chester, a black war correspondent for the *Philadelphia Press,* interviewed a newly released white officer who had been captured more than two months earlier in the Battle of the Crater at Petersburg, Virginia. "The Captain has witnessed the rebels bayoneting wounded colored troops begging piteously to be spared," Chester reported. "In the charge before Petersburg, the enemy rushed upon them with the cry of no quarter, and afterwards slaughtered the wounded without mercy. He saw a rebel officer place the muzzle of a pistol to the head of five dying negroes and blow their brains out." Maj. Matthew N. Love, a Confederate who fought at the Crater, corroborated Chester's account in a letter home: "Such Slaughter I have not witnessed upon any battle field any where Their men were principally Negroes and we shot them down untill we got near enough and then run them through with the Bayonet. . . . we was not very particular whether we captured or killed them the only thing we did not like to be pestered berrying the Heathens."[16]

Recent scholarship questions whether the Union army threw off all inhibitions and waged total war against the Confederate people. When it came to preserving the South's established social order, however, many Confederates acted with the same murderous ruthlessness that became all too common in the twentieth century's most horrible conflicts. Confederates not only targeted the United States Colored Troops (USCT) but also fugitive slaves of all ages and both sexes. Feeling betrayed by the runaways, Rebel troops assumed the role of wronged lovers and took their revenge. Any form of black resistance had to be crushed lest the contagion spread to the rest of the slave population. While the Union army's eventual embrace of "hard war" policies blurred the line between attacking enemy armies and enemy civilians, racial fear and the hatred it engendered compelled Confederate troops to cross that line. The Confederate denial of civilian immunity in matters of race control is an aspect of the Civil War that needs to be paid closer attention.[17]

The Civil War witnessed moments where white combatants treated each other with such savagery. The guerrilla conflict that raged in the hill country of the Border States and the Confederacy generated numerous massacres and summary executions. Union soldiers who strayed into the countryside to loot or burn Southern homes could expect little mercy if they fell into Rebel hands. During the famous March to the Sea and subsequent Union operations in the Carolinas, Rebel soldiers and guerrillas executed at least 173 Yankee "bummers." These lapses, however, occurred because combatants felt that their enemies had committed outrages that placed them beyond the protection of the rules of war. For the most part, white soldiers tended to grant quarter to surrendering or wounded white opponents.[18] Confederates denied black Union soldiers the same respect and consideration, not so much for any crimes they may have committed but for who they were and the social revolution that they represented. As a Virginia doctor blurted to a Union lieutenant a few months after the war's end, "We will not allow niggers to come among us and brag about having been in the yankee army. It is as much as we can do to tolerate it in white men."[19]

In a larger context, Confederate racial atrocities can be seen as part of the venerable American tradition of lynching. The public associates vigilante violence with the Wild West, but it was just as prevalent in more settled parts of the United States well into the twentieth century. In addition, American vigilantes targeted far more "uppity" blacks than bank robbers or cattle rustlers. "Vigilantism has had a special affinity for the persecution of minorities," wrote Linda Gordon, "including ideological dissenters but particularly often racially subordinated groups."[20]

Of course, Confederates have not been the only American fighting men to surrender to such madness. A combination of racism, atrocity, and retaliation prompted elements of the U.S. Army and Marine Corps to prosecute wars without mercy against American Indians, Filipino insurgents, Japanese military personnel, and the Vietcong. Allied veterans of World War II's Pacific Theater bitterly criticize Japan for its stubborn refusal to admit culpability for such war crimes as the Rape of Nanking, the Bataan Death March, and the Burma-Siam "Railroad of Death." Yet, when it comes to the Civil War, Americans are no more inclined to confront the dark side of their history than the Japanese.[21]

The one certain thing about atrocities is that they invite reprisals. Black Civil War soldiers considered their cause too important to be intimidated by Confederate terror tactics. Exhibiting a surprising affection for a country that had treated them as pariahs, they fought first and foremost to liberate their race—not only from slavery but also from the social and political fetters fastened to African Americans in the so-called free states. "If we understand the Declaration of Independence," wrote "E. W. D." of the celebrated 54th Massachusetts Volunteer Infantry, "it asserts the freedom and equality of all men. We ask nothing more. Give us equality and acknowledge us as men, and we are willing to stand by the flag of our Union and support the leaders of this great Government, until every traitor shall be banished from our shore."[22]

If the Rebels raised the black flag of no quarter, the U.S. Colored Troops pronounced themselves willing to live by the same code. A black crewman on a Union gunboat belonging to the Potomac Flotilla wrote on May 14, 1864: "I had the pleasure of conversing with some of the colored soldiers who were wounded [and] brought here to be transported to Washington. I am told by them that their officers could not manage them, they were so eager to fight.

Whenever they caught a rebel they cried out, 'No quarter! Remember Fort Pillow! No quarter for rebs,' &c. . . . They are all eager to go back to retaliate for the Fort Pillow massacre."

When correspondent Thomas Morris Chester visited the USCT regiments belonging to the Army of the James three months later, he learned that these vengeful impulses had not diminished. "Between the Negroes and the enemy it is war to the death," Chester related. "The colored troops have cheerfully accepted the conditions of the Confederate Government, that between them no quarter is to be shown. Those here have not the least idea of living after they fall into the hands of the enemy, and the rebels act very much as if they entertained similar sentiments with reference to the blacks. Even deserters fear to come into our lines where colored troops may be stationed."[23]

Some historians of the black experience in the Civil War classify such testimony as exaggerated and consign it to the realm of tough talk. When African American soldiers gained custody of enemy prisoners, they usually restrained themselves—or were restrained by their white officers—and committed no atrocities. In most cases, the worst they did was threaten captured Rebels with summary execution. On February 14, 1865, Thomas Morris Chester watched seven hundred exchanged Confederates board a truce ship authorized to convey them to friendly lines. "Some of our colored troops, who were near by," Chester noted, "amused themselves by assuring them that, if they ever fell into their hands during an engagement, the Government would not be annoyed with complicated questions of exchange, so far as they were concerned. They reminded the Johnnies that they had not forgotten Fort Pillow, which was still their battle-shout." W. R. Murphy belonged to a Confederate artillery unit captured near Mobile, Alabama, in April 1865. Afterward, Murphy recalled, he and his comrades were "guarded by a 'nigger' company, who told us they would have killed us. They also told us that they did not think we would be alive on the morrow."[24]

As in the Confederate army, however, discipline and humanity did not always prevail, and some USCT commands perpetrated war crimes. On April 9, 1865, a black infantry division helped storm Fort Blakely, a huge earthwork complex defending the eastern approaches to Mobile. The 33d Iowa Infantry, a white regiment, arrived on the scene soon after Blakely's fall. One of the 33d's officers, Lt. John S. Morgan, scribbled in his diary: "The negros in the charge are said to have taken few prisoners on account of one of their men having been shot who was captured (this is all rumor)."[25] A white lieutenant in one of the black assault regiments confirmed the rumor in a letter home: "The niggers did not take a prisoner, they killed all they took to a man."[26]

There were some Northerners who felt that retaliation for racial atrocities should become official Union policy. On April 18, 1864, a black New Yorker urged Secretary of War Edwin M. Stanton, "If the murder of the colored troops at Fort Pillow is not followed by prompt action on the part of our government, it may as well disband all its colored troops for no soldiers whom the government will not protect can be depended upon." Although the Lincoln administration threatened to reply in kind if Confederates failed to treat African American soldiers as honorable combatants, it did not make good on that pledge. Many high-ranking Union commanders did not like blacks or approve of their recruitment. Such officers rarely took note of Confederate excesses against black soldiers or civilians, let alone protest such incidents. Mary Mann, a representative of the U.S. Sanitary Commission, was appalled by the callous attitude that Federal authorities at Helena, Arkansas, exhibited toward African Americans in general. "Who then will care," she wrote a friend in early 1863, "for the murder of the poor Negro?"[27]

When Maj. Gen. William Tecumseh Sherman ordered the expulsion of civilian residents from Atlanta in September 1864, he received a letter from his leading Confederate opponent, Gen. John Bell Hood, who declared that Sherman's decision exceeded "in studied and ingenious cruelty, all acts ever before brought to my attention in the dark history of war." A furious Sherman responded with a lengthy list of Confederate excesses. He accused the Rebels of plunging a peaceful and prosperous republic into "dark and cruel war," daring Northerners to fight with insults to the flag, seizing federal arsenals and forts, and imprisoning regular army garrisons "sent to protect your people against Negroes and Indians," trying to force Kentucky and Missouri into rebellion, persecuting and impoverishing thousands of Southern Unionists, and defaulting on debts owed to Northern banks and businesses. Nowhere in this catalog of horrors did Sherman mention the murder of captured black soldiers and fugitive slaves. Such reticence on the part of the Union army's senior leadership serves as another explanation for why the issues explored in this volume do not command a central position in Civil War memory.[28]

During the March to the Sea, one of Sherman's generals actually delivered a large crowd of blacks to the vengeful mercies of pursuing Confederate cavalry. As Sherman made his way from Atlanta to Savannah, the slaves living along his route perceived the rampaging Federals as an army of liberation and trailed in their destructive wake. Sherman and many of his officers considered the fugitives a nuisance and an encumbrance to their movements. On December 9, 1864, Brig. Gen. Jefferson C. Davis, commander of Sherman's 14th Corps, erected a pontoon bridge to permit his troops to march over Ebenezer Creek. As soon as the last blue-clad soldier had crossed the bridge, Davis ordered it disassembled, stranding approximately 650 blacks on the far side of the stream. Blind panic gripped the abandoned runaways at the approach of Rebel horsemen, and many blacks tried to cross the stream on their own. Some succeeded with makeshift rafts or logs thrown into the creek by compassionate Yankees, but a significant number drowned. A Minnesota soldier who witnessed the tragedy expressed his shame in the form of a question: "Where can you find in all the annals of plantation cruelty anything more completely inhuman and fiendish than this?"[29]

The Civil War was not the chivalrous contest that white America prefers to remember. Adherence to that myth provides a reassuring vision of the nation's past, but it becomes a false foundation for any discussion of current racial problems. A people afraid of their history cannot be expected to scrutinize their own times with an objective eye. Under such circumstances, history with the darkness left out furnishes the present with insufficient guidance, and a people desperate to establish a sense of unity in a multicultural milieu will find themselves undermined by the failure to recognize what some Americans have done, on racial grounds, to others. It is time for the Civil War community to adopt a new spirit of candor. The conflict's unsettling facets must be addressed head-on. There should be no color line, even an invisible one, in Civil War studies. Americans of European and African descent did not create separate countries, and their trials and achievements should not be consigned to separate histories. It is hoped that the essays that follow will stimulate the research that will lead all Americans to see the Civil War not merely as a string of titanic battles but as a social revolution that still influences what it means to be American. The Civil War is too important to be turned into a latter-day Roman circus, where devotees fixate on the spectacle of massive violence and ignore the problems that caused the war and the enduring problems that the war caused.

Although this book emphasizes war crimes, its purpose is not to depict the average Confederate soldier as a war criminal. History should be a tool for understanding, not a weapon to make people feel ashamed of their ancestors. While some Johnny Rebs killed black prisoners and runaway slaves, many others chose not to do so. Some black Federals slew enemy prisoners and wounded for racial reasons, and many white Federals inflicted various forms of vicious abuse on the South's African American population, including murder.[30]

What makes this book especially relevant are the terrorist attacks of September 11, 2001. Americans can now better appreciate the state of siege that gripped the Confederate people from 1861 to 1865. Americans today find themselves confronted by enemies they view as bloodthirsty fanatics who operate outside of the rules of war. Americans feel that everything they hold dear—their lives, their loved ones, their property, and their personal liberties—are endangered. As the struggle with al Qaeda unfolds in the coming years, it remains to be seen if fear, anger, hatred, and a desire for revenge will stampede Americans into embracing the savage excesses that represent the most painful memories of their great Civil War.

Anne J. Bailey sets the tone for this collection with a thoughtful examination of how Texas Confederates reacted after they seized Union enclaves defended by black soldiers and populated by fugitive slaves. In the summer of 1863, Col. William H. Parsons and his Texas cavalry brigade attacked enemy outposts on the Louisiana side of the Mississippi River opposite Vicksburg. These raids did not save Vicksburg from Maj. Gen. Ulysses S. Grant's besieging army, but they provided the Texans with the opportunity to murder about a dozen captured soldiers from the 1st Arkansas Regiment of African Descent and an undetermined number of black civilians. Bailey concludes that the Texas troopers, most of whom did not own slaves, still acted out of their common heritage as white Southerners.

Not all Confederate soldiers murdered black prisoners, but such acts of mercy created unforeseen complications for their superiors. On July 8–9, 1863, the 54th Massachusetts Volunteer Infantry, the North's most famous black regiment, joined a Union army assembled to capture Charleston, South Carolina. By mid-August, more than forty of the 54th's enlisted personnel had fallen into enemy hands alive. The Confederate government had threatened to treat captured black soldiers not as prisoners of war but as rebellious slaves to be returned to bondage or otherwise punished. Yet, Rebel officials realized that if they openly implemented this policy, the Lincoln administration would retaliate in kind against Southern troops in Northern prison camps. Howard C. Westwood reconstructs the tortuous path trod by Confederate and South Carolina officials as they wrestled with this dilemma. He also recounts the sufferings of the 54th's captured personnel as they waited for the enemy to decide their fate.[31]

James G. Hollandsworth Jr. makes clear that the white officers who commanded the U.S. Colored Troops had as much reason to dread capture as their black subordinates. Although Southern slaveholders subscribed to the myth of black savagery, they could not conceive of their chattels having any legitimate reason to rebel against bondage. Those blacks who offered any kind of resistance to the slave system were assumed to have been corrupted by outsiders. Before the Civil War, Northern abolitionists played the villains in this imaginary scenario. With the promulgation of the Emancipation Proclamation, Confederates assigned that role to USCT officers.

By March 26, 1864, there were sixty thousand African Americans enrolled in the Union army, and the increased use of USCT regiments in combat operations witnessed a corresponding increase in Confederate racial atrocities.[32] David J. Coles presents new evidence regarding the aftermath of the Battle of Olustee, Florida, where the 54th Massachusetts and two other black regiments saw action on February 20, 1864. When the defeated Federals retreated that evening, they abandoned numerous wounded and missing men to the enemy, including black troops. The Rebels killed many African Americans and subjected those they spared to various forms of abuse.

The most infamous massacre of U.S. Colored Troops occurred on April 12, 1864, when Maj. Gen. Nathan Bedford Forrest captured Fort Pillow, Tennessee. A strong Forrest cult exists among fans of the Lost Cause, and Confederate apologists have composed elaborate arguments to deny that the general and his cavalrymen were guilty of any war crimes at Fort Pillow. In 1958, Albert Castel published his now-classic article that proved the victorious Rebels had slaughtered surrendering and wounded African Americans. Castel's work has stood the test of time and continues to be the starting point for all serious studies of this event.

Fort Pillow was not the first racial massacre of the Civil War, nor was it the largest, but politics invested it with a prominence that overshadowed all other outrages of its type. Derek W. Frisby charges Ohio senator Benjamin F. Wade and other Radical Republicans on the Joint Committee on the Conduct of the War with presenting a distorted and sensationalized account of the battle. The Radicals hoped to move the Lincoln administration toward harsher war policies by fanning the fires of hatred among the Northern public. The anti-Southern images created by Wade and his colleagues would figure prominently in the "bloody shirt" rhetoric that characterized postwar politics even well after the Republican Party finally abandoned Reconstruction and its black allies in the South.

When I set out to research the Battle of Poison Spring (also known as Poison Springs), Arkansas, I thought I would deal only with the near-annihilation of the 1st Kansas Colored Infantry Regiment on April 18, 1864. A combination of new and forgotten sources led me to discover that two other racial massacres reddened Arkansas soil in that gruesome April. A week after Poison Spring, Confederate troops cut down more than a hundred fugitive slaves at Marks's Mills. Then on the last day of the month, the 2d Kansas Colored Infantry avenged its sister regiment by murdering wounded Rebels left on the battlefield at Jenkins's Ferry. The findings suggest that scholars need to give closer attention to reports of black atrocities.

Next to meeting former slaves in combat, nothing inflamed Confederates more than having to fight white Southern Unionists. The fact that Fort Pillow's garrison consisted of both black and white Southerners accounts in large part for the homicidal passions that animated General Forrest's gray troopers. Some historians believe that this same inflammatory dynamic was in play when Brig. Gen. Robert F. Hoke's seven-thousand-man Confederate army captured Plymouth, North Carolina, on April 20, 1864. In a scrupulously fair and exhaustively researched investigation, Weymouth T. Jordan Jr. and Gerald W. Thomas conclude that Plymouth's Confederate conquerors may have murdered captured black soldiers and runaway slaves but not necessarily a significant number of white Southern Unionists. At the same time, Jordan and Thomas provide a methodological model for identifying unreliable massacre reports.

With the exception of Olustee, the events dealt with in the aforementioned contributions to this collection involved black units of regimental size or smaller. An entire USCT division containing nine infantry regiments participated in the Battle of the Crater on July 30, 1864, at Petersburg, Virginia. The Union high command's botched handling of this assault placed an unprecedented number of black troops in Confederate hands. Employing simple statistical analysis, Bryce A. Suderow concludes that the Crater witnessed the Civil War's largest racial massacre.

The fear and hatred that filled Confederates at the sight of black men in blue uniforms did not disappear when the Civil War ended. Throughout the remainder of Reconstruction, ex-Confederates and former slaves squared off in a prolonged political struggle all across Dixie. Reverting to the merciless tactics common during wartime, Southern whites targeted their black adversaries for a campaign of bloody intimidation. Chad L. Williams's account of the panic that seized Southern whites in the winter of 1865–66 reveals that the reign of terror that eventually toppled Reconstruction could trace some of its roots to the lingering indignation former Rebels harbored over black service in the Union army. The political violence that robbed African Americans of the political equality that they enjoyed ever so briefly during Radical Reconstruction is another subject that deserves closer scrutiny than it usually receives.[33]

Mark Grimsley of Ohio State University provides a summative essay expressly written for this collection. Grimsley comments upon and synthesizes the book's first ten essays by placing them in a wider context. He compares the racially motivated atrocities that Confederate forces committed against the U.S. Colored Troops with parallel episodes that occurred during the same general period in the Far West and societies outside of the United States.

This volume concludes with a select bibliography of books and articles to allow readers to explore some of the many other publications that cover the merciless quality that racial hatred inspired on so many Civil War battle-fields. This secondary literature is extensive and growing, and it can only be hoped that it will someday occupy a more prominent place in the nation's historical memory.

Notes

1. Observers outside of the Civil War community credit McPherson and Burns with reviving interest in the period. Undoubtedly, they helped spread the "bug" to the uninitiated, but the massive response they elicited was evidence of a widespread, preexisting condition. See James M. McPherson, *Battle Cry of Freedom: The Civil War Era* (New York: Oxford University Press, 1988); and Robert Brent Toplin, ed., *Ken Burns's The Civil War: Historians Respond* (New York: Oxford University Press, 1996). McPherson's epic tome was recently superseded by Russell F. Weigley, *A Great Civil War: A Military and Political History, 1861–1865* (Bloomington: Indiana University Press, 2000).

2. Walt Whitman, "Specimen Days (1882–83)," in *". . . The Real War Will Never Get into the Books": Selections from Writers During the Civil War,* ed. Louis P. Masur (New York: Oxford University Press, 1993), 281.

3. Barbara A. Gannon, "Sites of Memory, Sites of Glory: African-American Grand Army of the Republic Posts in Pennsylvania," in William Blair and William Pencak, eds., *Making and Remaking Pennsylvania's Civil War* (University Park: Pennsylvania State University Press, 2001), 166–68. See also Gaines M. Foster, *Ghosts of the Confederacy: Defeat, the Lost Cause, and the Emergence of the New South* (New York: Oxford University Press, 1985); Charles Reagan Wilson, *"Baptized in Blood": The Religion of the Lost Cause, 1865–1920* (Athens: University of Georgia Press, 1980); Thomas L. Connelly and Barbara L. Bellows, *God and General Longstreet: The Lost Cause and the Southern Mind* (Baton Rouge: Louisiana State University Press, 1982); Ralph Lowell Eckert, *John Brown Gordon: Soldier, Southerner, American* (Baton Rouge: Louisiana State University Press, 1989); David W. Blight, *Frederick Douglass' Civil War: Keeping Faith in Jubilee* (Baton Rouge: Louisiana State University Press, 1989); and Kirk Savage, *Standing Soldiers, Kneeling Slaves: Race, War, and Monument in Nineteenth-Century America* (Princeton: Princeton University Press, 1997).

4. David W. Blight, *Race and Reunion: The Civil War in American Memory* (Cambridge: Harvard University Press, 2001), 272–83; W. J. Cash, *The Mind of the South* (New York: Knopf, 1941); Fred A. Bailey, "Textbooks of the Lost Cause: Censorship and the Creation of Southern State Histories," *Georgia Historical Quarterly* 75 (fall 1991): 507–33; Fred A. Bailey, "Free Speech at the University of Florida: The Enoch M. Banks Case," *Florida Historical Quarterly* 71 (July 1992): 1–17; Fred A. Bailey, "Free Speech and the 'Lost Cause' in Texas: A Study of Censorship and Social Control in the New South," *Southwestern Historical Quarterly* 97 (Jan. 1994): 433–78; Fred A. Bailey, "Free Speech and the 'Lost Cause' in the Old Dominion," *Virginia Magazine of History and Biography* 103 (Apr. 1995): 237–66; Fred A. Bailey, "Free Speech and the 'Lost Cause' in Arkansas," *Arkansas Historical Quarterly* 55 (summer 1996): 143–66; Lynn J. Shaw, "The Turncoats among Us," *Confederate Veteran* 32 (Nov. 1984): 4.

5. *Arkansas Gazette,* Jan. 1, 1988; Ralph Green, letter to author, Jan. 9, 1988.

6. Collin Pulley, "Forward the Colors: A Report from the Heritage Committee," *Confederate Veteran* 6 (1998): 5. My quarrel with the SCV is covered in Bob Lancaster, "Old Signs There Are Not Forgotten: The Rebel Flag, and Contrary Emotion, Still Fly High in Arkansas," *Arkansas Times,* Apr. 11, 1997, 10–13. See also *Washington (D.C.) Times,* Sept. 28, 1996. The best look at the neo-Confederate movement and its role in America's current culture wars is Tony Horwitz, *Confederates in the Attic: Dispatches from the Unfinished Civil War* (New York: Pantheon Books, 1998).

7. William Blair, "The Brothers' War: *Gettysburg* the Movie and American Memory," in Blair and Pencak, *Pennsylvania's Civil War,* 246–54, 257–58.

8. Blight, *Race and Reunion,* 4.

9. Ibid., 2–4, 9, 31, 38, 55, 65, 189, 199–200.

10. William W. Freehling, "Why Civil War Military History Must Be Less than 85 Percent Military," *North and South,* Feb. 2002, 15; Mark Grimsley, "Race in the Civil War," *North and South,* Mar. 2001, 38. See also William W. Freehling, *The South Versus the South: How Anti-Confederate Southerners Shaped the Course of the Civil War* (New York: Oxford University Press, 2001).

11. James C. Bates to Mootie Johnson, May 14, 1862, in Richard Lowe, ed., *A Texas Cavalry Officer's Civil War: The Diary and Letters of James C. Bates* (Baton Rouge: Louisiana State University Press, 1999), 119–20.

12. Quoted in Blight, *Race and Reunion,* 298–99.

13. James C. Bates to "Dear Sister," June 16, 1862, in Lowe, *Texas Cavalry Officer's Civil War,* 134. See also Bertram Wyatt Brown, *Southern Honor: Ethics and Behavior in the Old South* (New York: Oxford University Press, 1983), 402–61; and James Oakes, *The Ruling Race: A History of American Slaveholders* (New York: Vintage Books, 1983), 22–24, 28–29, 49, 179–90, 218–19.

14. *Helena Southern Shield,* Oct. 25, 1856. For more on this theme, see Steven A. Channing, *Crisis of Fear: Secession in South Carolina* (New York: W. W. Norton, 1974).

15. *True Democrat,* Apr. 22, 1863.

16. Michael Fellman, "At the Nihilist Edge: Reflections on Guerrilla Warfare During the American Civil War," in Stig Forster and Jorg Nagler, eds., *On the Road to Total War: The American Civil War and the German Wars of Unification, 1861–1871* (Cambridge: Cambridge University Press, 1997), 522, 531, 533; James C. Bates to "My Dear Ma," Sept. 12, 1863, in Lowe, *Texas Cavalry Officer's Civil War,* 273; R. J. M. Blackett, ed., *Thomas Morris Chester, Black Civil War Correspondent: His Dispatches from the Virginia Front* (Baton Rouge: Louisiana State University Press, 1989), 146; Love quoted in J. Tracy Power, *Lee's Miserables: Life in the Army of Northern Virginia from the Wilderness to Appomattox* (Chapel Hill: University of North Carolina Press, 1998), 135, 139.

17. This total-war/hard-war debate is handled with admirable skill in Mark Grimsley, *The Hard Hand of War: Union Military Policy Toward Southern Civilians, 1861–1865* (Cambridge: Cambridge University Press, 1995). See also Mark E. Neely Jr., "Was the Civil War a Total War?" in Forster and Nagler, *On the Road,* 35, 37. For the lengths to which Confederates would go to keep slaves under control, see Winthrop D. Jordan, *Tumult and Silence at Second Creek: An Inquiry into a Civil War Slave Conspiracy* (Baton Rouge: Louisiana State University Press, 1993); Michael Fellman, *Inside War: The Guerrilla Conflict in Missouri During the American Civil War* (New York: Oxford University Press, 1989); and Michael Fellman, "Emancipation in Missouri," *Missouri Historical Review* 83 (Oct. 1988): 36–56.

18. Fellman, "At the Nihilist Edge," 522–26, 532; Joseph T. Glatthaar, *The March to the Sea and Beyond: Sherman's Troops in the Savannah and Carolinas Campaigns* (New York: New York University Press, 1985), 127–28; Gregory J. W. Urwin, *Custer Victorious: The Civil War Battles of General George Armstrong Custer* (Rutherford, N.J.: Fairleigh Dickinson University Press, 1983), 174–75; Roberta E. Fagan, "Custer at Front Royal: 'A Horror of the War'?" in *Custer and His Times: Book Three,* ed. Gregory J. W. Urwin and Roberta E. Fagan (Conway: University of

Central Arkansas Press, 1987), 17–81; Eric J. Wittenberg, *Glory Enough for All: Sheridan's Second Raid and the Battle of Trevilian Station* (Washington, D.C.: Brassey's, 2001), 219, 233–34.

19. Fellman, "At the Nihilist Edge," 531–33; Marcus S. Hopkins to James Johnson, Jan. 15, 1865, in Ira Berlin, Joseph P. Reidy, and Leslie S. Rowland, eds., *The Black Military Experience*, ser. 2, vol. 1 of *Freedom: A Documentary History of Emancipation, 1861–1867* (Cambridge: Cambridge University Press, 1982), 800.

20. Linda Gordon, *The Great Arizona Orphan Abduction* (Cambridge: Harvard University Press, 1999), 258–68. See also Ray Stannard Baker, *Following the Color Line: American Negro Citizenship in the Progressive Era* (1908; reprint, New York: Harper Torchbooks, 1964); David M. Chalmers, *Hooded Americanism: The History of the Ku Klux Klan* (Durham: Duke University Press, 1987); and George C. Rable, *But There Was No Peace: The Role of Violence in the Politics of Reconstruction* (Athens: University of Georgia Press, 1984). The white South's reliance on lynching and the threat of lynching to suppress the region's black population is a recurring theme in Edmund Morris's recent account of Theodore Roosevelt's presidency, *Theodore Rex* (New York: Random House, 2001).

21. One of the finest studies of the racial dimensions of modern warfare is John W. Dower, *War Without Mercy: Race and Power in the Pacific War* (New York: Pantheon Books, 1986). Some enlightening discussions on the nature of war crimes may be found in Aleksandar Jokic, ed., *War Crimes and Collective Wrongdoing: A Reader* (Malden, Mass.: Blackwell, 2001).

22. *Christian Recorder,* June 25, 1864.

23. *Christian Recorder,* May 21, 1864; Blackett, *Thomas Morris Chester,* 109–10. Outrage over the Fort Pillow Massacre even affected the behavior of some white Union troops for several weeks. As a lieutenant with the 10th Massachusetts Volunteer Infantry wrote from Virginia: "The prisoners who came in report that there are lots of others who want to come but our boys fire at them so they cannot, our men are much opposed to taking prisoners since the Fort Pillow affair, that has cost the Rebels many a life that would otherwise have been spared." Charles Harvey Brewster to "Dear Mother," May 24, 1864, in David W. Blight, ed., *When This Cruel War Is Over: The Civil War Letters of Charles Harvey Brewster* (Amherst: University of Massachusetts, 1992), 304.

24. Blackett, *Thomas Morris Chester,* 262; Mamie Yeary, ed. and comp., *Reminiscences of the Boys in Gray, 1861–1865* (Dallas: Smith and Lamar, 1912), 555; Joseph T. Glatthaar, *Forged in Battle: The Civil War Alliance of Black Soldiers and White Officers* (New York: Free Press, 1990), 154–55, 158, 201–2. See also A. F. Sperry, *History of the 33d Iowa Infantry Volunteer Regiment, 1863–6,* ed. Gregory J. W. Urwin and Cathy Kunzinger Urwin (Fayetteville: University of Arkansas Press, 1999), 158.

25. Jim Cullen, "'I's a Man Now': Gender and African American Men," in *Divided Houses: Gender and the Civil War,* ed. Catherine Clinton and Nina Silber (New York: Oxford University Press, 1992), 88; "Diary of John S. Morgan, Company G, Thirty-Third Iowa Infantry," pt. 2, *Annals of Iowa* 13 (Apr. 1923): 588; Glatthaar, *Forged in Battle,* 158, 167–68.

26. Gus to wife, May 6, 1864, quoted in Glatthaar, *Forged in Battle,* 158.

27. Theodore Hodgkins to Edwin M. Stanton, Apr. 18, 1864, in Berlin, Reidy, and Rowland, *Black Military Experience,* 587; William S. McFeely, *Grant: A Biography* (New York: W. W. Norton, 1982), 71–72, 238–40; Dudley Taylor Cornish, *The Sable Arm: Black Troops in the Union Army, 1861–1865* (1956; reprint, Lawrence: University Press of Kansas, 1987), 121–23, 274; Michael Fellman, *Citizen Sherman: A Life of William Tecumseh Sherman* (New York: Random House, 1995), 70–72, 79, 153–54, 156–70, 242–44; John F. Marszalek, *Sherman: A Soldier's Passion for Order* (New York: Vintage Books, 1994), 45–46, 59, 192–93, 254–55, 313–14; Glatthaar, *March to the Sea,* 57; Theodore Lyman to his wife, May 18, 1864, in George R. Agassiz, ed., *Meade's Headquarters, 1863–1865: Letters of Colonel Theodore Lyman from the Wilderness to Appomattox* (Boston: Atlantic Monthly, 1922), 102; Mary Mann to "Dear Elisha," Feb. 10, 1863, Mary Mann Papers, Library of Congress, Washington, D.C.

28. William T. Sherman, *Memoirs of General William T. Sherman,* 2 vols. (New York: Appleton, 1875), 2:119-20.

29. Glatthaar, *March to the Sea,* 64; Fellman, *Citizen Sherman,* 162-64; Jacob D. Cox, *Sherman's March to the Sea: Hood's Tennessee Campaign and the Carolina Campaigns of 1865* (1882; reprint, New York: Da Capo, 1994), 37-38; David Nevin, *Sherman's March: Atlanta to the Sea* (Alexandria, Va.: Time-Life Books, 1986), 71-73.

30. See Power, *Lee's Miserables,* 138-39; Bell I. Wiley, *The Life of Billy Yank: The Common Soldier of the Union* (1952; reprint, Baton Rouge: Louisiana State University Press, 1978), 114-15; and Glatthaar, *March to the Sea,* 56-59.

31. The *Richmond Examiner* described a parallel case in the summer of 1863 when a light-skinned African American was found among captured Union soldiers at Belle Isle. "He gave the name of Hascall, (intended rascal,) and said he enlisted in Massachusetts," the paper reported tersely. "The black sheep was removed from the white flock, and provided with quarters becoming his importance." *Richmond Examiner,* July 21, 1863.

32. Cornish, *Sable Arm,* 172-77.

33. For documents detailing a small portion of the violence and harassment that white Southerners directed against black Union veterans and the latter's families, see Berlin, Reidy, and Rowland, *Black Military Experience,* 761-62, 799-810, 819.

A Texas Cavalry Raid

1

Reaction to Black Soldiers and Contrabands

ANNE J. BAILEY

In June 1863, when Maj. Gen. Ulysses S. Grant's army bottled up the Confederates in Vicksburg, the Union campaign to gain control of the Mississippi River moved into its final stage. As summer began, many Southerners feared the army defending the town could not hold out much longer. Nevertheless, Confederate troops on the west side of the river displayed guarded optimism that they still might offer some support to their besieged comrades. Early in June, therefore, Texas infantry assaulted enemy positions on the Louisiana bank opposite Vicksburg, and late in the month, Texas cavalry raided Federal strongholds in the same region. The former, an attack on Milliken's Bend, has often been utilized by historians to point out atrocities that accompany war. The latter, a cavalry raid just over three weeks later, had much the same result but has never been examined carefully. Neither of these forays, however, made any difference to the ultimate fate of the river port. The major result of the fighting "was to publicize the controversy surrounding northern employment of black troops."[1]

Events in the Trans-Mississippi have never received the same recognition as those in other theaters. Perhaps one reason little is known of the Texas cavalry raid in Louisiana is because any account of Southern brutality toward blacks fades in comparison with Nathan Bedford Forrest's infamous assault upon Fort Pillow in April 1864. Forrest's biographer, Robert S. Henry, correctly observed, "Fort Pillow was *the* 'atrocity' of the war." Certainly, historians have evaluated and reevaluated the incident over and over.[2]

The use of former slaves as soldiers in the United States Army often aroused heated emotions. With enmity widespread, it is surprising there were not more of these violent racial incidents. Historian James M. McPherson, who has masterfully chronicled the uphill struggle of blacks during the Civil War, concluded, "The southern response to emancipation and the enlistment of black troops was ferocious—at least on paper and, regretably [*sic*], sometimes in fact as well."[3] Without the sensitive issue of Confederate treatment of contrabands, the cavalry raid along the Louisiana shore—less than a week before Vicksburg's surrender—would have scant importance.

To Confederates along the Mississippi, Vicksburg was only a fragment of a much larger picture—Federal forces threatened vital areas of Louisiana. To meet this emergency, soon after Lt. Gen. Edmund Kirby Smith had assumed command of the Trans-Mississippi Department early in 1863, he had started concentrating available troops to reinforce Maj. Gen. Richard Taylor's District of Louisiana. By June, Maj. Gen. John Bankhead Magruder, in charge of the District of Texas, reported he had forwarded almost five thousand men across the Sabine River.[4] From Arkansas, Lt. Gen. Theophilus H. Holmes sent Maj. Gen. John G. Walker's Texas Infantry Division.[5] These reinforcements did not arrive in time to prevent a Federal push up the Red River toward Alexandria, but after occupying the town, Maj. Gen. Nathaniel P. Banks halted his advance. Urged by Grant to take part in a joint campaign along the Mississippi, Banks concentrated his men near the Confederate stronghold of Port Hudson. By late May, Banks had moved to a position outside the fortification, while Grant threatened Vicksburg.

The Confederate situation along the river was critical. Taylor had to utilize most of his available troops to confront Banks's army. Moreover, Taylor recognized the futility of offering substantial support to Vicksburg. He later pointed out, however, that "public opinion would condemn us if we did not try *to do something*."[6] Thus, to exhibit concern for the defenders in Vicksburg, Confederates raided Union positions in northeast Louisiana. These movements, too late and ineffectual to alter the outcome of Grant's campaign, scarcely concerned the Federal commander, but the Texans' alleged murder of blacks did produce a reaction.

Early in June, Walker's division of Texas infantry assaulted Milliken's Bend, a Federal supply depot on the Mississippi. One important detail, often overlooked by historians, is that this was the first actual combat situation for many of these Texans, and their reaction to fighting blacks in Federal blue only reinforced what Bell I. Wiley believed—most Southerners "felt as the Mississippian who wrote his mother: 'I hope I may never see a Negro Soldier,' he said, 'or I cannot be . . . a Christian Soldier.'" Many blacks were brutally murdered; Federal commissioner Abraham E. Strickle claimed the slaughter at Milliken's Bend was "butchery." When Rear Adm. David Porter arrived on the scene, he had described "quite an ugly sight. The dead negroes lined the ditch inside of the parapet, or levee, and were mostly shot on the top of the head."[7] The charges of atrocity coupled with the stubborn resistance of the black troops only served to help relieve widespread prejudice against blacks in combat. Charles Dana, the assistant secretary of war, believed the bravery of the soldiers in the fight "completely revolutionized the sentiment of the army with regard to the employment of negro troops."[8]

Yet, the foray had brought no military rewards, and Taylor considered transferring Walker's command south of the Red River to assist his troops around Port Hudson. When Kirby Smith disapproved, Taylor decided instead to hold the force in the northeastern part of the state until the events at Vicksburg developed.[9] To harass Union positions along the river, Walker needed mounted reinforcements; therefore, Kirby Smith ordered Holmes to forward a mounted brigade toward Louisiana, where the troops were to raze locations under Federal control. "All such should be destroyed," he instructed, "and the negroes captured."[10]

Holmes ordered a brigade of Texas cavalry commanded by Col. William Henry Parsons to Louisiana. He decided not to send the entire brigade, however, for fear he might weaken his own defenses around Little Rock. Holmes released the 12th and 19th Texas Cavalries and one section of the 10th Texas Field Battery but kept the remainder of the brigade in Arkansas.[11] These men were seasoned veterans—the 12th Texas had been among the first regiments to arrive in Arkansas in 1862 and had since earned the reputation as an outstanding fighting unit. The 19th Texas and the battery had just returned from Missouri after taking part in Brig. Gen. John S. Marmaduke's unsuccessful raid upon Cape Girardeau.

Colonel Parsons, who viewed this opportunity to assist the defenders at Vicksburg with solemn regard, recognized that to be effective with his small force he must carefully plan his strategy. Over a year's experience assaulting enemy supply trains and patrols in Arkansas had taught him the importance of every detail. Thus, he preceded his men to Louisiana in order to reconnoiter the situation personally. When the two regiments crossed the Louisiana border late in June, the colonel had already determined the enemy's strengths and weaknesses. He had, according to a member of the 12th Texas, in a letter to a Houston newspaper, scouted "single-handed and alone, on his own hook, thro' the swamps, keeping his own counsel and learning the whereabouts of the Federals, and finding the best point for striking a telling blow; which self-imposed task, as the sequel proved, he accomplished most successfully."[12]

Parsons reunited with his men June 27 near Lake Providence, where he told them what he had learned during the reconnaissance. He spoke of the planned campaign, and his manner of deliverance strengthened the men's loyalty and their determination to follow him in battle. Henry Orr, a private

in the 12th Texas, recalled that the colonel addressed the troops "in an eloquent and patriotic strain, gave the soldiers great encouragement, and said
he was glad that we are privileged to strike a blow for Vicksburg."[13] Another
member of the 12th who listened to the "stirring, eloquent speech" observed,
"it forcibly struck me, much as a father would talk to his boys, of whom he was
proud." Parsons, he wrote, told "them of the brave garrison at Vicksburg . . .
that he could not take them there, but that he would take them where they
would hear the sullen boom of the Vicksburg cannon." The men, he observed,
"resolved to follow where he would lead, and nobly do or die for Vicksburg."[14]

Just after sunrise the next morning, the troops, stimulated by Parsons's
enthusiasm, left on the scout toward Lake Providence in the "highest spirits." A member of the 19th Texas pointed out, "Under the leadership of our
deservedly popular and able commander (for he's nothing less) we proceeded so cautiously and securely."[15] When the troops stopped to rest in the
camps of Walker's division, J. P. Blessington, a private in the 16th Texas Infantry commented, "As they passed by us, I could not but admire their horse-
manship; they all appeared to be excellent horsemen, and at a distance their
general appearance was decidedly showy and gallant." Although he noticed
their uniforms "contained as many colors as the rainbow," the rifles and
swords just issued to the command impressed him. Of this flashy force, he
noted, "their arms consisted mostly of Enfield rifles, slung to their saddles,
while around the waist of each was buckled a heavy cavalry sword, which
clattered at every movement of their horses. A pair of holster pistols attached
to the pommels of their saddles completed their equipment."[16]

Parsons joined Walker's infantry on a raid through the region between
Milliken's Bend and Lake Providence. "The object of the expedition," a
member of the 19th Texas reported to the *Dallas Herald,* "proved to be to
break up a nest of federals who were cultivating cotton and corn in the valley of Bayou Mason [Maçon] and on the Miss. on the free labor system that
is to say with hired negroes." Walker had left on this march in late June and
had broken up several plantations, burning the picked cotton, and had returned numerous slaves to their owners.[17]

Parsons had authorization to lead an independent action against Federal
garrisons near the Mississippi. After leaving Walker's camp on Monday, June
29, Parsons's two regiments joined Brig. Gen. James C. Tappan's Arkansas
brigade and Col. Horace Randal's Texas brigade, both infantry, accompanied by their scouts, Col. Isaac F. Harrison's Louisiana cavalry. The latter
was temporarily placed under Parsons's command, along with two batteries, one from Mississippi and the other from Louisiana.[18]

Parsons divided his force. Harrison's cavalry, accompanied by one of the batteries, took a road leading toward Goodrich's Landing on the Mississippi between Milliken's Bend and Lake Providence. Parsons headed his Texans along with the other battery toward a fortified position built on an old Indian mound. The infantry followed with the intention of reinforcing where needed.[19]

The cavalry's first objective was a fort manned by black troops under the command of white officers. Located about ten miles below Lake Providence and about one and one-half miles from the Mississippi, this stronghold, built on the top of an ancient Indian burying ground, supplied protection for the Federal plantations. Stationing black troops along the fertile regions of the Mississippi served a dual purpose: They not only safeguarded former slaves working on the plantations but their presence released white soldiers from this duty.[20]

As the Texans emerged from the dense undergrowth of bushes and briers, the position, identified by one Texan as De Soto Mound, presented an impressive appearance. Rising about eighty to one hundred feet from an extensive open field, it was described by George Ingram, a lieutenant in the 12th Texas, as "the most peculiar looking mound I ever saw."[21] The main fort was situated on the summit, which, measuring around thirty or forty feet square, was only accessible by a single pathway on the south side. To discourage anyone from trying to storm the slope, the Federals had loosened the dirt for a distance of fifteen to twenty feet from the top so that anyone attempting to climb up would lose his footing.[22]

The soldiers at the garrison had made preparations for an assault. The first line of defense was a secure trench surrounding the entire position some two and one-half to three feet deep, with the dirt thrown up in front to provide a light breastwork. Waiting in the ditch were troops of the 1st Arkansas Volunteers (African Descent), adequately armed with Enfield rifles. Upon the top of the mound were other blacks poised behind heavy timbers, placed there for the purpose of rolling them down on anyone rash enough to try to scale the precipitous sides if the first line broke.[23] There was no artillery, although the Federals had attempted to fabricate a cannon. Upon approaching the fortification, however, the Texans realized that what appeared to be a formidable 8-pounder was only a wooden log with a "vicious looking hole, some three inches in diameter, bored in one end of it."[24]

Parsons formed his men into a line of battle. The 12th Texas took the right, the 19th Texas the left, and the battery the center. When eight hundred yards from the Federal position, Parsons ordered a halt and instructed the battery to open fire. Lieutenant Ingram later informed his wife that the blast from the four Confederate guns "caused the rascals in the fort to hide their heads." As the Texans cautiously neared the garrison, Parsons ordered the 12th to form at right angles to the 19th.[25]

Parsons judged he could not storm the fort without great loss of life. The colonel detailed some of his men as sharpshooters in order to pick off the enemy exchanging rifle fire with the Confederates, and a company from the 19th Texas deployed on the top of a smaller mound, about one hundred fifty yards from the main location. As the two sides traded fire, Federal riflemen killed one Texan and wounded several.[26] However, the timely arrival of the infantry under Tappan provided the cavalry with reinforcements. With his numbers greatly increased, Parsons recognized, and the officers atop the mound quickly realized, that resistance by the Federals was futile. Just as Parsons ordered the men to form a line of battle, he directed a flag of truce toward the enemy demanding unconditional surrender.[27]

The fort capitulated without further bloodshed. The white officers acceded on the promise their captors would treat them as prisoners of war but requested to surrender the armed blacks unconditionally. Since Brigadier General Tappan had arrived, Parsons consulted with him before accepting the terms, and then 113 blacks and 3 white officers grounded their arms.[28]

The problem of black prisoners exacerbated acrimony on both sides. Walker reported, "I consider it an unfortunate circumstance that any armed negroes were captured." And Taylor had already received a warning from Grant. After hearing rumors that Walker's troops were guilty of hanging several black soldiers as well as a white captain and a white sergeant at Milliken's Bend, Grant had written Taylor that he hoped there was "some mistake in the evidence" or that "the act of hanging had no official sanction, and that the parties guilty of it" would be punished. "It may be you propose a different line of policy toward black troops and officers commanding them, to that practiced toward white troops," observed Grant. "If so, I can assure you," he warned, "that these colored troops are regularly mustered into the service of the United States. The Government and all officers serving under the Government are bound to give the same protection to these troops that they do to any other troops." Yet Pvt. John Simmons of the 22d Texas Infantry wrote that as the foot soldiers escorted the prisoners back to camp, about "12 or 15" blacks died before they arrived.[29]

Actually facing former slaves in blue uniforms was a new experience for many of the Texans. Parsons, who disliked the necessity of engaging black soldiers, had declared, "I would not give one of my brave men for the whole of them." Yet, another participant had indicated surprise with the obstinate stand of the black troops: "These negroes were *well drilled,* and used their guns with a precision equal with any troops, and here were killed three of the four men we lost."[30]

Parsons, nevertheless, had no desire to remain at the mound any longer than necessary, and he quickly resumed his raid. As the Texans rode toward the Mississippi, they burned houses, gins, and cotton and captured all the black field hands they came upon. Brig. Gen. Alfred W. Ellet, commanding the Union's Mississippi Marine Brigade (an army unit, despite its name), observed the destruction the next morning. "In passing by the negro quarters on three of the burning plantations," he reported, "we were shocked by the sight of the charred remains of human beings who had been burned in the general conflagration. No doubt they were the sick negroes whom the unscrupulous enemy were too indifferent to remove. I witnessed five such spectacles myself in passing the remains of three plantations that lay in our line of march and do not doubt there were many others on the 20 or more other plantations that I did not visit which were burned in like manner." Perhaps the Texans felt much the same as Forrest, who, in McPherson's astute description, showed "a killer instinct" for "blacks in any capacity other than slave."[31]

The brutality of these Confederates toward blacks was not an isolated incident. An important point to note is that this was not the first time there were charges against Parsons's 12th Texas for murdering blacks. When the regiment had raided a Federal supply train at L'Anguille River in northeastern Arkansas in 1862, there were reports they killed several refugee slaves accompanying the detachment. A Wisconsin soldier had claimed after the fighting, "The rebels . . . took possession of the camp, and with the most fiendish barbarity murdered many negroes, both men and women, plundered and burned the train, and then, with forty-seven prisoners besides negroes, returned, as rapidly as they came."[32]

But in Louisiana in 1863, blacks were not the only ones to feel the wrath of the Texans—Union sympathizers also suffered at the hands of the Southern raiders. As the Confederates moved south, they razed all the homes they suspected of housing traitors. Ellet recalled he had "found the road strewn with abandoned booty." Rear Adm. David D. Porter listed among the plunder such items as "furniture, pianos, pictures." Ellet concluded, however, the Southerners' primary objective was not pillaging but securing "the negroes stolen from the plantations along the river, some hundreds of whom they had captured."[33]

The path of destruction led from the Indian mound toward Lake Providence. Parsons hoped to arrive at the town before local Unionists spread news of his coming. Anxious to employ the element of surprise, he urged his troops to speed. The men in the 19th Texas, whose mounts had not yet recovered from the raid into Missouri with Marmaduke just a few weeks before, could not keep the pace and fell behind. When the Confederates neared the little town, the 12th Texas was well in advance of the rest of the force.[34]

News of the advance had preceded the Southerners, and Federal soldiers had prepared a reception. As the Texans emerged from a skirt of timber interspersed with heavy undergrowth, they rode into an ambush. Parsons promptly formed the 12th Texas into a line of battle, and a man near the colonel recalled, "I don't know whether I was scared or not, but I do know that I was not too *badly* scared to observe him closely. I *know* that *he* was not scared. He watched every movement and gave his orders as deliberately as though he was in no danger." In the midst of the firing, Parsons rode everywhere, "and though the balls rattled all around him, he gave his orders and directions as coolly as if he was on a drill."[35]

The battle, although fierce, proved short. Parsons, in front of his men, gave orders to dismount all but one squadron. Armed with recently arrived rifles, the Texans rushed toward the enemy on foot, fighting "Indian or Texas fashion."[36] As the dismounted cavalrymen drove the troops of the 1st Kansas Mounted Regiment back in a "pretty hot fight" about two to three hundred yards, Parsons ordered one squadron to charge on horseback.[37]

For a second time that day, the fortuitous arrival of reinforcements saved further destruction. As the 19th Texas rode up, Parsons ordered them to charge. A participant recalled with pride that if one could "have heard the real Texan yell they sent forth and seen those brave determined men, as they dashed off, urging on their jaded horses, you would have cried with me, the 'Lone Star' is in hands of which she may well be proud; and thus the exciting race continued for five miles, and within a mile of the town of Providence. But the Federal horses, being fresh, outran our horses and the jaded condition of both man and beast" forced Parsons to call a halt. Brig. Gen. Hugh T. Reid, commanding Federal troops in the vicinity of the town, reported his men had found the rebels "too strong, and had to fall back, skirmishing to within 3 miles of town, where the progress of the enemy was stopped."[38]

The cavalry headed back to join the main infantry force. But a gunboat, the *Romeo,* along with a transport mounting two guns on the hurricane deck, the *John Raine,* shelled the Confederate column as it marched down the levee.[39] One Texan observed, "their shells burst harmlessly above and around us, doing no other damage than killing three negroes." Porter claimed the gunboat pursued the Confederate column for fifteen miles but was unable to prevent further destruction of houses and property.[40]

The Confederates left the fertile land in ruins. All around them, columns of black smoke rose from burning houses, the red flames casting a sullen glow on the horizon. When the boom of signal guns bore the news of the fighting, one of Parsons's men proudly noted that the cannon informed the Confederates at Vicksburg "that a blow had been struck for [them]," and to "the besiegers, that a blow had been struck *against* them." As twilight fell, the strange scene, enhanced by the sobs of hundreds of black captives, observed the writer, was "grand, gloomy and peculiar."[41] Union commander Hugh Reid observed the damage and confirmed, "it was a part of Parsons' brigade of cavalry which did the mischief in this vicinity."[42]

Federal pursuit came immediately. By two o'clock the following morning, Ellet had debarked his entire force at Goodrich's Landing—infantry, artillery, and cavalry; at sunrise, he started in search of the raiders. Sending the cavalry in advance of the main force, Ellet's mounted men found the Confederates resting on the west bank of Tensas Bayou, where spirited firing erupted. Parsons, directing his men in person, attempted to cross the bayou and turn Ellet's right flank, but an advance line of Union skirmishers repulsed the assault. One Texan believed the Federals were "afraid to come out into an open space and give us a fair fight." Ellet, however, insisted the arrival of his artillery, which opened up on the Confederate position, convinced the Southerners to "precipitately" retreat.[43] But before leaving, Parsons ordered the bridge burned. Then, in obedience to Walker's orders, the Texas cavalry began to fall back, covering the infantry's rear.

Porter's reaction to the raid was matter-of-fact. "I am much surprised that this has never been attempted before," he observed, as "the temptation to plunder is very great, and there is nothing but the black regiments to protect the coast." Porter criticized the plantation system by pointing out its excessive cost to the government. Moreover, he believed unobstructed navigation of the Mississippi under this arrangement required a large army of white soldiers and gunboats to safeguard the blacks, whom he believed had proved unable to protect themselves.[44]

The raid, although successful, brought few material benefits. On the positive side, the Confederates had captured between thirteen and fifteen hundred blacks, over four hundred horses and mules, cattle, and camp equipage, and—important to the department—Southern wagons now held over two hundred Federal arms. But retaining Confederate troops opposite

Vicksburg late in June offered no military rewards. As Richard Taylor later observed, "The time wasted on these absurd movements cost us the garrison of Port Hudson, nearly eight thousand men," he conceded, "but the pressure on General Kirby Smith to *do something* for Vicksburg was too strong to be resisted."[45]

In reality, the Confederates in Louisiana could do nothing to aid their comrades across the river. Walker informed Kirby Smith on July 3: "If there was the slightest hope that my small command could relieve Vicksburg, the mere probability of its capture or destruction ought not, and should not, as far as I am concerned, weigh a feather against making the attempt, but I consider it absolutely certain, unless the enemy are blind and stupid, that no part of my command would escape capture or destruction if such an attempt should be made." Walker noted that at no time did his force amount to more than 4,700 men, and with the bad weather and "deleterious effect of the climate," the number was reduced to barely 2,500 fit for duty. Although he had been reinforced by Tappan, there were never more than 4,200 effectives.[46] And when Pemberton, besieged by Grant's army, ceased fighting the next day, Private Orr of the 12th Texas wrote his sister, "The news of the surrender [of] Vicksburg was received with regret."[47]

Although the raid made no significant military difference, few would have predicted it would bring the issue of blacks to the forefront. Moreover, public opinion in the South often condoned such acts. Kate Stone, a young Louisiana refugee living in east Texas, noted in her diary in June of Walker's fight at Milliken's Bend: "It is hard to believe that Southern soldiers—and Texans at that—have been whipped by a mongrel crew of white and black Yankees. There must be some mistake. . . . It is said the Negro regiments fought there like mad demons, but we cannot believe that. We know from long experience they were cowards." On September 1, she wrote: "There are quite a number of Yankee prisoners at Tyler [Texas], captured while in command of black troops. It does seem like they ought to be hanged. . . . The detestable creatures!"[48]

What happened to the captured blacks? Confederate soldiers seldom mentioned them in their correspondence, and the question is difficult to answer since they were treated as captured property. That status was clear in an order Colonel Parsons issued on August 16, which prohibited soldiers from keeping or selling any property taken during raids—specifically "mules or negroes." Significantly, Parsons (whose birthplace was New Jersey) owned only one slave, an old woman who had apparently come with his wife upon their marriage.[49]

Nevertheless, fighting along the Mississippi had brought the disagreeable question of black prisoners into the spotlight for both sides. Not only had Grant cautioned Taylor about the treatment of black soldiers opposite Vicksburg but persistent rumors of murdered blacks in the fighting around Port Hudson surfaced. Although in May the United States War Department had taken a stand on the position of troops of African descent in the army, Southerners seldom worried about punishment threatened by Abraham Lincoln's government.

In fact, Texans in the Trans-Mississippi simply ignored Washington's warnings of retaliation. For example, in April 1864, the 30th Texas Cavalry, which joined Parsons's Texas Cavalry Brigade shortly before the war ended, would take part in the most publicized massacre of blacks recorded in the department. Within days of Nathan Bedford Forrest's infamous assault on black troops at Fort Pillow, Tennessee, on April 12, 1864, Confederates fighting in Arkansas brutally murdered former slaves wearing Federal uniforms. On April 18, at Poison Spring, the Southerners slaughtered many black soldiers. The historian Robert L. Kerby has concluded: "The so-called battle of Poison Spring was a onesided massacre: the Union soldiers were torn to shreds," and the Confederates "deliberately drove captured wagons back and forth over the fallen Negro wounded, and execution squads went about the field shooting incapacitated prisoners." Kirby Smith confided to his wife that the Southerners had taken "some 200 prisoners and left 600 reported dead on the field principally negroes who neither gave or recd quarter. . . . I saw but two negro prisoners." When Private Orr of Parsons's 12th Texas visited the battle site in November, he wrote his sister that a "great many Negroes were killed. The Yankees were invited to come and bury them after the battle; three days after they came and threw a little dirt over them, but the hogs rooted them up; I reckon I saw half a wagonload of *bones*."[50]

To decide whether there was any consistent attitude toward blacks among these Texas cavalrymen serving in the Trans-Mississippi Department, it is necessary to consider all three incidents: L'Anguille River in 1862, the Louisiana raid in 1863, and Poison Spring in 1864. The atrocities committed against blacks along the banks of the Mississippi in northern Louisiana in 1863 were no different from those committed by Texans in Arkansas in 1862 and what they would continue to do in 1864. Moreover, it is important to look at the men involved. In each encounter, many of the Confederates were members of the 12th, 19th, or 30th Texas Cavalries. For example, James Frazier, a private in the 12th Texas who took part in the Louisiana raid, had one brother serving in the 19th Texas Cavalry and another serving in the 30th Texas. The majority of the troops in these regiments came from north central Texas—an area settled predominantly by families from the Upper South, an area without plantations and little cotton production, where few inhabitants were recorded owning any slaves in the 1860 Federal census.[51]

Why then did these Texans, many nonslaveholders from the Texas frontier, react as they did toward blacks? There appear to be three reasons. First, the majority of these Texans shared a common heritage—as Southerners, they acted as many Southerners would have done in the same situation. In 1862, when they first encountered contrabands following the Union soldiers, they responded as their culture had taught them—an almost natural wartime reaction to seeing blacks in any other capacity than that of slaves. Second, since all of the incidents described occurred in the Trans-Mississippi, there was not as great a chance of publicity or condemnation. By the time of the raid along the Mississippi in 1863, the troops had long since realized that the hierarchy in Richmond generally overlooked or even ignored their department. Finally, these Texas cavalry regiments served most of the war as scouts and raiders on the fringe of Union-occupied areas; they had a strong determination to prevent Federal soldiers from reaching their home state. When the United States Army amassed a two-front assault toward Texas in the spring of 1864, the Texans had to halt the advance or possibly concede north Texas to the enemy. The thought that soldiers—black soldiers—could have marched toward their homes sent fear and anger through the Texans, and the result was the massacre at Poison Spring. The reaction of Texas cavalrymen serving in the Trans-Mississippi to black soldiers and contrabands, therefore, stemmed from their cultural heritage, the separateness of their department from the rest of the Confederacy, and probably most decisive, their strong desire to protect their families in Texas from the ravages of war.

Notes

This essay was originally published in *Civil War History* 35 (June 1989): 138–52. Reprinted with permission of the Kent State University Press.

1. James M. McPherson, *Battle Cry of Freedom: The Civil War Era* (New York: Oxford University Press, 1988), 634. See also Richard Lowe, "Battle on the Levee: The Fight at Milliken's Bend," in *Black Soldiers in Blue: African American Troops in the Civil War Era*, ed. John David Smith (Chapel Hill: University of North Carolina Press, 2002), 107–35.

2. Robert Selph Henry, *"First with the Most" Forrest* (1944; reprint, Wilmington, N.C.: Broadfoot, 1987), 248. See also John Cimprich and Robert C. Mainfort Jr., "Fort Pillow Revisited: New Evidence about an Old Controversy," *Civil War History* 28 (Dec. 1982): 293–306; Albert Castel, "The Fort Pillow Massacre: A Fresh Examination of the Evidence," *Civil War History* 4 (Mar. 1958): 37–50, and "Fort Pillow: Victory or Massacre?" *American History Illustrated* 9 (Apr. 1974): 4–11, 46–48; Charles W. Anderson, "The True Story of Fort Pillow," *Confederate Veteran* 3 (Nov. 1895): 326; and John L. Jordan, "Was There a Massacre at Fort Pillow?" *Tennessee Historical Quarterly* 6 (June 1947): 122–32.

3. McPherson, *Battle Cry of Freedom,* 565.

4. *The War of the Rebellion: A Compilation of the Official Records of the Union and Confederate Armies,* 128 vols. (Washington, D.C.: Government Printing Office, 1880–1901), ser. 1, 26 (pt. 2): 58 (hereafter cited as *OR;* all citations are to series 1, unless otherwise noted).

5. *OR,* 15:1041, 1042–43; *OR,* 22 (pt. 2): 828; Richard Taylor, *Destruction and Reconstruction* (London: William Blackwood and Sons, 1879), 178–79; John D. Winters, *The Civil War in Louisiana* (Baton Rouge: Louisiana State University Press, 1963), 198.

6. Taylor, *Destruction and Reconstruction,* 179. By June, Taylor believed that he should place his major emphasis on relieving the Confederates at Port Hudson rather than operating opposite Vicksburg. See also Robert L. Kerby, *Kirby Smith's Confederacy: The Trans-Mississippi South, 1863–1865* (New York: Columbia University Press, 1972), 112–15.

7. Bell Irvin Wiley, *The Life of Johnny Reb: The Common Soldier of the Confederacy* (1943; reprint, Baton Rouge: Louisiana State University Press, 1987), 314; *OR,* 24 (pt. 2): 453–54, 455–56. See also Herbert Aptheker, "Negro Casualties in the Civil War," *Journal of Negro History* 32 (Jan. 1947): 10–80.

8. Charles Dana quoted in Dudley Taylor Cornish, *The Sable Arm: Negro Troops in the Union Army, 1861–1865* (1956; reprint, New York: W. W. Norton, 1966), 145.

9. Jackson Beauregard Davis, "The Life of Richard Taylor," (master's thesis, Louisiana State University, 1937), 75–76; *OR,* 24 (pt. 2): 461–62, 466. For a detailed account of Confederate operations west of the Mississippi River, see Edwin C. Bearss, "The Trans-Mississippi Confederates Attempt to Relieve Vicksburg," *McNeese Review* 15 (1964): 46–70, 16 (1965): 46–67. Walker's division consisted of the brigades of Henry McCulloch, Horace Randal, and James Hawes. An excellent narrative of Walker's operations along the Mississippi River can be found in Norman D. Brown, ed., *Journey to Pleasant Hill: The Civil War Letters of Captain Elijah P. Petty, Walker's Texas Division, C.S.A.* (San Antonio: Institute of Texan Cultures, 1982), 234–45.

10. *OR,* 22 (pt. 2): 856–57.

11. Not accompanying Colonel Parsons to Arkansas were Col. George W. Carter's 21st Texas Cavalry, several companies in a battalion under Maj. Charles L. Morgan, and a section of the battery under Maj. Joseph H. Pratt. Ibid., 851, 864, 866.

12. Soldat, "Col. Parsons' Cavalry Raid in the Valley of the Mississippi, Nearly Opposite Vicksburg . . . ," *Houston Weekly Telegraph,* Aug. 4, 1863. Soldat, sometimes spelled *Solidat,* was a member of the 12th Texas, probably on the colonel's staff, who wrote numerous articles for the Houston paper. His letters, which have proved quite accurate, provide information on events not otherwise recorded.

13. Ibid.; Henry Orr to father, June 27, 1863, in John Q. Anderson, ed., *Campaigning with Parsons' Texas Cavalry Brigade, CSA: The War Journals and Letters of the Four Orr Brothers, 12th Texas Cavalry Regiment* (Hillsboro, Tex.: Hill Junior College Press, 1967), 110–11.

14. Soldat, "Col. Parsons' Cavalry Raid."

15. Orr to father, 110–11; J. E. T., "Letter from Burford's Regiment," July 18, 1863, *Dallas Herald,* Aug. 5, 1863. J. E. T. was probably James E. Terrell, adjutant of the regiment, who died at Jackson, Mississippi, in November 1863 while on his way to Richmond.

16. J. P. Blessington, *The Campaign of Walker's Texas Division by a Private Soldier* (New York: Lange, Little, 1875), 113–14. Blessington mistakenly dated this account May instead of June.

17. J. E. T., "Letter from Burford's Regiment"; Report of Walker, 466; Winters, *Civil War in Louisiana,* 203; Brown, *Journey to Pleasant Hill,* 234–45.

18. Winters incorrectly identifies Parsons's command as "two Arkansas regiments to Tappan's cavalry." Winters, *Civil War in Louisiana,* 203.

19. Soldat, "Col. Parsons' Cavalry Raid."

20. For a complete account of the decision to station troops along the Mississippi River, see Cornish, *Sable Arm,* 115–19, 163–69. A description of life on a Federal plantation is found in Tho-

mas W. Knox, *Campfire and Cottonfield: Southern Adventure in Time of War: Life with the Union Armies, and Residence on a Louisiana Plantation* (New York: Blelock, 1865), 305–90, 417–54.

21. Soldat, "Col. Parsons' Cavalry Raid"; George W. Ingram to Martha Ingram, July 18, 1863, in *Civil War Letters of George W. and Martha F. Ingram, 1861–1865,* comp. Henry L. Ingram (College Station: Texas A&M University Press, 1973), 55–56.

22. J. E. T., "Letter from Burford's Regiment"; Soldat, "Col. Parsons' Cavalry Raid."

23. Winters, *Civil War in Louisiana,* 203–4; J. E. T., "Letter from Burford's Regiment"; Soldat, "Col. Parsons' Cavalry Raid."

24. Soldat, "Col. Parsons' Cavalry Raid."

25. George Ingram to Martha Ingram, 55–56; J. E. T., "Letter from Burford's Regiment"; Soldat, "Col. Parsons' Cavalry Raid."

26. James J. Frazier to mother, brothers, and sisters, July 7, [1863], Frazier Family Papers, Barker Texas History Center, Austin; J. E. T., "Letter from Burford's Regiment"; Soldat, "Col. Parsons' Cavalry Raid."

27. J. E. T., "Letter from Burford's Regiment"; Soldat, "Col. Parsons' Cavalry Raid."

28. Winters, *Civil War in Louisiana,* 203–4; J. E. T., "Letter from Burford's Regiment"; Soldat, "Col. Parsons' Cavalry Raid."

29. *OR,* 24 (pt. 2): 466; *OR,* 24 (pt. 3): 425–26, 443–44, 469; John Simmons to Nancy Simmons, July 2, 1863, in Jon Harrison, ed., "The Confederate Letters of John Simmons," *Chronicles of Smith County, Texas* 14 (summer 1975): 33–34. For a detailed discussion of the use of black soldiers, see Cornish, *Sable Arm,* 163–73.

30. Soldat, "Col. Parsons' Cavalry Raid." It should be pointed out that the black troops had also received what James McPherson described as "a somewhat left-handed compliment" from their Confederate adversaries after the fighting at Milliken's Bend. James M. McPherson, *The Negro's Civil War: How American Negroes Felt and Acted During the War for the Union* (New York: Vintage Books, 1965), 186–87. See also *OR,* 24 (pt. 2): 467–70.

31. Soldat, "Col. Parsons' Cavalry Raid"; *Official Records of the Union and Confederate Navies in the War of the Rebellion,* 30 vols. (Washington, D.C.: Government Printing Office, 1894–1922), ser. 1, 25:215–16 (hereafter cited as *ORN;* all citations are to series 1 unless otherwise noted); McPherson, *Battle Cry of Freedom,* 402.

32. William De Loss Love, *Wisconsin in the War of the Rebellion* (Chicago: Sheldon & Co., 1866), 557.

33. *ORN,* 25:212–14, 215–16.

34. The 19th and 21st Texas along with Morgan's companies and Pratt's Battery had joined Marmaduke on his raid upon Cape Girardeau, Missouri, from April 17 until May 2, 1863. For more on the expedition, see Stephen B. Oates, *Confederate Cavalry West of the River* (Austin: University of Texas Press, 1961), 121–31; and Anne J. Bailey, *Between the Enemy and Texas: Parsons's Texas Cavalry in the Civil War* (Fort Worth: Texas Christian University Press, 1989).

35. J. E. T., "Letter from Burford's Regiment."

36. George Ingram to Martha Ingram, 55–56; J. E. T., "Letter from Burford's Regiment"; Soldat, "Col. Parsons' Cavalry Raid."

37. Henry Orr to sister, July 2, 1863, in J. Anderson, *Campaigning with Parsons' Texas Cavalry Brigade,* 111–13.

38. Soldat, "Col. Parsons' Cavalry Raid"; *OR,* 24 (pt. 2): 450.

39. Porter reported to the secretary of the navy that the *John Raine* had arrived "as the rebels were setting fire to the so-called Government plantations, and supposing her to be an ordinary transport they opened fire on her with fieldpieces, but were much surprised to have the fire returned with shrapnel, which fell in among them, killing and wounding a number." The *Raine* was soon joined by the gunboat *Romeo,* which commenced shelling the enemy troops. *ORN,* 25:212–14.

40. Soldat, "Col. Parsons' Cavalry Raid"; *ORN,* 25:212–14.

41. Soldat, "Col. Parsons' Cavalry Raid." He goes on to say it was "the grandest sight I ever witnessed, and, were I to live threescore years and ten more, perhaps will never see again."

42. *OR,* 24 (pt. 2): 450.

43. Soldat, "Col. Parsons' Cavalry Raid"; *ORN,* 25: 215–16.

44. *ORN,* 25:212–14.

45. Soldat, "Col. Parsons' Cavalry Raid"; J. E. T., "Letter from Burford's Regiment"; Taylor, *Destruction and Reconstruction,* 181. See also Kerby, *Kirby Smith's Confederacy,* 115.

46. *OR,* 24 (pt. 2): 466; Winters, *Civil War in Louisiana,* 203–5; Kerby, *Kirby Smith's Confederacy,* 115.

47. Henry Orr to sister, July 15, 1863, in J. Anderson, *Campaigning with Parsons' Texas Cavalry Brigade,* 113–14.

48. Kate Stone diary, June 10, Sept. 1, 1863, in John Q. Anderson, ed., *Brokenburn: The Journal of Kate Stone, 1861–1868* (Baton Rouge: Louisiana State University Press, 1955), 218–19, 239.

49. Special Order No. 2, Aug. 16, 1863, Special Order Book of Parsons's Brigade, Collection of Parsons's Brigade Association Texas Cavalry, Sims Library, Waxahachie, Tex. Parsons had been born in New Jersey of Puritan ancestors. His family, however, had moved to Montgomery, Alabama, when he was a small child, and he had received his education in the South. There is a great deal of information concerning Parsons's ancestors, as his younger brother Albert moved north following the war and was among those executed for the killings at Chicago's Haymarket Square Riot in May 1886. See Lucy E. Parsons, ed., *Life of Albert R. Parsons* (1889; reprint, Chicago: Lucy E. Parsons, 1903), 12–15; Philip S. Foner, ed., *The Autobiographies of the Haymarket Martyrs* (New York: Humanities Press, 1969), 27–29; Paul Avrich, *The Haymarket Tragedy* (Princeton: Princeton University Press, 1984), 3–5; and Carolyn Ashbaugh, *Lucy Parsons, American Revolutionary* (Chicago: Charles H. Kerr, 1976), 13–14.

50. Kirby Smith quoted in Kerby, *Kirby Smith's Confederacy,* 312; Henry Orr to sister, Nov. 12, 1864, in J. Anderson, *Campaigning with Parsons' Texas Cavalry Brigade,* 149–50.

51. Frazier Family Papers, Barker Texas History Center; Frazier Papers, Confederate Research Center, Hillsboro, Tex.; Bureau of the Census, Eighth Census of the United States: Population Schedule, Hill County, Texas (microfilm, Washington, D.C.); Terry G. Jordan, "The Imprint of the Upper and Lower South in Mid–Nineteenth Century Texas," *Annals of the Association of American Geographers* 57 (1967): 667–90.

Captive Black Union Soldiers in Charleston 2
What to Do?

HOWARD C. WESTWOOD

"Thirteen prisoners Fifty-fourth Massachusetts, black. What shall I do with them?" That message, hastily penned by Confederate Brig. Gen. Johnson Hagood on the night of July 16, 1863, near the beginning of the Union attack on Fort Wagner, also noted that two of the blacks were "refugee" slaves, the rest free.[1]

The general's question posed a conundrum. The Confederacy had been struggling with it for months and would continue to struggle with it until the war was dwindling to an end. By mid-1863, the Union, after long hesitation, was taking blacks into its army by the thousands. Inevitably, some had become Confederate captives. In time there were many more. Some had been slaves in the state where they were captured. Some had been slaves in another of the Confederate states. Some had been slaves in a Union slave state. Some had been free, residents of a Union state or even of the Confederacy (notably Louisiana). Many blacks had donned the Union uniform voluntarily; but not a few, especially among slaves of Confederate states, had been forced into the army, either by formal conscription or by irregular means. Nearly all would be in the ranks, and eventually, some would be commissioned. Captive, too, would be some of their white officers. Finally, among the captives there would be officers and men of white units operating in conjunction with black units. The law of every Confederate state made slave insurrection or aiding such insurrection a crime; and as viewed by the Confederates, slaves in arms as Union soldiers were engaged in insurrection. The conundrum: Were all these captives regular prisoners of war or were they all common criminals? Or were some the former and some the latter? Or were some captives something in between, in some new, unprecedented status? Or were some simply to be slain, without ceremony? Confederate statesmen, politicians, military commanders, judges, lawyers, and ordinary soldiers and civilians were to face this puzzle. Nowhere in the Confederacy was it posed more starkly than in Charleston. For, from late 1862 until almost the end of the war, in Charleston and its near regions, there was repeated conflict with Union forces that included slaves of the local citizenry and, by 1863, slaves from elsewhere as well as free blacks.

General Hagood's query, after receipt at district headquarters, was forwarded at once to Gen. Pierre G. T. Beauregard, commander of the Department of South Carolina, Georgia, and Florida, headquartered in Charleston. With it went word that the captive blacks had been ordered to the city under a strong guard and "without their uniforms."[2] On the next day, July 17, the department sent a copy of Hagood's note to South Carolina governor M. L. Bonham. At the same time, Beauregard informed Richmond that he had black prisoners from the Union forces, several of whom "claim to be free, from Massachusetts." He asked, "Shall they be turned over to State authorities with the other negroes?"[3]

It reflected the confusion in the Confederacy at that time—the time of Chancellorsville, Gettysburg, Vicksburg, and Port Hudson—that neither General Beauregard nor Governor Bonham yet knew that on May 1, 1863, President Jefferson Davis had approved a joint resolution of the Confederate Congress that, as we shall see, answered Beauregard's question. The general and the governor both thought that President Davis's proclamation of December 23, 1862, promulgated on Christmas Eve, was still applicable: that "all negro slaves captured in arms be at once delivered over to the executive authorities of the respective States to which they belong to be dealt with according to the laws of said States," and that "like orders be executed in all cases with respect to all commissioned officers of the United States when found serving in company with armed slaves."[4]

Doubtless, Beauregard thought that the proclamation had been carefully formulated, for it had followed by less than a month quite different instructions that he had received from Secretary of War James A. Seddon. In mid-November 1862, one of Beauregard's district commanders had captured four slaves, armed and in Union uniform, and Beauregard immediately had sought Seddon's guidance. After checking with the president, Seddon on November 30 had instructed Beauregard to avoid a dilemma. On the one hand, delay and "military inconvenience" would be caused by turning the slaves over to civil tribunals, and on the other hand, they could not be recognized as "soldiers subject to the rules of war and to trial by military courts." The way between the dilemma's horns, Seddon instructed, was to have the "general commanding the special locality of the capture" inflict on the slaves "summary execution."[5] Obviously, Davis's proclamation, coming so soon after Seddon's harsh instruction, must have been thought through. And notably, it said nothing about free blacks. So Beauregard wanted further guidance. Indeed, as it turned out, most of the black captives claimed that they had not been slaves.

A very recent episode had shown Beauregard that he was in a delicate area. It had been only a month since General Hagood had forwarded a report that several young Confederate soldiers had been captured by Union forces at an observation outpost along one of the coastal waters. They were "sons of wealthy planters or themselves owners of slaves" and were lodged in the Beaufort jail instead of being treated as prisoners of war subject to exchange. It was said that the young men were kept hostage for black Union troops or their officers who might be captured by the Confederates.[6]

It was well for Beauregard to take warning from that report, for the facts behind it were sobering. It seems that the young Confederates were a sergeant and eight privates captured by the Union navy and that the navy had acceded to a demand of Union Maj. Gen. David Hunter, then army commander in the Sea Islands region, that they be turned over to him. Hunter knew that regiments of former slaves in his command had been one of the causes for the institution of a Confederate policy denying prisoner-of-war treatment to blacks and their officers. When he had found that among the navy's prisoners were "young darlings" of Southern families, "rich, powerful and malignant," "pets of the aristocracy," he wanted them as hostages.[7] Moreover, on the very day of the report that Hagood had forwarded, Hunter had instructed the commander of one of his black regiments, a one-time Jayhawker, Col. James Montgomery, that "every rebel man you may capture, citizen or soldier, you will send in irons to this place to be kept as hostages for the proper treatment of any of your men who may accidentally fall into the hands of the enemy."[8] While Beauregard would not have known of Hunter's instruction to Montgomery, he did know of a letter that Hunter had written to President Davis as recently as April 23, 1863, that revealed his attitude. Back in August 1862, when Hunter was first trying to take slaves into his army, Davis had his War Department issue an order declaring Hunter an outlaw and providing for his execution as a felon on presidential order, if captured, and the execution of any other captured Union officer engaged in "instructing slaves, with a view to their armed service in this war." In his April letter, Hunter had announced to Davis that if the August order were not revoked, "I will at once cause the execution of every rebel officer and every rebel slaveholder in my possession."[9]

While by the time of the Union expedition against Fort Wagner, Hunter had been superseded by Brig. Gen. Quincy Adams Gillmore as the Union army commander,[10] it was obvious enough to Beauregard that measure and countermeasure, retaliation met by retaliation, might soon make war uncivilized, and that he should exercise caution in his treatment of captive blacks. Indeed, there already had been a breakdown of the Union-Confederate prisoner exchange cartel so that any exchange was limited to "special agreements." The Confederate treatment of blacks had been one of the principal causes of the breakdown and would persist as an obstacle to repair.[11]

While Beauregard was writing Richmond, Governor Bonham was asking his state attorney general what evidence was required to render blacks captured in arms "amenable" for delivery to the state's executive under the presidential proclamation. On the next day, July 18, the attorney general opined that, since 1740, "by the laws of South Carolina a negro is presumed to be a slave until the contrary appears." Moreover, he advised, authoritative commentary had declared that "color is prima facie evidence that the party bearing the color of a negro, mulatto or mestizo is a slave." Hence, he concluded, General Beauregard must deliver to the governor all blacks captured in arms in South Carolina "unless by evidence before him he is satisfied that the prima facie presumption of slavery arising from color has been rebutted."[12]

The governor sent Beauregard a copy of his attorney general's opinion, and they conducted "some informal proceedings."[13] Though more blacks than those first reported by General Hagood were being captured, of the few who did not claim to be free, none was a South Carolinian. The presidential proclamation had ordered that slaves should be turned over to the executive of the state "to which they belong." Also, among the captives, there were white officers of black units, and the proclamation had ordered that "like orders be executed" for such men. Beauregard apparently thought that the proclamation meant what it said; that his slave captives and their officers were not to be turned over to South Carolina authorities but, presumably, were to be sent to the "belonging" state. The governor—who was a lawyer and formerly had been both a United States and a Confederate congressman[14]—read words not for what they said but for what they intended; in his view, however strained, the state "to which they belong" was intended to be the state where the "offense" of slave rebellion and the capture had occurred—South Carolina. But on the question of the free blacks, Beauregard and the governor did agree that further word from the president was needed.

As a result, on July 21, Beauregard followed up his recent inquiry to Richmond with a wire: "What shall be done with the negro prisoners who say they are free? Please answer."[15] And on the next day, the governor wrote Beauregard, formally demanding custody of the captured slaves and white officers and asking that the free blacks be retained—not exchanged or paroled—pending word from Richmond. As to the slaves, said the governor, if Beauregard disagreed with his interpretation of "to which [state] they belong," they also should be retained until the president could resolve the question. On the following day, July 23, the governor wrote Secretary of War Seddon, enclosing a copy of his letter to Beauregard, requesting not only the slaves and white officers but also the free blacks; the latter, he said, had violated a South Carolina statute of 1805 prescribing death for any person "concerned or connected with any slave or slaves in a state of actual insurrection within this State."[16]

On the day the governor had written Beauregard, Seddon had wired the general that, pursuant to a resolution of the Confederate Congress, "all negroes taken in arms" were "to be handed over to the authorities of the State where captured to be dealt with according to the laws thereof." And on the day the governor wrote Seddon, Beauregard wired the secretary of war that he did not know of the resolution, that, indeed, a congressman had informed him that "it failed to pass."[17] But finally, the governor located a copy of the resolution and, on July 27, sent it to the general.[18]

This was the resolution of May 1. It provided, as Seddon's wire had indicated, that all "negroes and mulattoes" (slave or free) who were "engaged in war . . . against the Confederate States" or who "give aid or comfort to the enemies of the Confederate States" shall, on capture, "be delivered to the authorities of the State or States in which they shall be captured to be dealt with according to the present or future law of such State or States."[19] Hence, on July 29, the governor was advised by Beauregard that the blacks, slave and free, were at his disposal. The governor, however, was not yet ready to take custody, and at his request, they were kept in Castle Pinckney, the military prison, until August 19, when they were transferred to the Charleston jail.[20]

For a time, however, the governor was confused about the white officers. Perhaps he had not read closely the congressional resolution before sending it to the general. For, on August 8, he wrote Seddon requesting that the officers also be delivered to him.[21] Two days later, though, he had found that the resolution explicitly provided that captured officers from black units would not be turned over to state authorities but would be tried by a Confederate military court and "be put to death or be otherwise punished at the discretion of the court," subject to the president's power to commute sentence.[22] Thus, on August 10, the governor wrote Seddon again, withdrawing his request for the officers. But in this further letter, Bonham raised a question: Would it be quite right for a free black to be given one sentence—South Carolina law, as we have seen, prescribed death, subject only to the governor's general power of commutation—but for his officer to be given a less severe punishment, as was possible under the congressional resolution? His letter suggested some arrangement between the state and Confederate authorities for uniformity of treatment. Bonham also advised Seddon that he would proceed with the trial of slaves and any free blacks from Confederate states but would delay action on free blacks from the North, hoping to hear word on the question he had raised.[23] The governor was beginning to glimpse something of the conundrum.

In the meantime, there was mounting public outrage that the defenders of Charleston were confronting armed blacks. The press reported that the Confederate troops were indignant at the thought that a white man might one day be exchanged for a black. The Northern blacks were described as "a mongrel set of trash." Incidents were reported of blacks, seeking to surrender, being summarily shot. To lend grim humor to the issue, there was quoted the story of a Frenchman who begged for quarter from a Scot: "'I canna stop to quarter ye,' he remarked, 'but I'll cut ye in twa.' And suiting his actions to his words he passed on." Indeed, the account of the opening engagement in the Fort Wagner attack told that the blacks "received no tender treatment during the skirmish, and the marsh in one place was thick with their dead bodies."[24]

One of the local papers, virulently anti-Davis, knowing that the governor had demanded that free black captives be turned over to him, assumed that their continued residence in Castle Pinckney was due to "that serbonian bog of indecision—Richmond."[25] The authorities were quick to correct the paper's misunderstanding; already the governor was preparing for criminal proceedings. On August 10, he had instructed his attorney general to convene a court for the trial of such of the captives as appeared to be slaves or to be free blacks of the Confederate states, and on the next day, Bonham ordered a three-man commission—two of his staff and another "prominent citizen"—to examine all the black prisoners.[26]

On August 14, the commission reported to the governor. There were, by then, twenty-four black captives other than hospitalized wounded. Each of the twenty-four was questioned separately. One prisoner seemed defiant; all the others were respectful. Only four appeared to be slaves. Of the twenty free men, none was from a Confederate state (though one seemed to be from Maryland). All were from the 54th Massachusetts Regiment (Colored). Questioning disclosed, however, that the entire unit contained not more than fifty or sixty blacks from Massachusetts and but a few more from other New England states; in fact, about a third of the regiment had come from Ohio.

The commissioners had, for the most part, believed the stories they heard, for they were convincingly similar. All but the one defiant captive were utterly disillusioned by their treatment in the Union army and were eager to return to civilian life. In substance, their complaints were three: their enlistment had been solicited by the promise that their service would not be for combat but merely for garrison and fatigue duty; promises of bounty and rates of pay had been grossly violated; and in battle, they had been put in the forefront "as breastworks for the White Troops" and were told by their officers that they would be shot from behind if they did not advance. Some said that their officers deserted them. Two prisoners were unarmed officers' servants, carrying into the attack only canteens for their officers.[27]

On August 14, the day the commission filed its report with the governor, Seddon wrote Bonham in reply to the letter of August 8, which had requested custody of the blacks' officers. Seddon pointed out that the congressional resolution superseded the presidential proclamation and that the officers were thus to be handled by the military. He assured Bonham that "appropriate proceedings will be instituted and severe punishment inflicted upon the officers taken in the unworthy and criminal service of commanding negroes, thereby inciting to servile insurrection and all its attendant horrors within your State."[28]

Though Seddon's letter was not, in fact, a reply to the governor's letter of August 10, in which he had withdrawn his earlier request but had raised the question of uniformity of punishment for free blacks and their officers, it seemed to say that the military would deal harshly with the officers. So, on August 19, with Seddon's letter received, the governor transmitted a copy to his attorney general, telling him to "defer no longer the trial of the free negroes of the Federal States found in arms with slaves."[29] By August 21, the governor had assigned as counsel to the blacks a very able Charleston lawyer, Nelson Mitchell; on that day, Bonham sent instructions to the Charleston sheriff to allow Mitchell and "lawyers associated with him" to have access to the prisoners "for the purpose of preparing for their defence."[30]

Soon—perhaps at Mitchell's request—the governor appointed as his co-counsel Edward McCrady, also a very able Charleston lawyer. The governor ordered the attorney general personally to prosecute the case, designating as his co-counsel one of the members of the commission that had examined the prisoners.[31] The matter was now coming to a head. On August 25, the court met and organized for the trial.[32] It was the police court for the Charleston District, sometimes called the provost marshal's court, with criminal jurisdiction over slaves and free blacks, and its decisions were not subject to appeal. The proceedings began on September 8; but only the four alleged slaves were brought to trial, despite the governor's instruction of August 19 that the free black captives were to be tried also.[33]

It is not known whether the trial was confined to the four slaves as a result of lawyers' tactics or as a result of the receipt by the governor of a further letter from Seddon, written on September 1, replying to Bonham's letter of August 10.[34] When the governor read this further letter, he was to find new confusion injected into Confederate policy. In Richmond, the complexity of the conundrum was becoming apparent. In early June, Seddon had written an old school friend, who had suggested that captured officers and men of black regiments be put to work "in the Chesterfield coal-pits," that the law required that slaves be turned over to the states, and that blacks "without free papers when not claimed by the owners" would "be liable to be sold as slaves."[35] But that easy dictate hardly met the problem. The problem was soon to be posed to Richmond more insistently by Lt. Gen. Edmund Kirby Smith, commanding the Department of the Trans-Mississippi.

In mid-June, Kirby Smith sent to Richmond copies of letters written to Maj. Gen. Richard Taylor, one of his district commanders who had custody of some blacks "captured in arms." Kirby Smith did not know of the congressional resolution; like Beauregard, he had understood that the legislation had not been adopted, leaving in force the presidential proclamation. One of the letters to Taylor had been sent by Kirby Smith's assistant adjutant general; it told Taylor that "no quarter" should be given to slaves in arms, but if quarter were given, they should be turned over to the executive authorities of the state where captured. (Apparently, Kirby Smith, like Governor Bonham, interpreted "to which they belong" in the proclamation not to mean what the words said.) The letter went on to say that if such blacks were executed by the military, Union retaliation would be provoked; but the author naively added that if they were turned over to the civil authorities to be tried under state law, "no exception can be taken." The other letter to Taylor was from Kirby Smith himself, who hoped that Taylor's subordinates "recognized the propriety of giving no quarter to armed negroes and their officers. In this way we may be relieved from a disagreeable dilemma." But if blacks were taken captive, Kirby Smith added, they should be turned over to state authorities for trial. In sending copies of the two letters to Richmond, Kirby Smith wrote, "Unfortunately such captures were made by some of Major-General Taylor's subordinates."[36]

With Kirby Smith's communication in hand by mid-July, Seddon had a reply sent that suggested a different policy. The reply did not mention officers, only the blacks. They, "as deluded victims," ought to be "treated with mercy and returned to their owners." However, "a few examples might perhaps be made," though "to refuse them quarter" would make them, "against their tendencies, fight desperately."[37] If, by the time Kirby Smith received this word, he had been informed of the congressional resolution, he must have wondered if his secretary of war intended to follow it; for the resolution was perfectly clear—all blacks, slave or free, were to be turned over to state authorities to be dealt with under state law; it made no provision either for refusing quarter or for the military's return of a slave to his owner.

In any event, Governor Bonham's letters, especially that of August 10 suggesting uniform treatment of free blacks and their officers, forced Seddon to seek instruction from his president. Perhaps he wanted such guidance because of a recent action by the president of the United States. On July 31, the Union's War Department had promulgated a proclamation by President Abraham Lincoln announcing that the Union would protect all of its citizens, "of whatsoever class, color, or condition," and that "for every soldier of the United States killed in violation of the laws of war a rebel soldier shall be executed, and for every one enslaved by the enemy or sold into slavery a rebel soldier shall be placed at hard labor on the public works."[38] When Seddon received Bonham's August 10 letter, he sent it to President Davis for instruction. The president returned it, inviting Seddon to state his own views. On August 23, Seddon resubmitted the letter with his endorsement, saying that "the free negroes should be either promptly executed or the determination arrived at and announced not to execute them during the war." They should not be treated as prisoners of war, said Seddon, but dealt with so as "to mark our stern reprobation of the barbarous employment of such inciters to insurrection." Seddon suggested that the way to do this "effectually" would be "by holding them to hard labor during the war." Seddon did not suggest how this course might be squared with the May 1863 congressional resolution.

On August 25, President Davis returned Bonham's letter to Seddon with his own endorsement added. He noted that the congressional resolution "gives no discretion to the Executive so far as the captured negroes are concerned." But, said Davis, the statute did provide, in the case of "white men serving with Negroes" (Davis did not say "officers"), that he had the power "to commute [the] penalty" that might be imposed by a military court. This, Davis noted, indicated "a purpose to make discriminations" between individual cases. So, Davis concluded, Bonham's suggestion that there be "the same line of action" by the state and by the Confederate governments (in their

respective treatment of free blacks and officers) could not be given a definite answer, "as each case must depend upon its circumstances"—unless
(and here the conundrum surely was confessed), "as you intimate," it were
decided "not to bring any case to trial." As to that possibility, Davis said that
he did "not know how far the power of the Governor extends."[39]

It was with the problem thus back in his lap that Seddon wrote to Bonham
on September 1. His letter quoted his own endorsement to the president and
the president's return endorsement. To the governor, he recommended that
"the captured negroes be not brought to trial, or if condemned, that your power
of executive clemency be exercised" to allow for the possibility of an "arrangement on this question, so fraught with present difficulty and future danger."
The difficulty and danger referred to, of course, was Union retaliation.[40]

Whether or not it was this word from Seddon that prompted the decision not to go forward with the trial of the free blacks when the four alleged
slaves were tried, that decision at least was consistent with a position then
being taken by the Confederate agent of exchange in a conference with his
Union counterpart on the breakdown of the prisoner exchange cartel. At the
conference, as the Union agent reported to his superior on August 25, the
Confederate agent said that his people would "die in the last ditch" before
giving up their right to send captured slaves back to slavery but that they were
willing to make "exceptions" for free blacks.[41] Obviously, the seeming neat
simplicity of the Confederate Congress's resolution was becoming befogged.

The trial of the four slaves, however, did proceed. It lasted for three days,
from September 8 to 10. The court was a five-man tribunal. There were two
charges: that being slaves, the defendants had been in insurrection against
the state; and that they had been "concerned and connected with slaves" in
insurrection. Allegedly, two of the defendants had been slaves in Missouri
and two in Virginia. The second of the two charges presumably was designed
to cover the case were it decided that only its own slaves could be deemed
to be in insurrection against South Carolina; the evidence was to show that,
in any case, the defendants had been encamped with two Union regiments
of South Carolina slaves.

At the trial, the only evidentiary conflict was whether or not one of the
defendants, in fact, had been a slave. Time was largely devoted to lawyers'
arguments, chiefly on the question of "the jurisdiction of the court, as a Civil
Tribunal, to try offenses committed by persons engaged as soldiers in the
act of war, and in the ranks of the enemy." The unanimous decision of the
judges, announced without elaboration, was that the court had no jurisdiction. Thereupon, the court ordered that the prisoners be recommitted to jail

and that the governor be notified of its decision.[42] The captives were subsequently held in the Charleston jail, month after dreary month, along with other captured blacks. Already in the jail when they had arrived were four black Union sailors, at least three of whom were free-born New Yorkers.

Despite the fact that from the Republic's early days, the Union to which the Confederate states had been parties had enlisted blacks in its navy (though not in its army),[43] the Confederates treated these black sailors harshly. As crew members of the Union gunboat *Isaac Smith,* they, with the boat's officers and the rest of the crew, had been captured in Charleston's waters in late January 1863. In time, the officers and white crewmen were exchanged. The Confederate exchange agent had included the names of the blacks in the exchange list furnished to the Union agent, but that had been a deception. Not until August did Union authorities hear that the blacks, in fact, were incarcerated in the Charleston jail. The three black New Yorkers had managed to have smuggled out a note to the United States consul in Nassau telling of their fate: "in close confinement," "almost dead," and fed "but a little corn bread and water." Their note was forwarded to Washington, where, on August 3, Secretary of the Navy Gideon Welles sent it on to Secretary of War Stanton for his "special attention." Maj. Gen. Ethan Allen Hitchcock, the Union commissioner for exchange, advised Stanton that there had been "other cases like this" and that, in his view, "they can only be effectually reached by a successful prosecution of the war." Stanton then ordered Hitchcock to have three South Carolina prisoners held "in close custody as hostages for the three colored men" and to communicate that action to Richmond.[44] Three captive privates of a South Carolina Confederate cavalry unit were put to "hard labor on the public works" in Washington.[45] But in the Charleston jail, the three New Yorkers and a fourth black crewman remained confined.[46]

For Governor Bonham, by mid-September, the conundrum had become most sharply posed. The Confederate Congress had decreed that all captured blacks were to be turned over to state authorities "to be dealt with according to" state law. But the governor's own state court had ruled that a South Carolina crime had not been committed by "persons engaged as soldiers in the act of war," even though they had been slaves. While Bonham later was to write Seddon that "the correctness" of that decision "may be questioned," he could hardly defy it. Aside from its finality under state law, the standing of the counsel involved gave it force. Prosecuted by the attorney general and defended by two of the state's leading lawyers—characterized by Bonham himself as "eminent"—the outcome of the case could not be shrugged off.[47] While the court's ruling, on its face, seemed applicable to slaves of South Carolina as well as other states, the governor, in time, did have at least some South Carolinian slaves tried before other state courts, and they were executed. But beyond that, he did not go; with his president fuzzily suggesting that blacks not be brought to trial, and with the secretary of war, obviously troubled by the problem of Union retaliation, recommending that the governor postpone a decision, Bonham simply "suspended further action," leaving the blacks in the Charleston jail at the expense of the state and local civil governments.[48] His bafflement must have increased when he found, as surely he soon did, that white officers of black units were not being given the severe treatment by the military that Seddon had so confidently predicted. With only a few exceptions, nowhere in the Confederacy was the pertinent provision of the congressional resolution actually carried out; the officers were treated rather as prisoners of war.[49]

Nearly a year after the Charleston trial, the governor picked up word from the Richmond press that further complicated the problem. It was reported that recently captured Union soldiers who had been slaves were being delivered to their former owners. Puzzled, on June 24, 1864, the governor wrote Seddon, asking for any pertinent regulations.[50] There is no record of a reply. Two months later, on August 23, he wrote Seddon again, saying that, in line with Seddon's letter of September 1, 1863, he had suspended action against all captive blacks except those who had been South Carolina slaves, but he wanted to bring the question "again to your attention, in order that something definite may be done if practicable." He explained that his term of office would end in December and that he would "be glad" to dispose of the matter before then.[51]

That the governor was in a mood to place the whole business behind him is suggested by the fact that his office had just requested the state auditor to recommend "a suitable and proper fee" to be paid to the lawyers who had conducted the prosecution and the defense in the trial of the previous September. In early September 1864, the auditor, after consulting "eminent members of the bar," recommended that a proper fee would be one thousand dollars "to each of the Council on the part of the State and on the part of the prisoners respectively."[52] This recommendation reached the governor just after he had received a reply from Seddon to his August 23 letter. Seddon's reply, dated August 31, must have made Bonham wonder whether all the trouble and expense undertaken by the state had been worth the candle.

Seddon said, in effect, that the Confederate executive and military were ignoring the congressional resolution of May 1, 1863, because of "embarrassments" from its "rigid enforcement." ("Embarrassments," of course, referred to Union retaliation.)

Moreover, some state authorities had objected to having blacks turned over to them and often complained about the "inability . . . to obtain criminal trials." So, said Seddon, captives who had been slaves were being returned to their owners under a statute of October 1862. But "free negroes of the North are held in strict confinement, not as yet formally recognized in any official dealing with the enemy as prisoners-of-war, but, except in some trivial particulars indicative of inferior consideration, are treated very much in the same manner as our other captives." Seddon concluded with advice that the governor deliver slaves to their owners and free blacks "to the Confederate authorities."[53]

The October 1862 statute referred to by Seddon had been adopted at the closing of the second session of the first Confederate Congress as a reaction to President Lincoln's preliminary Emancipation Proclamation. The new law had provided that the secretary of war should establish depots in each state to hold slaves captured by the Confederate military. Each slave would be returned to his owner on due proof of the owner's claim; newspaper advertisements of the slave would be published, and until proof of the claim was forthcoming, the slave would be employed by the military on public works. The bill whence came the statute had provided also that captured free blacks should be delivered to the governor of the state where captured "to be dealt with according to the laws of such State," but the House committee handling the bill had eliminated that provision.[54] Thus, the measure was very different from the severe congressional resolution of May 1, 1863. Indeed it may be that the 1862 statute had been intended initially to apply only to noncombatant slaves, fugitive or seized by Union forces, who were captured by the Confederate military; and it certainly had not been designed to cover the case of slaves of a non-Confederate state (Delaware and Maryland).[55] In any case, whatever the intended scope of that statute, and even though the 1863 resolution had not amended it in express terms, the latter most certainly had superseded the former with respect to slaves captured in arms. But now the Confederate executive, by sheer fiat, had superseded the 1863 measure in its entirety with the much narrower and milder 1862 statute.

If, on Governor Bonham's reading of Seddon's August 31 letter, he questioned what the military would do with free blacks "not as yet formally recognized . . . as prisoners-of-war," that uncertainty was removed in a letter sent a few weeks later, at Seddon's instruction, by Gen. Robert E. Lee to Lt. Gen. Ulysses S. Grant. This letter, sent on October 19, defended the propriety of the Confederates' returning to their owners captured Union soldiers or sailors who had been slaves of "citizens or residents of the Confederate States" but stated, unambiguously, that all other blacks in the Union armed services "are regarded as prisoners of war, being held to be proper subjects of exchange, as I recently had the honor to inform you. No labor is exacted from such prisoners by the Confederate authorities."[56]

When, if ever, that authoritative word reached Bonham, it must have heightened his confusion. Obviously, in his Charleston jail there were many free blacks, and they certainly were not being treated as prisoners of war. Further, he felt that some among his prisoners had been slaves, and Seddon's August 31 letter had advised that they be delivered to their owners, not kept in jail. But from the evidence available to him, Bonham could not identify either the slaves or their owners. Even as to the four who had been tried the year before, there was a problem. As to one, an alleged Virginia slave, evidence of his slavery was not clear; he may have been a free-born Ohioan. Two of the others were from Hannibal, Missouri, and the third from Norfolk, Virginia.[57] Identifying their owners and returning them would be, to put it mildly, impractical at that stage of the war. Finally, as the end of his term loomed near, the governor gave up. On December 8, he wrote Seddon that on that day he had ordered the Charleston sheriff to deliver all the prisoners to the Confederate military. "A few of them, it is supposed, may be slaves," he wrote, "but the State has no means of identifying them or their masters." He told Seddon that he had given the military "the evidence from which it is supposed that some of them may be slaves."[58]

In the meantime, for nearly a year and a half, the blacks had been suffering a jail confinement with the scantest fare and most miserable conditions.[59] Neither the Confederacy nor the state ever had notified the Union authorities of their identity; they had been nonpersons. While rumors reached the North that there were black prisoners in South Carolina, there was no way for the Union authorities to know who of the missing were dead and who were imprisoned. But, finally, there came in August 1864 another smuggled note brought by an exchanged white officer. The note pleaded that something be done to release the prisoners from their "destitute condition." The note was signed "Mass." but appended to it was a list of forty-six blacks in the Charleston jail as of June 13, 1864, most from the 54th Massachusetts, including the four who had been defendants in the trial of the preceding September. In a few days, the list was published in the New York press.[60] But, as we have seen, the blacks remained in jail until turned over to the Confederate military in December.

From that time, their circumstances, miserable as they had been, worsened. For their destination was the military prison stockade at Florence, South Carolina, which rivaled Andersonville. Disease was rife, and some died, including two of those who had been defendants at the September trial, victims of fever.[61] The Confederacy was disintegrating. By late January 1865, Brig. Gen. John H. Winder, in charge of prisons in the area, wanted to move his Florence prisoners; but he was "at a loss to know where," for "in one direction the enemy are in the way. In the other the question of supplies presents an insuperable barrier." He urged "paroling the prisoners and sending them home." Bonham's successor as governor and Brig. Gen. James Chesnut Jr., a leading South Carolinian, agreed with him.[62] But Winder's proposal was not accepted. Instead, the prisoners were moved from place to place in North Carolina.[63] In the meantime, by the end of January, the Confederate Congress had drastically amended the May 1, 1863, resolution so that it became nothing more than a condemnation of the employment of Confederate slaves as Union soldiers and a mere authorization to the president to retaliate as he thought proper. President Davis approved the amendment on February 8.[64] Finally, in early March, as Maj. Gen. William T. Sherman drove northward, most if not all of the black captives who had survived were released near Goldsboro, North Carolina. It is uncertain from records whether they were paroled, exchanged, or simply released.[65] No matter! The nonpersons had become persons again. And in Charleston, the struggle with the conundrum was no more. On February 18, Charleston had been occupied by the Union army.

Notes

This essay was originally published in *Civil War History* 27 (Mar. 1982): 28–44. Reprinted with permission of the Kent State University Press.

1. *The War of the Rebellion: A Compilation of the Official Records of the Union and Confederate Armies,* 128 vols. (Washington, D.C.: Government Printing Office, 1880–1901), ser. 2, 6:660–63 (hereafter cited as *OR;* all citations are to series 2, unless otherwise noted). See also F. W. Pickens and M. L. Bonham Papers, vol. 3, 519, Library of Congress, Washington, D.C. (hereafter cited as Bonham Papers; all citations are to volume 3).

2. *OR,* 6:124.

3. Bonham Papers, 519; *OR,* 6:125.

4. *OR,* 5:795–97. In his message of Jan. 12, 1863, opening the third session of the first Confederate Congress, President Davis said that he would treat the "enlisted soldiers" (meaning whites) as "unwilling instruments" of crime and would release them on parole. See *Messages and Papers of the Confederacy,* ed. James D. Richardson, 2 vols. (Nashville: United States Publishing, 1905), 1:290–91.

5. *OR,* 4:945–46, 954.

6. *OR,* 5:970.

7. It is virtually certain that the captives in the Beaufort jail were the Confederate soldiers

captured by the Union navy, whose custody as hostages Hunter had demanded of Rear Adm. Samuel F. Du Pont, naval commander in the area, of Secretary of the Navy Gideon Welles, and of President Abraham Lincoln. See *OR*, 5:646–47, 659, 666, 697, 698, 708, 711–13. Hence, I infer that Hunter's demand had been met.

8. *OR*, 5:770.

9. *OR*, ser. 1, 14:448–49, 599; *Charleston Mercury*, June 9, 1863.

10. *Charleston Mercury*, June 9, 13, 1863.

11. *OR*, 6:136; William Best Hesseltine, *Civil War Prisons* (1930; reprint, New York: F. Ungar, 1964), 87–89, 112–13, 186–88, 216–30.

12. Bonham Papers, 521.

13. *Charleston Mercury*, Aug. 15, 1863.

14. Edward McCrady Jr. and Samuel A. Ashe, *Cyclopedia of Eminent and Representative Men of the Carolinas,* 2 vols. (Madison, Wis.: Brant and Fuller, 1892), 1:88–90; Charles Edward Cauthen, *South Carolina Goes to War* (Chapel Hill: University of North Carolina Press, 1950), 166.

15. *OR*, 6:134.

16. Ibid., 139–40, 145–46; Bonham Papers, 523.

17. *OR*, 6:139, 145.

18. *Charleston Mercury*, Aug. 15, 1863.

19. *OR*, 5:940–41.

20. *Charleston Mercury*, Aug. 13, 15, 20, 1863; commitment to jail of Alfred Whiting and other Negro soldiers, Commitments, 1863, 1864, Penal System Papers, 1860–65, 7:238, dr. 3, South Carolina Department of Archives and History, Columbia, S.C.

21. *OR*, 6:190–91.

22. *OR*, 5:940–41.

23. *OR*, 6:193–94; Bonham Papers, 535.

24. *Charleston Courier*, July 17, 20, 22, Aug. 1, 1863; *Charleston Mercury*, Aug. 15, 1863.

25. *Charleston Mercury*, Aug. 11, 12, 1863.

26. *Charleston Mercury*, Aug. 13, 15, 1863; Bonham Papers, 536.

27. Bonham Papers, 540–41. In the Bonham Papers, 542–49, immediately following the commission's report, are notes of interviews with each of the twenty-four blacks; legibility is limited. (At that time, there were twenty-odd hospitalized wounded black captives in addition to those held in Castle Pinckney. See *OR*, 6:187–88; and *Charleston Courier*, Aug. 11, 1863.) The professed disillusionment of the blacks probably was not feigned. Early in 1863, Gov. John A. Andrew of Massachusetts secured authority from the War Department to raise and organize black troops; thus was created the 54th Massachusetts. But there were few blacks in Massachusetts or even in all of New England. An intensive recruiting drive was launched throughout much of the North. Unquestionably, recruiters offered strong inducements. The failure to make good on promised compensation is a familiar story. Familiar, too, is the fact that Col. Robert Gould Shaw, commanding the 54th, sought and secured a lead spot in opening assaults in the Fort Wagner operation. See Dudley Taylor Cornish, *The Sable Arm: Negro Troops in the United Army, 1861–1865* (1956; reprint, New York: W. W. Norton, 1966), 105–10, 150–56, 184–96. Interestingly, though the preliminary Emancipation Proclamation had not referred to blacks becoming soldiers, the final proclamation had announced that the freed slaves would be received into the armed service "to garrison forts, positions, stations, and other places and to man vessels." See House Misc. Doc. 210, 53d Cong., 2d sess., 1897, in *Compilation of the Messages and Papers of the Presidents, 1789–1897,* ed. James D. Richardson (Washington, D.C.: Government Printing Office, 1907), 8:96–98, 157–59. When general recruitment of blacks began in early 1863, many had the impression that they would be assigned to garrison and fatigue duty. See Cornish, *Sable Arm,* 240.

28. *OR*, 6:202.

29. Bonham Papers, 553.

30. Ibid., 560.

31. *OR,* 7:673. The attorney general's co-counsel was A. P. Aldrich, who had been a member of the examining commission subscribing to the report to the governor. See Bonham Papers, 541.

32. *Charleston Courier,* Aug. 26, 1863.

33. Bonham Papers, 568–72. This citation is to the report on the trial made to the governor by what appears to have been the five members of the tribunal conducting it. The report refers to the court as "Police Court for Charleston District." The governor referred to it as "the provost-marshal's court for Charleston district." See *OR,* 7:673. See also Bonham Papers, 536, 597; and *Charleston Courier,* Aug. 26, 1863. The court had been recently created. Its creation and powers are recounted in a letter to the author from William L. McDowell, deputy director, South Carolina Department of Archives and History, Oct. 21, 1980.

34. *OR,* 6:245–46; Bonham Papers, 561–64.

35. *OR,* 5:960, 966–67.

36. *OR,* 6:21–22.

37. Ibid., 115. It seems that a little later Seddon wrote Kirby Smith suggesting that captured white officers "be dealt with red-handed in the field, or immediately thereafter." See Herbert Aptheker, *To Be Free—Studies in American Negro History,* 2d ed. (New York: International, 1968), 94.

38. *OR,* 6:163; *Charleston Mercury,* Aug. 10, 1863.

39. *OR,* 6:193–94.

40. Ibid., 245–46, 194; Bonham Papers, 561–64. The South was keenly aware of the threat of retaliation. See *Charleston Courier,* Oct. 2, 1863.

41. *OR,* 6:225–26.

42. Bonham Papers, 568–72.

43. Herbert Aptheker, "The Negro in the Union Navy," *Journal of Negro History* 32 (Apr. 1947): 169, 170–74, 179.

44. *OR,* ser. 1, 14:199–202; *OR,* 5:708, 823–27; 6:171–72, 188.

45. Elon A. Woodward, comp., *The Negro in the Military Service of the United States—A Compilation* (1888), microcopy M-858, roll 5, 4224, National Archives, Washington, D.C.

46. Luis F. Emilio, *History of the Fifty-Fourth Regiment of Massachusetts Volunteer Infantry, 1863–1865,* 2d ed. (Boston: Boston Book, 1894), 413. Emilio's history, though based on painstaking research, including interviews with survivors, was written before records were fully organized and has some errors, including, on pages 97 and 406, a mistaken identification of the prisoners tried by the Charleston court.

47. Both defense counsels, Nelson Mitchell and Edward McCrady, had been prominent members of the state legislature in prewar days and were leaders of the Charleston bar. See *Biographical Directory of the South Carolina House of Representatives,* 5 vols. (Columbia: University of South Carolina Press, 1974–92), 1:356, 360, 364, 369, 373, 376; Mary C. Simms Oliphant and T. C. Duncan Eaves, eds., *The Letters of William Gilmore Simms,* 5 vols. (Columbia: University of South Carolina Press, 1954), 3:221 n. 250; Mitchell obituary, *Columbia Daily Southern Guardian,* Apr. 21, 1864; *Biographical Directory,* 364, 369, 373, 376; and McCrady and Ashe, *Cyclopedia,* 1:151–58. According to Emilio, *History of the Fifty-Fourth,* 97, 406–8, Mitchell suffered obloquy and poverty as a result of his representation of the defendants. The statement is based on hearsay, principally an unsigned letter appearing in *Harper's Weekly* of April 8, 1865. Quite inconsistent with any such statement is the fact that both Mitchell and McCrady were selected as members of a citizens' committee to welcome President Davis on his visit to Charleston in November 1863, several weeks after the trial. See *Charleston Courier,* Oct. 30, 31, and Nov. 2, 1863. Inconsistent, too, is the highly commendatory obituary published after Mitchell's death in February 1864. See Mitchell obituary; and Henry A. DeSaussure, "Death Records," *South Carolina Historical Magazine* 59 (Apr. 1958): 116. It is notable also that McCrady again was elected to the state legislature in 1864. McCrady, incidentally, had been a member of the state convention of December 1860 and had voted for secession. See *Biographical Directory,* 392; McCrady and Ashe, *Cyclopedia,* 151–58; and Cauthen, *South Carolina Goes to War,* 65–66.

48. *OR*, 6:1081–82; *OR*, 7:673.

49. Brainerd Dyer, "The Treatment of Colored Union Troops by the Confederates, 1861–1865," *Journal of Negro History* 20 (July 1935): 273, 282; Aptheker, *To Be Free*, 94–95.

50. *OR*, 7:409.

51. Ibid., 673.

52. Bonham Papers, 597–98.

53. *OR*, 7:703.

54. *Public Laws of the Confederate States of America, First Congress, 2d Sess.*, ed. James M. Matthews (Richmond: R. M. Smith, Printer to Congress, 1862), 89–90; *Journal of the Congress of the Confederate States of America*, 58th Cong., 2d sess., 1904, S. Doc. 234, 5:537–38.

55. *OR*, 7:583; Dyer, "Treatment of Colored Union Troops," 275–77.

56. *OR*, 7:990–93, 1010–12. Grant's reply to Lee refused to discuss "the slavery question," adhering to the position that all captured Union soldiers" regardless of color . . . must be treated as prisoners of war"; *OR*, 7:1018–19, 1029–30.

57. The Charleston court's report to the governor identified the Missourians as Henry Kirk and William Harrison, the Virginians as George Council and Henry Worthington. Evidence conflicted, it said, as to whether Worthington was a slave. See Bonham Papers, 568–72. The descriptive roll of Company B, 54th Massachusetts (Colored), RG 94, National Archives, shows George Counsel—not "Council." The roll of Company H shows the other three names. The rolls show the residence of each. Worthington is listed as being from Ohio, where, according to his file in the Compiled Military Service Records (RG 94), he was born. There were two men in Company H named William H. Harrison, one shown as "1st," the other as "2d." Their files in the Compiled Military Service Records show the "1st" as having been captured and the "2d" as having been killed at Fort Wagner in July 1863.

58. Bonham to Seddon, Dec. 8, 1864, in *OR*, 7:673.

59. Emilio, *History of the Fifty-Fourth*, 402–3, 414–15.

60. Ibid., 218, 395, 411–13; files of Henry Kirk, William H. Harrison "1st," and Henry W. Worthington, Company H, 54th Massachusetts, Compiled Military Service Records, RG 94, National Archives.

61. Emilio, *History of the Fifty-Fourth*, 419–22, 431. Worthington died on Jan. 12, Harrison on Jan. 26, both at Florence, according to their files in the Compiled Military Service Records, RG 94, National Archives.

62. *OR*, 8:96.

63. Emilio, *History of the Fifty-Fourth*, 422–23.

64. *OR*, 8:197; *Journal of the Confederate Congress*, 4:501, 503, 507, 510, 520, 545; 7:521, 528.

65. Emilio, *History of the Fifty-Fourth*, 422–23; files of George Counsel, Company B, 54th Massachusetts, and Henry Kirk, Company H, 54th Massachusetts, Compiled Military Service Records, RG 94, National Archives.

The Execution of White Officers from Black Units by Confederate Forces During the Civil War

3

JAMES G. HOLLANDSWORTH JR.

On May 1, 1863, both chambers of the Confederate Congress passed a resolution in response to the Emancipation Proclamation declaring that "every white person being a commissioned officer" who commanded, armed, trained, organized, or prepared black men for military service was guilty of "inciting servile insurrection, and shall, if captured, be put to death or be otherwise punished." Dudley Taylor Cornish drew attention to the resolution in his important book *The Sable Arm,* when he quoted Charles W. Eliot's comments during the dedication of the Shaw Monument on the Boston Common: "The white officers, taking life and honor in their hands, cast in their lot with men of a despised race unproved in war and risked death as inciters of servile insurrections if taken prisoners, beside encountering all the common perils of camp, march, and battle."[1] References such as these sparked my curiosity. The fact that the Confederate Congress had adopted the controversial resolution is beyond dispute. Yet, to what extent was the threat implemented?

Federal military records provided the answer. At the end of the war, the federal government published the *Official Army Register of the Volunteer Forces of the U.S. Army, 1861–1865,* containing a roster of all officers who served in the infantry, cavalry, and artillery regiments constituting the United States Colored Troops. If the Confederate government's policy was carried out in the field, the names of its victims would be found here.

The *Official Army Register* lists 7,773 Civil War officers from black units. One of my graduate students, Lisa Moon, went through these names and identified every officer who died of noncombat causes. She also compiled a list of officers who were recorded as "missing" and presumably dead.[2] Her research determined that 9 officers were "murdered," "executed," or "killed" under circumstances not involving combat, while 10 others are listed as "missing." To put these figures into perspective, one must consider that 18 officers died during the war of accidental causes and 160 men were killed in action. Another 94 died of disease.

Armed with the names of those killed or missing, I visited the National Archives in Washington and reviewed the compiled military service and pension records for each man. I also consulted the *Official Records* for references to these individuals. My findings regarding individuals killed under noncombat conditions are presented in table 3.1. Three of the nine (Anson Sanborn, Jacob Schwartz, and Eben White) were killed by civilians behind

TABLE 3.1. OFFICERS "KILLED" IN SITUATIONS OTHER THAN COMBAT

NAME	UNIT	DISPOSITION
2d Lt. Ellis Bentley	3d HA (1st Tenn. HA)	"Killed by guerillas Sept. 22, 1864, near Wacomah Creek south of Memphis."
2d Lt. George L. Conn	49th Inf. (11th La.)	Captured at Milliken's Bend, June 7, 1863. "Reported to have been hung by the enemy; murdered by the rebels at Monroe, La., during Aug., 1863."
2d Lt. David G. Cooke	12th Inf.	Killed near Columbia, Tenn., Dec. 22, 1864.
Asst. Surgeon Eli M. Hewitt	15th Inf.	"Killed by guerillas near Springfield, Tenn., July 24, 1864."
2d Lt. John A. Moulton	67th Inf. (3d Mo.)	Captured at Mount Pleasant Landing, La., on May 15, 1864. "Information has been received of his being killed 12 hours after capture."
Capt. Charles G. Penfield	44th Inf.	"Murdered by Capt. Harvey Scouts, Forrest's Cavalry, near Columbia, Tenn., Dec. 22, 1864." (Had also been captured at Dalton, Ga., on October 13, 1864, and paroled two days later.)
2d Lt. Anson L. Sanborn	1st Inf.	"Killed by Dr. Wright at Norfolk, Va., July 11, 1863, while on recruiting service."
2d Lt. Jacob Schwartz	59th Inf. (1st Tenn.)	"Killed by 3 men names unknown at Memphis, Tenn., Sept. 13, 1864." Also "Assassinated in South Memphis on the evening of the 11th Sept., 1864."
2d Lt. Eben White	7th Inf.	"Murdered by John H. Southoron & son, Oct. 20, 1863, at Benedict, Md., while on recruiting duty."

Source: Individual compiled military service and pension records in the National Archives, Washington, D.C.
Note: All units are U.S. Colored Troops unless otherwise indicated. *HA* indicates Heavy Artillery.

the front lines. Although their affiliation with black units may have contributed to these murders, violent acts by civilians in Union-controlled territory tells us little about the enforcement of official Confederate policy. I consequently focused my attention on the remaining six officers, who were apparently killed by Confederate troops.[3]

The compiled military service and pension records of the ten missing officers generated a less consistent picture, as can be seen in table 3.2. Three of the ten (Alman Bassett, John Cochran, and James Wilson) were dismissed from active duty. The search did not produce any records regarding a fourth man (F. Comstock), who was also presumably rejected by the army. Of the remaining six missing officers, Elisha Dewitt was reported to have been paroled after his capture at Milliken's Bend. Five others were captured, four in battle and one while on recruiting duty near Washington, Louisiana. One of the latter five, Capt. Corydon Heath, was reportedly murdered near Monroe, Louisiana. The other four—William B. Hamblen, Oscar Orillion, David W. Parmenter, and James C. Spry—were never heard from again. These five names plus the six men noted earlier thus constitute my list of candidates for the dubious honor of having been victims of the Confederate government's policy regarding white officers serving in black units:

> Bentley, 2d Lt. Ellis. Killed: Sept. 22, 1864, Memphis, Tenn. Death reported. Confederate operation: Forrest raids north Alabama and middle Tennessee.
> Conn, 2d Lt. George L. Killed: June 7, 1863, Milliken's Bend, La. Death reported. Confederate operation: Taylor attempts to relieve Vicksburg.
> Cooke, 2d Lt. David G. Killed: Dec. 22, 1864, Columbia, Tenn. Death reported. Confederate operation: Forrest retreats from Nashville with Hood.
> Hamblen, 2d Lt. William B. Killed: March 22, 1864, Washington, La. Death reported. Confederate operation: Taylor moves against Banks on Red River.
> Heath, Capt. Corydon. Killed: June 7, 1863, Milliken's Bend, La. Death reported. Confederate operation: Taylor attempts to relieve Vicksburg.
> Hewitt, Asst. Surgeon Eli M. Killed: July 24, 1864, Springfield, Tenn. Death not reported. Confederate operation: Forrest chases A. J. Smith in north Mississippi.
> Moulton, 2d Lt. John A. Killed: May 15, 1864, Mount Pleasant Land-

ing, La. Death not reported. Confederate operation: Wirt Adams disrupts leased plantations.

Orillion, 2d Lt. Oscar. Killed: Aug. 6, 1863, Jackson, La. Death reported. Confederate operation: Lyon orders harassment of Federal troops.

Parmenter, 2d Lt. David W. Killed: April 20, 1864, Plymouth, N.C. Death not reported. Confederate operation: Hoke undertakes 1864 offensive in North Carolina.

Penfield, Capt. Charles G. Killed: Dec. 22, 1864, Columbia, Tenn. Death reported. Confederate operation: Forrest retreats from Nashville with Hood.

Spry, 2d Lt. James C. Killed: July 7, 1864, Johns Island, S.C. Death not reported. Confederate operation: Jones directs operations around Charleston.

Out of the eleven cases, I was able to locate reports regarding seven, one of the earliest of which involved Lt. Oscar Orillion.[4] On August 3, 1863, Confederate cavalry swept down on a detachment of Union infantry near Jackson, Louisiana. Twenty-two black enlisted men and Orillion were among the Federal prisoners. The next morning, Col. John L. Logan, who commanded the raiders, ordered a guard from the 17th Arkansas Mounted Infantry to march the prisoners toward Confederate lines with Orillion at the head of his men. The guard set out several hours before the main body broke camp, took the wrong road, and eventually rejoined the main column later, minus the prisoners. Col. John Griffith, who commanded the 17th Arkansas, reported that four of the black soldiers had attempted to escape and were fired upon, which "created some excitement and a general stampede among them, all attempting to effect their escape." Col. Frank Powers, commander of Logan's cavalry, was more explicit. "I ordered the guard to shoot them [the four escapees] down. In the confusion the other negroes attempted to escape likewise. I then ordered every one shot, and with my six shooter assisted in the execution of the order." Lt. James W. Shattuck of Scott's cavalry later boasted of having killed thirteen of the prisoners himself. Although neither Griffith or Powers mention Orillion by name, he was probably killed along with his men.[5]

Another account of an officer being shot "while trying to escape" involved Lieutenant Hamblen, who was captured while on recruiting duty near Washington. In January 1868, Hamblen's mother placed an advertisement in the *New Orleans Times* for information regarding her son. The notice attracted the attention of one Crouch, formerly of the 173d New York Infantry, who

TABLE 3.2. OFFICERS LISTED AS MISSING AND PRESUMED DEAD

NAME	UNIT	DISPOSITION
2d Lt. Alman Bassett	54th Mass. Inf.	Commission dated Feb. 14, 1863. "Not accepted."
1st Lt. John Cochran	93d Inf. (25th Cd'A)	"Failed boards, Nov. 25, 1863, dismissed for incompetency, July 10, 1865."
1st Lt. F. Comstock	3d HA (1st Tenn. HA)	No compiled military service or pension record.
Capt. Elisha Dewitt	5th HA (9th La. Inf.)	Captured at Milliken's Bend, La., June 7, 1863. "Absent on parole of honor," July 10, 1863.
2d Lt. William B. Hamblen	4th Cav. (1st Cav. Cd'A)	On recruiting service, "captured March 22, 1864, near Washington, La." Still no record as of Feb. 28, 1866.
Capt. Corydon Heath	5th HA (9th La. Inf.)	"Was taken prisoner and murdered by the enemy at or near Monroe, La., June, 1863."
2d Lt. Oscar Orillion	73rd Inf. (1st NG)	"Missing at Jackson, La., Aug. 6, 1863." No information as of Sept. 1864.
2d Lt. David W. Parmenter	10th Inf.	Captured at Plymouth, N.C., April 20, 1864. "Not been heard from since and dropped from the Rolls."
2d Lt. James C. Spry	26th Inf.	"Wounded and taken prisoner at the Battle of Bloody Bridge," Johns Island, S.C., July 7, 1864.
Capt. James Wilson	57th Inf. (4th Ark.)	Commission revoked and dismissed from the service, Feb. 29, 1864.

Source: Individual compiled military service and pension records in the National Archives, Washington, D.C.
Note: All units are U.S. Colored Troops unless otherwise indicated. *Cd'A* indicates Corps d'Afrique; *HA,* Heavy Artillery; and *NG,* Native Guard.

claimed to have been a prisoner in Opelousas when young Hamblen was captured. Crouch reported to Hamblen's mother that her son was ordered to Texas, presumably to the Confederate prison at Camp Ford, but "was shot dead by the guard" about five miles from the town. Crouch stated that Opelousas residents were aware of the incident, talked about it among themselves, and justified the guard's actions because Hamblen had been "recruiting and running off negroes from the Plantations."[6]

Actually, this was the second account the family had received regarding Hamblen's death. In May of the year before, Robert M. McClermont, formerly of the 11th New York Cavalry, had written Hamblen's brother-in-law from Baton Rouge to give the following report:

> I was captured on the 14th of Nov. 1864, by Confederate forces of this state [Louisiana]. While a prisoner at one time there were three (3) sergeants appointed to guard me also to conduct me to a place of safety in the interior—Jackson, Miss. At one time the three sergeants held a sort of a council as to the propriety of shooting me, and accounting for it on the plea that I had made an attempt to escape, as the Vice President's son had been served. I immediately spoke up and denied their ever having the Vice President's son in their custody. They positively affirmed it and stated when and where he had been captured—which I have now forgotten. . . . I understood them to say that Young Hamblen was recruiting in this state for some Negro Regiment, and that they thought he was the Vice President's son, on account of his name and his being a New England Yankee. He was placed under the charge of a young Texan Cavalry man who shot Willie in the back of the head killing him dead, for attempting to escape. The sergeant who told me about it saw the young man's dead body, and heard the shot.[7]

McClermont made it safely to Jackson and was exchanged six weeks later. His report seems plausible, although it should be noted that McClermont was captured east of the Mississippi River, while Hamblen's murder occurred in the Trans-Mississippi Department. Nevertheless, the pension office accepted his account and awarded a pension to Hamblen's mother in 1890.[8]

Two months prior to Lieutenant Orillion's demise, 2d Lt. George Conn and Capt. Corydon Heath, respectively of the 9th and 11th Louisiana Infantry, African Descent, were captured at Milliken's Bend on the west bank of the Mississippi River near Vicksburg. Shortly thereafter, Thomas Cormal claimed that a white captain and all of the black soldiers taken in that battle had been hung in Richmond, Louisiana, in the presence of district commander Maj. Gen. Richard Taylor and his staff. Maj. Gen. Ulysses S. Grant wrote directly to Taylor to inquire about the charge. Taylor responded with a strong denial, adding that he had "remained at Richmond and its vicinity for several days after the skirmish to which you allude, and had any officer or negro been hung the fact must have to come to my knowledge, and the act would most assuredly have met with the punishment it deserved." Grant accepted Taylor's denial, and there is no evidence to suggest that Taylor was lying. In fact, the black troops captured at Milliken's Bend were not killed but were sent to Texas, where they survived the war to return to their regiments after the Trans-Mississippi Department surrendered. Yet, Lieutenant Conn and Captain Heath were never heard from again.[9]

As Grant and Taylor exchanged messages over Cormal's allegations, several citizens living in the vicinity of Monroe came forward with another report of a violent end for two white officers from black units captured about the same time. They told Capt. W. H. Welman of the 59th Indiana Infantry that two white officers captured by Confederate troops near Lake Providence, Louisiana, had been taken into the woods one night and shot. They identified the gunmen as Maj. M. W. Sims and Lieutenant Sparks, both members of Brig. Gen. Paul O. Hebert's staff (Hebert was commander of the subdistrict of northeast Louisiana). In fact, 3 white officers from the 1st Arkansas Infantry, African Descent (later the 46th Infantry, USCT), had been captured along with 113 of their men by Parsons's Texas Cavalry near Lake Providence on June 29, 1863. The Federals occupied a stout fortification on top of a large Indian mound. The white officers had offered to trade their strong defensive position for a promise of proper treatment but agreed to surrender the black soldiers unconditionally. Col. William Henry Parsons accepted the terms, but apparently something went wrong. One of the white soldiers, Lt. John East, did make it safely to Camp Ford, where he remained until his release at the end of the war. The other two officers disappeared.[10]

The fate of the two officers captured with East is clouded further by the absence of any reference to them in the *Official Army Register*. Of the five fatalities among officers in the 1st Arkansas during the course of the war, the *Official Army Register* indicates that four died of disease and one drowned in the Gulf of Mexico. No one is listed as missing or killed. I hoped to resolve this discrepancy when I learned that Major Sims had been captured by Federal troops in July 1863 as he attempted to cross the Mississippi River with dispatches for Gen. Joseph E. Johnston. After a brief stay in Northern prison camps, Sims returned to Vicksburg, where he was jailed until he could be court-martialed for the murder of the still unidentified officers. Unfortunately, this writer could find no evidence in the National Archives that Sims's court-martial ever took place. What I did find was a pardon for Sims after the war, ordered by President Andrew Johnson and signed April 23, 1866. Thus, the question of whether Sims and Sparks murdered two men and, if so, who they were remains unanswered.[11]

The most credible of the execution reports concerns another pair of fatalities. This time the accuser, 1st Lt. George W. Fitch of the 12th Infantry, USCT, was an eyewitness to the event, and his statement is riveting.

I was captured on the 20th of December fourteen miles in a southeasterly direction from Murfreesborough, [Tennessee,] in company with two other officers, Lieut. D. G. Cooke, Twelfth U.S. Colored Infantry, and Capt. Charles G. Penfield, Forty-fourth U.S. Colored Infantry, by a company of scouts belonging to Forrest's command, numbering thirty-six men, commanded by Captain [Addison] Harvey. As soon as captured we were robbed of everything of any value, even clothing. We were kept under guard for three days with some other prisoners . . . until we reached a small town called Lewisburg, some eighteen miles south of Duck River. There the officers were sent under a guard of four men to report, as I supposed, to General Forrest's headquarters. The guard told [me] that was their destination. They took us along the pike road leading from Lewisburg to Moorsville, about four miles, and then left the road and turned to the right for the purpose, as they said, of stopping at a neighboring house for the night.

After leaving the road about half a mile, as we were walking along through a wooded ravine, the man in advance halted us, partially turned his horse, and as I came up, drew his revolver and fired on me without a word. The ball entered my right ear just above the center, passed through and lodged in the bone back of the ear. It knocked me senseless for a few moments. I soon recovered, however, but lay perfectly quiet, knowing that my only hope lay in leading them to believe they had killed me. Presently I heard two carbine shots, and then all was still. After about fourteen minutes I staggered to my feet and attempted to get away, but found I could not walk. About that time a colored boy came along and helped me to a house nearby. He told me that the other two officers were dead, having been shot *through the* head. That evening their bodies were brought to the house where I lay. Next morning they were decently buried on the premises of Col. John C. Hill, nearby.[12]

Fitch eventually made his way back to Union lines and reported the incident to Maj. Gen. George H. Thomas, who wrote to Gen. John Bell Hood on January 13, 1865, to express his outrage. Hood did not reply, possibly because he was forced to relinquish command of the Army of Tennessee a few days later.[13]

Did any white officers from black units who were captured live to tell about it? Thirty such instances are known to have occurred. As noted earlier, Capt. Elisha Dewitt was evidently paroled after his capture at Milliken's Bend, although corroborative evidence of his release has not been found. Records also indicate that Captain Penfield, who met his fate at the hands of Forrest's scouts in December 1864, had been captured and paroled at Dalton, Georgia, only two months earlier. Second Lt. Joseph K. Nelson of the 11th Infantry, USCT, was captured near Sulphur Branch Trestle, Alabama, on September 25, 1864, only to be paroled less than two months later. First Lt. George B. Coleman of the 10th Infantry, Corps d'Afrique (later, the 82d Infantry, USCT), was taken prisoner in August 1863 near Jackson, Louisiana, and survived to return to duty at the very end of the war, as did Lt. John East.[14]

A particularly interesting incident involved Capt. Albert Allen and 2d Lt. Charles E. Page of the 6th and 9th Infantry, Corps d'Afrique (later, the 78th and 81st Infantry, USCT), respectively. Maj. Gen. Nathaniel P. Banks wrote General Taylor in August 1863 to protest the detention of the two officers "in close confinement and in irons" at Shreveport because they served as officers in black regiments. Taylor made an inquiry and reported to Banks a few weeks later that the allegation was "incorrect and without foundation," although he admitted that the two men were no longer under his control. When Allen and Page were exchanged a year later, both reported that they had been "kept in close confinement in *irons* forty days, on account of being suspected of belonging to a colored regiment." Their denial may have worked, for both men were exchanged and eventually given a discharge from the Union army.[15]

Certainly, the single largest capture of white officers from black units occurred during the Battle of the Crater outside of Petersburg, Virginia, during which a group of eleven fell into Rebel hands. "What disposition was made of these officers?" Gen. Robert E. Lee's assistant adjutant general asked. In spite of the Confederate resolution, they were sent to Columbia, South Carolina, as prisoners of war. By Christmas, at least three of them had been exchanged, with the remaining eight reaching the Federal exchange point at Annapolis, Maryland, by early March 1865. Furthermore, my examination of a list of Union officers held prisoner at Columbia turned up the names of eleven additional officers from black regiments who were held there. Seven of these had been captured before Petersburg, while three others had caught up with Maj. Gen. Nathan Bedford Forrest at Brice's Crossroads. The eleventh prisoner had been captured at Olustee, Florida. These officers also survived the war and were duly discharged or mustered out of the Union army at the end of the conflict. This evidence suggests that by mid-1864 white officers from black units were being treated in the same manner as officers from white regiments, particularly if they were fortunate enough to fall into the hands of frontline Confederate troops.[16]

It is probable that Abraham Lincoln's well-publicized threat to retaliate in equal measure was a major reason why the Confederate government failed to carry through with the terms of the congressional resolution of May 1, 1863. The correspondence between the commissioners of exchange is full of references regarding the proper treatment of these officers. In fact, the threat of retaliation was so effective that Confederate authorities and commanders in the field consistently denied that the policy was being carried out.[17] For example, Gen. Joseph E. Johnston directed Maj. Gen. Stephen D. Lee "to inquire into the truth of the report that after the recent action [August 3, 1863,] near Jackson, La., twenty-three prisoners (one white officer and twenty-two colored and negro privates) were put to death in cold blood and without form of law, and if it is true, to bring the culprits to trial." This was the skirmish in which Lieutenant Orillion was captured. However, this writer could find no evidence that Griffith, Powers, Shattuck, or any of the guard from the 17th Arkansas were punished. The "shot while trying to escape" excuse apparently worked.[18]

Although the Confederate threat to execute white officers from black units was not carried out officially, there was another way in which the spirit of the decree could be followed without fear of retaliation. Confederate troops could avoid taking prisoners in the first place. This was precisely the position Lt. Gen. Edmund Kirby Smith took when he learned that a number of black soldiers and their officers had been inadvertently captured at Milliken's Bend. Writing to General Taylor on June 13, 1863, Kirby Smith put the matter bluntly: "I have been unofficially informed that some of your troops have captured negroes in arms. I hope this may not be so, and that your subordinates who may have been in command of capturing parties may have recognized the propriety of giving no quarter to armed negroes and their officers. In this way we may be relieved from a disagreeable dilemma."[19] It should not be surprising, therefore, that when Confederate troops overran positions held by black soldiers, the number of prisoners they took was usually far less than when the defenders were white. This can be documented by incidents at Milliken's Bend, Poison Spring, the Crater, and Fort Pillow. In these instances, the white officers were less likely to survive than the black troops they commanded. As is well known, the Rebel battle cry at Milliken's Bend was "No quarter for white officers, kill the damned abolitionists, but spare the niggers."[20]

In summary, the evidence suggests that the Confederate government did not officially carry out its threat to execute white officers who volunteered to command black troops in the Union army. On the other hand, there were a number of instances in which individuals serving in the Confederate army carried out the spirit, if not the letter, of the law by shooting prisoners who, they claimed, were trying to escape. As far as can be determined, none of these persons were ever brought to trial for their crimes, in spite of official condemnation of their acts by superior officers.

Although the number of white officers from black units executed by Confederate forces during the war was not great (none died of accidents), the death of each man was still tragic. This point was brought home to this writer when he encountered the following letter while reviewing Oscar Orillion's compiled military service record.

New Orleans, September 20, 1864

General:

My brother Oscar Orillon [*sic*] duly commissioned by Maj. Gen. Banks First Lieut. of the 1st Regt. of the Louisiana Native Guards have been made a prisoner since the month of August last in a place nearby Port-Hudson[.] I have been for all that whole time deprived of any news concerning his situation or whereabouts[.] After much inquiry, they tell me that you, only you Sir, could give to an affectionate sister some consolation, and calm the anxiety that I suffer on account of my beloved brother, being my support, and enlist for the purpose of aiding me in my living, being a widow with two little children. I am sure Sir that you will understand uneasiness about him and that you will excuse a poor Sister who comes to trouble you in your camp duty to have some news of dear brother who was for the present all my hopes in this world.

If you can let me have any information, Sir, I shall be in the future very grateful to you, and will learn to my young ones to pray for you, and to respect your name, and I shall be for ever one of your most faithful Servant

Rosella Debergue Orillon[21]

There ends the record of Lt. Orillion's military service in the United States Army.

Notes

This essay was originally published in *Louisiana History* 35 (fall 1994): 475–89. Reprinted with permission of *Louisiana History*.

1. Dudley Taylor Cornish, *The Sable Arm: Negro Troops in the Union Army, 1861–1865* (1956; reprint, New York: W. W. Norton, 1966), 161–68, 224.

2. *Official Army Register of the Volunteer Forces of the U.S. Army, 1861–1865*, 8 vols. (Washington, D.C.: Government Printing Office, 1865). Deaths after May 26, 1865, were not included, although several white officers from black units were killed after the collapse of the Confederate government. These incidents cannot be viewed as official acts of a deceased government, although the sentiments that provided the impetus for the resolution in the first place may have survived.

3. For the identities of the civilians involved with these murders, see *War of the Rebellion: A Compilation of the Official Records of the Union and Confederate Armies*, 128 vols. (Washington, D.C.: Government Printing Office, 1880–1901), ser. 1, 29 (pt. 2): 364 (hereafter cited as *OR*); *OR*, ser. 2, 6:106, 157, 187, 216, 323, 360.

4. Orillion was actually black, one of the free men of color to receive a commission in the 1st Regiment of Butler's Native Guards (later the 73d Infantry, USCT) when it was organized. Race did not play a part in his execution, however, as the lightness of his complexion caused his captors to mistake him for white. Orillion's name appears on the list of officers dated Sept. 27, 1862, in box 44 (69–75th U.S. Colored Infantry), Regimental Papers, RG 94, National Archives, Washington, D.C.

5. *OR,* ser. 2, 6:244, 258–59, 289, 960–61.

6. William F. Perkins to C. T. Hamblen, Jan. 23, 1868, file of William B. Hamblen, Compiled Military Service and Pension Records, National Archives. The advertisement alleged that the 2d Louisiana Cavalry had been responsible for Hamblen's capture. The author was unable to verify that Crouch served in the 173d New York Infantry. That name does not appear in the Compiled Military Service index for that regiment.

7. Affidavit of R. M. McClermont, Jan. 21, 1868, William B. Hamblen file, National Archives.

8. Ibid.

9. *OR,* ser. 1, 24 (pt. 3): 425–26, 443–44, 469, 537, 590; *OR,* ser. 2, 6:394; Cyrus Sears, *The Battle of Milliken's Bend* (Columbus: F. J. Heer, 1909), 15; Affidavit of Herman Lieb, Jan. 9, 1873, in pension record for Corydon Heath, National Archives.

10. *OR,* ser. 1, 34 (pt. 2): 450, 466. The *Official Army Register* indicates that four officers were captured by Parsons's troops, which is confirmed in a letter written by one of the Confederate soldiers shortly after the incident. See John Q. Anderson, ed., *Campaigning with Parsons' Texas Cavalry Brigade, CSA: The War Journals and Letters of the Four Orr Brothers, 12th Texas Cavalry Regiment* (Hillsboro, Tex.: Hill Junior College Press, 1967), 111–12. The reports in the *OR,* however, refer to only three. A more recent study of Parsons's brigade also accepts three as the correct number. See Anne J. Bailey, *Between the Enemy and Texas: Parsons' Cavalry in the Civil War* (Fort Worth: Texas Christian University Press, 1989), 240. The evidence suggests that East was the only officer serving in a black unit who was held at Camp Ford. See "List of Officers, Prisoners of War at Camp Ford," in *The Old Flag, 1864: Fiftieth Anniversary, 1914: First Published by Union Prisoners at Camp Ford, Tyler, Texas, 1864* (Bridgeport, Conn.: "The Old Flag," 1914). There were several exchanges of prisoners from Camp Ford after East was captured, but he did not gain his release until two days after Lt. Gen. Simon B. Buckner surrendered the Department of the Trans-Mississippi to Maj. Gen. Edward R. S. Canby in New Orleans. East lived to start drawing his pension in 1883. Pension record for John East, National Archives.

11. *Official Army Register,* 6:122, 8:219; *OR,* ser. 1, 24 (pt. 3): 590; *OR,* ser. 2, 6:394; M. W. Sims's Application for Pardon, dated Apr. 20, 1866, and granted Apr. 23, 1866, pardon records, National Archives.

12. *OR,* ser. 2, 8:19–20.

13. *OR,* ser. 1, 45 (pt. 2): 578–79. See also *OR,* ser. 1, 45 (pt. 1): 546.

14. Compiled Military Service Records for George B. Coleman, John East, Joseph K. Nelson, and Charles G. Penfield, National Archives; *OR,* ser. 2, 8:19–20.

15. *OR,* ser. 2, 6:213, 264; Albert Allen to George B. Drake, Aug. 6, 1864, file of Albert Allen, and Charles E. Page to George B. Drake, July 26, 1864, file of Charles E. Page, Compiled Military Service Records, National Archives.

16. *OR,* ser. 2, 7:6, 198, 540, 956; *Official Army Register,* 8:174, 179, 190, 194, 201, 202; John L. Ransom, *Andersonville Diary, Escape, and List of Dead, with Name, Co., Regiment, Date of Death and No. of Grave in Cemetery* (Auburn, N.Y.: J. L. Ransom, 1881).

17. For Lincoln's response to the Confederate resolution, see *OR,* ser. 2, 6:163; *OR,* ser. 3, 3:148–64. For examples of general correspondence, see *OR,* ser. 2, 5:737; 6:33, 73, 115, 185, 226, 230, 244, 248, 349, 594–97.

18. *OR,* ser. 2, 6:244.

19. Ibid., 21–22.

20. *OR,* ser. 1, 24 (pt. 1): 102; 26 (pt. 2): 478; 24 (pt. 1): 746, 753, 792; *OR,* ser. 2, 6:817–18; *OR,* ser. 3, 3:452–53; William Wells Brown, *The Negro in the American Rebellion: His Heroism and His Fidelity* (1867; reprint, New York: Johnson Reprint, 1968), 232; Joseph T. Glatthaar, *Forged in Battle: The Civil War Alliance of Black Soldiers and White Officers* (New York: Free Press, 1990), 156, 159–62; Randall C. Jimerson, *The Private Civil War: Popular Thought During the Sectional Conflict* (Baton Rouge: Louisiana State University Press, 1988), 113–15; Ira Don

Richards, "The Battle of Poison Spring," *Arkansas Historical Quarterly* 18 (1959): 348–49; Sears, *Battle of Milliken's Bend,* 9. When Confederate troops failed to overrun a position held by black troops, the ratio of killed to wounded in black and white units was comparable.

21. Rosella Debergue Orillon [*sic*] to "General," Sept. 20, 1864, file of Oscar Orillion, Compiled Military Service and Pension Records, National Archives.

"Shooting Niggers Sir"

4

Confederate Mistreatment of Union Black Soldiers at the Battle of Olustee

DAVID J. COLES

On the evening of February 20, 1864, a defeated Union army abandoned large numbers of wounded and missing troops during its retreat from the bloody Olustee battlefield. A substantial percentage of these soldiers came from three black regiments that had composed a significant part of the defeated Northern force. Of the 1,861 casualties suffered by the Federals, 626 came from the ranks of the 8th United States Colored Infantry (USCI), the 35th USCI, and the 54th Massachusetts. The latter figure included at least 158 missing troops, some undoubtedly killed during the confused fighting and others left wounded or simply lost on the battlefield. The close of the battle did not end the suffering of these men, because in the hours and days that followed, they endured varying degrees of cruelty and abuse inflicted upon them by the victorious Confederates. This mistreatment of black Union soldiers at Olustee remains a subject largely ignored by historians.[1]

Political and military considerations both played a role in the 1864 Florida Expedition that ended in the Battle of Olustee. It was a presidential election year, and two factions within the Republican Party both hoped to organize a loyal Florida government under the provisions of President Abraham Lincoln's Reconstruction Proclamation of December 1863. This would enable a small group of Florida Unionists to play a role at the 1864 nominating convention as well as the general election. Treasury Secretary Salmon P. Chase, viewed as Lincoln's principal rival, had already begun to establish a network of supporters in the state. Direct tax commissioners, appointed by the secretary under the provisions of the 1862 Direct Tax Law, began operating in Union-occupied Fernandina and St. Augustine. The most controversial of these appointees was Lyman D. Stickney, who let few opportunities pass to promote Chase and to encourage an increased Federal military presence in the state.[2]

In 1863, Stickney met with Maj. Gen. Quincy Adams Gillmore, the newly appointed commander of the Department of the South, which included the Union-held coastal portions of South Carolina, Georgia, and Florida. Stickney encouraged an expedition to reoccupy Jacksonville, which had been briefly occupied three previous times in 1862 and 1863, at the earliest opportunity. The commissioner reported to Chase that Gillmore seemed to support both the expedition as well as the Chase nomination movement. The commissioner met with Gillmore a second time in December 1863, at which time the two made definite plans for an early movement into northeast Florida. On December 15, Gillmore requested permission from the War Department to commence operations in Florida. The objectives were to "recover all the most valuable portion of that state, cut off a rich source of the enemy's supplies, and increase the number of my colored troops."[3] He made no mention of possible political motives for the campaign at that time. Meanwhile, Stickney organized Unionist meetings in occupied Key West and St. Augustine, in preparation for the restoration of a loyal government. During this period, he also contacted President Lincoln and described conditions in Florida. While Stickney's motives remain unclear, historian Ovid Futch writes that he was simply "making an effort to ingratiate himself with the President, so that he would be in line for political rewards regardless of the outcome of the contest."[4] Undoubtedly aware of Stickney's character, Lincoln instead commissioned his private secretary, John Hay, as a major and sent him to Florida to supervise the registration of loyal citizens and to "engineer the business there."[5] On January 13, 1864, the president also wrote directly to General Gillmore, informing him of Hay's appointment and of his plans for the state: "I understand an effort is being made by some worthy gentlemen to reconstruct a loyal state government in Florida. . . . I wish the thing done in the most speedy way possible, so that, when done, it lie within the range of the late proclamation on the subject. . . . I shall be greatly obliged if you will give it such general supervision as you can find consistent with your more strictly military duties."[6]

Gillmore subsequently contacted Maj. Gen. Henry Halleck, the Union general-in-chief, and Secretary of War Edwin M. Stanton to receive final authorization for a movement into Florida. He informed them of Lincoln's interest in Florida and also outlined the main military objectives of the expedition: to procure an outlet to the north for Florida products; to stop the flow of cattle, salt, and other supplies being sent from Florida to the other Confederate states; and to obtain contrabands to add to the ranks of his department's black regiments.[7]

By February 1, Gillmore had received his final authorization, and he began selecting units to participate in the operation. Over the next three days, he assembled his force at Hilton Head, South Carolina. While Gillmore would accompany the expedition during its early phases, he placed Brig. Gen. Truman B. Seymour in actual command. Some thirty-eight transports, tugs, and warships from Rear Adm. John A. Dahlgren's South Atlantic Blockading Squadron would be needed to transport the Union soldiers to Florida. On the night of February 5–6, approximately seven thousand Federal soldiers boarded their ships for the short voyage to the mouth of the St. Johns River, which they reached early on the morning of February 7. The Florida Expedition had begun.[8]

Supported by gunboats, the Union transports moved up the St. Johns River on February 7 and began landing the Federal infantry at Jacksonville. General Seymour ordered a detachment of the 54th Massachusetts under Maj. John Appleton to disperse the few Confederate pickets stationed there and to help secure the town. They found Jacksonville largely deserted, though a black soldier of the 54th recalled that the few women he saw displayed "a sort of Parisian disgust as the well-appointed Union army, composed in part of Lincoln's 'niggers,' filed through the streets."[9]

With disembarkation of his troops completed by noon on February 8, Seymour advanced his command towards Camp Finegan, a Confederate position located about eight miles west of the town. He sent his cavalry under Col. Guy Henry ahead of the slower-moving infantry. The mounted soldiers surprised a Rebel force of about 350 men under the command of Col. Abner McCormick of the 2d Florida Cavalry at Camp Finegan and then moved on to Ten Mile Run, where a second Rebel force was surprised and a number of men captured. Over the next several days, Henry's command continued to Baldwin, an important railroad junction farther west, and then to Sanderson, which they occupied the evening of February 10. By the following morning, the Union horsemen had advanced nearly all the way to Lake City, some sixty miles west of Jacksonville. They encountered a stronger force of Confederates in a strong defensive position about three miles east of the town. After several hours of skirmishing, Henry's troopers withdrew to Sanderson. While the Southern force had prevented Henry's troopers from moving farther west and perhaps destroying an important railroad bridge over the Suwannee River, the Federal cavalry had accomplished part of the military goals of the campaign—the disruption of Florida's railroad and supply lines. Several smaller cavalry raids to Gainesville and Callahan were undertaken over the next several days for the same purpose.[10]

Despite these early successes, General Seymour had grown pessimistic about the expedition. "I am convinced that a movement upon Lake City is not, in the present condition of transportation, admissible," he wrote Gillmore on February 11, "and indeed that what has been said of the desire of Florida to come back now is a delusion. The backbone of rebeldom is not here."[11] Gillmore ordered Seymour to concentrate his advanced forces at Sanderson, and he notified his subordinate that he was sending part of the 54th Massachusetts to Baldwin for support. On February 14, Gillmore and Seymour met in Jacksonville to discuss future operations. After ordering Seymour to construct defenses at Jacksonville, Baldwin, and Barber's Plantation, Gillmore placed his subordinate in command of the newly created District of Florida. "I considered it well understood at that time," Gillmore later reported, "that no advance would be made without further instructions from me, or until the defenses were well advanced."[12] He returned the next day to his departmental headquarters at Hilton Head, South Carolina.

Seymour's pessimism about the expedition, so evident in his earlier letter to Gillmore, quickly evaporated. He soon determined to maintain the forward elements of his command at Barber's Station, and he wrote to his department commander that he now intended to advance to the Suwannee River, west of Lake City. "[B]y the time you receive this I shall be in motion," he informed the startled Gillmore.[13] The department commander dispatched his chief-of-staff, Brig. Gen. John Turner, to Florida with orders for Seymour to stop his advance, but stormy weather delayed Turner's voyage, and he did not arrive in Florida until after the Battle of Olustee. Because of the scarcity of Seymour's manuscript material, historians can only speculate on the general's state of mind in mid-February 1864. At a council of war held a day or two before the Olustee fight, most of Seymour's subordinates felt "that it would be impossible to hold permanently a position out toward the center of the state," but the general "thought it his duty to go on." His objective may have been Florida's capital, Tallahassee, located some one hundred miles west of Lake City, though he probably only intended to occupy the latter town and then advance and destroy the railroad bridge located on the Suwannee.[14]

John Hay has given perhaps the best description of the general's odd behavior: "Seymour has seemed very unsteady and queer since the beginning of the campaign. He has been subject to violent alternations of timidity & rashness, now declaring Florida loyalty was all bosh, now lauding it as the purest article extant, now insisting that [Gen. Pierre G. T.] Beauregard was in front with the whole Confederacy & now asserting that he could whip all the rebels in Florida with a good brigade."[15] Perhaps Seymour hoped to regain with a victory in the Florida pines some of the prestige he had lost the previous July, when he had commanded Union forces in the unsuccessful assault on Fort Wagner near Charleston. Following the repulse, Northern papers bitterly criticized Seymour for the defeat, as well as for his alleged mishandling and lack of concern for the black troops under his command.[16]

Whatever the motivations of its commander, early on the morning of February 20, the small Union army advanced westward from its encampment at Barber's Station. Seymour had divided his force into three brigades, commanded by Cols. Joseph Hawley, William Barton, and James Montgomery. Hawley's brigade consisted of the 7th New Hampshire, the 7th Connecticut, and the 8th USCI. The latter unit had no previous combat experience. Organized at Camp William Penn near Philadelphia in late 1863 and early 1864, the 8th included in its ranks free blacks from Pennsylvania and Delaware, as well as contrabands. "Our camp thronged with visitors, and darkees who wanted to enlist," wrote a white officer. "There are hundreds of them, mostly slaves, here by now, anxiously waiting for the recruiting officer."[17] Col. Charles W. Fribley of Lycoming County, a veteran of the 84th Pennsylvania Volunteers, commanded the regiment, which at the time of the Florida Expedition had not yet completed its training. Its inexperience proved disastrous in the upcoming battle.[18]

The 47th, 48th, and 115th New York Infantry Regiments, commanded by Col. William Barton, comprised Seymour's 2d Brigade. During the upcoming engagement, the New Yorkers would suffer severe casualties while defending the center of the Union line. The last Union brigade was led by the controversial Col. James Montgomery, who had participated in the brutal Kansas-Missouri border warfare of the 1850s as a lieutenant of the infamous James Lane. After serving in Kansas at the war's outbreak, he was authorized by the War Department in early 1863 to recruit a black regiment for the Department of the South. Historian Dudley Taylor Cornish described Montgomery as a "primitive patriarch uninhibited by any effete Eastern notions of the rules of civilized warfare, and his Old Testament kind of warfare was completely at odds with the Harvard tradition of fair play."[19] Montgomery demonstrated his brutality by burning the small Georgia town of Darien in June 1863. By the time of the Florida Expedition, Montgomery had risen to the command of a small, two-regiment brigade, consisting of the famous 54th Massachusetts and the 1st North Carolina Colored Infantry (later known as the 35th USCI).

One of the first black regiments organized in the Northern states, the 54th consisted almost entirely of free blacks. It had earned a proud reputation the preceding July, when Col. Robert Gould Shaw led his black soldiers in a heroic, yet unsuccessful assault against Battery Wagner. Shaw and more than 250 of his men fell in the assault. Now commanded by Col. Edward N. Hallowell, the regiment would see its first real combat since Battery Wagner on the Florida Expedition. In contrast to the 54th, the 1st North Carolina was comprised of ex-slaves from Virginia and the Carolinas. Col. James Beecher, brother of *Uncle Tom's Cabin* author Harriet Beecher Stowe, commanded the inexperienced regiment, which had seen little previous combat. To his everlasting regret, Beecher was on recruiting duty in the North when his regiment went to Florida. Lt. Col. William Reed would lead the 1st North Carolina at Olustee. In addition to his three infantry brigades, Seymour's column, which totaled between five thousand and five thousand five hundred men, contained a number of mounted troops and artillery batteries.[20]

After leaving Barber's Station shortly after daybreak, the Federal army moved westward toward Lake City along roads paralleling the Florida, Atlantic, and Gulf Central Railroad. The troops passed through Sanderson shortly after noon, and within several hours they were within a few miles of the railroad station of Olustee. Shortly after leaving Sanderson, a few Confederate pickets appeared to contest the Union advance. The Rebels' numbers increased, and sharp skirmishing broke out as the Northern column approached Olustee. In the days since the Federal landing, Brig. Gen. Joseph Finegan, the Irish-born commander of the Confederate District of East Florida, had received reinforcements from Savannah and Charleston until he, like Seymour, commanded a force of between five thousand and five thousand five hundred men. Most important among these was a brigade of Georgia veterans commanded by Brig. Gen. Alfred H. Colquitt. Finegan ordered the construction of a series of breastworks along a north-south line that crossed the railroad tracks near Olustee Station. A large lake, Ocean Pond, anchored Finegan's left, while impassable swamps protected his right. The position was, according to Confederate engineer officer M. B. Grant, the "only point offering any advantages whatever between Lake City and the south prong of the Saint Mary's River." Finegan planned to draw the Union troops toward his lines and fight from behind his strong entrenchments. He consequently ordered forward his cavalry, along with the 64th Georgia Infantry and elements of the 32d Georgia, for skirmishing duty. The fighting to the east of the Confederate defensive line gradually escalated as both Seymour and Finegan sent additional troops piecemeal into the battle.[21]

As the fighting intensified, Finegan ordered General Colquitt, his most experienced subordinate, to go forward with a portion of his brigade and take command of the troops actively engaged. Finegan, still hoping to force the Federals to attack his prepared defensive positions, would wait with the remainder of his forces near Olustee Station. Contrary to Finegan's expectations, a full-scale battle would eventually develop some two miles to the east of the Confederate field works. Faced with stiffening Rebel resistance, Seymour ordered his lead infantry brigade under Joseph Hawley to deploy for battle. One of Hawley's regiments, the 7th Connecticut, was already engaged in skirmishing when the colonel ordered forward the 7th New Hampshire and the 8th USCI. Apparently because of a misunderstood deployment order, the veteran 7th New Hampshire soon fell into confusion and retired. This allowed the Confederates to focus their attention on the inexperienced 8th USCI. The unit quickly came under heavy fire and many commissioned and noncommissioned officers fell wounded or dead. After ordering his men to slowly retire, Col. Fribley toppled over dead with a bullet through the heart. The 8th's second-in-command subsequently fell wounded, as did three members of the regiment's color guard. Lt. Oliver Norton, a veteran of Gettysburg, remembered the Confederate fire at Olustee as "the most destructive . . . I ever knew." The inexperienced black troops at first "were stunned, bewildered, and knew not what to do . . . but gradually they recovered their senses and commenced firing."[22] The 8th had suffered a rude baptism of fire. Sent into a dangerous position with little preparation or support, the unit had performed as well as could be expected. Some of its enlisted personnel had fled, while others had fought and died. Of the 554 men the regiment brought into the battle, more than 300 became casualties.[23]

With the defeat of Hawley's brigade, Seymour hurriedly brought forward the three New York regiments commanded by William Barton. The New Yorkers valiantly held the Union line against increasing Confederate pressure as General Finegan also sent forward more troops. At a critical juncture, both sides ran low on ammunition, and the firing slackened while each brought up additional supplies. In an effort to drive the Federal army from the field, General Finegan then deployed the last of his reserves, and the Confederate line commenced a general advance.[24]

The arrival on the battlefield of Finegan and his remaining troops threatened to overwhelm the Union position. Seymour ordered forward his final reserves—the brigade of black soldiers commanded by Col. James Montgomery. The 54th Massachusetts and the 1st North Carolina Infantry had spent the battle guarding the Union supply train, and the troops were anxious to enter the fight. As they moved forward, other Union soldiers warned them of the desperate situation, shouting "We're badly whipped! You'll all get killed," while General Seymour exclaimed to Colonel Hallowell of the 54th, "The day is lost; You must go in and save the corps."[25] The arrival of the black regiments eased the pressure on Barton's New Yorkers and allowed them to retire. Montgomery's small brigade could not, however, check the Confederate advance, and Seymour soon ordered a general withdrawal. The Federal cavalry, along with the 7th Connecticut Infantry and a portion of the 54th Massachusetts, covered the retreat. Lt. Col. Henry N. Hooper of the 54th gathered his men together and, according to Major Appleton, told them, "Well boys we must hold this line, we must fix bayonets and die in our tracks." Hooper's inspiring words had the desired effect, as related by Appleton: "The men shouted 'we can do it.' They gathered all the cartridges from the field they could, and as the enemy advanced, at times passing sixty yards beyond our flanks, the men would cheer so that the Rebels thought it was a trap and fell back."[26]

That night, the exhausted Federals retired all the way to Barber's Plantation, where the day had begun with such promise. Though all available transportation was filled to capacity with Union wounded, many men were abandoned on the battlefield. The black soldiers in particular hoped to avoid capture. "The endurance of some of the colored soldiers was almost incredible," wrote a white soldier in the 40th Massachusetts. "We overtook and passed many who were crawling upon their hands and knees, preferring that painful mode of escape to capture, as the enemy threatened tortures more than death to any 'niggers' that might fall into their hands."[27] During the retreat, a train loaded with wounded soldiers broke down. To prevent their comrades' capture, a group of men from the 54th Massachusetts attached ropes to the engine and dragged the cars to safety. The men's actions "ought to ensure [them] a higher praise than to hold the field in the face of a victorious foe," reported a Dr. Marsh of the U.S. Sanitary Commission. "They knew their fate if captured; [but] their humanity triumphed. Does history record a nobler deed?"[28]

By February 22, Seymour's army had retired to its Jacksonville defenses, where Northern gunboats protected it from attack. Finegan pursued slowly, and the Southern commander received some criticism for allowing the battered Federals to escape. Nonetheless, the Confederates had inflicted an embarrassing military defeat on the Federal forces. The Olustee debacle also effectively ended Union efforts to reconstruct a loyal Florida government in time for the 1864 elections. While both sides for a time reinforced their armies in Florida, eventually it became obvious that another major battle would not take place there. Jacksonville would remain in Union hands until the end of the war, but Olustee ended large-scale military operations in the state.[29]

The three black regiments at Olustee had lost heavily in the battle, and the suffering of many black soldiers did not end with the retreat of the Union army on the evening of February 20. Those unfortunates left on the battlefield would endure torment and abuse in the hours and days that followed. In early 1864, black Federals faced an uncertain future if captured by the enemy. African American troops abandoned at Olustee and other battlefields paid the price of the two combatants' failure to implement a comprehensive, humane policy relative to black prisoners of war. The abuses suffered by black troops in the 1864 Florida campaign can be divided into two major categories: the treatment of wounded and captured blacks in the hours immediately following battle, and the handling of those blacks who survived the postbattle abuses and were sent to Confederate prisoner-of-war camps. In addition, the treatment given to captured white officers of black units merits study.

Following the retreat of the Union army, Confederate soldiers roamed over the battlefield. They discovered huge amounts of abandoned weapons, food, clothing, and equipment, much of which the ill-equipped Rebels gratefully appropriated for their own use. They also encountered the human wreckage present after every battle—the lifeless bodies of Union and Confederate soldiers, as well as groups of wounded and dazed survivors, wandering through the debris. The Union survivors included members of the heavily engaged 8th and 35th USCI and a lesser number from the 54th Massachusetts. These men had either been left wounded on the field or gotten separated from their commands in the hasty retreat toward Jacksonville.[30]

From the primary evidence available, much originating from Confederate participants, it appears certain that at least some black troops were killed by vengeful foes after the battle's close. The harsh attitude of some Rebel soldiers toward their black enemies is illustrated in the postwar reminiscences of Lawrence Jackson of the 2d Florida Cavalry. Jackson recalled that before his unit entered the battle, Col. Abner McCormick delivered the following address to his troopers:

> Comrades and soldiers of the 2nd Florida Cavalry, we are going into this fight to win. Although we are fighting five or six to one, we will die but never surrender. General Seamore's army is made up largely of negroes from Georgia and South Carolina, who have come to steal, pillage, run over the state, and murder, kill, and rape our wives, daughters and sweethearts. Let's teach them a lesson. I shall not take any negro prisoners in this fight.[31]

More illuminating than Jackson's account is a detailed memoir written after the war by William Penniman, a trooper in the 4th Georgia Cavalry. Immediately following the fight, he rode over the battlefield, observing the carnage and destruction. Penniman heard firing "going on in every direction," which "sounded almost frequent enough to resemble the bark of skirmishers." These sounds confused him until he met a Confederate officer and asked him about the cause. The officer said that his men were "Shooting niggers Sir. I have tried to make the boys desist but I can't control them." When Penniman replied that he thought it a shame to kill wounded prisoners, the other soldier responded: "That's so Sir, but one young fellow over yonder told me the niggers killed his brother after being wounded, at Fort Pillow, and he was twenty three years old, that he had already killed nineteen and needed only four more to make matters even, so I told him to go ahead and finish the job."[32]

Riding farther along, Penniman heard the sounds of firing continue. The Georgian later recalled visiting the battlefield early the next day:

> The results of the shooting of the previous night became all to apparent. Negroes, and plenty of them, whom I had seen lying all over the field wounded, and as far as I could see, many of them moving around from place to place, now . . . all were dead. If a negro had a shot in the shin another was sure to be in the head.
>
> A very few prisoners were taken, and but a few at the prison pen. One ugly big black buck was interrogated as to how it happened that he had come back to fight his old master, and upon his giving some very insolent reply, his interrogater drew back his musket, and with the butt, gave him a blow that killed him instantly. A very few of the wounded were placed on the Surgeon's operating table—their legs fairly flew off, but whether they were at all seriously wounded I have always had my doubt.[33]

Written long after the war, Jackson's and Penniman's accounts alone cannot be considered definitive proof that atrocities occurred at Olustee. Indeed, some historians have been skeptical of their allegations, and it appears that Penniman in particular embellished his account. The two claims are, however, substantiated by a number of other first-person reminiscences.

In a letter written to his wife immediately following the battle, James Jordan of the 27th Georgia Infantry reported that "desperate slaughtering" had taken place and that the black Federals "were badly cut up and killed." More ominously, Jordan commented, "Our men killed some of them after they had fell in our hands wounded."[34] Another Georgian, Henry Shackelford of the 19th Infantry, published a letter in the *Atlanta Daily Intelligencer* soon after the fight. Shackelford admitted that the black troops fought well, noting the Confederates "walked over many a wooly head as we drove them back. . . . How our boys did walk into the niggers, they would beg and pray but it did no good."[35]

Edwin Tuttle, a soldier in the 26th Virginia, who arrived in Florida soon after the battle, mentioned Confederate atrocities in a letter written home to his family. "The Yankee forces consisted mostly of Negrows and foreigners," he wrote. "I tell you our men slayed the Negrows & if it had not been for the officers their would not one of them been spaired."[36] Although strongly religious, Tuttle's view of Christian charity did not pertain to blacks. After viewing a group of captured white and black prisoners, Tuttle reflected: "I deeply pitied the Whites but I am afraid I did not have the right spirit toward the nigs. If their does a Battle come of here Shortly it will be a desperate one for we know we will not meet with any mercy if we fall into the hands of niggers & I tell you they do not meet with mercy from us."[37] Tuttle's comments illustrate the animosity that existed between the combatants during the Florida campaign, based largely on the Union's use of black regiments. This emotionally charged atmosphere undoubtedly contributed to the Rebels' postbattle brutality.

Confederate chaplain Edmund C. Lee confirmed the accounts of mistreatment. Although it is unclear whether he was present at Olustee, Lee was in Savannah in early March 1864, when many of the Confederate wounded from the battle arrived there. Lee heard from these survivors that wounded Union blacks had remained on the battlefield until all the white prisoners had received treatment. Many of these blacks died unattended in the streets of Lake City, while others were "knocked in the heads like dogs" and killed while awaiting medical attention.[38] In a postbattle letter to his wife, Winston Stephens, a captain in the 2d Florida Cavalry, also indicated that Union blacks were mistreated. Stephens, a slave owner himself, instructed his wife: "Tell the negroes if they could have seen how the [Union] negroes were treated I think it would cure them of all desire to go. One of the yankee negroes offered to shake hands with one of the negroes in camp & the one in camp killed the other telling him not to offer to speak to him."[39]

Several other self-serving accounts describe the antipathy directed toward captured black Federals by the black servants and cooks of Confederate officers. Edwin Tuttle observed that "some of the Black cooks in the Georgia Regts went on the Battle Field & knocked many of the Wounded in the head with light wood knots."[40] An article in the *Atlanta Daily Intelligencer* related a similar, possibly apocryphal, incident:

After the battle, a gentleman, accompanied by his body servant, went over the field, looking for the dead and wounded negroes. Having proceeded some distance, the servant's attention was attracted by an excellent pair of boots on the feet of a negro soldier, lying near where they stood, and, after getting his master's consent, seized one of the boots to pull it off. He had hardly done so when the wounded negro commenced kicking furiously, and cried out, "Let my boots alone; I am not dead!" The servant startled, stepped back and asked, "What did you say?" "I say let my boots alone; I ain't dead." The servant picked up a lightwood knot, and coming back said, "You ain't dead!" "No, I ain't," replied the soldier. "Well, den, if you ain't dead, I'll deaden you," and immediately despatched him with a lightwood knot, and bore off the coveted boots.[41]

Joab Roach, a Georgia soldier present at Olustee, confirmed this particular method of killing Union blacks: "The Yankees brought theare negro troops out to fight us[.] We cild [killed] and wounded agrat menney of them and after the battle the boys went over the battlefield and knoct the most of the wouded negros in the head with lightwood knots."[42]

Federal soldiers on the battlefield also recorded their experiences. An anonymous member of the 48th New York Volunteers left a particularly graphic account of the battle and its aftermath. Wounded and abandoned during the fighting, this soldier concealed himself in some bushes, where he observed Confederates moving about the battlefield:

I could see the rebels come to our wounded, and take their money, watches, and whatever they found on their persons; while they stripped the dead altogether. The wounded negroes they bayoneted without mercy. Close beside me was a fine-looking negro, who was wounded in the leg: his name was Brown, an orderly sergeant in one of the companies of the Eighth United States Regiment. A rebel officer happened to see him, and says, "Ah, you black rascal, you will not remain here long!" and, dismounting from his horse, placed his revolver close to the negro's head, and blew his brains out.[43]

Sgt. Henry Lang of the 48th New York was also abandoned during the retreat. Years later, he recalled lying on the darkening battlefield, listening to the "blasphemous language of some marauding soldiers who were ill-treating wounded negroes." Ironically, Lang noted the kind treatment afforded him by several Confederates, who built a fire and gave him a blanket, water, and tobacco.[44]

It is impossible to determine with any degree of precision the number of missing black soldiers who were killed during the battle, murdered by Southern troops in the aftermath of the fight, or captured and sent to prisoner-of-war camps. Certainly, not all of the missing black soldiers were killed by Confederate troops. Muster rolls in the National Archives and casualty reports in the published records indicate 158 men missing from the three black units engaged at Olustee, although it appears that the Federal units did not compile their casualty lists uniformly. Some may have listed men known to be wounded and left behind during the retreat as wounded, although other units might have listed these individuals as missing. It is, therefore, difficult to determine how many men were actually abandoned on the battlefield following the retreat.[45] A postbattle report by a Rebel surgeon sent to Jacksonville via a flag of truce lists 102 wounded black enlisted men in Confederate hands, while preliminary studies from unit records indicate that 50 to 60 of these men were actually sent to Southern prisons. A reasonable estimate might conclude that between 25 and 50 black troops may have been killed after the battle's close.[46]

Those soldiers who survived the battle and its immediate aftermath still faced a harrowing future. Civil War prisons, North and South, were deadly. Disease, lack of food, shelter, clothing, and other essentials, and the incompetence or brutality of prison administrators all contributed to staggering death rates. As appalling as conditions were for all captives, African American soldiers suffered inordinately. Confederate policy toward captured black soldiers was confused, particularly during their early employment by Union armies in 1863. Some were returned to slavery, and others were forced into hard labor or dealt with as insurrectionists. By 1864, some modification in the Confederate position had evolved. Many captured blacks who were not summarily executed were treated as prisoners of war, although they were considered ineligible for parole and often subjected to worse treatment than their white comrades.[47]

The surviving black prisoners from Olustee were confined at Lake City in the days after the battle. The more severely wounded prisoners, white and black, stayed in hospitals and private dwellings in that city, while the remainder were sent to Tallahassee and Madison. In a letter that appeared in the *Savannah Republican,* a certain "J. B." recalled seeing wounded blacks housed in a Lake City stable, with most of the white captives accommodated in churches, hospitals, or houses. Some white troops were also eventually placed in this stable.[48]

Charles Colcock Jones of the Chatham Artillery missed the Battle of Olustee, arriving in Florida several days later. On February 25, he passed through Madison by train and saw "144 Federal Prisoners among them a few negroes." Jones proceeded to Lake City, where he confirmed the presence of wounded black prisoners:

In a stable near the Depot were lying some 30 or 40 white and black wounded prisoners, most of them severely and several mortally wounded. One of them was dying. Poor fellow had both of his eyes shot out and numbers were shot through the legs and body. It was a sad sight, and I pitied the poor Devils. Proceeding up the street I came to a house in which our Surgeons were busily engaged amputating legs and arms of wounded Federals, a Federal Surgeon was also busily operating. I looked in for a little while but the atmosphere was so oppressive and the sight so revolting that I did not feel inclined to remain in the further indulgence of . . . a morbid curiosity.[49]

John Ash, a trooper in the 5th Georgia Cavalry, visited Lake City on February 27, one week after the battle. He observed "about a dozen" black prisoners, along with a similar number of whites, all wounded.[50] Some wounded Federals remained at Lake City into April, as a hospital inspection report dated the tenth of that month records several hospital wards holding prisoners.[51] A memorandum of the same date lists "8 Yankees" present in ward number three, under the care of one white and one black nurse. Conditions in this ward were "in tolerable order only—clean bedding wanted & particular supports."[52] In addition, the April 12 morning report for the Lake City General Hospital listed twelve "U.S. Prisoners" present.[53]

The Confederates confined the unhurt and the less seriously wounded prisoners for a time in the Masonic Hall in Tallahassee. They eventually transported the captives to the Apalachicola River, placed them on steamers, and sent them north to Fort Gaines, Georgia. From there, they traveled by rail to the prison camp at Andersonville. Some prisoners remained at Tallahassee well into the summer of 1864, before they, too, were transported north. Regimental returns show that several blacks died while confined at Tallahassee.[54]

Conditions at Andersonville defy description, and the available evidence indicates that black prisoners suffered even worse treatment than whites. The first black Olustee prisoners probably arrived at Andersonville on March 14, 1864, as a fellow prisoner noted their appearance on that day.[55] Many of the blacks were wounded, and Sgt. Warren Lee Goss, a white prisoner from the 2d Massachusetts Heavy Artillery, observed that some "were victims of atrocious amputations performed by rebel surgeons.... [W]hen there had been a case of amputation, it had been performed in such a manner as to twist and distort the limb out of shape."[56] This supports William Penniman's claim that some blacks suffered from unnecessary or brutally performed amputations after the battle.

Illinois cavalryman John McElroy agreed that black prisoners received little consideration from their captors:

The wounded were turned into the Stockade without having their hurts attended to. One stalwart, soldierly Sergeant had received a bullet which had forced its way under the scalp for some distance, and partially imbedded itself in the skull, where it still remained. He suffered intense agony, and would pass the whole night walking up and down the street in front of our tent, moaning distressingly. The bullet could be felt plainly with the fingers, and we were sure that it would not be a minute's work, with a sharp knife, to remove it and give the man relief. But we could not prevail upon the Rebel Surgeons even to see the man. Finally inflammation set in and he died.[57]

Several other white prisoners later described the conditions endured by blacks at Andersonville. Henry C. Lull of the 146th New York testified that blacks were given no medical treatment and that he once saw an African American soldier whipped by Rebel guards because he refused to work.[58] Elgin Woodlin of the 11th Massachusetts reported that blacks "were treated worse than dumb brutes, and the language used toward them by the rebels was of the most opprobious character."[59] Oliver B. Fairbanks of the 9th New York Cavalry felt the Confederates "seemed to have a particular spite toward the colored soldiers, and they had to go without rations several days at a time on account of not daring to go forward and get them."[60]

Union prisoners remembered between fifty and two hundred blacks present at Andersonville, though some had been captured at battles other than Olustee. The Confederates forced these men to labor on fortifications and to carry dead prisoners out of the stockade and bury them in the prison cemetery. John McElroy recalled seeing black captives organized into squads to labor outside the stockade. They worked under the supervision of a white Union sergeant, who, McElroy claimed, was shot "without any provocation whatever," because of the Confederates' hatred for his black subordinates. McElroy wrote, "the sergeantcy was then offered to me, but as I had no accident policy, I was constrained to decline the honor."[61]

By the later summer of 1864, Confederate officials transferred many prisoners from Andersonville to other camps. This became necessary as Maj. Gen. William T. Sherman's Union army moved closer to Atlanta and the threat of a cavalry raid on Andersonville seemed likely. The Confederates moved some prisoners to other sites within Georgia, while the majority were transported to camps in South Carolina. Fortunately for the emaciated survivors of prisoner-of-war camps like Andersonville, the prisoner exchange system reopened in early 1865. The Confederates included few black soldiers in these exchanges, and most Olustee survivors returned to their regiments only at the conclusion of the war.[62]

A preliminary examination of the regimental records of the three African American units engaged at Olustee located the names of between 20 and 25 soldiers originally reported missing but later exchanged as prisoners. These men represent the only survivors of the 158 soldiers officially listed as missing in action at Olustee. The remainder had either been killed during the battle itself or by Confederates soon afterward, or they had died in prison camps.[63]

In addition to mistreating black enlisted captives, Confederate officials refused to care for the captured white officers of African American regiments in the same manner as those of all-white units. While Southerners occasionally showed pity toward captured blacks—considering them ignorant pawns in corrupt Yankee hands—they reserved a special hatred for those whites commanding blacks in battle. Maj. John Appleton of the 54th Massachusetts heard such sentiments several days before Olustee, when he conversed with a Florida woman. "Do you know you are in a terrible position young man?" the woman said to him. When Appleton asked why, the woman replied, "Because you expect to fight here and if you are taken prisoner you will surely be hung because you command nigger troops."[64]

The experiences of a white officer captured at Olustee further illustrate this sentiment. Maj. Archibald Bogle was the second-in-command of the 35th USCI during the battle and assumed command of the regiment upon the wounding of the unit's lieutenant colonel. Toward the end of the fight, Bogle fell wounded through the leg and was abandoned and captured on the field.[65] While he was not executed, Bogle's captors refused to treat him with the deference usually accorded to officers of similar rank, solely because of his association with blacks. In a postwar letter describing his experiences, Bogle recalled: "I was conveyed to the Olustee Depot where I was exposed all day, listening to such exclamations as 'shoot him! hang him!' The prejudice at that time against Colored Troops was very great."[66] Another Union prisoner described the Confederates' mistreatment of Bogle: "They seemed to delight in the torture they inflicted upon him: telling him hanging was too good; that he ought to be buried alive, with one of his Negroes beneath him, and one above him."[67]

Bogle was eventually transported to Lake City and held in the Presbyterian Church. A Confederate civilian wrote, "At first it was difficult to get our ladies to attend him but humanity prevailed, and he has no cause to complain of his treatment."[68] Bogle agreed that he was "kindly treated" by the authorities and civilians at Lake City.[69]

Unfortunately for the young officer, he was soon moved to Andersonville, where he found his new captors much less humane. Although designed to house only enlisted prisoners, Bogle endured several months of captivity there. Prison authorities denied him medical attention and stopped a fellow prisoner from dressing his wounds. "Turn him out with his God damned Niggers," Bogle overheard a Rebel exclaim.[70] When he again tried to enter the prison hospital, a steward threatened the other prisoners, "If you don't get that God damned Nigger Major out of there I will shoot him and put a ball and chain on you." When finally admitted to the hospital in June 1864, Bogle's weight had dropped from 170 to between 70 and 80 pounds.[71] Despite the fact that "no opportunity to insult 'the nigger officer' was neglected," a prisoner recalled that Bogle "bore it all with dignified self-possession."[72]

In November 1864, Bogle's captors transferred him to another stockade, but he found his new location not much of an improvement. Upon his arrival at the Millen, Georgia, prison camp, a Confederate officer informed his clerk to "put [Bogle] in the stockade—God damn him, don't register his name, he will never be exchanged, as long as I am in command of the post."[73] Bogle, however, soon left Millen and was incarcerated in several other Southern prisons, until his eventual parole at Goldsboro, North Carolina, in February 1865. His treatment might not seem overly harsh when compared to that given captured enlisted soldiers, but it was distinctly inferior to the normal Confederate handling of officers from white Union regiments.[74]

Further indication of the Southern attitude toward white officers belonging to the U.S. Colored Troops can be found in correspondence between Truman Seymour and Confederate Brig. Gen. William M. Gardner, commander of the District of Middle Florida. Shortly after Olustee, the widow of Col. Charles Fribley traveled to Florida, hoping to obtain information about her husband. Through a flag of truce, Gardner forwarded several personal items found on the battlefield but informed Seymour: "That I may not be misunderstood, it is due to myself to state that no sympathy with the fate of any officer commanding negro troops, but compassion for a widow in grief, had induced these efforts to recover her relics which she must naturally value."[75]

A vitriolic letter published in the *Savannah Daily Morning News* in March 1864 denounced Fribley more directly. After describing the mass burial of Union dead at Olustee, the writer added:

> Such was the case with the redoubtable Col. Frieble, of a negro regiment, in whose pocket was found a letter from his wife (query, white or black?) asking him to "confiscate" for her "a nice saddle when he reached Tallahassee."

Yes! The black-hearted Frieble had a dog's burial. A leader of a horde of infuriated negroes, on a mission of murder, robbery and rape, ought he not to have been
left to rot on the plain, to the obscene birds to fatten on his vitals, and the great wolves
to gnaw his bones?[76]

Due largely to the remoteness of the Olustee battlefield and the Union
army's immediate retreat from the vicinity, Northerners never realized the
extent of Confederate mistreatment of captured blacks. In the weeks after
the battle, little information reached the North regarding the fate of the large
number of Union missing. Most of the news received came from sources such
as Confederate deserters and newspapers. Coupled with this lack of hard
evidence was the apparent desire of some Union officials to downplay or
disregard any information indicating that blacks suffered abuse after capture.
The primary reason for this attitude, apparently, was the fear that such information might restrict black enlistment and turn Northern public opinion
against the continued recruitment of black soldiers.[77]

Truman Seymour, defeated at Olustee but retained for a time as commander of the Union District of Florida, seemed particularly adamant in his
insistence that black prisoners received humane treatment at Confederate
hands. In a letter written soon after the battle, the general informed Col.
James Beecher of the 35th USCI of information he had obtained regarding the
condition of Major Bogle and the captured black enlisted men: "From rather
indefinate information, I am led to believe, that Major Boyle was taken to
Lake City, and has been cared for precisely like all other officers—and without respect to his belonging to a colored Regiment. So far as I can ascertain,
all prisoners have been treated alike. Further inquiry shall be made by the
first opportunity."[78] Three days later, Seymour sent an even more optimistic note to Beecher, which read in part, "I may assure you, I believe, that the
colored soldiers and their officers are treated by the Confederates precisely
as are those of white Regiments."[79]

Why Seymour maintained such an optimistic outlook is unclear, considering that virtually all his information came from Confederate sources—hardly
the most reliable or unbiased available. Seymour was accused during and after the war of having a low opinion of black units in general, but whether his
seemingly naive attitude stemmed from a deliberate lack of concern for black
troops or simply a mistaken estimate of the situation is not known.[80] In the
weeks following the battle, Seymour corresponded with the various Confederate commanders in Florida, mostly regarding the status of Union prisoners and wounded. The Rebel officers eventually provided a list of all the
wounded prisoners in their hands. Perhaps this act convinced Seymour that,

from the beginning, black prisoners had received treatment similar to whites.[81] In the spring of 1864, the U.S. Congress's Joint Committee on the Conduct and Expenditures of the War investigated the Florida campaign. During the interrogation of various Northern officers, the committee made inquiries about the fate of black prisoners. Once again, the Union high command seemed to avoid or downplay the issue. Brig. Gen. John Turner, General Gillmore's chief of staff and chief of artillery, told the committee that, to the best of his knowledge, white and black prisoners received identical treatment.[82]

Some Union leaders doubted Confederate assurances of equal treatment for whites and blacks. On September 25, 1864, Brig. Gen. John Porter Hatch, the new commander of the District of Florida, sent Maj. Gen. Ethan Allen Hitchcock, the Union commissioner for the exchange of prisoners, a letter that told a horrific story:

> Soon after the battle of Olustee, in Florida, a list of wounded and prisoners in the hands of the enemy was forwarded to our lines by the commander of the rebel army. The very small number of colored prisoners attracted immediate attention, as it was well known that the number left wounded on the field was large.
>
> It is now known that the most of the wounded colored men were murdered on the field. These outrages were perpetrated, so far as I can ascertain, by the Georgia regulars and the Georgia volunteers in Colquitt's brigade.
>
> As many of these troops are now in our hands as prisoners, an investigation of circumstances might easily be made.
>
> All accounts represent the Florida troops as not engaged in the murders.[83]

As far as can be ascertained, Federal authorities did not act upon Hatch's suggestion of an investigation into Olustee atrocities, and the matter ended.

Until recent years, the Florida campaign has received relatively little attention from historians. Consequently, the issue of Confederate atrocities has also remained largely ignored. Mark Boyd, the author of a generally reliable secondary account of the campaign, does not mention Rebel atrocities. Historian Richard McMurry was one of the first Olustee authors to examine the issue. While acknowledging the statements made in the recollections of Penniman and Jackson, McMurry argued that "the accounts . . . were written so long after the battle and are so at variance with the more immediate evidence that they should not be given credence. At the most, there may have been a few cases of individual abuse of black prisoners by Confederates; even the evidence that such mistreatment occurred is very weak."[84] McMurry, however, did not have access to the numerous additional primary sources indicating that some abuses did, in fact, take place.

An earlier historian of the battle, William T. Bauskett, author of a history of Florida commissioned by the state legislature but never published, dared to explore the possibility of Southern atrocities:

> It was charged by Federal officers unofficially that the Confederates gave no quarter to the negro soldiers enlisted against them. This charge has been denied again and again, but it was the general rule in the Confederate army to give little consideration to either the negro soldiers or those who fought with them. The north suppressed the facts in this respect, knowing that an insurmountable fear would be raised in the breast of the negro. The author has discussed this battle of Olustee with many Confederate officers who participated in it and has heard Confederate and Federal officers discuss it together, and, from what they say, he believes that the negro soldiers were given little consideration when they offered themselves as prisoners. ... There was no order for no quarter of the negro troops, but the frenzied resentment of the Southerners that their own property should be used for their destruction left scant mercy in their souls.[85]

William Nulty, author of the most detailed study of the Olustee campaign, virtually ignored the issue in his original dissertation on the subject. In his subsequent, published version, he briefly examined the atrocity charges utilizing sources gathered primarily from a master's thesis on the battle. "The treatment of black prisoners is still an open area of inquiry," he concluded.[86]

As previously noted, a substantial number of accounts left by individuals present at the conclusion of the battle describe Confederate mistreatment of wounded and captured blacks. While some eyewitnesses probably exaggerated, the preponderance of evidence indicates that abuses did occur. Some sources deny such charges, but in most cases these were written by persons not present at the battle's end and thus cannot be considered as reliable.[87]

The evidence presented above, coupled with the knowledge of similar Confederate actions when facing black troops in other battles, proves beyond a reasonable doubt that at least some atrocities occurred at Olustee. The exact number of victims, however, will never be known. Only the remoteness of the battlefield, the apparent lack of concern of Union officials, and the previous lack of detailed historical research into the battle has kept this aspect of Olustee from gaining notoriety. Unfortunately, the largest battle in Florida history must take its place alongside Fort Pillow, Saltville, the Crater, and other engagements as an example of Confederate war crimes directed against black Union soldiers.

Notes

1. *The War of the Rebellion: A Compilation of the Official Records of the Union and Confederate Armies,* 128 vols. (Washington, D.C.: Government Printing Office, 1880–1901), ser. 1, 35 (pt. 1): 298 (hereafter cited as *OR;* all citations are to series 1, unless otherwise noted). For overviews of the Olustee campaign, see William H. Nulty, *Confederate Florida: The Road to Olustee* (Tuscaloosa: University of Alabama Press, 1990); Mark F. Boyd, *The Federal Campaign of 1864 in East Florida* (Tallahassee: Florida Board of Parks and Historic Memorials, 1956); and David James Coles, "Far from Fields of Glory: Military Operations in Florida During the Civil War, 1864–1865" (Ph.D. diss., Florida State University, 1996).

2. Overviews of the political intrigue surrounding the campaign are Ovid Leon Futch, "Salmon P. Chase and Radical Politics in Florida, 1862–1865" (master's thesis, University of Florida, 1952), and "Salmon P. Chase and Civil War Politics in Florida," *Florida Historical Quarterly* 32 (Jan. 1954): 163–88; George Winston Smith, "Carpetbag Imperialism in Florida, 1862–1868," *Florida Historical Quarterly* 27 (Oct. 1948, Jan. 1949): 99–130, 260–99; Jerrell H. Shofner, *Nor Is It Over Yet: Florida in the Era of Reconstruction, 1863–1877* (Gainesville: University Presses of Florida, 1974); and Coles, "Far from Fields of Glory," 1–39.

3. *OR,* 28 (pt. 2): 129; Lyman Stickney to Salmon P. Chase, June 6, Dec. 11, 1863, and Feb. 4, 1864, Salmon P. Chase Papers, Manuscripts Division, Library of Congress, Washington, D.C.

4. Futch, "Chase and Radical Politics," 63.

5. Ibid.; Tyler Dennett, ed., *Lincoln and the Civil War in the Diaries and Letters of John Hay* (New York: Dodd, Mead, 1939), 110. See also Michael Burlingame and John R. Turner Ettlinger, eds., *Inside Lincoln's White House: The Complete Civil War Diary of John Hay* (Carbondale: Southern Illinois University Press, 1997), 134–35.

6. Roy P. Basler, ed., *The Collected Works of Abraham Lincoln,* 8 vols. (New Brunswick, N.J.: Rutgers University Press, 1953–55), 7:126.

7. *OR,* 35 (pt. 1): 278.

8. Dennett, *Diaries and Letters of John Hay,* 155; *OR,* 35 (pt. 1): 279–81; Nulty, *Confederate Florida,* 76–81; Boyd, *Federal Campaign of 1864,* 4.

9. Virginia Adams, ed., *On the Altar of Freedom: A Black Soldier's Civil War Letters from the Front* (Amherst: University of Massachusetts Press, 1991), 113.

10. Nulty, *Confederate Florida,* 76–111; Boyd, *Federal Campaign,* 5–12; Coles, "Far from Fields of Glory," 48–57.

11. *OR,* 35 (pt. 1): 282.

12. Ibid., 277.

13. Ibid., 284–85; Nulty, *Confederate Florida,* 114–19.

14. *OR* 35 (pt. 1): 262–77, 284–86; Joseph R. Hawley, "Comments on General Jones's Paper by Joseph R. Hawley, Brevet Major-General, U.S.V.," in Robert Underwood Johnson and Clarence Clough Buel, eds., *Battles and Leaders of the Civil War,* 4 vols. (1887–88; reprint, New York: Thomas Yoseloff, 1956), 4:79.

15. Dennett, *Diaries and Letters of John Hay,* 164.

16. See particularly *New York Evening Post,* Feb. 29, Mar. 1, 7, 14, Apr. 9, 19, 1864; and *New York Tribune,* Mar. 1, 2, 14, 17, 1864.

17. Oliver Willcox Norton, *Army Letters, 1861–1865* (Chicago: O. L. Deming, 1903), 196.

18. Samuel Penniman Bates, *History of Pennsylvania Volunteers, 1861–5,* 5 vols. (Harrisburg: S. Singerly, State Printer, 1869–71), 5:965–68; Norton, *Army Letters,* 180–97; Frank H. Taylor, *Philadelphia in the Civil War, 1861–1865* (Philadelphia: City of Philadelphia, 1913), 186–91.

19. Dudley Taylor Cornish, *The Sable Arm: Negro Troops in the Union Army, 1861–1865* (New York: Longmans, Green, 1956), 150.

20. Luis F. Emilio, *History of the Fifty-Fourth Regiment of Massachusetts Volunteer Infantry, 1863–1865* (1894; reprint, New York: Johnson Reprint, 1968), 1–22, 34, 81–82; Russell Duncan, ed., *Blue-Eyed Child of Fortune: The Civil War Letters of Colonel Robert Gould Shaw* (Athens: University of Georgia Press, 1992) is the definitive collection of Shaw's writings and contains a biographical sketch of the officer on pp. 1–68; Milton Rugoff, *The Beechers: An American Family in the Nineteenth Century* (New York: Harper and Row, 1981), 451–66; Francis Beecher Perkins, "Two Years with a Colored Regiment: A Woman's Experience," *New England Magazine* 17 (Feb. 1898): 533–43; *OR*, 35 (pt. 1): 298.

21. *OR*, 35 (pt. 1): 321–26, 338; W. H. Lloyd to Mrs. Parramore, June 17, 1909, vol. 3, Florida Division, United Daughters of the Confederacy Scrapbooks, Florida State Archives, Tallahassee, Florida.

22. Quoted in Norton, *Army Letters,* 198; Edwin S. Redkey, ed., *A Grand Army of Black Men: Letters from African-American Soldiers in the Union Army, 1861–1865* (Cambridge: Cambridge University Press, 1992), 41; *Brooksville (Pa.) Republican,* Feb. 23, 1864.

23. *OR*, 35 (pt. 1): 298, 311–14.

24. Nulty, *Confederate Florida,* 145–69; Boyd, *Federal Campaign,* 25–28; Coles, "Far from Fields of Glory," 131–41.

25. Emilio, *History of the Fifty-Fourth Regiment,* 162–63; John Appleton journal, Feb. 20, 1864, John W. M. Appleton Papers, University of West Virginia Library, Morgantown.

26. Appleton journal, Feb. 20, 1864.

27. Charles A. Currier, "Recollections of Service with the 40th Massachusetts Volunteers," 85, Charles A. Courier Papers, United States Army Military History Institute, Carlisle Barracks, Pa.

28. Quoted in Emilio, *History of the Fifty-Fourth Regiment,* 174–75.

29. See Nulty, *Confederate Florida,* 170–202, 219–25; Boyd, *Federal Campaign,* 28–37; and Coles, "Far from Fields of Glory," 186–247, for details on the battle's aftermath and for post-Olustee military operations in northeast Florida. In addition, see Richard A. Martin and Daniel L. Shafer, *Jacksonville's Ordeal by Fire: A Civil War History* (Jacksonville: Florida Publishing, 1984), 212–77.

30. Numerous sources describe conditions following the battle. Among the most graphic are *A Voice from Rebel Prisons; Giving an Account of Some of the Horrors of the Stockades at Andersonville, Milan, and Other Prisons: By a Returned Prisoner of War* (Boston: G. C. Rand and Avery, 1865), 4; *Atlanta Daily Intelligencer,* Mar. 3, 1864; and *Savannah Daily Morning News,* Mar. 30, 1864.

31. Lawrence Jackson, "As I Saw and Remember the Battle of Olustee, Which Was Fought February 20, 186[4]," Lawrence Jackson Papers, P. K. Yonge Library of Florida History, University of Florida, Gainesville.

32. William Penniman reminiscences, 60, William Penniman Papers, Southern Historical Collection, University of North Carolina, Chapel Hill. The reference to Fort Pillow is confusing and almost certainly incorrect. In April 1864, two months after Olustee, Confederate forces under Nathan Bedford Forrest captured Fort Pillow, Tennessee. Forrest's troops did not immediately accept the surrender of the black soldiers that made up a portion of the Union garrison, and an undetermined number were murdered on the field. There would have been no opportunity for black soldiers to kill Confederate troops trying to surrender.

33. Ibid., 60–61.

34. James M. Jordan to wife, Feb. 21, 1864, typescript, in "Letters from Confederate Soldiers, 1861–1865," 2:481, Georgia Division, United Daughters of the Confederacy, Georgia Department of Archives and History, Atlanta.

35. *Atlanta Daily Intelligencer,* Mar. 2, 1864.

36. Edwin Tuttle to parents, Mar. 7, 1864, Edwin Tuttle Papers, Robert W. Woodruff Library, Emory University, Atlanta, Ga.

37. Ibid.

38. Edmund Lee to "Dear Sarah," Mar. 14, 1864, "Civil War Letters" of Edmund C. Lee, copied by Historical Records Survey, State Archives Survey, 1937, Florida Room, State Library of Florida, Tallahassee.

39. Winston Stephens to Octavia Stephens, Feb. 21, 1864, Stephens-Bryant Papers, P. K. Yonge Library of Florida History, University of Florida, Gainesville.

40. Tuttle to parents, Tuttle Papers.

41. *Atlanta Daily Intelligencer*, Mar. 19, 1864.

42. Joab Roach to Miss Fannie, Mar. 5, 186[4], Joab Roach Papers, Georgia Historical Society, Savannah.

43. *Voice from Rebel Prisons*, 4.

44. Quoted in Abraham J. Palmer, *History of the Forty-Eighth Regiment* (Brooklyn: Veteran Association of the Regiment, 1885), 136.

45. *OR*, 35 (pt. 1): 298. See also Regimental Books and Regimental Papers of the 8th USCT, 35th USCT, and 54th Massachusetts, Adjutant General's Office, Regimental Records, U.S. Volunteers, RG 94, National Archives.

46. Regimental Books and Regimental Papers of the 8th USCT, 35th USCT, and 54th Massachusetts; *New York Times*, Apr. 19, 1864.

47. Cornish, *Sable Arm*, 157–80; Walter L. Williams, "Again in Chains: Black Soldiers Suffering in Captivity," *Civil War Times Illustrated*, May 1981, 36–43.

48. *Savannah Republican*, Mar. 3, 1864.

49. Charles Colcock Jones Jr. to wife, Feb. 27, 1864, Charles Colcock Jones Papers, Special Collections Division, University of Georgia Library, Athens.

50. John Ash diary, Feb. 27, 1864, John H. Ash Papers, Robert W. Woodruff Library, Emory University, Atlanta, Ga.

51. "Report of Inspection of the General Hospital at Lake City, Fla., April 10th 1864," War Department Collection of Confederate Records, Letters Received, Department of South Carolina, Georgia, and Florida, RG 109, National Archives.

52. "Memorandum of General Condition of Wards in General Hospital at Lake City, Fla., April 10 1864," Collection of Confederate Records.

53. "Morning Report of General Hospital, Lake City, Florida, April 12th 1864," Collection of Confederate Records.

54. *Voice from Rebel Prisons*, 4–6. See also David J. Coles, "Southern Hospitality: A Yankee Prisoner at Olustee, Tallahassee, and Andersonville," *Apalachee* 10 (1984–90): 19–28.

55. Emilio, *History of the Fifty-Fourth Regiment*, 426.

56. Quoted in ibid., 427.

57. John McElroy, *Andersonville: A Story of Rebel Military Prisons* (Toledo: D. R. Locke, 1879), 163.

58. Emilio, *History of the Fifty-Fourth Regiment*, 429.

59. Quoted in ibid.

60. Quoted in ibid.

61. McElroy, *Andersonville*, 163. See William Marvel, *Andersonville: The Last Depot* (Chapel Hill: University of North Carolina Press, 1994), 324, which is highly critical of McElroy's accuracy, calling the work "dubious" and "highly embellished."

62. Regimental Books and Regimental Papers, 8th USCT, 35th USCT, and 54th Massachusetts; Marvel, *Andersonville*, 201–2, 304; Cornish, *Sable Arm*, 172.

63. Regimental Books and Regimental Papers, 8th USCT, 35th USCT, and 54th Massachusetts.

64. Appleton journal, Feb. 13, 1864.

65. Archibald Bogle to General Lorenzo Thomas, May 26, 1865, and Archibald Bogle to U. S. Grant, Apr. 27, 1866, file of Archibald Bogle, Compiled Military Service Records of Volunteer Union Soldiers, RG 94, National Archives.

66. Bogle to Grant, Bogle file.

67. *Voice from Rebel Prisons,* 4.

68. *Savannah Republican,* Mar. 3, 1864.

69. Bogle to Thomas, Bogle file.

70. Quoted in ibid. See also McElroy, *Andersonville,* 162.

71. Quoted in Bogle to Thomas, Bogle file.

72. McElroy, *Andersonville,* 162.

73. Quoted in Bogle to Thomas, Bogle file.

74. Ibid.

75. Quoted in *American Annual Cyclopedia and Register of Important Events for the Year 1864* (New York: Appleton, 1872), 51.

76. *Savannah Daily Morning News,* Mar. 30, 1864.

77. Cornish, *Sable Arm,* 157–80.

78. Truman Seymour to James Beecher, Mar. 14, 1864, Bogle file.

79. Truman Seymour to James Beecher, Mar. 17, 1864, Bogle file.

80. The controversial attack on Fort Wagner on July 18, 1863, raised questions about Seymour's attitude toward blacks. Maj. John Appleton, for example, criticized Seymour in this regard. Appleton journal, Feb. 1, 1864.

81. *OR,* 35 (pt. 1): 330, 493, 496; *OR,* 35 (pt. 2): 3, 7.

82. U.S. Congress, Senate, *Report of the Joint Committee on the Conduct and Expenditures of the War,* 38th Cong., 1st sess., 1864, S. Rept. 47, 10.

83. *OR,* ser. 2, 7:876.

84. Richard McMurry, "The President's Tenth and the Battle of Olustee," *Civil War Times Illustrated,* Jan. 1978, 23. See also Boyd, *Federal Campaign.*

85. Unpublished history of the state of Florida by William T. Bauskett, 139–40, William T. Bauskett Papers, Florida State Archives, Tallahassee.

86. William Nulty, "The 1864 Florida Federal Expedition: Blundering into Modern Warfare," (Ph.D. diss., University of Florida, 1985); Nulty, *Confederate Florida,* 210; David J. Coles, "'A Fight, a Licking, and a Footrace': The 1864 Florida Campaign and the Battle of Olustee" (master's thesis, Florida State University, 1985).

87. See, for example, Charles Duren to mother, Apr. 9, 1864, Charles Duren Papers, P. K. Yonge Library of Florida History, University of Florida.

Lt. Gen. Edmund Kirby Smith, the commander of the Confederacy's Trans-Mississippi Department, who advised his subordinates to summarily execute members of the U.S. Colored Troops to avoid having to deal with black prisoners of war. (Library of Congress)

Gen. Pierre G. T. Beauregard, commander of the Department of South Carolina, Georgia, and Florida, who hesitated to enforce the draconian policies authorized by the Confederate government after his subordinates captured black Union troops during the siege of Charleston, S.C. (Library of Congress)

Confederate Secretary of War James A. Seddon, who advocated the summary execution of captured black Federal soldiers in November 1862. By the following summer, Seddon was calling former slaves in Union service "deluded victims" who should be "treated with mercy and returned to their owners." (Library of Congress)

The 54th Massachusetts Volunteer Infantry Regiment assaults Fort Wagner near Charleston, S.C., July 18, 1863. (U.S. Army Military History Institute)

A fatigue party of enlisted men from the 54th Massachusetts (*at left*) rests in a sap before Fort Wagner, whose sandy south wall rises in the background. (Massachusetts Commandery, Military Order of the Loyal Legion of the United States, and U.S. Army Military History Institute)

Enlisted men from the 54th Massachusetts (*at bottom left*) inside Fort Wagner, after its evacuation by Confederate forces in September 1863. The fact that most of the 54th's rank and file were free blacks created legal complications for their Rebel foes. (Massachusetts Commandery, Military Order of the Loyal Legion of the United States, and U.S. Army Military History Institute)

Robert Gould Shaw, the first colonel of the 54th Massachusetts, who died leading his regiment against Fort Wagner on July 18, 1863. The Confederates showed their contempt for Shaw by mistreating his body and burying him in a pit beneath twenty-five of his slain soldiers. (Massachusetts Commandery, Military Order of the Loyal Legion of the United States, and U.S. Army Military History Institute)

Capt. Luis F. Emilio of the 54th Massachusetts, who claimed that it took extra courage to accept a commission in a black regiment because of Confederate threats to execute Union officers captured while leading black troops. (Massachusetts Commandery, Military Order of the Loyal Legion of the United States, and U.S. Army Military History Institute)

Brig. Gen. Truman B. Seymour, who led the Union's Florida Expedition to a humiliating defeat at Olustee on February 20, 1864. Seymour also directed the failed assault on Fort Wagner the previous July. (U.S. Army Military History Institute)

First Sgt. Charles W. Fribley of the 84th Pennsylvania Volunteer Infantry Regiment poses with his wife early in the war. Fribley served as the colonel of the 8th U.S. Colored Infantry during the Florida Expedition, and he died at Olustee. (David L. Richards Collection and U.S. Army Military History Institute)

Maj. Gen. Nathan Bedford Forrest, the captor of Fort Pillow. Though heralded as the most outstanding cavalryman of the Civil War, Forrest's reputation was forever tarnished by the Fort Pillow Massacre. (Massachusetts Commandery, Military Order of the Loyal Legion of the United States, and U.S. Army Military History Institute)

Sen. Benjamin F. Wade of Ohio, a domineering and calculating Radical Republican, who chaired the Joint Committee on the Conduct of the War. The hasty investigation orchestrated by Wade ensured that the Fort Pillow Massacre would become the Civil War's most famous racial atrocity. (Library of Congress)

Col. Samuel J. Crawford of the 2d Kansas Colored Infantry (seen here as a brevet brigadier general), who avenged the Poison Spring Massacre by leading his "Iron Clads" in a charge that captured two Confederate cannon at the Battle of Jenkins's Ferry, April 30, 1864. (U.S. Army Military History Institute)

Three officers of the 2d Kansas Colored Infantry *(left to right):* Lt. John J. Bertholf (the regimental adjutant), Capt. J. C. Ball, and Capt. Edward C. McFarland. In response to the Poison Spring Massacre, the officers of the 2d Kansas swore to "take no prisoners so long as the Rebels continued to murder our men." (U.S. Army Military History Institute)

Surgeon William L. Nicholson of the 29th Iowa Infantry, who witnessed the murder of wounded black prisoners from the 2d Kansas Colored Infantry in a field hospital on the Jenkins's Ferry battlefield and later at Princeton, Ark. (U.S. Army Military History Institute)

Five black sailors from the 137-man crew of the USS *Miami*, one of the gunboats the Union navy assigned to assist in the defense of Plymouth, N.C. (U.S. Naval Historical Center)

Maj. Gen. Benjamin F. Butler, the commander of the Department of Virginia and North Carolina, who may have solicited false testimony from a purported member of the 2d U.S. Colored Cavalry to substantiate rumors that massive racial atrocities accompanied the Confederate capture of Plymouth, N.C., on April 20, 1864. (Library of Congress)

Brig. Gen. Edward Ferrero, who commanded the black 4th Division in the Army of the Potomac's 9th Corps at the Battle of the Crater, near Petersburg, Va., on July 30, 1864. (Library of Congress)

Brig. Gen. William Mahone, who became a Confederate hero by leading the counterattack that stemmed the Union breakthrough at the Battle of the Crater. Mahone initially exhorted his men to take no black prisoners but later reportedly ordered his subordinates "not to kill quite all of them." (National Archives)

Pvt. Louis Troutman, Company F, 118th U.S. Colored Infantry. To newly emancipated blacks, men like Troutman symbolized freedom, security, and the idea that racial equality was no longer just a dream. To white Southerners, the U.S. Colored Troops were galling reminders of military defeat and the death of the traditional Southern way of life. (Michael J. McAfee)

The Fort Pillow Massacre

An Examination of the Evidence

ALBERT CASTEL

A feeling of horror swept across the North during the month of April 1864. From the banks of the Mississippi down in Tennessee came news that the Union garrison at Fort Pillow had been brutally massacred by the Confederate cavalry of Nathan Bedford Forrest. Not only had the Confederates murdered most of the garrison after it had surrendered but they had buried black soldiers alive, set fire to tents containing Federal wounded, and committed other terrible atrocities. Outraged people throughout the North demanded vengeance, and President Lincoln promised retaliation should the reports from Tennessee prove true.[1]

Although Lincoln never ordered reprisals, the "Fort Pillow Massacre" became fixed in the mind of the North as a deed of "inhuman, fiendish butchery." The Joint Congressional Committee on the Conduct of the War, after collecting a large quantity of sworn testimony from the survivors of the garrison, issued a widely read report that provided official documentation for this belief.[2] On the basis of the evidence contained in the report, Horace Greeley bluntly asserted that "If human testimony ever did or can establish anything, then [Fort Pillow] is proved a case of deliberate, wholesale massacre of prisoners of war after they had surrendered."[3] Subsequent Northern historians, without any notable exception, have basically accepted this conclusion.[4]

Southern historians, however, especially the many biographers of Forrest, have heatedly and skillfully challenged the Northern view.[5] They have questioned the objectivity of the Committee on the Conduct of the War, criticized its procedures, and pointed to contradictions and errors in the statements of the witnesses who appeared before it. Above all, they have offered an impressive amount of testimony, much of it sworn, from Confederate participants in the attack on Fort Pillow. This is in fundamental opposition to the Northern testimony. Backed by this Southern evidence, they have in effect declared that if human testimony ever did or can establish anything, then Fort Pillow was not a case of deliberate, wholesale massacre of prisoners of war after they had surrendered.

In the writer's opinion, neither side in this controversy is altogether wrong or altogether right; they are both guilty, in varying degrees, of prejudice and error. Consequently, the discussion in the following pages is an attempt to reexamine the evidence concerning Fort Pillow solely on its own merits and to arrive at the closest approximation to the historical truth possible. The fact that, because of his Kansas birth, the author might be considered a "Yankee" is, he trusts, balanced by the fact that prior to undertaking this study he was a wholehearted believer in the Southern point of view concerning Fort Pillow.

The historical debate over Fort Pillow divides itself into three categories: the capture of the fort, the massacre, and the atrocities.

The Capture of the Fort

Fort Pillow stood atop a bluff overlooking the Mississippi River. It consisted of a dirt parapet 6 to 8 feet high and from 4 to 6 feet thick, with a ditch 5 feet wide and about 8 feet deep immediately in front. The parapet extended for about 125 yards in the form of a rough semicircle and faced only to the east. The rear, or river side, of the fort was open to the bluff, which descended sharply to the riverbank below. The terrain on the land side of the fort was rough and hilly and covered with a low undergrowth. At distances varying from 10 to 150 yards, the ground sloped downward from the works into a ravine that projected from a rivulet named Coal Creek on the north side of the fort and ran completely about the fort until it merged with the river bluff on the south. On the slope leading to the south side of the fort were several rows of storehouses and barracks. The garrison of 295 white and 262 Negro troops was commanded by Maj. Lionel F. Booth. A gunboat, the *New Era,* commanded by Capt. James Marshall, supported the fort from the river. Booth and Marshall had a prearranged system of signals by which Booth was to indicate the points on land where the heavy naval guns would be most effective against an assailing force.[6]

During the early spring of 1864, Forrest's cavalry corps was engaged in raiding Federal rear areas in west Tennessee and Kentucky in an attempt to delay Sherman's forthcoming invasion of Georgia. On April 10, from Jackson, Tennessee, Forrest sent Brig. Gen. James R. Chalmers's division of fifteen hundred men to "attend to" Fort Pillow. Chalmers arrived before the fort at dawn on the morning of April 12. One of his brigades, commanded by Col. Tyree H. Bell, deployed to the northern and eastern sides of the fort, while the other, under Col. Robert McCulloch, moved into position on the south. They then advanced, quickly overcame the "very slight resistance" of the Federal pickets, and by 8:00 AM had the fort completely invested and under heavy rifle and artillery fire. Shelling by the *New Era* did them little damage, and the cannons of the fort were equally ineffective. A Confederate sharpshooter picked off Major Booth, who was succeeded in command by Maj. William F. Bradford.[7]

Forrest arrived on the field at 10:00 AM and took personal charge of the operation. He reconnoitered the approaches to the fort and discovered that if he could get his men into the buildings on the south side of the fort and into the ravine formed by Coal Creek on the north and east, they would be sheltered from the garrison's fire and in advantageous positions for an assault. Accordingly, he ordered these objectives seized. By 11:00 AM, McCulloch's men were firmly ensconced among the buildings on the south side.[8] As Forrest had foreseen, they were protected from the Northern fire. Wrote Lt. Mack J. Leaming of the garrison in his official report on the battle: "Owing to the close proximity of these buildings to the fort, and to the fact that they were on considerably lower ground, our artillery could not be sufficiently depressed to destroy them, or even render them untenable for the enemy."[9] Bell's brigade likewise successfully achieved its objective on the northeastern approaches, where it was also immune to the guns of the garrison.

Forrest believed that his forces were now in position to storm the fort and that consequently it would be useless and senseless for the garrison to continue resisting. He waited until 3:30 PM in order to replenish his ammunition supply and then sent forward a flag of truce with a note addressed to Major Booth: "The conduct of the officers and men garrisoning Fort Pillow has been such as to entitle them to being treated as prisoners of war. I demand the unconditional surrender of the garrison, promising you that you shall be treated as prisoners of war. My men have received a fresh supply of ammunition, and from their present position can easily assault and capture the fort. Should my demand be refused, I cannot be responsible for the fate of your command."[10] The threat at the end of the communication was a customary device of Forrest's, which he had used often before to bluff or frighten an enemy commander into quick surrender.

Bradford, wishing to conceal Booth's death, signed that officer's name to his reply: "I respectfully ask for one hour for consultation with my officers and the officers of the gunboat. In the meantime no preparation to be made on either side."[11]

While awaiting this answer, Forrest noticed three Federal steamers bearing on the fort, one of them "apparently crowded with troops." This caused him to suspect that the request for an hour's delay was merely intended to gain time for these vessels to bring reinforcements. Therefore, he informed the Union commander that he had but twenty minutes in which to decide to surrender or fight. In less than the stipulated time, he received Bradford's final answer: "I will not surrender."[12]

At this point, we come to the crux of the controversy surrounding the capture of the fort. The report of the Committee on the Conduct of the War accused the Confederates of taking advantage of the truce flag to advance their lines closer to the fort and, by implication, alleged that they would not have been able to seize the fort had they not committed this violation of the laws of war. Without exception, all the Federal participants in the Fort Pillow action whom the committee questioned made the same charge.

A close examination of the Union testimony indicates, however, that the Confederates were not supposed to have moved nearer the fort on all sides but only on its northeastern approach. Thus, Lieutenant Leaming stated that while the garrison's attention was occupied with the truce flag, the Confederates advanced to "within 20 yards" of the fort on the east and north. And Captain Marshall of the *New Era* testified that during the truce, "he saw the rebels coming down the ravine above the Fort, and taking positions there."[13] Since the only ravine "above the Fort" and "within 20 yards" of it was Coal Creek ravine, Forrest was alleged to have unfairly seized a position that Bell's brigade had in fact possessed at least two and one-half hours prior to the cease-fire.

Actually, although Union witnesses had some justification for believing that Forrest had violated the truce, they were mistaken in regard to the nature of the violation and also in the implication that that "violation" was responsible for the fall of the fort. While the cease-fire was still in effect, Forrest became increasingly concerned over the approach of the Northern steamships. He decided to take precautions against them and sent two detachments of two hundred men each to the riverbank below the fort to prevent the steamers from landing troops or taking off the garrison. One detachment, under Capt. Charles W. Anderson, posted itself in some abandoned trenches to the south, practically to the rear, of the fort. The other detachment, led by Col. C. R. Barteau, moved down Coal Creek ravine and stationed itself on the riverbank north of the fort.[14] In all likelihood, Leaming, Marshall, and other Federal witnesses mistook the movement of Barteau's detachment for a Confederate advance. It must have appeared to them from their positions in the fort and on the gunboat that the Confederates were shifting their lines on the northeast nearer to the fort.

Another reason for believing that the Union witnesses were mistaken lies in the fact that Forrest had no motive for using the truce to cover an advance on the fort. Both Northern and Southern testimony positively establishes that the Confederates in the buildings on the south slope already were so close to the fort that they were immune to its artillery fire. This position alone made it unnecessary, not to say superfluous, for Forrest to obtain other positions nearer the fort by trickery. The most that can be charged against Forrest is that he violated the cease-fire by stationing Anderson's and Barteau's detachments along the riverbank. But even here it can be reasonably argued that he was justified in believing that the approaching steamships intended to aid the garrison and, therefore, in taking measures to forestall this action.

In brief, the weight of evidence and logic supports the Southern point of view concerning the capture of Fort Pillow: namely, that the fort fell before the superior strength and strategy of Forrest, not as the result of a devious ruse.

The Massacre

Upon receiving Bradford's refusal to surrender, Forrest ordered his troops to prepare for the assault. When everything was ready, his bugler sounded the attack. The Confederates sprang forward with a shrill "rebel yell." A weak, erratic volley from the defenders failed to halt them. They quickly covered the few yards separating them from the outer ditch and jumped down into it. Scarcely pausing, they scrambled up the side of the ditch and over the parapet. To the Federal troops, it seemed as if they rose "from out the very earth."[15]

According to the report of the congressional committee, the following ghastly spectacle ensued: The Union troops, seeing that continued resistance was hopeless, threw down their weapons in token of surrender. But the Confederates ignored this sign of submission and began shooting and bayoneting the helpless defenders. The panic-stricken Federals then ran down the bluff to the riverbank below. There they sought refuge behind trees, logs, and bushes, or even in the river itself. But to no avail. The Confederates came after them shouting, "No quarter! No quarter!" and "Kill the damned niggers; shoot them down!" All who attempted to escape were hunted down and shot. Many who raised their hands in surrender also were shot down, especially the black soldiers. Pleas for mercy were answered with curses and bullets.[16]

Confederate witnesses and Southern historians declare the above description to be grossly inaccurate and offer a radically different account of the events following the capture of the fort. According to their version, the garrison never surrendered but instead fell back down the bluff to the riverbank, where many Federal soldiers continued to resist until killed, wounded, or captured. Others drowned or were shot while trying to escape by swimming out into the river. Still more fell when they failed to heed commands to stop running away. No doubt some of the men slain or wounded probably should not have been, it is argued, but there definitely was not an organized, wholesale massacre of surrendered prisoners.[17]

The points of disagreement between the Northern and Southern versions are readily discernible and raise several questions. The first, and perhaps basic, one, is: Did the garrison surrender after the Confederates stormed the fort, or did it retreat to the riverbank with the intention of continuing the battle? Union testimony is unanimous that the garrison abandoned its arms before, or in the act of, fleeing down the bluff and that it attempted no further resistance. The Confederates, however, all agreed that the Union troops retreated to the river with arms in hand. Captain Anderson, commander of one of the detachments posted by Forrest along the riverbank, wrote after the war that following the battle he supervised a detail that picked up 269 Federal rifles along the riverbank and found 6 cartridge cases open and ready for use. The discovery of the rifles and particularly of the cartridges, asserted Anderson, proved that the garrison withdrew to the riverbank as part of a prearranged plan to maintain the struggle after the fort itself had fallen.[18] This is possible. When questioned by the congressional committee, Captain Marshall of the *New Era* stated that he had arranged a plan with Bradford by which the garrison, if forced to evacuate the fort, would withdraw under the bluff. His gunboat, then, would "give the rebels canister."[19] But Marshall is the only person to mention this plan. None of the survivors of the garrison referred to it. They all testified, or implied at least, that their retreat was inspired by necessity, not strategy. Neither Bradford nor any of the other Federal officers are reported to have ordered a withdrawal. Instead, several witnesses said that the officers endeavored to rally the men inside the fort. Bradford, far from instructing his command to retreat, cried out, "Boys, save your lives!" and then ran "down to the creek."[20] If Bradford and Marshall had a plan for a last-ditch defense along the river, it was never put into execution.

Once they reached the riverbank, what did the defeated and frightened Union soldiers do, and what happened to them? By their own testimony, they attempted to surrender but were shot down by blood-lusting rebels shouting "No quarter!" The alleged massacrers, on the contrary, testified that most of the Federal troops tried to escape by fleeing along the bank and that many of them kept on fighting. Captain Anderson, in a sworn statement made in 1898 and subscribed to by fifty other former members of Forrest's command, related that "when driven from the works, the garrison retreated towards the river, with guns in hand, and firing back."[21] In his official report, made soon after the battle, and in an article written for the *Confederate Veteran* in 1895, Anderson further stated that as the Union troops came running down the bluff, his and Barteau's detachments "poured into them an enfilading and deadly fire, at a distance of 40 to 100 yards. The assaulting line in the meantime had gained the brow [of the bluff] and mowed down their rear."[22]

According to Barteau, in an interview published in 1884, the garrison, after evacuating the fort, "made a wild, crazy, scattering fight. They acted like a crowd of drunken men. They would at one moment yield and throw down their guns, and then would rush again to arms . . . and renew the fire."[23]

A similar story was recorded in the journal of one of Forrest's officers, DeWitt Clinton Fort: "The wildest confusion prevailed among those who had run down the bluff. Many of them had thrown down their arms while running and seemed desirous to surrender while many others had carried their guns with them and were loading and firing back up the bluff at us with a desperation which seemed worse than senseless. We could only stand there and fire until the last man of them was ready to surrender."[24]

Colonel Bell and Captain Anderson, in statements made in the 1890s to John Allan Wyeth for his biography of Forrest, remembered the firing following the fall of the fort as having lasted only a few minutes.[25] The reason that the Confederates continued to fire at all after storming the works, aside from combating the efforts of the garrison to escape or resist, explained Anderson in his official report, was that the men in the detachments under the bluff "had no means of knowing or reason for believing that the fort was in . . . [Confederate] possession, as they could from their position see the flag but could not see the fort." "For the survivors [of the garrison]," he added, "it was . . . a fortunate occurrence that some of our men . . . pulled down their flag." When the flag disappeared from view, "firing was stopped at once."[26] And Confederate Colonel McCulloch was certain that "not a gun was fired, nor a prisoner . . . shot . . . after the surrender [hauling down the flag] was made."[27]

Southern writers vehemently deny the charge made in the congressional committee's report that the "slaughter" of the garrison was the result of a "policy deliberately decided upon and unhesitatingly announced" by Forrest and his officers. On this point, they are supported not only by Confederate sources but by Federal testimony as well. Union Pvt. Elias Wells related that the Confederates "killed all the men after they surrendered" until orders came from Forrest to stop firing. Lieutenant Leaming testified that when a

Confederate started shooting at the "darky soldiers," an officer rode up and said, "Stop that firing; arrest that man." And Capt. John G. Woodruff of the Union army reported a conversation with Chalmers the day after the battle, in which Chalmers said that he and Forrest had "stopped the massacre as soon as they were able to." This agrees with the statement of Confederate Col. D. M. Wisdom, who recalled that he was instructed by Forrest to go down below the bluff and stop "any and all firing." A number of other Confederate participants testified to the same effect, one saying that Forrest personally "rode down the line and commanded and caused the firing to cease."[28] Some of Forrest's men, however, apparently believed, or pretended to believe, that their commander had ordered no quarter be shown the garrison. Wrote a Confederate sergeant to his family a week after the battle: "I with several of the others tried to stop the butchery and at one time had partially succeeded but Gen. Forrest ordered them shot down like dogs and the carnage continued."[29] Obviously, if Confederate soldiers thought that Forrest had ordered a massacre, it was only natural that many of the Union survivors got the same impression, which they passed on to the committee when they testified.

Accepted uncritically, the Southern version of the events following the fall of the fort would seem to exonerate Forrest's troops almost completely of the charge that they massacred the garrison after it surrendered. But a close examination of the testimony on which this version is based reveals a number of significant contradictions. To begin with, the postbellum assertions of Bell and Anderson that the Confederates stopped firing within a few minutes after the fall of the fort runs counter to the contemporary testimony of DeWitt Clinton Fort, who recorded in his private journal that "Gabriel's trumpet" could not have been heard "for at least thirty minutes after we were in possession of the fort."[30] Secondly, the Confederates claimed that they had to keep firing at the Union troops huddled along the riverbank because some of them continued to fight and would not surrender. Yet, the Confederates gave two opposed reasons for this alleged resistance: that it was in accordance with a prearranged plan; and that the garrison "acted like a crowd of drunken men," that is, fought without any plan. And thirdly, the Confederates gave three contradictory accounts of how and why they ceased firing: the flag of the fort came down; the garrison abandoned its efforts to resist and escape; and Forrest and his officers "commanded and caused the firing to cease."

However, despite these contradictions in testimony, the Confederates probably were basically correct in claiming that a portion of the Union troops attempted to fight back after retreating to the riverbank, thereby giving the attackers no alternative except to continue firing until all resistance ceased. But, if this were the case, why then did the Union men keep on fighting, especially when it was so futile to do so? Could it not have been because they found that Forrest's men were not taking prisoners? Several Union witnesses specifically stated that as soon as the Confederates entered the fort they began shooting surrendered men and that the main reason the garrison fled to the riverbank was that the victors were not giving quarter.[31] Furthermore, according to Confederate sources, the black troops fought harder than the white ones. Was this because of the superior courage and discipline of the blacks, or was it, as seems more likely, because they realized they had more to fear from the Southern soldiers? Forrest's men took 168 whites prisoner, but only 58 black ones.[32] And, finally, it is difficult to accept fully the statements of Anderson, Fort, Barteau, and Bell that the Confederates simply stood on top of the bluff and fired into the men on the riverbank until they surrendered, in view of the testimony of Captain Marshall of the *New Era* and of other Union men who survived the attack. Marshall stated that the Union and Confederate troops were so intermingled following the fall of the fort that he could not carry out the plan to "give the rebels canister" when the garrison evacuated the fort. Further, numerous wounded Union survivors testified that they were shot at point-blank range.[33]

Amidst this welter of conflicting and often ambiguous testimony, both Northern and Southern, one fact establishes itself: The Union troops at Fort Pillow were massacred—massacred in the sense that they were shot down in great numbers without being able to offer effective resistance or to inflict casualties commensurate to their own losses. Out of a garrison of about 560 men, an estimated 231 were killed and approximately 100 more seriously wounded. Confederate losses, in contrast, were 14 killed and 86 wounded.[34] Quite possibly, as the Confederates contended, a high proportion of the Union losses occurred during the storming of the fort and the flight of the garrison to the riverbank and hence may be considered "legitimate." But even so, there can be little doubt that in a great many individual instances—many more than the Confederates cared to admit—Union soldiers were shot after they, personally, had stopped fighting and were trying to surrender.

As one historian has shrewdly commented, Forrest "did not need" to order a massacre at Fort Pillow.[35] Half of the force holding Fort Pillow were blacks, former slaves now enrolled in the Union army. Toward them, Forrest's troops had the fierce, bitter animosity of men who had been educated to regard blacks as inferior and who, for the first time, had encountered them armed and fighting against white men. The sight enraged and perhaps terrified many of the Confederates and aroused in them the ugly spirit of a lynch mob. Black witnesses before the congressional committee told of being shot by Southern soldiers who made such remarks as "Damn you, you are fighting against your master" and "Kill all the niggers."[36] In short, the massacre at Fort Pillow was essentially an outburst of racial antagonism.

The other half of the garrison consisted of Tennessee Unionists, many of them deserters from Forrest's command. Forrest's soldiers, most of whom were also from Tennessee, felt that these men were traitors to their state, to the Southern cause, and, because they were fighting in company with blacks, to their race. Moreover, Forrest's men believed that the Tennessee Unionists at Fort Pillow were responsible for various outrages and hardships allegedly suffered by Confederate adherents in the region of the fort.[37]

Finally, the Confederate troops had been fighting all morning and for most of the afternoon when they stormed the fort; they were tired, nervous, and angry. They had offered the garrison a chance to surrender, but it had chosen to maintain a futile struggle. So, to the racial, political, and personal passions of Forrest's soldiers was added the bitterness of men who were forced to risk their lives in an assault that they deemed unnecessary, had the garrison exercised common sense. The result: "The slaughter was awful," wrote a Confederate soon afterwards.[38]

The Atrocities

The most horrifying testimony gathered by the congressional investigating committee related to Union soldiers being buried alive. Daniel Taylor described his own burial and escape, and Frank Hogan, another black soldier, said that he saw a wounded man buried. Surgeon Horace Wardner confirmed these stories, stating that two men under his care gave accounts of being buried alive with others who also were not dead.[39]

Southern writers have attempted to refute this testimony by contending that the Union dead were buried by the survivors of the garrison, not by Forrest's men, thereby making it impossible for the Confederates to have committed this crime. As evidence, they cite Forrest's official report, which states that "details were made, consisting of the captured Federals and negroes, in charge of their own officers, to collect together and bury the dead."[40] But the following letter, written by a member of Forrest's command, is to be found in the *Atlanta Appeal* of June 14, 1864:

> You have heard that our soldiers buried Negroes alive at Fort Pillow. That is true. At the first fire, after Forrest's men scaled the walls, many of the Negroes threw down their arms and fell as if they were—dead. They perished in the pretence, and could

only be restored at the point of the bayonet. To resuscitate some of them, more terrified than the rest, they were rolled into the trenches made as receptacles for the
fallen. Vitality was not restored until breathing was obstructed, and then the resur-
rection began.[41]

On the basis of this letter, it is necessary to conclude that the Confederates participated in the burial of the Union dead. In all probability, they supervised or guarded the Federal burying parties and while doing so "resus-
citated" a number of blacks who had feigned death by the methods so
jocularly described in the letter. In any case, the letter provides a reasonable
explanation of how some of the blacks came to be buried alive and makes it
impossible to dismiss the stories told by Taylor, Hogan, and Wardner as mere
fabrications, as some Southern writers have done.

Another charge the investigating committee levied against Forrest's troops
was that they deliberately set fire to buildings and tents containing Union
wounded. Two Northern witnesses, Ransom Anderson and Frank Hogan,
said that they heard the screams of men being burned in the fort hospital.
Anderson said that the burning occurred during the night, a statement supported by only one other witness. All the other witnesses stated that the
burning took place in the morning of April 13. Lieutenant Leaming reported
that early in the morning a gunboat started shelling the shore, whereupon
the Confederates began setting fire to all the buildings and tents about the
fort.[42] Leaming's account harmonizes with the testimony of Chalmers's adjutant, Capt. W. A. Goodman:

> On the following morning, (the 13th,) a detail was sent to the Fort to collect and
> remove the remaining arms, and to bury such of the dead as might have been over-
> looked on the day before. They had been at work but a short time when a gunboat
> ... came up and began to shell them. As this became annoying, the officer command-
> ing the detail ordered the tents which were still standing in the Fort to be burned,
> intending to abandon the place.[43]

Captain Anderson negotiated a truce with the gunboat, and from 9:00 AM
to 4:00 PM the Federal wounded were transferred aboard Union ships. While
this work went on, persons from the boats walked about the riverbank and
the bluff, where some of them noticed the charred or burning bodies of
black men among the smoking remnants of the tents and shacks. Lt. William Clary, among others, later testified that he saw "five negroes burning.
... It seemed to me as if the fire could not have been set more than half an hour
before. Their flesh was frying off them, and their clothes were burning."[44]
This testimony, although at first glance damaging to the Confederates, is

consistent with Goodman's explanation of the origin of the reports of Northern wounded being burned: "In doing this [setting fire to the tents about the fort], the bodies of some negroes who had been killed in the tents, on the day before, were somewhat burned; and this probably gave rise to the horrible stories about burning wounded prisoners which were afterwards invented and circulated."[45]

The final category of atrocity of which the congressional committee accused Forrest's soldiers was "sparing neither age nor sex." Survivors told such stories as these to the committee:

> Some of them came along, and saw a little boy belonging to company D. One of them ... shot the boy down.

> There were two negro women, and three little boys, some 8, 9 or 12 years old, about 25 steps from us. The secesh ran upon them and cursed them, and said, "Damn them;" they thought they were free to shoot them. All fell but one, a little fellow, and they took the breech of a gun and knocked him down.

> I saw two women shot by the river bank, and their bodies thrown into the river after the place was taken.[46]

Forrest's men indignantly denied these stories, and Southern historians have endeavored to disprove them through the testimony of Captain Marshall and Dr. C. Fitch, surgeon of the garrison, who said that all the women and children present at Fort Pillow were removed to boats prior to the Confederate attack, and that consequently, there were none to be murdered.[47] This evidence would be conclusive and would do much to impugn all Northern testimony, were it not for a sentence in Forrest's own report: "We captured ... about 40 negro women and children."[48] So, perhaps the strongest evidence—but not proof—that the Confederates did not kill women and children lies in the fact that no one reported seeing the bodies of women and children among the slain.

No review of the evidence concerning Fort Pillow would be complete without some word as to the reliability of the evidence itself. On this point, Southern writers have challenged the integrity of the congressional investigating committee and the veracity of the witnesses who appeared before it and have asserted that the committee's report was simply a propaganda document designed to stir up hatred of Confederates in the North. In support of their contentions, they stress various alleged contradictions and flaws in the Union testimony and claim that the heads of the committee, Sen. Benjamin F. Wade and Rep. Daniel W. Gooch, were both extreme Radicals dedicated to the destruction of the South.[49] Much of their criticism is more or less justified, particularly in regard to the propaganda intent of the committee's report.[50] Nevertheless, it is the considered opinion of the writer that the testimony gathered by the committee is of historical and scholarly value, if used, as all ex parte evidence of its type must be, with critical discrimination. While it does contain certain contradictions and weaknesses, most of these are attributable more to the physical and psychological condition of the witnesses— many of whom were wounded, and all of whom, most likely, were bitter toward the Confederates—than to the political and personal motivations of the investigators. In other words, the writer is totally unable to accept the Southern charge that the committee's report was a conspiracy of falsification and fabrication. On the contrary, he finds the testimony it contains strong, consistent, and convincing on the main point of issue: massacre of the garrison after it had quit fighting. Moreover, much of the testimony is repeated in affidavits independently obtained by the Federal military authorities. Finally, the Confederate testimony not only contains a sizable number of contradictions and errors but was obviously motivated throughout by a desire to soften the facts of the massacre and to exonerate the great Southern military hero, Forrest.

An analysis of both the Northern and Southern evidence leads to the conclusion that Forrest's troops, having captured Fort Pillow as a result of superior strength and tactics, out of a combination of race hatred, personal animosity, and battle fury then proceeded to kill a large number of the garrison after they had either ceased resisting or were incapable of resisting.

Notes

This essay was originally published as "The Fort Pillow Massacre: A Fresh Examination of the Evidence," *Civil War History* 4 (Mar. 1958): 37–50. Reprinted with permission of the Kent State University Press.

1. *Chicago Tribune,* Apr. 16, 1864; *New York Daily Tribune,* Apr. 15, 1864; *Indianapolis Daily Journal,* Apr. 22, 1864; *Harper's Weekly,* Apr. 30, 1864; Roy P. Basler, ed., *The Collected Works of Abraham Lincoln,* 8 vols. (New Brunswick, N.J.: Rutgers University Press, 1953), 7:302–3.

2. *Harper's Weekly,* Apr. 30, 1864; U.S. Congress, Joint Committee on the Conduct of the War, *Fort Pillow Massacre,* 38th Cong., 1st sess., 1864, H. Rept. 65 (hereafter cited as *Fort Pillow Report*).

3. Horace Greeley, *The American Conflict,* 2 vols. (Hartford, Conn.: O. D. Case, 1864–66), 2:620.

4. See, for example, Dudley Taylor Cornish, *The Sable Arm: Negro Troops in the Union Army, 1861–1865* (New York: Longmans, Green, 1956), 173–76; T. Harry Williams, "Benjamin F. Wade and the Atrocity Propaganda of the Civil War," *Ohio State Archeological and Historical Quarterly* 48 (Jan. 1939): 40; and Carl Sandburg, *Abraham Lincoln: The War Years,* 4 vols. (New York: Harcourt Brace, 1939), 3:36–40.

5. See the following: Thomas Jordan and J. P. Pryor, *The Campaigns of Lieut. Gen. N. B. Forrest* (New Orleans: Blelock, 1868); John Allan Wyeth, *Life of General Nathan Bedford Forrest*

(New York: Harper, 1899); John L. Jordan, "Was There a Massacre at Fort Pillow?" *Tennessee Historical Quarterly* 6 (June 1947): 99–133; and Robert Selph Henry, *"First with the Most" Forrest* (New York: Bobbs Merrill, 1944).

6. *The War of the Rebellion: A Compilation of the Official Records of the Union and Confederate Armies*, 128 vols. (Washington, D.C.: Government Printing Office, 1880–1901), ser. 1, 32 (pt. 1): 613–14 (hereafter cited as *OR;* all citations are to series 1, volume 32, part 1); *Fort Pillow Report*, 3; Jordan and Pryor, *Campaigns of Gen. Forrest*, 432 (map of Fort Pillow).

7. Wyeth, *Life of General Forrest*, 339–42.

8. *OR*, 538, 559, 609, 613–14, 620–21; Lois D. Bejach, ed., "The Journal of a Civil War 'Commando,' DeWitt Clinton Fort," *West Tennessee Historical Society Papers* 2 (1948): 19; Charles W. Anderson, "The True Story of Fort Pillow," *Confederate Veteran* 3 (Nov. 1895): 322–23.

9. *OR*, 560.

10. Ibid., 596, 614, 621; Wyeth, *Life of General Forrest*, 343–44; Bejach, "Journal of a Civil War 'Commando,'" 19.

11. *OR*, 596.

12. Ibid., 596–97, 614.

13. Ibid., 561; *Fort Pillow Report*, 86.

14. *OR*, 615; Wyeth, *Life of General Forrest*, 345; Anderson, "True Story of Fort Pillow," 323.

15. *OR*, 561, 615.

16. *Fort Pillow Report*, 4–6.

17. *OR*, 610, 615–16; Anderson, "True Story of Fort Pillow," 323–24; Wyeth, *Life of General Forrest*, 350–81; Bejach, "Journal of a Civil War 'Commando,'" 20.

18. Anderson, "True Story of Fort Pillow," 324. See also Jordan and Pryor, *Campaigns of Gen. Forrest*, 437.

19. *Fort Pillow Report*, 86.

20. Ibid., 39, 42, 48; *OR*, 539, 566. Bradford was eventually captured and killed by Confederates under circumstances that became and remain highly controversial. See *OR*, 588–93.

21. Quoted in Wyeth, *Life of General Forrest*, 386.

22. *OR*, 597; Anderson, "True Story of Fort Pillow," 325–26.

23. Quoted in Henry, *"First with the Most,"* 256.

24. Bejach, "Journal of a Civil War 'Commando,'" 20.

25. Wyeth, *Life of General Forrest*, 383, 386–87.

26. *OR*, 597.

27. Quoted in Wyeth, *Life of General Forrest*, 384, 386.

28. *Fort Pillow Report*, 15, 40; *OR*, 558; Wyeth, *Life of General Forrest*, 378, 386, 389.

29. Quoted in Henry, *"First with the Most,"* 264.

30. Bejach, "Journal of a Civil War 'Commando,'" 19.

31. *OR*, 529–30, 540; *Fort Pillow Report*, 27, 42, 55–59, 82, 84–87, 92–93, 100.

32. Wyeth, *Life of General Forrest*, 359–61.

33. *Fort Pillow Report*, 42, 55–59, 86, 93.

34. Wyeth, *Life of General Forrest*, 361; *OR*, 622.

35. Cornish, *Sable Arm*, 175.

36. *Fort Pillow Report*, 2–4, 13, 15, 17–18, 20–21, 48.

37. Wyeth, *Life of General Forrest*, 369–70.

38. Quoted in Henry, *"First with the Most,"* 264.

39. For Federal testimony concerning the alleged burial of living men, see *Fort Pillow Report*, 14, 17–18, 48, 87, 95.

40. *OR*, 615. At least one Union soldier testified that he took part in such work. See *Fort Pillow Report*, 96.

41. Quoted in George W. Williams, *A History of the Negro Troops in the War of the Rebellion* (New York: Harper and Brothers, 1888), 265.

42. *Fort Pillow Report,* 31–32, 39–40, 94.

43. Quoted in Jordan and Pryor, *Campaigns of Gen. Forrest,* 443.

44. *Fort Pillow Report,* 52–53.

45. Quoted in Jordan and Pryor, *Campaigns of Gen. Forrest,* 443.

46. *Fort Pillow Report,* 13, 15, 20–21, 47, 51; *OR,* 537.

47. *Fort Pillow Report,* 86; Dr. C. Fitch to Chalmers, May 13, 1879, in *Southern Historical Society Papers* 7 (Aug. 1879): 440.

48. *OR,* 616.

49. See Jordan and Pryor, *Campaigns of Gen. Forrest,* 452–53; Jordan, "Was There a Massacre?" 127–28, 132–33; and Henry, *"First with the Most,"* 260.

50. See T. Harry Williams, "Benjamin F. Wade," 34–37, 40.

DEREK W. FRISBY

News of the "Fort Pillow Massacre" arrived at a crucial time in Washington, D.C. Speculation abounded throughout the country about the upcoming 1864 presidential election, a contest many viewed as a referendum on the nation's will to continue the war and decide the character of postwar Reconstruction. For the last three years, a Democratic resurgence and divisions within his own party had diminished considerably the political fortunes of Republican President Abraham Lincoln. A reelection bid in 1864 would be difficult; no incumbent president had been elected to a second term since Andrew Jackson in 1832 or had even secured his party's renomination since 1840. With a war-weary electorate and internal strife splintering the Republicans, these trends appeared in little danger of being reversed in November.

A small group of congressional Radical Republicans had grown impatient with Lincoln's political and military leadership. Some also worried that Lincoln might waver in his commitment to securing the postwar rights of freedmen in the South. These Radicals had incessantly criticized Lincoln's management of the war and demanded that the president end conciliatory overtures toward the Rebels. Instead, they favored a war of conquest that would dismantle the political and economic power of the Southern planter class with terms of surrender that guaranteed the permanency of emancipation and freedmen's rights, especially suffrage. Radical leaders now feared that the current political climate might lead to a Democratic takeover of both Congress and the White House in the fall elections. Such a result, combined with the current military stalemate, would almost certainly lead to a negotiated settlement, thereby allowing the seceded states to reenter the Union without extending permanent rights to freedmen, or, worse yet, granting the Confederacy independence. Thus, the Radicals viewed the campaign of 1864 as their last opportunity to build public momentum for their measures.

One of their most potent weapons for accomplishing this mission was the Joint Committee on the Conduct of the War.[1]

Although many Americans lacked formal military training and were rather contemptuous of a professional military establishment before the war, numerous civilian and congressional experts on military strategy suddenly appeared after the attack on Fort Sumter. Under increasing public pressure to suppress the rebellion before the first ninety-day enlistment periods expired, Lincoln ordered a green Union army to move on Richmond in July 1861 in search of a decisive victory. The ensuing Battle of Manassas shattered any illusions Northerners held for a quick, decisive conflict with minimal casualties.[2]

As the struggle for battlefield supremacy continued throughout the remainder of 1861 and into early 1862, political battles raged in Washington over the conduct of the war and future conditions for reunion.[3] Contrary to the president's conciliatory attitude, the Radicals favored an all-out national mobilization and military assault upon the Confederate armies to dismantle the foundations of Southern society, especially slavery. In response to Lincoln's reluctance to adopt emancipation as a war objective and after a few small, but ignominious, military defeats, the Radicals manifested their displeasure with their commander-in-chief in December 1861 by creating the Joint Committee on the Conduct of the War.[4] This committee would serve as an investigative body "to inquire into the causes of the disasters that have attended the public arms" and "to enlighten the public . . . which carries on this war, and which furnishes the means for carrying it on."[5] Congress chose Sen. Benjamin F. Wade of Ohio, an ardent abolitionist and a leading Radical, to chair this committee. During the committee's initial meetings in 1862, Wade quickly established himself as that body's central figure by aggressive use of his power as chair. Through the sheer force of Wade's domineering personality, the committee's policies and those of its chairman became practically indistinguishable.[6]

In December 1863, the president announced an amnesty and reconstruction program to begin restoring Southern states to the Union. Under Lincoln's plan, when 10 percent of the voters in a state formerly in rebellion had reaffirmed their allegiance to the Union, that state could reconstitute a government. It also included provisions for granting pardons to former Confederates. Angry Radicals condemned the plan for being too lenient, infringing upon Congress's authority over Reconstruction, and ignoring the postwar status of emancipated blacks.[7] Wade was among the most vocal critics of the president's plan, calling it a "usurpation" of congressional powers.

Like other Radicals, he feared conciliatory Northern Democrats would ally with Southern plantation owners to restore the antebellum status quo. Rep. Thaddeus Stevens of Pennsylvania best expressed the dissatisfaction Wade and other Radicals felt for the presidential plan when he said, "The foundation of [the South's] institutions . . . must be broken up and relaid, or all our blood and treasure have been spent in vain."[8]

By late March 1864, the ability of Wade and the committee to influence the conduct of the war was waning. The committee's investigations into early Union military reverses, particularly those at First Manassas and Fredericksburg, while having some positive effect, had unintentionally provided Lincoln political cover to exert greater executive control over the army and military strategy. Furthermore, the committee's constant attempts to expose "Copperheadism" within the Union high command had eroded the committee's credibility. Yet, the conflicts over the postwar status of freedmen and jurisdictional authority for Reconstruction remained unresolved. In these areas, at least, the committee still hoped to exert some influence. Wade accordingly turned the committee's efforts toward marshalling the Northern public's will to achieve a total victory and support a tougher Reconstruction policy.[9]

To gain public support for their program, the Radicals would first have to rekindle the fire in the Northern heart. Maj. Gen. Ambrose E. Burnside's declaration before the committee that Union soldiers did not "adequately hate" Confederates to fight them with due severity had greatly disturbed Wade and the other Radicals.[10] Earlier in the war, Wade and the committee had sponsored and circulated several accounts of Confederate atrocities perpetrated upon Union soldiers. These ghoulish stories were intended to generate a greater level of animosity among soldiers for their enemy and encourage the nation to fight a "hard war" to destroy the institutions of Southern society, but they had little lasting effect.[11] Now, with Lincoln's Proclamation on Amnesty and Reconstruction, Radicals again feared their prior "achievements might still be annulled in the very hour of victory," and they attempted with renewed vigor to wrest control of the war and Reconstruction from the president. They enthusiastically threw their support behind Maryland Rep. Henry Winter Davis's bill, which proposed giving Congress full control over Reconstruction. Wade was so impressed by Davis's legislation that he became its cosponsor and personally guided it through the Senate. Moreover, several Radicals secretly began seeking a delay of the June 1864 Republican convention in hopes of finding a Radical candidate to replace Lincoln on the party's presidential ticket.[12] As the convention approached and the Wade-Davis bill neared an important House vote, the committee seized upon an opportunity provided by the Battle of Fort Pillow to charge Southerners with additional fiendish behavior and thereby demonstrate the need for Radical military and Reconstruction policies.

Fort Pillow sat atop high bluffs overlooking the Mississippi River, about sixty miles north of Memphis, Tennessee. Artillery positioned there could easily impede navigation around the sharp river bend below. The Rebels began constructing an extensive stronghold on this commanding spot at the outbreak of the war but were forced to evacuate three months after the fort's completion because the Federal capture of Corinth, Mississippi, on May 30, 1862, jeopardized the garrison's line of retreat. Federal forces sporadically occupied the works thereafter but never with any sizable contingent, confident the Confederates could not mount a serious attack against them.[13] Believing this position secure, they even established a small civilian trading post near the fort's boat landing to assist freedmen and white Tennessee Unionists.[14] This was a move that Maj. Gen. William T. Sherman later described as the "first fruits of the system of trading posts designed to assist the loyal people of the interior. All these stations are a weakness, and offer tempting chances for plunder."[15]

In January 1864, Sherman directed that Fort Pillow be "abandoned" and its present garrison join other units preparing for the Meridian campaign.[16] Instead of seeking victory through decisive battle, Sherman and Maj. Gen. Ulysses S. Grant would begin targeting the Confederate infrastructure to demoralize the Southern population and deny the Rebel armies material and moral support. Cutting a swath of devastation from Vicksburg to Meridian, Mississippi, Sherman's twenty one thousand men destroyed more than a hundred miles of railroad and at least twenty valuable locomotives, devastated cropland, and dismantled warehouses, arsenals, and factories. The elimination of the Meridian railroad hub greatly impaired the South's ability to mount offensives in the Western Theater and allowed Sherman to begin concentrating his forces against Atlanta. The Meridian campaign and the increased confiscation of Confederate property were the first manifestations of Grant's and Sherman's hard war strategy.[17]

Contrary to Sherman, Maj. Gen. Stephen A. Hurlbut, commander of the Memphis District, considered Fort Pillow too important to desert and disregarded his commander's order to abandon it. Hurlbut did withdraw the 52d Indiana Infantry but sent Maj. William Bradford's 14th Tennessee Cavalry to reoccupy Fort Pillow and establish a recruiting point. In accordance with the Union's new hard war approach, Bradford's orders authorized him to seize any supplies he needed from "both the loyal and disloyal, giving vouchers only to those who might furnish unmistakable evidence of their loyalty."[18] Bradford's 268 men used the fort as a base from which to join other Tennessee Unionist units in bringing hard war to the citizens of west Tennessee throughout February and March 1864.[19]

Meanwhile, Confederate Maj. Gen. Nathan Bedford Forrest was returning to Jackson, Tennessee, to refit and reorganize his command. Learning of recent property confiscations and depredations by Tennessee Unionist militias in the Jackson vicinity, Forrest's men demanded retaliation against these "renegade Tennesseans" who were preying upon Confederate families.[20] Forrest finally agreed to attack the staging areas for these Unionists, not solely for revenge but to obtain the provisions a weakened Confederate government could not provide and to restore confidence in the Confederacy's ability to protect its citizenry. After two weeks' rest, Forrest divided his force into two raiding parties to hit the supply depots at Paducah, Kentucky, and Union City, Tennessee, almost simultaneously.[21]

Forrest personally led one column, consisting of about 2,500 men from Col. Abraham Buford's division, toward the lucrative cache at Paducah. Already alerted to the Confederate advance, the 665 Union troops at nearby Fort Anderson braced for a seemingly imminent attack. The garrison included 275 members of the 1st Kentucky Heavy Artillery (Colored). Forrest deployed sharpshooters in several buildings surrounding the fort to pin down the Federals while his men plundered the supply depot. The Confederates rapidly swept through the undefended warehouses within the town, taking horses and other stores, including valuable medical supplies. Forrest left the docks and rail yard in flames but attempted no direct assault on Fort Anderson, believing such a move would be a waste of effort and his men's lives. The other Rebel column, approximately 475 men from the 7th Tennessee Cavalry (C.S.A.) led by Col. W. L. Duckworth, had reached Union City the previous day, March 24, and quickly surrounded the town's defenses. Duckworth's initial assault met with a repulse, but he shifted strategy and successfully executed an elaborate ruse that convinced the Federal commander, Col. Isaac Hawkins, to surrender his 7th Tennessee Cavalry (U.S.A.), even though Union reinforcements were en route from nearby Cairo, Illinois. It was the second time in the war Hawkins had been fooled into surrendering his entire command to Forrest's troopers. Stunned and embarrassed upon discovering Duckworth's deception, Hawkins's soldiers ridiculed their leader for again succumbing too easily to the enemy and even denounced him as a traitor.[22]

Regrouping his forces at Jackson on April 4, Forrest assessed the intelligence gathered during the two raids. The Federals appeared spread out among lightly garrisoned outposts throughout the region. "It is clear," Forrest determined, "that they are concentrating all their available force . . . at Chattanooga."[23] He promptly reported these observations to his superior, Maj. Gen. Leonidas Polk, commander of the Confederate Department of Alabama, Mississippi, and East Louisiana, and requested rifled artillery to interdict the enemy's river supply routes. Forrest probably realized the futility of this request because of the logistical problems now plaguing the Confederacy. He had faced similar supply shortages before, but he had usually filled deficiencies by seizing what he needed from the enemy. Recently, scouts had spotted several rifled artillery pieces at Fort Pillow and reported that a relatively small force was assigned to protect them. Forrest immediately began devising a plan to take them.[24]

On March 28, Hurlbut had moved to check any potential movement by Forrest across the Mississippi River by sending Maj. Lionel Booth's 1st Battalion, 6th U.S. Heavy Artillery, Colored (USHAC), from Memphis to Fort Pillow. Booth's force of 224 former slaves, two 12-pound cannon, and two 10-pound rifled Parrott guns, along with 41 newly mustered black soldiers from Company D, 2d U.S. Light Artillery (Colored) and their section of two 6-pound cannon, augmented Bradford's battalion. The Parrotts' longer range and greater penetration capability gave the garrison substantial firepower to defend itself and control the river.[25] However, neither Booth, a former quartermaster sergeant, nor Bradford, a frontier lawyer, had any significant experience constructing defenses or leading troops in combat.[26] Hurlbut created instant confusion and tension in the chain of command by insisting that Booth confer "freely and fully" in all decisions with the lower-ranking Bradford, whom Hurlbut described in the same order as "a good officer, though not of much experience." Hurlbut also instructed Booth to segregate his men from Bradford's and to keep his black troops from interacting with the local populace. In closing, Hurlbut reassured Booth that Forrest would not attack the fort and promised Booth that his men would immediately return to Memphis, once the threat had subsided.[27]

Following Booth's arrival, the two units set about segregating their living quarters and improving the fortifications. Booth's soldiers pitched camp on the higher of two bluffs located inside the old Confederate works and above the river landing. In addition, the black troops erected an M-shaped breastwork, approximately eight feet high, enclosed by a six-foot ditch around their camp. Along the southeast edge of a ravine that nearly circled the new fortifications, they also dug a series of rifle pits. Meanwhile, the white soldiers accomplished little else besides building a number of small cabins for themselves outside Booth's works along a road leading to the fort's southern entrance.[28] In Booth's last report to Memphis on April 3, he communicated to Hurlbut that Fort Pillow was "perfectly safe" and that the surrounding area was quiet.[29]

But all was not quiet. After a forced night march through heavy rain, fifteen hundred Confederates under Brig. Gen. James Chalmers (Forrest's second-in-command) converged upon an unsuspecting Fort Pillow on the morning of April 12, 1864. Despite the recent defensive improvements, the fort was still highly vulnerable. Rebel sharpshooters promptly captured several high points overlooking the Federal positions and began firing into the fort's interior. This forced the defenders to stay hidden below the berm and prevented any observation of the enemy's movements. Forrest arrived around 10:00 AM and directed the Confederates to occupy the ravine in front of the fort, bringing his troops to within fifty yards of the fort's primary breastworks. The Union gunboat *New Era* fired in support of the fort from the river, but the crew was unable to elevate the guns sufficiently to reach over the high bluffs and sweep the ravine that afforded the Rebels cover.[30]

By noon, Forrest had surrounded the fort and requested the garrison's surrender. Unknown to Forrest, snipers had killed both Major Booth and his adjutant while they were trying to raze Bradford's cabins, which obstructed the Union artillery's field of fire. Booth's death left Bradford in sole command of Fort Pillow, but he continued to sign Booth's name to all correspondence, hoping to create the illusion that his senior commander was still alive. Bradford was well aware of the shameful reputation another Tennessee Unionist, Isaac Hawkins, had earned in surrendering to Forrest's ruses too quickly, and he did not want to be similarly regarded as a coward, or worse, a traitor. Unable to determine the true size of the enemy, he refused the Confederates' surrender demand three times.

During the numerous truces called to discuss surrender, Bradford continued to formulate a plan for the fort's defense. According to his plan, when the Confederate charge began, the African American troops defending the ramparts would begin a fighting retreat down the bluff to the river's edge, offering only token resistance. Once the African Americans reached a designated point near the water, where Bradford's men remained hidden, the white soldiers would open fire on the advancing Confederates from their concealed position and lead both groups in a counterattack back into the main fort, while the gunboat raked the fleeing Rebels with canister. Bradford was so confident in his ability to hold the fort that he refused assistance from two or more passing steamboats loaded with potential reinforcements.[31] After distributing ammunition and perhaps some whiskey to his troops to bolster their morale, Bradford waited for a Confederate assault and the opportunity to implement his plan.[32]

Frustrated by the garrison's refusal to surrender and smarting from a fall off his horse while personally reconnoitering the lines, Forrest ordered a determined attack at approximately 4:00 PM.[33] Veteran Confederates armed with shotguns, carbines, and revolvers swarmed over the parapet and poured a withering fire into the poorly trained and inadequately armed blacks, who responded with a lone volley from their single-shot muskets before falling back, as planned, toward the river. To Bradford's dismay, the *New Era* suddenly sailed upriver out of sight, her guns fouled and unserviceable from firing more than three hundred rounds during the day.[34] The gunboat's support was lost. Bewildered by this unexpected development and overwhelmed by the assault's momentum, Bradford panicked and yelled, "Boys, save your lives. . . . It is of no use anymore."[35] Next to him at the fort's flagpole, the ranking officer of the 6th USHAC, Lt. Peter Bischoff, countermanded Bradford's order and implored his men to continue fighting. Confused by the contradictory commands, some brave blacks continued to resist, while the remainder ran toward the river.[36] Those retreating found themselves caught in a murderous cross fire as Bradford's men unleashed a premature fusillade at the advancing Confederates before their black comrades could scurry out of the way. The fighting raged out of control, often at hand-to-hand range, for the next fifteen to thirty minutes. Many Union soldiers who attempted to surrender were shot and left for dead by the marauding Confederates. When the firing finally ceased, the Confederates had emerged victorious, losing about twenty dead and sixty wounded.[37] Nearly three hundred Union soldiers were killed or reported missing, with approximately two-thirds of these casualties coming from the African American units.[38] Forrest believed his victory at Fort Pillow had decisively demonstrated the Confederacy's resolve to shield its citizens from Unionist depredations, but more importantly, he had acquired the rifled artillery he needed to harass Sherman's build-up in Middle Tennessee.[39]

The next morning, the gunboat *New Era,* escorting two steamers, the *Platte Valley* and *Silver Cloud,* returned to Fort Pillow and arranged for a truce to gather the Federal casualties. During their transport to hospitals in Cairo, Illinois, the wounded and about fifty other survivors rescued from the riverbank recounted details of the assault to the passengers and reporters aboard. Telegraph wires soon began relaying the story of the "Fort Pillow Massacre" throughout the country.⁴⁰ *Harper's Weekly* described the battle as an "indiscriminate butchery of the whites and blacks, including the wounded." The paper particularly emphasized the fate of the black troops and their families, who reportedly "were killed in cold blood . . . [and] piled in heaps and burned."⁴¹

Almost immediately after the first sketchy reports of the "Fort Pillow Massacre" reached Washington, Radical Republican senators appeared on the Senate floor to denounce the behavior of the Confederate troops. On April 18, Congress debated a request for an on-site investigation by the Committee on the Conduct of the War, to be led by Chairman Wade and Rep. Daniel Gooch of Massachusetts. This was an extraordinary request because, until that moment, the committee had restricted its personal visits to areas in the Eastern Theater close to Washington. Moderate Maine Republican William Fessenden expressed his opposition to the excursion, claiming that "unless in cases of extreme urgency, it is hardly worth the while for members of Congress to make these inquiries. . . . It is the duty of the War Department to look into these matters." Michigan's Jacob Howard, recognizing the importance of the manpower supplied by African American troops to the Union war effort, rebuked Fessenden. "It would be a disgrace to the nation not to avenge promptly this gross wrong," he said. "It concerns the national honor to protect the men who fight our battles and those who wear our uniform. If this [investigation] is not done, the black troops, by reason of these threatened terrors, at some critical hour in battle, might lose us the day." Apparently swayed by Howard's admonition, Congress approved the resolution after attaching an amendment directing the committee to determine why reinforcements never reached Fort Pillow or why an evacuation did not take place.⁴²

President Lincoln, speaking at the Sanitary Fair in Baltimore, also addressed the public's apprehension over the "Fort Pillow Massacre" and the Union's use of African Americans as soldiers. "There seems to be some anxiety in the public mind," he observed, "whether the government is doing its duty to the colored soldier." Lincoln then reiterated his support for their continued enlistment: "Having determined to use the Negro as a soldier, there is no way but to give him all the protection given to any other soldier." But as to the "painful rumor" of Fort Pillow, he stressed, "We do not today know that a colored soldier . . . has been massacred. . . . We fear it, believe it, I may say, but we do not *know* it." Lincoln concluded: "We are having the Fort Pillow affair thoroughly investigated. . . . If there has been the massacre of three hundred there, or even the tenth part of three hundred, it will be conclusively proved; and being so proved, retribution shall as surely come."[43] The following day, April 19, Wade and his entourage boarded a westbound train, eager to provide the president with the incontrovertible proof he claimed was needed to justify swift, harsh retaliation against the South. Wade's overzealousness caused him to discount the abundance of reliable accounts detailing Rebel atrocities and to ignore other evidence that might have contributed to the fort's fall, in favor of more sensational and less credible testimony to emphasize Southern depravity and the need for a Radical program of Reconstruction.[44]

The subcommittee conducted the first of its interviews on April 22 in Cairo, Illinois. Wade and Gooch took testimony from the district's key commanders, the surgeons attending the survivors, and the survivors themselves. In three days, the committee traveled down the Mississippi to Fort Pillow and Memphis, gathering evidence, interviewing approximately seventy people, and entering into the record statements from about forty others. In typical fashion, Wade dominated these inquiries. He permitted the admission of hearsay evidence and distorted testimony and the submission of ex parte statements, often preventing cross-examination of witnesses who were less than credible or objective.[45]

The first witness, Cairo District commander Brig. Gen. Mason Brayman, painted a bleak portrait of the Federal situation in the Mississippi Valley. Corruption and illegal trade were rampant, according to Brayman, and the forces stationed to guard supplies were "wholly inadequate," given the amount of government property within striking distance of the Confederates. Furthermore, the weapons and fortifications were "unfit for service, and the supply of ammunition deficient and defective."[46] Though Wade appeared concerned about these allegations, they did not provide the type of incendiary testimony the committee sought, and he dismissed Brayman from the proceedings.

Next, surgeons described in gory detail the wounds of their patients and speculated about how the wounds had been inflicted, though none of the doctors had been present at the battle or had visited the field. Chief Surgeon Horace Wardner of the Mound City Hospital testified, "They were the worst butchered men I have ever seen." "Nearly all," he added, were attacked "after they had thrown down their arms, surrendered, and asked for quarter." He related the case of one young black boy brought to the hospital in an "insensible," or comatose, condition on April 13, but who had inexplicably managed to recount the battle's details before he died the following day. Wardner testified that the boy was lying with a fever in the Fort Pillow hospital when the attack began. "The rebels entered the [fort's] hospital, and with a sabre hacked his head, no doubt with the intention of splitting it open. The boy put up his hand to protect his head, and they cut off one or two of his fingers." Dr. Wardner further supposed that "about four hundred [were] massacred—murdered there."[47]

Following the medical testimony, the subcommittee proceeded to the various wards and took testimony from those wounded who were able to bear examination. Due to the "broken language some of them used," the subcommittee took the liberty of transcribing their statements into "grammatical form."[48] The statements again described in graphic detail incidents in which Confederates allegedly shot, burned, or mutilated defenseless African American soldiers. Curiously, many of the incidents reported to the subcommittee could not be corroborated by other soldiers. Despite having served alongside each other for several months, few witnesses were able to recall the names of comrades who were the victims of these alleged atrocities, and accounts of the same incident varied greatly among them.[49] For example, some witnesses to the death of Fort Pillow's quartermaster, 1st Lt. John Ackerstrom, claimed the Rebels had murdered him, mutilated his corpse, and nailed it to a structure inside the fort before setting both the building and body ablaze. Neither the officers aboard the steamers retrieving the wounded nor the details assigned to bury the Federal dead, however, made mention of seeing Ackerstrom's body in such a condition on April 13. Yet, two officers of Bradford's battalion, who had been in Memphis during the battle, testified they had seen Ackerstrom's charred body still nailed to the floor of a burned structure almost two days after Federal forces had retaken the fort and buried all the bodies.[50]

In addition to accepting easily impeachable testimony as fact, the subcommittee ignored information that was critical of the garrison's discipline, training, and equipment, choosing to hear only what supported the "massacre" charge.[51] The testimony of Henry Weaver, a white noncommissioned officer with Company C, 6th USHAC, was edited to exclude what happened before the fort fell. Weaver's written statement in the *Official Records* was more critical of factors that contributed to the heavy casualties, including faulty ammunition, confused commands, and poor tactical decisions. Contradicting the Federal officers' testimony, he said that the garrison had taken considerable casualties as a result of sniper fire prior to the final assault. Furthermore, the larger artillery pieces had been positioned outside the fort's parapets to make room for encampments inside the works until the first warning of the attack came.[52]

Weaver's statement tends to support the theory that these African American "artillerymen" had never been intended to engage in battle. Hurlbut had issued cannons to Weaver's unit just hours before it had embarked on March 28.[53] It is plausible that many of the black soldiers had received no instruction at all on artillery operations until that very morning. After almost two weeks at Fort Pillow, gun platforms had not been constructed, and Bradford's troops had been allowed to build cabins within the cannons' fields of fire. Therefore, Weaver's men spent the initial hours of the siege hastily constructing gun platforms, only to learn that Bradford's cabins obstructed their fire. Major Booth and others had attempted to destroy the cabins, but snipers had killed them as soon as they stepped out from behind the fort's walls. When Weaver's cannon finally did fire, "not more than one in five of the shells burst, owing to poor fuses."[54] This significant information was omitted in the published report through Wade's skillful interrogation. In the report, Wade instructed Weaver to limit his testimony to the period "particularly after the capture."[55]

Statements not related to Fort Pillow directly but forwarded to Washington at the same time lend further credibility to Weaver's written account describing the unserviceable weaponry supplied to the African American troops. The Union army's adjutant general, Brig. Gen. Lorenzo Thomas, under direct orders from Lincoln to investigate the problems of freedmen and African American soldiers along the Mississippi River, had inspected eight African American regiments on Ship Island, Mississippi, on April 8, 1864, and questioned their combat readiness. He reported to Secretary of War Edwin M. Stanton: "This regiment, like most of this class of soldiers, have old flintlock muskets, altered to percussion, which have been in use for a long time. The muskets of this regiment were condemned at once."[56] With untrained troops and defective arms, Fort Pillow's garrison would have been at a great tactical disadvantage before the engagement even began.

These reports of ill-equipped and poorly trained troops begged an answer to the question as to why "a fort, with uninterrupted water communication above and below, could possibly be without a garrison strong enough to hold it for a few hours."[57] Brigadier General Brayman wrote to his wife shortly after his appearance before the committee: "I have made a long report of testimony in the Ft. Pillow affair.... All will be published. I must also write an elaborate report of operations since I came. There has been blundering. The blame must fall on somebody. It shall not be *me*."[58] Indeed, blame would have to fall on somebody, but given the controversy and uproar created by Wade's previous attacks on Union officers, it would appear the committee had learned that it was better to blame the Rebels than one of their own.

Important rifts had also surfaced among the region's senior officers during the investigation, but like the other evidence exposing Union maladministration, the subcommittee left this issue unexplored. On April 16, Sherman told the *Washington Star*, "We are satisfied that the loss of Fort Pillow was simply the result of a mistake made by the local commander [Hurlbut], who occupied it against direct orders."[59] Earlier in the day, he had also written Grant in exasperation concerning the battle and General Hurlbut's command in Memphis. "I don't know what these men were doing at Fort Pillow. I ordered it abandoned before I went to Meridian, and it was so abandoned. . . . I don't know what to do with Hurlbut."[60]

Hurlbut, a lawyer and state legislator in Illinois before the war, enjoyed the backing of important political allies, such as President Lincoln. Hurlbut had been appointed by the president as one of three representatives sent to evaluate the situation at Fort Sumter in South Carolina's Charleston Harbor in April 1861. Hurlbut was a former resident of Charleston, but Lincoln did not know that he had been forced to leave the city under a cloud in the 1840s. Viewing a military command as a springboard for further political success and personal redemption, Hurlbut joined the Union war effort by obtaining an appointment as a brigadier general with help from his friend in the White House. Discouraged by his inability to secure a promotion and transfer to the Judge Advocate General's office, he began drinking heavily and started trading illegally with government contractors to supplement his military salary. Later, Hurlbut marched with Grant through Tennessee to Shiloh in 1862 and finally distinguished himself at the Hornet's Nest by aiding the defense of this critical position in the Union center. Despite his courage at Shiloh, Hurlbut had caused considerable embarrassment for the Lincoln administration since his arrival in Memphis. Embezzlement, extortion, bribery, forgery, fraud, and frequent drinking binges had plagued his administration of Union-occupied West Tennessee.[61]

For several days after the Fort Pillow battle, both Grant and Sherman seemed reluctant to dismiss Hurlbut because of his close relationship with Lincoln. The president still considered the staunch Illinois Republican a valuable and loyal political ally for Reconstruction, despite his liabilities.[62] Deeply concerned that Forrest's raids and Hurlbut's incompetence might endanger preparations for the Union army's coordinated spring campaigns, Grant relieved Hurlbut on April 16 for what Sherman described as "marked timidity."[63] Sherman noted, "In making up our fighting force, we have left inferior officers on the river." The style of warfare he and Grant intended to employ in future operations required what Grant called more "sober and energetic" commanders.[64] Grant then appointed Maj. Gen. C. C. Washburn, the brother of Rep. Elihu B. Washburne of Illinois, a Republican who was Grant's and Lincoln's personal and political champion, to command West Tennessee, indicating to Sherman that Washburn "will obey your instructions and establish no posts, except where you order them."[65]

Nervousness and tension seemed to take a toll on the beleaguered Hurlbut during his interview with the subcommittee on April 24. Hurlbut vehemently denied the accusation that Sherman had ordered the fort "abandoned," even when presented with the order itself. In testy exchanges with Wade, he steadfastly held to the belief that the river passage was essential to keeping the Mississippi River open, although other testimony suggested he had stationed troops there to protect and assist a local cotton speculator, Edward Benton, in raising a potentially lucrative cotton crop.[66] Nevertheless, Hurlbut had been an early advocate of abolition and favored recruiting more African American units. Such opinions must have endeared him to Wade, who was apparently reluctant to impugn Hurlbut's reputation publicly and allowed Grant's private censure to serve as the deposed district commander's only reprimand. Besides, Confederate conduct, not matters of Union governance and leadership, were the immediate focus of investigation. Consequently, the subcommittee chose to ignore Hurlbut's inept administrative conduct, the confusion that allowed the fort to be reoccupied, its inadequate defense, or the circumstances that prevented its reinforcement.

Returning to Washington just days before the Republican nominating convention in Baltimore, Wade rushed the government's printing office into publishing and distributing an unprecedented sixty thousand copies of the committee's summary findings. Secretary of War Stanton suggested that the Joint Committee on the Conduct of the War should attach photographs and statements from returned Union prisoners recovering at Annapolis as an addendum to the full report to increase its shock value. Wade agreed.[67] According to historian T. Harry Williams, Stanton "appreciated to the full the vast importance of the press as a medium for shaping mass opinion." Like many Radicals, he believed that the only way to force the administration to adopt a harsher Southern policy was by "stirring up public opinion." John M. Forbes, a Radical New England industrialist and founder of a pro-Union propaganda outlet called the Loyal Publication Society, voiced the same sentiments: "Governments are always timid about new measures without precedents. . . . Let the people speak, and the government must follow."[68]

Certainly, the widespread availability of the gruesome battle details and the descriptions of Confederate prison conditions in the full *Fort Pillow Report,* as well as the shorter pamphlet summaries, quickly intensified Union outrage and marked a change in the public's attitude for conducting the war. Calls for reprisal echoed throughout the Northern press, and news of African American soldiers swearing oaths to avenge Fort Pillow began to circulate.[69] "The massacre was, no doubt, intended to intimidate our people in regard to employing colored soldiers . . . but it will fall short of its purpose," said the *Hamilton (N.Y.) Republican*. Instead, the editorial continued, "it will band us closer together the loyal hearts; it will add vigor to our policy, and the law of retribution to our military code."[70] A correspondent for the *New York Tribune* reported from Knoxville, Tennessee: "The Universal sentiment is—'Let no quarter be shown to these dastardly butchers of Forrest's command while the war lasts.'"[71] Such comments probably pleased Wade, who had wanted to create the level of "hate" he felt was necessary to fight a hard war.

Far from being an objective investigation of the battle, Wade's report on Fort Pillow reads more like a literary composition designed to rekindle the level of emotional outrage generated earlier by Harriet Beecher Stowe's *Uncle Tom's Cabin*. Wade sought to portray all Confederates, especially former planters and slave owners like Forrest, as morally bankrupt members of a slave society that would never recognize the humanity of African Americans.[72] To support this impression, Wade sprinkled his official findings with stories of Forrest's command violating flags of truce, murdering prisoners in violation of the laws of war, and killing civilian men, women, and children.[73] In one such incident, Rebel troops at Paducah allegedly mingled with groups of women and children seeking safety across the river, using the noncombatants as human shields to advance on key positions and wound several Union officers and men. Wade claimed that this tactic compelled Union forces to hold their fire and give up these positions "out of regard for the lives of women who were made use of in this most cowardly manner."[74]

According to the *Chicago Tribune,* "The whole civilized world will be shocked by the great atrocity at Fort Pillow, but in no respect does the act misrepresent the nature and precedents of Slavery."[75] William Lloyd Garrison's *Liberator* rhetorically asked: "Can [Southerners] have ever been American citizens? What has transformed them into the shape of fiends?" "Slavery!" it answered. "In no other school could human beings have been trained to such readiness for cruelties like these. . . . Accustomed to brutality and bestiality all their lives, it was easy for them to perpetrate the atrocities."[76] The *Boston Journal* was even more direct. "The massacre at Fort Pillow was the legitimate out-cropping of that imperious, barbarous, remorseless spirit, born, bred, and ingrained by slavery," wrote the anonymous editorialist, "a spirit which regards the larger part of the human race as created to forego all comforts, all culture, all rights of man or womanhood, in order that the few may laxily lord it over the many."[77] Wade's aunt by marriage expressed similar reactions after reading the accounts of the massacre and mistreatment of Union prisoners. She related to Wade's wife, Caroline, that the accounts contained in the report filled her "with horror." She wrote that they were "sufficient to convince one of the awful depravity of the slave holding system. . . . How long, O Lord, how long," she closed, "shall the wicked rule?"[78] Wade's investigation, therefore, reinforced the notion among Northerners that only military defeat followed by a harsh reconstruction policy could infuse the South with the necessary "Yankee virtue" needed to "repair the harmful effects of slave society" and bring civilization to the "savages" and "barbarians" of that region.[79]

Wade's report, like Stowe's novel, also indicted those Northerners showing leniency toward or abetting the slaveholding Confederacy. The document called particular notice to a report about Union army officers inviting members of Forrest's command aboard a transport at Fort Pillow for drinks the day following the battle, while burial details were still interring the dead. In the committee's opinion, these Union officers "so lost every feeling of decency, honor, and self-respect, as to make themselves disgracefully conspicuous in bestowing civilities and attention upon the rebel officers, even while they were boasting of the murders they had there committed." Although unable to identify the officers involved, Wade denounced them for committing this "most astounding and shameful act . . . [that had] inflicted so foul a stain upon the honor of our army."[80] This careful choice of words expressed more than Wade's indignation at Southerners; it implied that any attempt to negotiate a peaceful settlement with the Confederacy would be seen as dishonorable. Perhaps the most trenchant comments came from a Connecticut woman writing to the *New York Independent*. "We cannot pass over the Fort Pillow massacre in silence. . . . Respond to the butchery on the Mississippi by giving black men the right of suffrage, and making them citizens," she recommended. "Such a response would be a greater protection to the black soldier. . . . He would be recognized as a man. It would do infinitely greater damage to the rebel cause; for it would be a blow aimed at its very cornerstone. We must remember that, while we deny to these blacks the rights of men, we share in the guilt of those who slaughter them like cattle."[81]

The *Fort Pillow Report* further served as a rallying point to invigorate soldiers to fight. Union soldiers, especially those in African American regiments, often compared the incident to the Alamo.[82] Badges emblazoned with "Remember Fort Pillow" adorned the uniforms of African American soldiers, and cries of "Remember Fort Pillow!" resonated from charging Union troops at the Petersburg Crater, Nashville, and seemingly everywhere else they met the enemy for the remainder of the war.[83] Cpl. Charles Musser of the 29th Iowa Infantry wrote: "I never Saw men So exasperated about anything as the troops here are about Fort Pillow. . . . Even the Colored troops are wild about it. If the rebels would now attack us, blood would run in torrents."[84] Henry Clay Weaver, a soldier in the 16th Kentucky Infantry, wrote of an African American unit at the Battle of Nashville: "I understand, at one place where the darkies carried the enemies works, they cried 'Fort Pillow' and made the gray Jackals suffer."[85] Even white Union soldiers were not immune to the fever. Commenting on the increasing brutality and retaliation practiced by the soldiers of both sides, a Union officer wrote, "'Remember Fort Pillow' had become the feeling if not the word."[86] Robert Hale Strong, an Illinois volunteer, recounted that after storming a Rebel position in Arkansas, he and his comrades noticed a Confederate soldier with a tattoo reading "Fort Pillow" crudely inscribed on one arm. "As soon as the boys saw the letters on his arm, they yelled, 'No Quarter for you!' and a dozen bayonets went into him and a dozen bullets were shot into him. I shall never forget his look of fear."[87]

While soldiers in the field dispensed their brand of unofficial justice, their leaders in Washington deliberated the best official response to the *Fort Pillow Report*. In several discussions of the report, cabinet members remained highly suspicious of the committee's findings. Secretary of the Navy Gideon Welles said, "I distrust Congressional Committees. They exaggerate."[88] Many believed that Wade's investigation was sensationalized and meant to tarnish the president's image. In reporting the details of the *Fort Pillow Report*, the pro-Confederate *Times* of London dismissed Wade's allegations of Confederate atrocities as just more political propaganda. "The European reader will know what estimate to place upon the extravagant stories [about Fort Pillow] with which the papers of the United States abound. . . . They remind one of the fables so extensively circulated [by Wade] just after the first battle of Manassas."[89] That Wade did not cover other atrocities (including those with more substantiation), because they fell outside of a politically expedient timetable or particular set of circumstances, attests to the *Fort Pillow Report*'s propagandistic purpose. It also emphasizes the prejudicial nature with which Wade's committee conducted the Fort Pillow inquiry. The committee did not act earlier to investigate William C. Quantrill's raid on Lawrence, Kansas, the massacre at Poison Spring, Arkansas (which occurred almost simultaneously with Fort Pillow), or the later Saltville murders.[90]

Lincoln received the *Fort Pillow Report* with skepticism and remained reluctant to retaliate in kind for the Fort Pillow atrocities. The president's dilemma was best expressed in the pages of the *Liberator*. In such a "barbarous case" as Fort Pillow, the problem "is to determine what shall be done, *without being equally diabolical*. Let the President have the *time to authenticate the facts* in this butchery, and to take counsel as to the *best manner of preventing a repetition of it*."[91] By this time, Ulysses S. Grant had been promoted to lieutenant general and named commander-in-chief of all the Union armies. Grant had suggested, even before the subcommittee had left to investigate Fort Pillow, harsher measures to end the war, but Lincoln hesitated to accept this advice. Lincoln believed abandoning conciliation for retribution would only increase hostilities and prolong postwar reconciliation and Reconstruction. Much to the chagrin of Stanton, Wade, and other Radicals, Lincoln only threatened to retaliate for Fort Pillow and never carried out any specific reprisals or individual punishments. While choosing not to retaliate in kind for Fort Pillow, Lincoln and Grant did implement harsher policies concerning the prisoner exchange system. Ostensibly, the change stemmed from the Rebel stance toward African American prisoners, but the more practical reason was to prevent the Confederacy from rebuilding its army with newly exchanged prisoners. Within days of the incident, the War Department ordered an end to the current prisoner exchange system until Rebel officials allowed African American soldiers to benefit from it. Of course, the Confederates refused. An unintended consequence of this new policy was the overcrowding of Confederate prison camps, particularly at Andersonville, Georgia. More than fourteen thousand Union soldiers, including more than two-thirds of the white Unionists captured at Union City and Fort Pillow, died due to the deteriorating conditions at this camp.[92] Wade attempted again in late 1864 to persuade the president to retaliate for the poor treatment of captured Federals. "Retaliation has in all ages of the world been a means of bringing inhuman and savage foes to a sense of their duty," he said. "It is a rather mawkish idea of humanity that fears to subject rebel prisoners to the same treatment that we know our own brave soldiers are subjected to." By this point in the war, however, Wade's influence had diminished considerably, and his resolutions to retaliate for Rebel atrocities were defeated.[93]

The joint committee's charges that the Confederate government openly supported the mistreatment of Union prisoners elicited a surprising response from Richmond. President Jefferson Davis issued public directives to his commanders concerning the treatment of prisoners, both white and black. That Davis's statement recognized African Americans as soldiers at all was unprecedented, for it elevated them to a status previously denied by their former masters. Several Rebel leaders later suggested the use of African American troops in their own armies, thereby sacrificing slavery for independence, but these plans were categorically rejected.[94] The *Fort Pillow Report* even failed to convince some Northerners of the vital African American contribution to the Union war effort. After the massacre and Wade's investigation, some Northern newspapers began to question the continued use of African American soldiers. "Dressing a *monkey* in the uniform of the government . . . cannot convert the monkey into a real soldier, and attach to him the rights and immunities of a prisoner of war," argued the *Portland Advertiser*. "If the United States elect to employ barbarian means and agencies against the South, they must expect barbarian usage in turn."[95]

Nevertheless, the *Fort Pillow Report* swelled the numbers of those supporting the continued and expanded role African Americans were taking in the Union war effort. *Harper's Weekly* charged that the Fort Pillow massacre was a "direct challenge to our Government to prove whether it is in earnest or not in emancipating slaves and employing colored troops." It concluded, "There should be no possibility of mistake in the reply. Let the action of the Government be as prompt and terrible as it will be final."[96] The *Boston Journal,* after noting the government's past mistreatment of African American soldiers, wrote that "the Government is strangely behind the people. . . . We consider [African American troops] the victims of an injustice . . . so surprising that we know not whether it proceeds from intentional ill will or thoughtless neglect. . . . At any rate, the policy ought to be reformed altogether, and as speedily as possible."[97] "At last," said Frederick Douglass, shortly after Fort Pillow, "there seems to be a purpose in Congress to award fair play to black soldiers. . . . Let us welcome the justice, tardy though it be. . . . It is cheering to notice in a portion of the press," he added, "these outrages . . . vehemently denounced and the full measure of justice urgently demanded. . . . This massacre will materially contribute to a repentant feeling throughout the nation towards the long persecuted colored American."[98]

Since mid-summer 1863, the issue of equal pay and pensions for African American soldiers had remained stalled in Congress. Major Booth's widow, thrust into national celebrity on account of the massacre, even visited the president to lobby for pensions for the families of Fort Pillow victims, regardless of race. After their meeting, Lincoln introduced Mary Elizabeth Booth to Sen. Charles Sumner, saying, "She makes a point which I think is very worth of consideration, which is, that widows and children in fact of colored soldiers who fall in service be placed in law the same as . . . the widows and orphans of white soldiers."[99] The deadlock over equal pay for white and black soldiers was finally broken on June 15, 1864, eighteen months after the debate had begun, but by no small coincidence, less than a month after the release of the *Fort Pillow Report*.[100] In addition, Congress allowed a greater number of African Americans to enlist and expanded opportunities for African American soldiers to become both noncommissioned and commissioned officers. Although the government had been slow to allow African Americans into the army, Frederick Douglass believed that "contrary to the expectations of some, this horrible massacre at Fort Pillow has given an impulse to enlisting. . . . Colored men manifest an eagerness for the chance to avenge their slaughtered brethren."[101] The prospect of large numbers of freedmen serving in the Union army and the termination of prisoner exchanges dealt the Confederacy, already low on manpower, a serious blow.[102]

Senator Wade's exploitation of the Fort Pillow affair strengthened Northerners' general belief that the Rebels had intensified the war's "meanness" by resorting to "uncivilized" methods.[103] So effective was Wade's use of the *Fort Pillow Report* that references to its horrifying contents persisted well into the postwar era. During Reconstruction, if defeat threatened a bill concerning policies affecting the former Confederate states, Radicals needed only to wave the "bloody shirt" to remind Northerners of the cruelties, like those at Fort Pillow, to illustrate "the savage and infernal spirit [of the Confederacy]," whose soldiers had unhesitatingly committed "acts so horrible that the nation stands aghast as they are told what has been done."[104]

The "great and indelible stain" at Fort Pillow tainted Forrest's reputation to his death in 1877 and beyond. The political cartoonist Thomas Nast often used Forrest's likeness, with some reference to Fort Pillow attached, to deride ex-Confederates' attempts to reestablish a "white man's government" during Reconstruction.[105] However, neither Forrest nor any of his men were ever prosecuted for the Fort Pillow massacre. Lincoln's assassination in April 1865 placed Tennessean Andrew Johnson in the White House, and the conservative Democrat needed all the political allies he could find in his battle against moderates and the Radicals. Though Johnson harbored a deep animosity toward the planter class, Forrest's political influence in west Tennessee and northern Mississippi after the war was undeniable and invaluable to the Democratic cause. Johnson therefore pardoned Forrest in 1868, ending any possibility that charges would be brought against him for culpability in the Fort Pillow incident.[106]

Reconstruction would end in 1877, but controversies over Fort Pillow refused to die. Allusions to Fort Pillow had cropped up frequently in Reconstruction political squabbles. Republican opponents of Confederate Brig. Gen. James Chalmers, one of Forrest's lieutenants in the battle, often taunted him with the label "villain of the 'Fort Pillow massacre'" during his Mississippi senate campaign.[107] An editorial advocating sectional reconciliation that appeared in the *New York Times* on November 1, 1877, proclaimed the "Fort Pillow Massacre" a "malignant partisan falsehood . . . [and] the whole subject of the alleged Fort Pillow massacre should be buried as deep as the dead Federal soldiers." Yet, Fort Pillow remained a contentious part of America's historical memory. Even into the twentieth century, the mere mention of Fort Pillow held sufficient sway to reawaken sectional animosities. In early 1941, Northern National Guardsmen, despite their silence concerning the segregation of the armed forces, protested the naming of a training facility in Tullahoma, Tennessee, Camp Forrest because of the general's connection with Fort Pillow. Today, the persistent attempts to remove statues and memorials to Nathan B. Forrest are fueled as much by his connection with Fort Pillow as his postwar involvement with the Ku Klux Klan.[108]

Since 1864, Fort Pillow historiography has been mired in debates over whether or not a massacre occurred there. Much of this debate centers on determining the validity of the testimony found in Wade's report to attach blame for the atrocities to certain individuals, namely Forrest and Chalmers, or to prove a racially motivated massacre occurred by quantitative analysis of the Federal casualty figures. Overwhelmingly, the available historical evidence from both Union and Confederate sources independent of Wade's investigation proves that atrocities were indeed committed. Thus, to paraphrase Lincoln, it mattered little whether thirty or three hundred were murdered, the Fort Pillow fight still qualifies as a massacre. But Fort Pillow was not the first or last time Rebel troops committed such outrages, nor was it even the largest racial massacre of the war. Nevertheless, this incident received a congressional investigation and held much of the public's attention during the crucial spring of 1864. The historical significance of Fort Pillow lies not in determining the number of black soldiers killed there or the manner in which they died but in how and why Union officials shaped the *perception* of the "Fort Pillow Massacre" and the effect this perception had on the Union war effort and Reconstruction. The *Fort Pillow Report* not only revealed what the Civil War had become but what the Radicals wanted the war to be: a hard war to overthrow the Southern slaveocracy and reconstruct the society that supported it. As George Julian said shortly after the report's publication, "A grand opportunity now presents itself for recognizing the principles of radical democracy in the establishment of new and regenerated states."[109]

In many ways, the Joint Committee on the Conduct of the War could stand as a model for subsequent and more systematic efforts by the government to "mold the American mind" during wartime. This new mentality required armies composed of "citizen-soldiers" to "adequately hate" their opponents and support the destruction of their enemy's society.[110] The Radicals had fought throughout the war to mobilize the entire North's manpower resources, including blacks, and to arouse public support for pursuing not just military victory but the recasting of Southern society. Wade and his colleagues welcomed the promotion and success of hard war as practiced by Generals Grant and Sherman but realized by early 1864 that Lincoln still seemed committed to a policy of political reconciliation. Therefore, they became determined to push for a war and a peace that favored Reconstruction over reconciliation.

Wade's atrocity propaganda, including the Manassas, Ball's Bluff, and Fort Pillow investigations, dehumanized the Southern enemy and prepared the country for hard war.[111] In detailing the inhuman qualities of the enemy, it was a fundamental part of the Radicals' plan to persuade Lincoln and the Northern populace into broadening Union strategy from a limited, and rather restrained, war against the Southern armies toward a more destructive war that included the transformation of Southern social and economic institutions as well. According to C. Vann Woodward, the Lincoln administration "moved from hesitant support of a limited war with essentially negative aims toward a total war with positive and revolutionary aims."[112] This change occurred in part because the Radicals gradually won over public support through a propaganda campaign that peaked with the *Fort Pillow Report.* Wade's efforts were further validated when Sherman garnered the Northern public's adulation during his 1864 "March to the Sea" for hard war tactics that a year earlier would have brought him condemnation and scorn. Ironically, Southerners later charged Sherman with the same "barbarity and cruelty" Wade had frequently attributed to them. "War is war and not popularity seeking," Sherman shot back at his critics.[113] But Wade and the Radicals knew differently. "Popularity seeking" was crucial to the evolving concept of modern warfare. Without the will of the people to endure long, costly wars, or their commitment to achieving the enemy's complete political over-

throw, now a necessary corollary to military victory, democracies could be
rendered impotent in future conflicts.

Notes

The author thanks George C. Rable, Lawrence F. Kohl, Harold Selesky, Forrest and Ellen
S. McDonald, Howard Jones, John Beeler, Gregory J. W. Urwin, Jon Wiarda, Mark A. Smith, Ed
Frank, and Andrew Ward for reading various revisions of this essay and for offering their informed
opinions. The late Thomas Shouse, former senior park ranger at Fort Pillow State Historical Park,
also conducted a fascinating personal park tour for me one blustery winter day. Additionally, the
University of Alabama History Department, the Tennessee Historical Society, and the West Ten-
nessee Historical Society provided encouragement and financial assistance. Above all, however,
I owe the greatest debt to my wife, Debbie, for her patience and loving support.

1. Works that support this interpretation of Lincoln's relations with the Radical Republicans
include T. Harry Williams, *Lincoln and the Radicals* (Madison: University of Wisconsin Press, 1941);
and, more recently, Bruce Tap, *Over Lincoln's Shoulder: The Committee on the Conduct of the War*
(Lawrence: University Press of Kansas, 1998). A revisionist view is offered by Hans Trefousse, *Radical Republicans: Lincoln's Vanguard for Racial Justice* (New York: Alfred E. Knopf, 1969).

2. William Pierson, "The Committee on the Conduct of the Civil War," *American Historical Review* 23 (Apr. 1918): 551; T. Harry Williams, "The Committee on the Conduct of the War:
A Study of Civil War Politics" (Ph.D. diss., University of Wisconsin, 1937), 8–11.

3. James M. McPherson, *Battle Cry of Freedom: The Civil War Era* (New York: Oxford University Press, 1988), 331–65, 698–713.

4. Determined not to let the war "degenerate into a violent and remorseless revolutionary
struggle," Lincoln had initially balked at using ex-slaves to assist the Union forces. He had dismissed Maj. Gen. John C. Frémont for summarily freeing Missouri slaves, refused to endorse Maj.
Gen. Benjamin F. Butler's plan to employ ex-slaves as Union laborers at Fort Monroe, Virginia,
and had reprimanded his first secretary of war, Simon Cameron, for suggesting the arming of
Southern slaves. The selection of Maj. Gen. George B. McClellan, a Democrat and avid critic of
abolitionists, to command the Army of the Potomac only further enraged the Radicals. See
McPherson, *Battle Cry of Freedom,* 358–63. See also William C. Harris, *With Charity for All:
Lincoln and the Reconstruction of the Union* (Lexington: University Press of Kentucky, 1997).

5. Pierson, "Committee," 553–55; David H. Donald, *Lincoln* (New York: Simon and
Schuster, 1995), 323–27; *Congressional Globe,* 37th Cong., 2d sess., 1861, pt. 1: 17, 30–31.

6. H. L. Trefousse, *Benjamin Franklin Wade, Radical Republican from Ohio* (New York:
Twayne, 1963), 157. Throughout 1862 and early 1863, the Joint Committee on the Conduct of the
War conducted a number of closed hearings into the causes of early Union defeats. The com-
mittee focused its attention on the large number of Union army staff officers and generals, par-
ticularly McClellan, who were thought to harbor Southern sympathies. The committee also
sought to exonerate officers who supported emancipation, such as Ambrose Burnside, Joseph
Hooker, Benjamin Butler, and John Frémont, of any culpability for military failure or inefficiency.
For an overview of these investigations, see Tap, *Over Lincoln's Shoulder.*

7. Article 4, Section 3, of the United States Constitution gives Congress the right to admit
new states and regulate "territory or other property belonging to the United States." Many Radicals insisted that this provision ensured congressional authority over Reconstruction because the
states had committed "suicide" and were subject to congressional reorganization. For an overview of reactions to Lincoln's "Amnesty and Reconstruction Proclamation," see McPherson,
Battle Cry of Freedom, 698–713; and Trefousse, *Benjamin Franklin Wade,* 220–21.

8. *Congressional Globe,* 38th Cong., 1st sess., 1864, 3449–51; *New York Herald,* Dec. 15, 1865.
Many Radicals initially supported the president's plan, but after more careful consideration and
election debacles in Louisiana, some Radicals believed Lincoln had devised the plan to attract

support for his upcoming nomination and presidential campaign. See Donald, *Lincoln,* 467–97; and McPherson, *Battle Cry of Freedom,* 698–713.

9. See Williams, *Lincoln and the Radicals,* 230–62; T. Harry Williams, "Benjamin F. Wade and the Atrocity Propaganda of the Civil War," *Ohio Archaeological and Historical Quarterly* 48 (Jan. 1939): 33–43; Tap, *Over Lincoln's Shoulder,* 192–93; and Trefousse, *Benjamin Franklin Wade,* 204–9.

10. Quoted in Williams, *Lincoln and the Radicals,* 206.

11. U.S. Congress, *Report of the Joint Committee on the Conduct of the War,* 8 vols., 37th Cong., 3d sess., 1863–66, S. Doc. 108; Williams, *Lincoln and the Radicals,* 259–62, 401–2.

12. Trefousse, *Benjamin Franklin Wade,* 220; Williams, *Lincoln and the Radicals,* 306–33.

13. James Dinkins, "The Capture of Fort Pillow," *Confederate Veteran,* Dec. 1925, 460.

14. *The War of the Rebellion: A Compilation of the Official Records of the Union and Confederate Armies,* 128 vols. (Washington, D.C.: Government Printing Office, 1880–1901), ser. 1, 32 (pt. 3): 382 (hereafter cited as *OR;* all citations are to series 1, unless otherwise noted).

15. Ibid.

16. *OR,* 32 (pt. 1): 367.

17. Mark Grimsley, *The Hard Hand of War: Union Military Policy Toward Southern Civilians, 1861–1865* (New York: Cambridge University Press, 1995), 4–6, 162–66.

18. Testimony of Capt. James Marshall, Apr. 25, 1864, U.S. Senate, Committee on the Conduct of the War, *Trade Regulations, &c.,* 38th Cong., 1st sess., 1864, S. Rept. 38-S, vol. 4, n. 142, pt. 3, serial 1214, 35; *OR,* 32 (pt. 2): 311, 318–19; *OR,* 32 (pt. 3): 176–77; Charles Lufkin, "Not Heard from since April 12, 1864: The Thirteenth Tennessee Cavalry, U.S.A.," *Tennessee Historical Quarterly* 45 (spring 1986): 287–315.

19. U.S. Senate, *Trade Regulations, &c.,* 26–44; Kevin McCann, *"Hurst's Wurst": A History of the Sixth Tennessee Cavalry* (Ashland City, Tenn.: privately printed, 1995), copy in Tennessee State Library and Archives, Nashville; and Noel Fisher, "'Prepare Them for My Coming': General William T. Sherman, Total War, and Pacification in West Tennessee," *Tennessee Historical Quarterly* 51 (spring 1992): 75–86.

20. *OR,* 32 (pt. 3): 663–65. See also Gary Blankenship, "Fielding Hurst and the Hurst Nation," *West Tennessee Historical Society Papers* 34 (Oct. 1980): 71–81, and "Fielding Hurst, Tennessee Tory: A Study of a West Tennessee Unionist of the American Civil War" (master's thesis, Memphis State University, 1977). Achilles V. Clark, letter to sister, Apr. 14[?], 1864, Confederate Collection, folder 19, Tennessee State Library and Archives, Nashville; Dinkins, "Capture of Fort Pillow," 460.

21. Brian S. Wills, *A Battle from the Start: The Life of Nathan Bedford Forrest* (New York: Harper Collins, 1992), 172–74.

22. For various accounts regarding the attack on Union City, see *OR,* 32 (pt. 1): 503–10, 543–45, 607–9. Col. W. L. Duckworth's force consisted of the 7th Tennessee Cavalry and elements of W. W. Faulkner's 12th Kentucky Cavalry and Charles McDonald's Tennessee Cavalry Battalion (also known as J. M. Crews's Tennessee Cavalry Battalion). Gen. Abraham Buford's division consisted of A. P. Thompson's brigade, Tyree H. Bell's brigade, and an Alabama regiment under the command of Jeffrey Forrest, the general's brother. James R. Chalmers's division included R. V. Richardson's Tennessee brigade, the 7th Tennessee Cavalry, and "Black Bob" McCulloch's brigade of Tennesseans, Texans, Mississippians, and Missourians. See Lonnie Manness, *An Untutored Genius: The Military Career of General Nathan Bedford Forrest* (Oxford, Miss.: Guild Bindery, 1990), 214–27. See also Ronald Huch, "Fort Pillow Massacre: The Aftermath of Paducah," *Illinois State Historical Society Journal* 66 (spring 1973): 62–70.

23. *OR,* 32 (pt. 1): 607–9.

24. Ibid., 608–9.

25. U.S. Congress, Joint Committee on the Conduct of the War, *Fort Pillow Massacre,* 38th Cong., 1st sess., 1864, H. Rept. 65, S. Rept. 38 (hereafter cited as *Fort Pillow Report*).

26. Born in Pennsylvania in 1838, Booth enlisted in the regular army at age twenty and then became the quartermaster sergeant of the 1st Missouri Light Artillery in 1862. He transferred to the 6th USHAC and became a major. According to unit records, Booth had asked for a leave of absence on Mar. 27, 1864, saying he had taken no leave since his enlistment. See John Cimprich and Robert Mainfort Jr., "Fort Pillow Revisited: New Evidence about an Old Controversy," *Civil War History* 28 (Dec. 1982): 294.

27. *OR,* 32 (pt. 1): 556–57.

28. Ibid., 538.

29. Ibid., 557.

30. Charles Anderson, "The True Story of Fort Pillow," *Confederate Veteran* 3 (Nov. 1895): 322–26.

31. *OR,* 32 (pt. 1), 559–63.

32. Whether drunkenness contributed to the fall of the fort has continued to be a point of contention among historians. The practice of giving troops alcohol to bolster their courage was not uncommon, and there were large caches of alcohol in the area, according to Brig. Gen. Mason Brayman's chief of staff, James Odlin, in his testimony before a Joint Committee on the Conduct of the War hearing on trading practices in the West. Furthermore, the April 20 *New York Times* reprinted a story from the *St. Louis Missouri Democrat* stating that a Captain Young, provost marshal of the 24th Missouri, said his Confederate brother kept a grog shop at the fort. Later, several jugs and "medicine bottles" containing stimulants, or "bitters," known to have high alcohol content were found inside the works. See U.S. Senate, *Trade Regulations &c.,* 26–44; and Robert Mainfort Jr., *Archaeological Investigations at Fort Pillow State Historical Area: 1976–1978* (Nashville: Division of Archaeology, Tennessee Department of Conservation, 1980).

33. Jack D. Welsh, *Medical Histories of Confederate Generals* (Kent, Ohio: Kent State University Press, 1995), 70–72; Wills, *Battle from the Start,* 181–82.

34. *OR,* 32 (pt. 1): 571–72.

35. Ibid., 566.

36. Ibid., 566–68.

37. Ibid., 609.

38. John Cimprich and Robert Mainfort Jr., "The Fort Pillow Massacre: A Statistical Note," *Journal of American History* 76 (Dec. 1989): 830–37.

39. *OR,* 32 (pt. 1): 609–11.

40. *New York Times,* Apr. 18, 20, 1864.

41. *Harper's Weekly,* Apr. 30, 1864.

42. Quoted in *New York Times,* Apr. 18, 1864.

43. Roy P. Basler, ed., *The Collected Works of Abraham Lincoln,* 8 vols. (New Brunswick, N.J.: Rutgers University Press, 1953–55), 7:301–3. The investigation Lincoln mentioned is the one initiated by Secretary of War Stanton before the Joint Committee on the Conduct of the War became involved. Once Wade and Gooch began their inquiry, Stanton, a staunch abolitionist and friend of the chairman, ordered Sherman to merge the Union army's investigation with the committee's.

44. Tap, *Over Lincoln's Shoulder,* 196–208.

45. Pierson, "Committee," 564–66, 574; Trefousse, *Benjamin Franklin Wade,* 201–3; Williams, "Committee on the Conduct of the War," 397. See also U.S. Congress, *Report of the Joint Committee* (1863), 3:281–82.

46. *Fort Pillow Report,* 8.

47. Ibid., 13–14.

48. Ibid., 14.

49. Ibid., 16.

50. Ibid., 106–9; John Jordan, "Was there a Massacre at Fort Pillow?" *Tennessee Historical Quarterly* 6 (June 1947): 122–25. John Charles Ackerstrom (a.k.a. Akerstrom) was a New York

native possibly living in Chicago in 1860. He joined Bradford's battalion as a second lieutenant on January 20, 1864, and Bradford appointed him Fort Pillow's post quartermaster on February 9. Ackerstrom's widow filed a pension request with the government for his service, but the claim was rejected because there was no proof Ackerstrom had ever served in the Union army, and the pension office had no proof of death. No reference is made in his pension file to the testimony in the *Fort Pillow Report* nor did any comrade provide supporting evidence of his service or his death, information typically requested and included in similar cases. See Civil War Pension File for Charles J. Akerstrom (Ackerstrom), alias John C. Akerstrom, 13th Tennessee Cavalry (Bradford's Battalion), W660316, RG 94, National Archives, Washington, D.C.; and Charles Akerstrom, Compiled Service Records, Bradford's Battalion, M395, reel 109 (microfilm), RG 94, National Archives.

51. Lufkin, "Not Heard from," 139–41. According to several witnesses from Bradford's battalion, discipline at Fort Pillow had been steadily deteriorating since their arrival because of command disputes, inhospitable weather, inadequate medical care, and the lack of pay. Major Bradford later reported: "The regiment has suffered considerable from desertions caused by the rivalry and intrigue of other recruiting regiments. Quite a number of the desertions have been apprehended and present prospects indicate that there will be but few if any more desertions and that it will fill up to the maximum." Maj. W. F. Bradford to Brig. Gen. R. P. Buckland, Feb. 23, 1864, file for William F. Bradford, Compiled Service Records, Bradford's Battalion, RG 94. See also service records for James Park and John F. Gregory in ibid., as well as pension files for William Read Johnson, Bradford's Battalion, file F320530-231780 and file M243909-200858, RG 94.

52. *OR,* 32 (pt. 1): 538–39.

53. *OR,* 32 (pt. 2): 556.

54. *OR,* 32 (pt. 1): 538–39.

55. Ibid., 538; *Fort Pillow Report,* 92–93.

56. Quoted in Benjamin Quarles, *The Negro in the Civil War* (New York: Da Capo, 1989), 205–6.

57. *Fort Pillow Report,* 123–25.

58. Brig. Gen. Mason Brayman to Mary Brayman, May 1, 1864, Bailhache-Brayman Papers Collection, Illinois State Historical Library, Springfield.

59. Quoted in *Washington Star,* Apr. 16, 1864, reprinted in the *New York Times,* Apr. 18, 1864.

60. See Jeffrey Lash, "Stephen Augustus Hurlbut: A Military and Diplomatic Politician, 1815–1882" (Ph.D. diss., Kent State University, 1980), 107–206, and "'The Federal Tyrant at Memphis': General Stephen A. Hurlbut and the Union Occupation of West Tennessee, 1862–64," *Tennessee Historical Quarterly* 48 (spring 1989): 15–28. Sherman used the term "marked timidity," but Grant officially ordered Hurlbut relieved by telegraph, at Sherman's request. *OR,* 32 (pt. 3): 381.

61. Lash, "Stephen Augustus Hurlbut," 116–61.

62. Ibid., 107–200.

63. *OR,* 32 (pt. 3): 366, 381–82.

64. Ibid., 366, 382.

65. Ibid., 382. C. C. Washburn dropped the "e" in his last name to distinguish himself from his brother, Elihu.

66. *Fort Pillow Report,* 63–68. Edward Benton, a civilian entrepreneur at the fort and a former Missouri beef supplier for the Union army, said he owned the land the fort rested upon and was planting cotton there just before the battle, through a common army practice of using blacks supplied to him from the army in Memphis. Curiously, Hurlbut never mentioned Benton in his testimony. A deposition from A. Guduth described the cotton speculation of senior Union officers in charge of confiscated Southern plantations. He stated that "almost all the members of the corps of officers, from General McPherson, Generals Hurlbut, McCarter, down to captains and quartermasters, are interested in trade and administration of plantations so as to form a perfectly linked chain of thieves." See U.S. Senate, *Trade Regulations, &c.,* 43. For Benton's testimony, see

Fort Pillow Report, 119. Before the battle at Fort Pillow, both Hurlbut and Bradford wrote Andrew Johnson, Tennessee's Union military governor, pleading for the dismissal of a circuit judge who had ruled against the confiscation of property by Union forces in West Tennessee and whose removal would have made it simpler to arrange situations like Benton's. See William Bradford to Andrew Johnson, Dec. 15, 1862, and Hurlbut to Johnson, Feb. 2, 1863, in Leroy Graf and Ralph Haskins, eds., *The Papers of Andrew Johnson,* vol. 6, *1862–64* (Washington, D.C.: Government Printing Office, 1963), 99–100 (Hurlbut's letter appears in the microfilm edition but not in the published volume). A letter from Maj. Gen. James B. McPherson, commander of the Army of the Tennessee, to Maj. Gen. H. W. Slocum, commanding the District of Vicksburg, warned that the government's policy of using abandoned plantations for the employment of freedmen and the establishment of trading posts along the river for Unionists left the occupants vulnerable to attack and corruption because the army did not have the forces to adequately defend these places. *OR,* 32 (pt. 3): 416–17; *Fort Pillow Report,* 65.

67. Williams, "Benjamin F. Wade and Atrocity Propaganda," 37–43.

68. Williams, *Lincoln and the Radicals,* 230–35; John M. Forbes to *New York Evening Post,* n.d., in Sarah Forbes Hughes, ed., *Letters and Recollections of John Murray Forbes,* 2 vols. (Boston: Houghton, Mifflin, 1899), 1:219–20.

69. *OR,* 32 (pt. 1): 586–623.

70. Editorial in *Hamilton Republican,* reprinted in *Liberator,* Apr. 29, 1864.

71. *New York Tribune,* reprinted in *Liberator,* May 6, 1864.

72. Williams, *Lincoln and the Radicals,* 254–57.

73. See *Fort Pillow Report,* 1–7.

74. Ibid., 3–4.

75. *Chicago Tribune,* Apr. 16, 1864.

76. *Liberator,* Apr. 22, 1864.

77. Editorial in *Boston Journal,* reprinted in *Liberator,* Apr. 29, 1864.

78. E. Hubbard to Caroline Wade, June 17, 1864, Benjamin F. Wade Papers, Manuscripts Division, Library of Congress, Washington, D.C.

79. Quoted in Randall Jimerson, *The Private Civil War: Popular Thought During the Sectional Conflict* (Baton Rouge: Louisiana State University Press, 1988), 133.

80. *Fort Pillow Report,* 6–7.

81. "Retaliation. By a Connecticut Woman," *New York Independent,* reprinted in *Liberator,* May 13, 1864.

82. *Liberator,* Apr. 22, 1864.

83. Kenneth Moore, "United States Colored Troops 1864," *Tennessee Historical Quarterly* 54 (summer 1995): 116. See also James McPherson, *Marching Toward Freedom: Blacks in the Civil War, 1861–1865* (New York: Facts on File, 1994), 85.

84. Barry Popchock, ed., *Soldier Boy: The Civil War Letters of Charles O. Musser, 29th Iowa* (Iowa City: University of Iowa Press, 1995), 129.

85. James Merrill and James Marshall, eds., "The 16th Kentucky and the End of the War: The Letters of Henry Clay Weaver," *Filson History Club Quarterly* 32 (1958): 338–39.

86. Gus to wife, May 6, 1864, quoted in Joseph T. Glatthaar, *Forged in Battle: The Civil War Alliance of Black Soldiers and White Officers* (New York: Free Press, 1990), 157.

87. Ashley Halsey, ed., *A Yankee Private's Civil War,* (Chicago: Henry Regnery, 1961), 15–16.

88. John T. Morse, ed., *The Diary of Gideon Welles,* 3 vols. (Boston: Houghton, Mifflin, 1911), 2:23–24.

89. Report of *Times* of London correspondent in Richmond, Virginia, reprinted in *Cairo (Ill.) Daily Journal,* June 19, 1864.

90. See Gregory J. W. Urwin, "'We Cannot Treat Negroes . . . as Prisoners of War': Racial Atrocities and Reprisals in Civil War Arkansas," *Civil War History* 42 (Sept. 1996): 193–210; and

Thomas Mays, *The Saltville Massacre* (Fort Worth: Ryan Place, 1995). See also Emory Thomas, *The Confederate Nation: 1861–1865* (New York: Harper and Row, 1979), 246–47.

91. *Liberator,* Apr. 22, 1864.

92. Statistics for the POW mortality rate for Bradford's battalion compiled from corresponding Compiled Service Records. See also McPherson, *Battle Cry of Freedom,* 790–96, 802; and Peggy Scott Holley, "The Seventh Tennessee Volunteer Cavalry: West Tennessee Unionists in Andersonville Prison," *West Tennessee Historical Society Papers* 42 (1988): 39–58.

93. *Congressional Globe,* 38th Cong., 2d sess., 1865, 364–65; 38th Cong., 2d sess., 1865, S.R. 95 and 97 (Jan. 18 and 26); Tap, *Over Lincoln's Shoulder,* 208–9. Senator Wade amended S.R. 97 on January 24 to strengthen the language advocating retaliation.

94. Thomas, *Confederate Nation,* 245–78; McPherson, *Battle Cry of Freedom,* 832–33.

95. Editorial in *Portland (Maine) Advertiser,* reprinted in *Liberator,* May 13, 1864.

96. *Harper's Weekly,* Apr. 30, 1864.

97. Editorial in *Boston Journal,* reprinted in *Liberator,* May 6, 1864.

98. Frederick Douglass, "Address at Twelfth Baptist Church, New York City, April 14, 1864," reprinted in *Liberator,* Apr. 29, 1864.

99. Quoted in *Liberator,* May 27, 1864.

100. Quarles, *Negro in the Civil War,* 202.

101. Douglass, "Address at Twelfth Baptist Church."

102. Donald, *Lincoln,* 470–71.

103. Gus to wife, May 6, 1864, quoted in Glatthaar, *Forged in Battle,* 157.

104. U.S. Congress, *Report of the Joint Committee on the Conduct of the War,* 1:iii–iv.

105. *New York Times,* Nov. 1, 1877. For examples of Nast's work incorporating Fort Pillow, see "This Is a White Man's Government," *Harper's Weekly,* Sept. 5, 1868; and "The Modern Samson," *Harper's Weekly,* Oct. 3, 1868.

106. Wills, *Battle from the Start,* 342–49.

107. C. Vann Woodward, *Origins of the New South, 1877–1913* (Baton Rouge: Louisiana State University Press, 1951), 101–2.

108. *Nashville Tennessean,* Jan. 26, and Feb. 19, 1941. See also the fall 1989 controversy over Middle Tennessee State University's mascot and student center, as well as the 1998 attempts to rename Forrest Elementary Schools in Gadsden, Alabama, and Jacksonville, Florida, in *Sidelines* (MTSU student newspaper), Aug.–Sept. 1989; *New York Times,* Jan. 1, 1998; and *USA Today,* Mar. 3, 1998.

109. George Julian, *Speeches on Political Questions* (New York: Hurd and Houghton, 1872), 223.

110. David Kennedy, *Over There: The First World War and American Society* (New York: Oxford University Press, 1980), 45–93.

111. Grimsley, *Hard Hand of War,* 4–6.

112. C. Vann Woodward, "Equality: The Deferred Commitment," in *The Burden of Southern History,* rev. ed. (Baton Rouge: Louisiana State University Press, 1968), 69–87.

113. William T. Sherman, *Memoirs of General William T. Sherman,* 2 vols. (Bloomington: Indiana University Press, 1957), 2:111. See *OR,* ser. 1, 38 (pt. 5): 794–95. See also Stig Forster and Jorg Nagler, eds., *On the Road to Total War: The American Civil War and the German Wars of Unification, 1861–1871* (Cambridge: Cambridge University Press, 1997).

"We *Cannot* Treat Negroes … as Prisoners of War"

7

Racial Atrocities and Reprisals in Civil War Arkansas

GREGORY J. W. URWIN

The Battle of Poison Spring, April 18, 1864, was one of the most complete victories ever won by Confederate forces in Arkansas. Fewer than four thousand cavalrymen sprang a cleverly laid ambush within the hearing of thirteen thousand Union soldiers in nearby Camden, capturing a large wagon train carrying food for their foes. As the exulting Rebels scattered the train's escort, they refused to take prisoners from its largest unit, the 1st Kansas Colored Volunteer Infantry Regiment. Thus, a glorious Confederate triumph was transformed into Arkansas's most notorious war crime.[1] The atrocities at Poison Spring, along with the retaliatory measures adopted by other African American troops serving in Arkansas, reveal the essence of a savage conflict whose central issue was race.

Though 140 years have passed since that terrible day, the memory of Poison Spring still troubles many of those who prefer to view the Civil War in romantic terms. The Arkansas Department of Parks and Tourism, which maintains a historic park at Poison Spring, has tended to ignore the dark deeds that stained that particular patch of hallowed ground. Despite such indifference, the murder of captured black soldiers at Poison Spring deserves a prominent place in any history of the Civil War west of the Mississippi River.[2]

The clash at Poison Spring marked the beginning of the end for the Camden Expedition, the last major Federal offensive in Arkansas. In late March 1864, Maj. Gen. Frederick Steele, the commander of the Union Department of Arkansas and 7th Army Corps, marched south with roughly fourteen thousand troops drawn from his garrisons at Little Rock and Fort Smith. The five thousand soldiers from the latter post belonged to Brig. Gen. John M. Thayer's Frontier Division and were veterans of successful operations in Indian Territory. Among Thayer's regiments were the 1st and 2d

Kansas Colored Infantry, composed of runaway slaves from Missouri and Arkansas and led by white officers. Steele's column penetrated further into southern Arkansas than the Federals had ever gone before. The expedition also represented the first time that black units in the state were employed as anything more than garrison or labor battalions. Both of these facts struck terror into the hearts of the region's white inhabitants.[3]

Steele carried orders to rendezvous at Shreveport, Louisiana, with a larger Union army and a gunboat flotilla under Maj. Gen. Nathaniel P. Banks. Once Steele joined him, Banks planned to invade Texas, seizing vast supplies of cotton in the process to enrich Northern speculators. But the two armies were destined never to meet.[4] Hampered by muddy roads and constantly harassed by more than six thousand Confederate cavalry, Steele pushed southward by starts and stops. A feint toward Washington, the capital of Confederate Arkansas since Little Rock's capture the previous year, threw the Rebels so off balance that Steele was able to march into the fortified town of Camden without a fight on April 15.[5]

The country through which Steele's army passed had been picked over by Confederate foragers since the autumn of 1863. By the time the Federals reached Camden, they had been on half rations for three weeks, and their rations were soon halved again. But relief lay close at hand. Capt. Charles A. Henry, Steele's chief quartermaster, learned of the existence of five thousand bushels of corn stored at a point sixteen miles west of Camden. Henry assembled a forage train of 198 wagons to secure the corn.[6]

Steele turned to the Frontier Division for an escort to guard the train, and General Thayer detailed a total of 1,170 troops for that purpose. There were 438 officers and men from the 1st Kansas Colored Infantry; 383 from the 18th Iowa Infantry; 291 troopers from the 2d, 6th, and 14th Kansas Cavalry; and 58 artillerymen manning 4 guns. Command of the escort went to James M. Williams, the 1st Kansas's colonel and an officer known for his zeal, competence, and courage. A lawyer in civilian life, Williams had distinguished himself at several battles in Indian Territory in 1863 and would end the war a brevet brigadier general of volunteers.[7]

The Confederates destroyed 2,500 bushels of corn before Williams could reach the scene on April 17, but the Federals saved the remainder and loaded it aboard their wagons by midnight. At sunrise the next day, Williams started his column back toward Camden, detaching small parties to gather additional corn from the farms lying near his route. After marching some four miles, Williams encountered Confederate Brig. Gen. John S. Marmaduke with 12 cannon and over 3,600 cavalry deployed for battle at Poison Spring.[8]

Marmaduke's hastily assembled force represented a cross section of Confederate mounted strength in the Trans-Mississippi theater: a brigade and an independent battalion containing 786 of Marmaduke's fellow Missourians; 1,500 Arkansans in brigades led by Brig. Gen. William L. Cabell and Col. William A. Crawford; and 655 Texans and 680 Choctaw Indians in a division brought from Indian Territory by Brig. Gen. Samuel B. Maxey. Most of these horsemen carried infantry rifles, weapons with greater range and stopping power than the Rebel cavalry's traditional carbines and shotguns.[9]

Colonel Williams deployed the 1st Kansas in an L-shaped line to shield the head and southern side of the forage train from the enemy's main thrust. The black soldiers had only gotten fifteen hours of rest during the past seventy-eight and were now caught in a three-way artillery cross fire. Nevertheless, they held their ground in the face of superior numbers, repulsing two Confederate attacks with rapidly delivered volleys. Many Rebels present, impressed by such tenacity but unwilling to concede that former slaves could match them as soldiers, later stated that the Federals had 1,500 black troops at Poison Spring instead of 438.[10]

By the time Marmaduke was ready to mount a third attack, the 1st Kansas's ranks had been badly thinned by death and wounds, and ammunition was running low. Advancing with cheers and war whoops, the Rebels turned the battered regiment's flanks and drove the crumbling blue line back through the parked wagons. Colonel Williams rallied as many men as he could and conducted a fighting withdrawal to the comparative safety of a swamp north of the battlefield. From there, he guided what was left of his escort on a circuitous retreat to Camden. The first of these weary fugitives began entering Steele's lines around 8:00 PM.[11]

A gloating Camden resident watched as Colonel Williams's men "held groups of soldiers in the streets in solemn silence, to hear the story of the fight at Poison Spa." The tales spread by the battle's survivors contained elements more horrifying than the experience of military defeat. As Williams himself reported: "Many wounded men of the First Kansas Colored Volunteers fell into the hands of the enemy, and I have the most positive assurances from eyewitnesses that they were murdered on the spot." The 1st Kansas's major and adjutant confirmed the colonel's accusations, as did other members of the escort.[12]

Williams's casualty figures told Steele's veterans at Camden that they could not dismiss these atrocity stories. Of the 301 men listed as killed, wounded, or missing from Williams's escort, 182 belonged to the 1st Kansas. That by itself proved nothing, as the blacks had borne the brunt of the battle. What aroused suspicion was the disclosure that the 1st Kansas had suffered 117 slain but only 65 wounded. "It will be seen," reasoned a trooper in Steele's 3d Missouri Cavalry, "that the number of our killed exceeds the number of our wounded in this engagement, an unusual occurrence in warfare of the present day, as it is generally found from the reports of the many battles being daily fought in our land, to be just the contrary. This can be accounted for when it is known as we were informed by one of the 2d Kansas Cavalry who made his escape a few minutes prior to the completion of the struggle, that the inhuman and blood thirsty enemy . . . was engaged in killing the wounded wherever found."[13]

In letters, diaries, reminiscences, and oral testimony handed down from generation to generation, the victors at Poison Spring described the fate that befell those black soldiers who failed to escape. Lt. William M. Stafford, a Texas artilleryman in Maxey's division, confided to his journal: "The surprise of the enemy was complete—at least 400 darkies were killed. [N]o black prisoners were captured." Three different Arkansas cavalrymen expressed pride in the fact that the Union dead were "mostly Negroes." A trooper in the 1st Arkansas Cavalry boasted that "we almost exterminated the troops that had the train in their charge." "I think there were 10 negroes killed to one white Fed," another Arkansas cavalryman wrote to a loved one in Arkadelphia. "If the negro was wounded our men would shoot him dead as they were passed and what negroes that were captured have . . . since been shot." Ordered to remove the captured wagons to a place of greater safety, Cabell's Arkansans drove over the dead and dying blacks, competing to see who could crush the most "nigger heads." When Gen. Edmund Kirby Smith, the commander of the Confederacy's Trans-Mississippi Department, reached the Camden vicinity two days later, his jubilant subordinates informed him that they had left six hundred Federal dead rotting at Poison Spring, "primarily Negroes who neither gave or rec'[eived] quarter." Local civilians were soon referring to the fight as the "Poison Spring Massacre."[14]

Of all those who succumbed to the homicidal frenzy at Poison Spring, none surpassed Col. Tandy Walker's Choctaws for sheer ferocity. As Lieutenant Stafford scribbled in his journal, "The havoc among the negroes had been tremendous—over a small portion of the field we saw at least 40 dead bodies lying in all conceivable attitudes, some scalped & nearly all stripped by the bloodthirsty Choctaws." "You ought to see Indians fight Negroes—kill and scalp them," marveled Pvt. Charles T. Anderson of the 2d Arkansas Cavalry. "Let me tell you, I never expected to see as many dead Negroes again. They were so thick you could walk on them." The Choctaws' behav-

ior was still a topic of conversation when Brig. Gen. Thomas J. Churchill's
Arkansas infantry division arrived in the Camden area a few days after Poison Spring. "The Chocktaw was at Camden when we came up," James
McCall Dawson of the 34th Arkansas wrote his family. "They caught out one
Regt of Steels negros and killed all of them[.] They take no prisoners[.] They
would shoot a negro as long as he could breathe." Elizabeth Godbold Watts,
whose home was close enough to Poison Spring to be pressed into service
as a field hospital, complained that her slave, Henry, did nothing to protect
her hogs from Choctaw foragers "for fear that someone will kill him since
the negroes were killed so in that fight."[15]

The Choctaws harbored so much animosity for their black victims that
killing them was not enough. In addition to scalping and stripping, the Indians devised other ways to desecrate the 1st Kansas Colored's dead. The
Washington (Ark.) Telegraph treated its readers to this example of "Choctaw
Humor": "After the battle of Poison Springs, the Choctaws buried a Yankee in an ordinary grave. For a headstone they put up a stiff negro buried to
the waist. For a footstone another negro reversed, out from the waist to the
heels." Three days after the battle, a Union burial detail discovered that three
dead white officers from the 1st Kansas had been scalped, stripped, and
turned on their faces as a sign of dishonor, while the corpses of their black
soldiers were laid in a circle around them.[16]

News of these atrocities traveled quickly throughout southern Arkansas.[17]
For years afterward, Martha Holcomb thrilled her children and grandchil-
dren in the little village of Moscow with this version of the battle:

> By noon Marmaduke's men had routed the Federals who had put into the front
> line of the battle the untrained negro slaves. It was easy enough for these Southern
> planters when faced to face with their own slaves, to attack with a rage which put to
> flight the unskilled . . . negroes. They fled in terror to hiding places and were pur-
> sued by their masters like infuriated demons.
>
> A few miles below the battle field was an old mill with its beautiful pond fed by
> an abundant spring; here was refuge for the fleeing negroes. These Southern sol-
> diers' revenge was not appeased by flight. The negroes were hunted and either shot
> or bayonetted in their hiding places.[18]

General Marmaduke and his senior officers never openly admitted that
their men had butchered black prisoners, but they strongly hinted that such
had been the case in their official reports. "The number of killed of the enemy was very great, especially among the negroes," noted General Cabell.
"You could track our troops by the dead bodies lying on the ground." Colo-

nel Walker asserted that during the engagement his "hungry, half-clothed Choctaws" had been animated solely by the desire to shed "the blood of their despised enemy." Col. Charles DeMorse, who led the Texas brigade in Maxey's division, offered this sinister revelation: "But few prisoners were brought in by my command."[19]

While acknowledging no complicity in any war crimes, some of Marmaduke's officers felt the need to justify the carnage committed by their troops. Colonel DeMorse implied that his Texans were outraged to find the Federal forage train "laden with corn, bacon, stolen bed quilts, women's clothing, hogs, geese, and all the *et ceteras* of unscrupulous plunder." Lt. Col. John M. Harrell of Cabell's brigade recalled that "little children's and women's clothing" were "piled upon the wagons," including "little baby frocks, shoes, stockings, women's bonnets, shawls and cloaks."[20]

It was only natural for Confederates to be infuriated by such discoveries. Brutalized by hunger and the frustrations of campaigning in rough and hostile territory, Steele's bluecoats blazed a path of destruction across southern Arkansas. But that does not explain why the winning side at Poison Spring made the 1st Kansas Colored the sole object of its vengeance. After all, the 1st Kansas composed less than half of Colonel Williams's escort, and the African Americans were so drained by a lack of food and rest that they were in poor shape to go ranging about the countryside collecting forage and plunder. By sunup on April 18, one hundred black infantrymen were so worn out that Williams classified them as "unfit for duty."[21]

The escort's 291 white Kansas cavalrymen were far better equipped to loot the farms along their route, and they apparently made the most of their opportunities. "Many of the cavalry, in violation of orders, straggled from their commands," Williams fumed. Shortly before the battle broke out, some of these wayward troopers showed up at the home of Sara Elizabeth Gillespie, about three miles from Poison Spring. "The soldiers," wrote Gillespie's great-granddaughter, "took what meal, hams and sides of meat, dried beans, peas and fruit that Sarah had not sent deep into the woods and buried."[22] According to the same source, the Kansans were even more ruthless in ransacking the farm next door: "A neighbor of Sarahs climbed up into her meal barrel when the soldiers started to take it, but the man just picked her up and set her out on the floor and took the barrel of meal away. They also took all of her silver. . . . She had one fork left that they did not find. The Federals took feather pillows and mattresses, ripped them open and emptied the feathers out, then used them as sacks to carry their 'loot' in. They could sling them across the backs of their horses if there was no room in the wagons."[23]

From the existing testimony of Confederate civilians who lived in and around Camden during Steele's occupation, it is incontestable that the Union troops to be most feared were white Kansans—especially cavalry-men.[24] "The real yankee's I was not afraid of," insisted Clara Dunlap, "they treated me gentlemanly enough, but the Kansas jay hawkers, that were most always sent with the wagon trains I was afraid off, they looked mean enough for any thing, & the officers, as bad as the men!" Dunlap testified that the Kansans "took all of our mules, *corn, sugar, molasses, flour, every thing* in the world we had to eat . . . , they even took all my *soap, candles, coffee & every hen, chicken,* turkey, *eggs* &c on the place except two or three setting hens, that ran off in the woods; all my *cooking vessels,* pans, *blankets* &c & then searched the house over, broke the lock on every trunk (but one) & took a good many little things all my good *shoes, stockings, soda,* spirits, even . . . took my *wedding slippers.*" The invaders ravaged the nearby farms of Dunlap's relatives with the same merciless thoroughness. Many of these "Jayhawkers" bore grudges against Southerners that dated back nearly a decade to "Bleeding Kansas" days, and they rarely missed a chance to settle old scores.[25]

In contrast to their white comrades, Steele's black troops were reasonably well behaved, and the guilt for relatively few depredations can be laid at their door. On the night of April 6–7, 1864, some of the 2d Kansas Colored may have burned a cotton barn south of Hot Springs, after word got out that the white men from that plantation "were all in the Southern army." A week later, two black soldiers forced their way into a house at Moscow, but all they demanded was food.[26]

For the most part, however, enlisted personnel from the 1st and 2d Kansas Colored gave Confederate civilians few legitimate grounds for complaint. "I did not find the negro soldiers impudent to a firm white man," an anonymous Camden resident informed the *Washington Telegraph.* During the Federal evacuation of the town on April 26, this same observer spotted a black regiment protecting a doctor's home from marauding white stragglers.[27]

Where Steele's black troops deliberately disregarded Southern white sensibilities was in their enforcement of the Emancipation Proclamation. Once at Camden, they wasted no time in notifying local slaves that they were now free to leave their masters and mistresses. Black soldiers also encouraged male slaves to enlist in the Union army, sometimes resorting to press gang tactics to snare recruits. Yet, in all these activities, the men of the 1st and 2d Kansas avoided direct confrontations with whites, and alert slave owners managed to hold onto most slaves who were too timid to go willingly with the Federals. When an armed black squad tried to spirit off the household servants of businessman Henry Merrell, he succeeded in talking the soldiers out of it: "I interposed a long-winded argument to the colored patriots & they listened respectfully enough, until suddenly the drums beat for 'Roll Call,' & my audience vanished in obedience to discipline." Merrell also obtained a speedy release for his body servant, Munroe, who was bullied into enlisting after other black soldiers threatened him with hanging.[28]

If Federal looting really was the primary cause of the Poison Spring Massacre, then the Confederates had as much reason to murder the 120 white prisoners who fell into their hands—and not just the African Americans. The fact that the victims of this massacre belonged exclusively to the 1st Kansas leads to the conclusion that the perpetrators' motives were racial. The *Washington Telegraph,* the voice of Confederate Arkansas, admitted as much seven weeks after the battle.[29]

With the onset of civil war, John R. Eakin, the *Telegraph*'s editor, dedicated his newspaper to ensuring unwavering public support for the Confederacy across southern Arkansas. His importance as an opinion maker received an enormous boost after Washington became the state's Confederate capital.[30] In a June 8, 1864, editorial titled "The Slave Soldiers," Eakin turned his persuasive talents to justifying Confederate excesses at Poison Spring:

> How shall we treat our slaves arrayed under the banners of the invader, and marching to desolate our homes and firesides? . . . It is a case in which it well becomes our rulers to pray most earnestly for Divine guidance. May they have it soon! Meanwhile the problem has met our soldiers in the heat of battle, where there has been no time for discussion. They have cut the Gordian knot with the sword. They did right. It was not theirs to untangle its knotty folds. It is far better for the deluded victims, as for us, that the fate which may perhaps be considered inevitable, should come upon them in hot blood, and the excitement of the battle field.[31]

African Americans are such a conspicuous and valued part of today's American military that it is difficult to appreciate the revolutionary nature of Abraham Lincoln's decision to let slaves become soldiers. Yet, when John Eakin proclaimed that "the crime of Lincoln in seducing our slaves into the ranks of his army" should be ranked "amongst those stupendous wrongs against humanity, shocking to the moral sense of the world, like Herod's massacre of the Innocents, or the eve of St. Bartholomew," multitudes of Confederates on both sides of the Mississippi would have agreed. "All minor and local massacres," Eakin added defensively, "pale before it."[32]

To Eakin and other guardians of Southern slavery, African Americans were always two persons rolled into one. On the one hand, they were simple and childlike souls, needing white care and guidance to lead happy and productive lives. On the other hand, they remained savages at heart, purportedly like their ancestors in Africa, and had to be restrained by slavery. If ever those bonds should slip, they would revert to their animal nature and attempt to kill every white person they came across.[33]

White Arkansans schooled in such prejudices viewed any Northern action against slavery as more than just a threat to their economic and social status but as a deliberate attempt to stir up servile insurrections. If slavery were abolished, whites would either have to exterminate blacks or suffer extermination themselves. The question was literally a matter of life and death, or so whites believed.[34]

When the Lincoln administration followed the Emancipation Proclamation with authorization to accept blacks into the Union army, Confederates in Arkansas fretted that the South's worst nightmare was about to come true. Little Rock's *True Democrat* accused the Federals of escalating the conflict into "a war for extermination, not only of men, but of women and children." The competing *Arkansas Gazette* anticipated this shift in enemy policy months before it took place, and its reaction was similar to the *Democrat*'s: "Our course is plain. A savage war has been forced upon us. We will have to meet, and deal with it as we find it." In particular, the *Gazette* urged the Confederate government to adopt the following course of action: "Arming negroes, as soldiers or otherwise, or doing any thing to incite them to insurrection is a worse crime than the murder of any one individual: Therefore, all officers and soldiers . . . guilty of such practices . . . should be punished as murderers."[35]

Arkansas journalists charged the North with violating the rules of civilized warfare by fielding black regiments. Only the most drastic action could save the Confederacy and what she represented. "It follows irresistably that we *cannot* treat negroes taken in arms as prisoners of war," proclaimed John Eakin, "without a destruction of the social system for which we contend. In this we must be firm, uncompromising, and unfaltering. We *must* claim the full control of all negroes who may fall into our hands, to punish with death, or any other penalty, or remand to their owners. If the enemy retaliate, we must do likewise; and if the *black flag* follows, the blood be upon their heads."[36]

Eakin's readers shared his indignation, especially after the 1st and 2d Kansas Colored appeared in their midst. Reflecting in 1911 on the depredations committed by white Federals during Steele's stay in Camden, Virginia

Stinson revealed: "Only one thing stirred my Southern blood to heat, was when a negro regiment passed my home going to fight our own dear men at Poison Springs. How fierce they did look, it was then that I gave vent to my feelings." When three wounded white prisoners from Poison Spring were delivered to the house of Elizabeth Watts, she taunted them by asking "if they felt as though they were fighting with their equals."[37]

These feelings prevailed at the highest command levels in the Trans-Mississippi Department. Ten months prior to Poison Spring, General Kirby Smith chided one of his senior officers in Louisiana: "I have been unofficially informed that some of your troops have captured negroes in arms. I hope this may not be so, and that your subordinates who may have been in command of capturing parties may have recognized the propriety of giving no quarter to armed negroes and their officers." Fear of Federal retaliation prevented the Confederate government from openly endorsing this draconian policy, but Kirby Smith's subordinates needed little prodding from above to put it into practice. In raids on Pine Bluff and Clarksville, Arkansas, between the fall of 1863 and the spring of 1864, Rebel irregulars shot or hanged captured black soldiers. Confederate guerrillas in Missouri habitually executed any male slaves caught trying to sneak off to Union recruiting stations. In a skirmish south of Lake Providence, Louisiana, on June 29, 1863, a Texas colonel directed his cavalry brigade to charge a fort held by two companies of black infantrymen and to "take none with uniforms on."[38]

As the first black combat unit in the Union army, the 1st Kansas was the paramount symbol of Yankee malice to every Confederate soldier and guerrilla in "Kirby Smithdom." In a clash that presaged Poison Spring, more than 150 Confederate bushwhackers surprised a foraging party of 25 men from the 1st Kansas at Sherwood, Missouri, on May 18, 1863. The black soldiers had stacked their rifles to load some corn into wagons, and most could not recover their arms before the Rebels were upon them. The guerrillas showed the defenseless Federals no mercy—shooting, stabbing, or beating 13 of them to death. The others saved themselves by fleeing into the brush.[39]

Despite this setback, the 1st Kansas Colored developed into a first-rate regiment, which maddened its enemies all the more. At the Battle of Honey Springs in Indian Territory on July 17, 1863, the 1st Kansas squared off in a head-to-head musketry duel with the dismounted 29th Texas Cavalry. The blacks outshot the 29th Texas, downing its colors twice and finally putting it to rout. The Texans never got over the humiliation of being bested by former slaves. When the 1st Kansas and 29th Texas next met at Poison Spring, the Texans recognized their opponents and shouted with vindictive glee: "You First Kansas Niggers now buck to the Twenty-ninth Texas!" After the fight, a black soldier feigning death heard the Texans chanting a macabre litany as they searched the battlefield for wounded men to kill. "Where is the First Kansas Nigger now?" one would crow. "All cut to pieces and gone to hell by bad management," another would answer.[40]

An African American did not have to bear arms for the Union to become the object of Confederate wrath. Simply running away to the Federals was considered enough of a threat to Southern society to warrant the severest penalty, as was seen at the Battle of Marks's Mills, Arkansas, April 25, 1864. Like Poison Spring, the clash at Marks's Mills was a consequence of General Steele's logistical problems at Camden. On April 23, he dispatched 240 wagons to Pine Bluff to pick up a load of supplies. Mindful now of the sting of the Confederate cavalry, Steele detailed an entire infantry brigade of 3 regiments (1,200 men), 240 cavalry, and 2 artillery sections under Lt. Col. Francis M. Drake as the train's escort. Drake noted that his column was accompanied by "a large number of cotton speculators, Arkansas refugees, sutlers, and other army followers, and 300 negroes." Two days out from Camden, Drake linked up with a relief party of 150 Union cavalry from Pine Bluff.[41]

That same day, 4,000 Confederate horsemen directed by Brig. Gens. James F. Fagan and Joseph O. Shelby converged on Drake's force at Marks's Mills. Hitting the Federals from two directions at once, the Rebels annihilated the escort in short order, taking 1,300 prisoners and the entire supply train. But according to General Fagan, only 150 of the 300 runaway slaves with Drake were taken into custody by the victors. What happened to the others?[42]

The diary of Lt. Benjamin Pearson of the 36th Iowa Infantry, captured with most of his regiment at Marks's Mills, provides a partial answer: "There was not an armed negro with us & they shot down our Colored servents & teamsters & others what ware following to get from bondage as they would shoot sheep dogs." A wounded Colonel Drake fell into enemy hands midway through the engagement, and he subsequently learned that "a large number [of] negroes . . . were inhumanly butchered by the enemy, and among them my own negro servant." A graphic account of this massacre comes from Confederate major John N. Edwards, the adjutant of Shelby's brigade. "The battle-field was sickening to behold," Edwards wrote in 1867. "No orders, threats, or commands could restrain the men from vengeance on the negroes, and they were piled in great heaps about the wagons, in the tangled brushwood, and upon the muddy and trampled road." An Arkansas soldier saw General Shelby himself bring a clubbed rifle crashing down on the head of a frightened slave. Then Shelby drew his revolver and casually shot the prostrate black man to death.[43]

The exact number of fugitive slaves killed at Marks's Mills will probably never be known, but it undoubtedly topped one hundred. The day after the fight, Lieutenant Pearson's captors allowed him to walk the battlefield to search for his son, who was listed as missing. "The number of Negroes I could not get," Pearson complained. "I saw perhaps near 30, & the Rebs pointed out to me a point of woods where they told me they had killed eighty odd negroes men women & children[.] this is their report to me & . . . I fully believe they are hartless enough to do any act that wicked men or devils could conceive." Those few runaways who survived the carnage were apparently hunted down by local whites and carried off to Texas for resale into slavery—much to the chagrin of their original owners.[44]

The war crimes at Poison Spring and Marks's Mills were not isolated outbursts of senseless racial violence but part of an ongoing program of racial intimidation that took its cues from the basic values of antebellum Southern society. As far as the men who did the killing were concerned, they had simply made examples of some disloyal slaves to deter other blacks from betraying their masters or giving further aid and comfort to the enemy. Fresh from the butchery at Poison Spring, one Arkansas trooper offered this rationalization for his comrades' merciless conduct: "Our men is determine[d] not to take negro prisoners, and if all the Negroes could have seen what occurred that day, they would stay at home."[45]

Despite the additional peril, there was no restraining the emancipation movement. When Steele's desperate Federals finally evacuated Camden on the evening of April 26, hundreds of slaves followed in their wake. Likewise, most black men already wearing Union uniforms were not demoralized by the Confederates' no-prisoners policy. A few weeks after Lt. William Blain of the 40th Iowa Infantry returned from Camden, he encountered a former servant named Alfred who had joined a black regiment at Little Rock. "I asked him," Blain wrote the next day, "if he intended to give the 'rebs' any quarter when he fought with them?" "No Sah," Alfred replied, "dey don't gib us any, and we don't intend to gib dem any. Why sah, dey just kill us like brutes and we's gwine to use dem de same way."[46]

Those were not empty words. Black troops had redeemed Alfred's harsh pledge a full month before Lieutenant Blain first heard it. Within a day of the bloodbath at Poison Spring, Col. Samuel J. Crawford called the officers of the 2d Kansas Colored Infantry into council at Camden to discuss the enemy's treatment of their sister regiment. Before they adjourned, Crawford and his officers solemnly swore "that in future the regiment would take no prisoners so long as the Rebels continued to murder our men."[47]

The 2d Kansas fulfilled that dreadful oath on April 30, 1864, when Kirby Smith and three Confederate infantry divisions overtook Steele's retreating army amid the flooded bottoms on the south side of the Saline River at Jenkins's Ferry. At one point in the battle, the Rebels unlimbered two cannon opposite Crawford and his black troops. Crawford accepted the challenge and ordered a charge, which was closely supported by the white 29th Iowa Infantry. With one volley, the blacks immobilized the enemy artillery by killing most of its horses, and with a second volley, they dispersed a supporting line of infantry. Then the 2d Kansas dashed forward with leveled bayonets, the men shouting "Poison Springs" and "Here comes your 'Iron Clads.'" The blacks easily overran the battery position, impaling every Confederate within reach, including three gunners who raised their hands in surrender. Only the timely arrival and forceful intervention of the 29th Iowa saved the lives of Lt. John O. Lockhart, the commander of the captured cannon, and his five remaining men.[48]

In his 1911 memoirs, Colonel Crawford admitted that the 2d Kansas used Jenkins's Ferry to repay the enemy for Poison Spring, but he insisted that his troops behaved in a humane fashion. "After the Poison Springs massacre," Crawford recalled, "we were resolved to take no prisoners. And yet, there lay scores of Rebel wounded all around us; but we left them as they were, to be cared for by their comrades." But Pvt. Milton P. Chambers of the 29th Iowa told a very different tale in a letter home seven days after the fight. "The negroes want to kill every wounded reb they come to," he wrote, "and will do it if we did not watch them."[49]

In the fury of their charge, Crawford's vengeful blacks drew no distinction between able-bodied or wounded foes. As Private Chambers related, "One of our boys seen a little negro pounding a wounded reb in the head with the but of his gun and asked him what he was doing. the negro replied he is not dead yet! I tel you they won't give them up as long as they can kick if they can just have their way about it."[50]

Yet, even after the heat of combat cooled, the 2d Kansas continued to exact revenge for Poison Spring. Having fought Kirby Smith to a standstill, Steele's white regiments started to disengage and slip across the Saline River, leaving behind the 2d Kansas for approximately two hours to cover their retreat. Crawford claimed that he utilized that interval to send "men all along where our lines had stood to pick up such of our wounded as might have been overlooked." His soldiers, however, combined this mission of mercy with acts of merciless cruelty.[51]

Earlier in the day, Pvt. John H. Lewis of the 18th Texas Infantry took a bullet in the leg and crawled behind a tree stump for shelter. "After awhile," Lewis explained, "the firing ceased and our army was gone. Soon I looked around and saw some black negroes cutting our wounded boys' throats, and I thought my time would come next." Forcing himself to walk on his wounded leg, Lewis hobbled away to a place of safety.[52]

Other Confederates, following the Federals at a prudent distance, eventually stumbled across the horrors described by Private Lewis. Surgeon Edward W. Cade of Col. Horace Randal's Texas brigade revealed: "Our command fell back, and when they again advanced they found several of our wounded who had their throats cut from ear to ear by the Negroes." James Dawson of the 34th Arkansas Infantry wrote his family that "the negros killed some of our Wounded." Assistant Surgeon Junius N. Bragg of the 33d Arkansas Infantry informed his wife that A. J. Williams, the regiment's acting sergeant major, "had his throat cut by a Negro" and lived long enough to tell about it. David S. Williams, the 33d's senior surgeon and A. J.'s brother, added more details in his own harrowing revelations: "We found that many of our wounded had been mutilated in many ways. Some with ears cut off, throats cut, knife stabs, etc. My brother . . . was shot through the body, had his throat cut through the windpipe and lived several days. I saw several who were treated in the same way. One officer . . . wrote on a bit of paper that his lower jaw and tongue were shot off after the battle was over or during the falling back as referred to above."[53]

News of these reprisals quickly became common knowledge throughout Steele's army, but no one censured the 2d Kansas Colored. "It looks hard," Private Chambers conceded, "but the rebs cannot blame the negroes when they are guilty of the same trick." Lieutenant Blain resigned himself to the increasing dehumanization of the conflict as symbolized by Poison Spring and Jenkins's Ferry: "The 'rebs' appear to be determined to show no quarter to Black troops or officers commanding them. It would not surprise me in the least if this war would ultimately be one of extermination. Its tendencies are in that direction now."[54]

Colonel Crawford liked to pretend that the retaliatory measures he sanctioned at Jenkins's Ferry taught the Rebels to stop killing black prisoners. He was mistaken. Of the 150 badly wounded men that the retreating Federals abandoned at a field hospital on that battlefield, 9 belonged to Crawford's 2d Kansas. Before sunset, some Confederate cavalry rode up to the hospital and began robbing the patients. "One," reported an indignant Surgeon William L. Nicholson of the 29th Iowa, "dressed like an officer, drew his revolver and shot three wounded 'niggers' who lay in the yard." Two weeks later, the

Confederates moved Nicholson and the 6 surviving 2d Kansas men to more permanent accommodations at Princeton, Arkansas, where the blacks were lodged in a small storehouse. Shortly after their arrival, Nicholson heard gunshots and someone shouting, "The niggers are catching it." Next, he saw a Rebel gripping a revolver in each hand emerge from the storehouse. "I went over at once," Nicholson related, "and found all the poor negroes shot through the head."[55]

The unfortunate 1st Kansas Colored had several more of its members murdered at a hay-cutting camp fifteen miles from Fort Gibson, Indian Territory, before 1864 came to a close. On September 16, Brig. Gen. Richard Gano and a brigade of 1,200 Texas cavalrymen fell on Company H of the 1st Kansas at Flat Rock. The company's 37 men took shelter in a ravine and kept the Rebels at bay for two hours until their ammunition ran out. At that, the blacks' white lieutenant told them to save themselves, but only 4 succeeded in getting away. Those few escapees relayed what happened next to Capt. John R. Graton, their acting regimental commander: "The men were all killed except a few who concealed themselves in a ravine until dark and then crawled away."[56]

Graton's words jibed well with Confederate accounts. "The negroes were nearly all killed in a little creek into which they had jumped," remembered Pvt. Jefferson P. Boze of the 30th Texas Cavalry. "The water was red with blood of the dead negroes." Pvt. W. T. Sheppard of the 5th Texas Partisan Rangers rejoiced: "The Federals were short a company of negro troops and after the battle they were all 'good' negroes." To their credit, some of Gano's Texans abstained from the general bloodletting and spared 6 blacks as prisoners, but up to 27 other Company H men were massacre victims.[57]

The racially motivated killings at Poison Spring, Marks's Mills, Jenkins's Ferry, Princeton, and Flat Rock sprang from deep-seated fears that had permeated white Southern society during two centuries of slavery. Such atrocities were not peculiar to the Trans-Mississippi, even though that theater had earned a reputation for brutality well before black troops entered the Union army. In 1864, incidents like the Poison Spring Massacre occurred from one end of Dixie to the other. To cite only the more conspicuous examples, Confederate soldiers refused to take black prisoners at Fort Pillow in Tennessee and in battles around Petersburg, Virginia.[58]

Confederates regarded the employment of African American soldiers as such a crime against humanity that they felt absolved from any obligation to treat black troops and their white officers as honorable opponents. Rebellious slaves and white abolitionist agitators had to be exterminated to keep other blacks in their place and save a social system based on racial subordination. These convictions added a unique element of savagery to the Civil War, and they persisted for a century after Appomattox. During Reconstruction, many Confederate veterans joined terrorist organizations that frequently assassinated assertive blacks who dared to press for political equality. As heirs to this heritage of racial oppression, the descendants of those veterans would preserve much of the old Southern order down to the 1960s. Thanks to the civil rights movement and the aggressive actions of the national government, expression of much of America's ingrained racial hatred has been driven underground, but students of the dark side of the Civil War should not be surprised to see it still surface from time to time.[59]

Notes

This essay was originally published as "'We Cannot Treat Negroes . . . as Prisoners of War': Racial Atrocities and Reprisals in Civil War Arkansas," *Civil War History* 42 (Sept. 1996): 193–210. Reprinted with permission of the Kent State University Press.

1. Henry Merrell, "Receipts" Book (diary), Apr. 18, 27, 1864, Henry Merrell Papers, Southwest Arkansas Regional Archives, Washington, Ark.; *Fort Smith (Ark.) New Era,* May 7, 21, 1864. For an overview of military operations in Arkansas that places the Poison Spring affair in context, see Mark K. Christ, ed., *Rugged and Sublime: The Civil War in Arkansas* (Fayetteville: University of Arkansas Press, 1994).

2. See Jay S. Miller and Elwin Goolsby, *The Red River Campaign in Arkansas* (Little Rock: Arkansas State Parks, 1989), 1–4; and *Arkansas Democrat Gazette,* Sept. 11, 1994.

3. Wiley Britton to his wife, "The Camden Expedition," June 1, 1864, pp. 1, 10, Wiley Britton Letters, J. N. Heiskell Historical Collection, H-4, 13, UALR Archives and Special Collections, UALR Library, University of Arkansas at Little Rock; Wiley Britton, *The Union Indian Brigade in the Civil War* (Kansas City, Mo.: Franklin Hudson, 1922), 346–47, 355–56; Dudley Taylor Cornish, "Kansas Negro Regiments in the Civil War," *Kansas Historical Quarterly* 20 (May 1953): 420–27; *Lafayette County (Ark.) Democrat,* July 8, 1971; John M. Harrell, "Arkansas," in Clement A. Evans, ed., *Confederate Military History,* vol. 10 (Secaucus, N.J.: Blue and Grey, 1975), 239; "An Abstract of Facts in Case of John Taylor, Co. C., 79th U.S.C. Troops," ca. 1891, Military File of John Taylor, Civil War (Union) Compiled Military Service Records, 79th U.S. Colored Infantry, Military Service Branch, Records of the Adjutant General's Office, 1780s–1917, RG 94, National Archives, Washington, D.C.

4. Ludwell H. Johnson, *Red River Campaign: Politics and Cotton in the Civil War* (1958; reprint, Kent, Ohio: Kent State University Press, 1993), 46–48, 81, 85.

5. James A. Campbell diary, Mar. 25, 1864, J. N. Heiskell Historical Collection, H-16, box 1, file 4, UALR Archives and Special Collections, UALR Library, University of Arkansas at Little Rock; *The War of the Rebellion: A Compilation of the Official Records of the Union and Confederate Armies,* 128 vols. (Washington, D.C.: Government Printing Office, 1880–1901), ser. 1, 34 (pt. 1):660–63 (hereafter cited as *OR;* all citations are to series 1, volume 34, part 1, unless otherwise noted); Roman J. Zorn, ed., "Campaigning in Southern Arkansas: A Memoir by C. T. Anderson," *Arkansas Historical Quarterly* 8 (autumn 1949): 241–42; John N. Edwards, *Shelby and His Men; or, The War in the West* (Cincinnati: Miami Printing and Publishing, 1867), 263; Harrell, "Arkansas," 238–39.

6. Carl H. Moneyhon, *The Impact of the Civil War and Reconstruction on Arkansas: Persistence in the Midst of Ruin* (Baton Rouge: Louisiana State University Press, 1994), 116, 129; Lenore Routon, "The Carrigans: Family History" (1945), p. 129, MsF no. 326, Southwest Arkansas

Regional Archives, Washington, Ark.; George Boddie to Mary E. Boddie, Feb. 2 and Feb. 12, 1864, in Sarah M. Fountain, ed., *Sisters, Seeds, and Cedars: Rediscovering Nineteenth-Century Life Through Correspondence from Rural Arkansas and Alabama* (Conway: University of Central Arkansas Press, 1995), 174–75; John W. Brown diary, Apr. 20, 1864, Arkansas History Commission, Little Rock; *OR,* 661, 679–80; Campbell diary, Apr. 15, 1864; A. W. M. Petty, *A History of the Third Missouri Cavalry from Its Organization at Palmyra, Missouri, 1861, up to November Sixth, 1864: With an Appendix and Recapitulation* (Little Rock: J. William Denby, 1865), 67–68; Merrell diary, Apr. 23, 1864; Britton, *Union Indian Brigade,* 360–61.

7. *OR,* 743–44, 746; Britton, *Union Indian Brigade,* 362–63; Glenn L. Carle, "The First Kansas Colored," *American Heritage,* Feb./Mar. 1992, 79–80, 82–90.

8. *OR,* 680, 743–44, 819, 828, 848, 849.

9. *OR,* 819, 828, 848, 849; James L. Skinner III, ed., *The Autobiography of Henry Merrell: Industrial Missionary to the South* (Athens: University of Georgia Press, 1991), 352; Harrell, "Arkansas," 238–39.

10. *OR,* 745, 751–54, 792, 818–19, 842; *Fort Smith New Era,* May 21, 1864; Britton, *Union Indian Brigade,* 369; William M. Stafford, "Battery Journal," Apr. 18, 1864, M. D. Hutcheson Papers, Camden, Ark.; Ethan Earle, "First Kansan Colored Vol. Reg't. Records," n.d., 53, R. Stanton Avery Special Collections Department, New England Historic Genealogical Society, Boston, Mass.

11. *OR,* 745–46, 752–53, 755–56, 829; Britton, *Union Indian Brigade,* 370–72.

12. *Washington Telegraph,* May 25, 1864; Campbell diary, Apr. 18, 1864; Merrell diary, Apr. 18, 1864; *OR,* 746, 748, 754, 756; *Fort Smith New Era,* May 7, 21, 1864; Britton, *Union Indian Brigade,* 372–73; Earle, "First Kansan Colored," 52.

13. *OR,* 746, 753; *Fort Smith New Era,* May 7, 28, 1864; Petty, *Third Missouri Cavalry,* 76.

14. Stafford, "Battery Journal," Apr. 18, 1864; John C. Wright, *Memoirs of Colonel John C. Wright* (Pine Bluff, Ark.: Rare Book, 1982), 142; J. T. Kidd, "The History of J. T. Kidd from March 18th, 1862, until May 28th, 1865," n.d., p. 12, SF no. 101, Southwest Arkansas Regional Archives; "A Confederate Veteran's Story," in Charlean Moss Williams, ed., *The Old Town Speaks: Washington, Hempstead County, Arkansas* (Houston: Anson Jones, 1951), 91; *Lafayette County Democrat,* July 15, 1971; [Alfred G. Hearn, Reuben C. Reed's Company, Newton's 10th Arkansas Cavalry?] to "Dear Sallie," Apr. 20, 1864, Solomon Spence Family Letters, Old State House Museum, Little Rock, Ark.; Ralph R. Rea, *Sterling Price: The Lee of the West* (Little Rock: Pioneer Press, 1959), 106; *Washington Telegraph,* May 11, 1864; Edmund Kirby Smith to his wife, Apr. 20, 1864, Edmund Kirby Smith Papers, Southern Historical Collection, Manuscripts Department, Wilson Library, University of North Carolina, Chapel Hill; Skinner, *Autobiography of Henry Merrell,* 367–68.

15. Stafford, "Battery Journal," Apr. 18, 1864; Zorn, "Campaigning in Southern Arkansas," 242–43; James McCall Dawson to "Dear Father Sister and Brothers," May 5, 1864, in James Reed Eison, ed., "'Stand We in Jeopardy Every Hour': A Confederate Letter, 1864," *Pulaski County Historical Review* 31 (fall 1993): 2; Elizabeth Godbold Watts to John Comer Watts, May 9, 1864, in "Poison Springs Battle Recalled by 1864 Letter," *Ouachita County Historical Quarterly* 19 (Sept. 1987): 14; *Fort Smith New Era,* May 21, 1864. For another account of the massacre by a different member of Dawson's regiment, see W. C. Braly to "My Dear Ma," May 7, 1864, Amanda Malvina Fitzallen McClellan Braly Papers, Special Collections Division, University of Arkansas Libraries, Fayetteville.

16. *Washington Telegraph,* May 11, 1864; Charles H. Lothrop, *A History of the First Regiment Iowa Cavalry Veteran Volunteers, from Its Organization in 1861 to Its Muster Out of the United States Service in 1866* (Lyons, Iowa: Beers and Eaton, 1890), 182. For more on the Choctaws' implacable hatred for black Union troops, see Henry Cathey, ed., "Extracts from the Memoirs of William Franklin Avera," *Arkansas Historical Quarterly* 22 (summer 1963): 103, 107; Wright, *Memoirs,* 146; John Hallum, *Reminiscences of the Civil War,* vol. 1 (Little Rock: Yunnah and Pittard, 1903), 115–16, 315–16; *Fort Smith New Era,* May 28, 1864; *Washington Telegraph,* Aug. 3, 1864; Skinner, *Autobiography of Henry Merrell,* 367–68; and *OR,* 843, 849.

17. Hellice Gillespie Burton, *Arkansas' Role in the War Between the States 1861–1865* (Houston: privately printed, 1986), 12; Cathey, "Memoirs of Avera," 107; Mary Elizabeth Moore Carrigan diary, May 2, 3, 1864, SMF 479, Southwest Arkansas Regional Archives; Merrell diary, Apr. 18, 1864.

18. Artie Whiteside Vardy, "The Battle of Moscow: As It Was Told to Me by My Grandmother, Martha Holcomb," n.d., p. 2, SMF 191, Southwest Arkansas Regional Archives.

19. *OR*, 781, 791–92, 820, 842–43, 847–49. For additional consideration of this point, see Ira Don Richards, "The Battle of Poison Spring," *Arkansas Historical Quarterly* 18 (winter 1959): 349; and Anne J. Bailey, "Was There a Massacre at Poison Spring?" *Military History of the Southwest* 20 (fall 1990): 161.

20. *OR*, 847; Harrell, "Arkansas," 250. See also *Lafayette County Democrat*, July 15, 1971.

21. Aside from officers of the 1st Kansas Colored, the Confederates may have murdered at least one white Federal soldier at Poison Spring. But the motive was racial even in this case, as the Unionist *Fort Smith New Era* reported: "An officer . . . saw a man who was wounded taken out of the ambulance by the rebels and asked what command he belonged to, he told them the 18th Iowa, they called him a *damned liar,* and said he belonged to the 12th Kansas, brigaded with the negroes and knocked his brain out with the butt of a gun" (*New Era,* May 7, 1864). *OR*, 743–44.

22. *OR*, 744, 748; Britton, *Union Indian Brigade,* 365; Burton, *Arkansas' Role,* 11.

23. Burton, *Arkansas' Role,* 12.

24. Brown diary, Apr. 17, 24, 1864; *Washington Telegraph,* May 25, 1864; United Confederate Veterans, Arkansas Division, *Confederate Women of Arkansas in the Civil War 1861–'65: Memorial Reminiscences* (Little Rock: H. G. Pugh, 1907), 41, 49–52. See also "The Federal Occupation of Camden as Set Forth in the Diary of a Union Officer," *Arkansas Historical Quarterly* 9 (autumn 1950): 216–17.

25. Clara Dunlap to "Dear Dear Sister," July 24, 1864, Fred J. Herring Collection, Small Manuscripts Collection, Arkansas History Commission. For more on the depredations committed by Kansas cavalrymen in the Trans-Mississippi, see Stephen Z. Starr, *Jennison's Jayhawkers: A Civil War Cavalry Regiment and Its Commander* (Baton Rouge: Louisiana State University Press, 1973); and Arabella Lanktree Wilson to William H. D. Wilson, Nov. 2, 1863, in James W. Leslie, ed., "Arabella Lanktree Wilson's Civil War Letter," *Arkansas Historical Quarterly* 47 (autumn 1988): 257–72.

26. Lonnie J. White, ed., "A Bluecoat's Account of the Camden Expedition," *Arkansas Historical Quarterly* 24 (spring 1965): 84; Vardy, "Battle of Moscow," 2.

27. *Washington Telegraph,* May 25, 1864.

28. Vardy, "Battle of Moscow," 2; Merrell diary, Apr. 18, 1864; Skinner, *Autobiography of Henry Merrell,* 372–73; Brown diary, Apr. 15, 17, 26, 1864; Virginia Mc'Collum Stinson, "Memories," in M. A. Elliott, comp., *The Garden of Memory: Stories of the Civil War as Told by Veterans and Daughters of the Confederacy* (Camden, Ark.: Brown Printing, 1911), 33–34.

29. *OR*, 820, 826.

30. Robert Freeman Smith, "John R. Eakin: Confederate Propagandist," *Arkansas Historical Quarterly* 12 (winter 1953): 316–26.

31. *Washington Telegraph,* June 8, 1864.

32. Ibid. For more on the Confederate reaction to blacks in the Union army, see Joseph T. Glatthaar, *Forged in Battle: The Civil War Alliance of Black Soldiers and White Officers* (New York: Free Press, 1990), 155–59; Dudley Taylor Cornish, *The Sable Arm: Black Troops in the Union Army, 1861–1865* (1956; reprint, Lawrence: University Press of Kansas, 1987), 157–80; and Michael Fellman, *Inside War: The Guerrilla Conflict in Missouri During the American Civil War* (New York: Oxford University Press, 1989), 69–70.

33. Skinner, *Autobiography of Henry Merrell,* 24, 38–39, 44, 260; Wright, *Memoirs,* 266–67; Clara Dunlap to Clarissa Dickson, Oct. 7, 1863, in Fountain, *Sisters, Seeds, and Cedars,* 152; *Washington Telegraph,* July 27, 1864, Jan. 13, 1865; *Arkansas Gazette,* Nov. 4, 1853, Apr. 6, June 15, 1855.

34. *Washington Telegraph,* Oct. 15, 1862, June 8, 1864; *Helena (Ark.) Southern Shield,* Dec. 20, 1862; *Arkansas Gazette,* Oct. 11, 1862; Moneyhon, *Civil War and Reconstruction,* 62, 81, 93–94.

35. *True Democrat,* Apr. 22, 1863; *Arkansas Gazette,* Oct. 11, 1862. See also *Washington Telegraph,* Oct. 15, 1862.

36. *Washington Telegraph,* June 8, 1864.

37. Stinson, "Memories," 31; Elizabeth Watts to John Watts, 14.

38. *OR,* ser. 2, 6:21–22; James G. Hollandsworth Jr., "The Execution of White Officers from Black Units by Confederate Forces During the Civil War," *Louisiana History* 35 (fall 1994): 475–89; J. S. Adamson, "Personal Reminiscences of the Civil War," *Pulaski County Historical Society Review* 7 (Mar. 1959): 2–3; *Fort Smith New Era,* Apr. 9, 1864; Glatthaar, *Forged in Battle,* 69–70; Michael Fellman, "Emancipation in Missouri," *Missouri Historical Review* 83 (Oct. 1988): 50; excerpt from testimony of R. A. Watt, Nov. 30, 1863, in Ira Berlin, Joseph P. Reidy, and Leslie S. Rowland, eds., *The Black Military Experience,* ser. 2, vol. 1 of *Freedom: A Documentary History of Emancipation, 1861–1867* (Cambridge: Cambridge University Press, 1982), 235–36; Henry Orr to "Dear Sister," July 2, 1863, in John Q. Anderson, ed., *Campaigning with Parsons' Texas Cavalry Brigade, CSA: The War Journals and Letters of the Four Orr Brothers, 12th Texas Cavalry Regiment* (Hillsboro, Tex.: Hill Junior College Press, 1967), 111–12; Junius N. Bragg to "My Dear Wife," July 1, 1863, in T. J. Gaughan, ed., *Letters of a Confederate Surgeon, 1861–1865* (Camden, Ark.: privately printed, 1960), 142–44; *OR,* ser. 1, 24 (pt. 2):450–66; Anne J. Bailey, "A Texas Cavalry Raid: Reaction to Black Soldiers and Contrabands," *Civil War History* 35 (June 1989): 138–52.

39. Britton, *Union Indian Brigade,* 176–77, 242; John R. Graton to "My Dear Wife," May 22, 1863, John R. Graton Papers, 1838–1910, Kansas State Historical Society, Topeka; Joseph T. Wilson, *The Black Phalanx: A History of the Negro Soldiers of the United States in the Wars of 1775–1812, 1861–1865* (Hartford, Conn.: American Publishing, 1890), 231–32; Cornish, "Kansas Negro Regiments," 425.

40. Charles DeMorse was the colonel of the 29th Texas at Honey Springs, and he took a bullet in the right arm in the first volley fired by the 1st Kansas Colored. Recovered from his wound, DeMorse commanded a brigade at Poison Spring (consisting of the 29th, 30th, and 31st Texas Cavalry), which, as he put it, took "but few prisoners." *OR,* ser. 1, 22 (pt. 1):447–52; Britton, *Union Indian Brigade,* 242, 277, 279–84, 367, 372–73; Cornish, "Kansas Negro Regiments," 425; *OR,* 848; Rea, *Sterling Price,* 105.

41. *OR,* 712–13; F. M. Drake, "Campaign of General Steele," in *War Sketches and Incidents as Related by Companions of the Iowa Commandery of the Loyal Legion of the United States,* vol. 1 (Des Moines: P. C. Kenyon, 1893), 65–66, 68–69; Charles H. Lothrop, "The Fight at Marks' Mills," n.d., p. 1, Civil War Manuscripts, State Historical Society of Iowa, Des Moines; Ira Don Richards, "The Engagement at Marks' Mills," *Arkansas Historical Quarterly* 19 (spring 1960): 54–55.

42. *OR,* 713–15, 788–99; Harrell, "Arkansas," 255, 259; Richards, "Marks' Mills," 55–60; Elizabeth Titsworth, ed., "The Civil War Diary of a Logan County Soldier," *Wagon Wheels* 1 (winter 1981): 19.

43. R. P. Marshall of Shelby's brigade defended the excesses committed by his comrades at Marks' Mills and other locations with these words: "People called us rough and Savages we had to be we had to lay aside the Golden Rule with the Federals and treat them just like they treat us. [A]nd as old David Haram said do it First." "Benjamin Pearson's War Diary" (pt. 5), *Annals of Iowa* 15 (Oct. 1926): 441; *OR,* 714–15; Edwards, *Shelby and His Men,* 279; Rea, *Sterling Price,* 110; Lurton Dunham Ingersoll, *Iowa and the Rebellion: A History of the Troops Furnished by the State of Iowa to the Volunteer Armies of the Union, Which Conquered the Great Southern Rebellion of 1861–5* (Philadelphia: J. B. Lippincott, 1866), 658; Cathey, "Memoirs of Avera," 107; R. P. Marshall to W. L. Skaggs, Feb. 20, 1912, W. L. Skaggs Collection, Arkansas History Commission.

44. "Pearson's War Diary," 441; George Boddie to Mary E. Boddie, June 11, 1864, in Fountain, *Sisters, Seeds, and Cedars,* 179. For more on the problem of stolen Arkansas slaves being sold illegally to new owners in Texas, see John Hudson to Harris Flanagin, May 30, 1864, Kie Oldham Papers, Arkansas History Commission; and John Hugh Reynolds, ed., "Official Orders of Governor Harris Flanagin, Commander in Chief of the Militia of Arkansas," in John Hugh Reynolds, ed., *Publications of the Arkansas Historical Association,* vol. 2 (Fayetteville: Arkansas Historical Association, 1908), 400–401.

45. *Washington Telegraph,* June 1, Aug. 3, 1864; Elizabeth Watts to John Watts, 14; Vardy, "Battle of Moscow," 2; [Hearn?] to "Dear Sallie," Apr. 20, 1864.

46. A. F. Sperry, *History of the 33d Iowa Infantry Volunteer Regiment, 1863–6* (Des Moines: Mills, 1866), 94; Stinson, "Memories," 33–34; Brown diary, Apr. 26, 1864; Clara Dunlap to "Dear Dear Sister"; William Blain to "Dear Wife," June 1, 1864, in Dolly Bottens, comp., *Rouse Stevens Ancestry and Allied Families* (Carthage, Mo.: privately printed, 1970), 110A.

47. Samuel J. Crawford, *Kansas in the Sixties* (Chicago: A. C. McClurg, 1911), 117; *Washington Telegraph,* May 25, 1864.

48. The 2d Kansas Colored was nicknamed the "Iron Clads" soon after its formation in 1863. *OR,* 697–98, 781, 813; *Unconditional Union,* May 13, 20, 1864; George Carr to "Dear Father," May 2, 1864, Eugene A. Carr Papers, Archives Branch, U.S. Army Military History Institute, Carlisle Barracks, Pennsylvania; John W. Long to "Sir," May 17, 1864, in "A Union Soldier's Personal Account of the Red River Expedition and the Battle of Jenkins Ferry," *Grassroots* 8 (July 1988): 3; Crawford, *Kansas in the Sixties,* 124, 128; White, "Camden Expedition," 87–88; William E. McLean, *Forty-Third Regiment of Indiana Volunteers: An Historic Sketch of Its Career and Services* (Terre Haute, Ind.: C. W. Brown, 1903), 26; Samuel J. Crawford to Joseph T. Wilson, Dec. 31, 1885, in Joseph Wilson, *Black Phalanx,* 242; *Fort Scott (Kans.) Union Monitor,* Oct. 22, 1863; Skinner, *Autobiography of Henry Merrell,* 368; Earle, "First Kansan Colored," 56.

49. Crawford, *Kansas in the Sixties,* 124; Milton P. Chambers to "Dear Brother," May 7, 1864, Milton P. Chambers Papers, Special Collections Division, University of Arkansas Libraries, Fayetteville.

50. Chambers to "Dear Brother," May 7, 1864, Chambers Papers.

51. Crawford, *Kansas in the Sixties,* 131–32; *OR,* 759; Crawford to Wilson, 245; William L. Nicholson, "The Engagement at Jenkins' Ferry," *Annals of Iowa* 11 (Oct. 1941): 511.

52. Quoted in Mamie Yeary, ed. and comp., *Reminiscences of the Boys in Gray, 1861–1865* (Dallas: Smith and Lamar, 1912), 437.

53. Edward W. Cade to "My dear Wife," May 6, 1864, Edward W. and Allie Cade Correspondence, John Q. Anderson Collection, Texas State Archives, Austin; Dawson to "Dear Father Sister and Brothers," 52; Junius N. Bragg to Anna Josephine Goodard Bragg, May 5, 1864, in Gaughan, *Letters,* 230; *OR,* 817; Yeary, *Reminiscences of the Boys in Gray,* 390, 799.

54. Chambers to "Dear Brother," May 7, 1864, Chambers Papers; *OR,* 671, 698; White, "Camden Expedition," 87; William Blain to "Dear Wife," May 17, 1864, in Bottens, *Rouse Stevens Ancestry,* 108B.

55. Nicholson, "Jenkins' Ferry," 509, 511–15, 519. Nicholson's story was corroborated by two other captured Union officers, Lt. John Hayes of the 2d Kansas Colored and Surgeon C. R. Stuckslager of the 12th Kansas Infantry, who were interviewed for the *Fort Smith New Era* following their release from prison camp. See *Fort Smith New Era,* June 16 and Aug. 6, 1864.

56. In another irony, Gano's brigade included three regiments that participated in the Poison Spring Massacre—the 29th, 30th, and 31st Texas Cavalry. Marvin J. Hancock, "The Second Battle of Cabin Creek," *Chronicles of Oklahoma* 39 (winter 1961–62): 416–18; Larry C. Rampp, "Negro Troop Activity in Indian Territory," *Chronicles of Oklahoma* 47 (spring 1969): 550–53; Britton, *Union Indian Brigade,* 437, 439–40; John R. Graton to "Dear Wife," Sept. 29, 1864, Graton Papers.

57. Yeary, *Reminiscences of the Boys in Gray,* 46, 352–53, 684, 812, 831; John R. Graton to "My Dear Wife," Mar. 12, 1865, Graton Papers.

58. For balanced accounts of these and other antiblack atrocities committed in 1864, see Brian Steel Wills, *A Battle from the Start: The Life of Nathan Bedford Forrest* (New York: Harper Collins, 1992); Richard L. Fuchs, *An Unerring Fire: The Massacre at Fort Pillow* (Rutherford, N.J: Fairleigh Dickinson University Press, 1994); Michael A. Cavanaugh and William Marvel, *The Battle of the Crater: "The Horrid Pit," June 25–August 6, 1864* (Lynchburg, Va.: H. E. Howard, 1989); Richard J. Sommers, *Richmond Redeemed: The Siege at Petersburg* (Garden City, N.Y.: Doubleday, 1981); and Edward J. Miller Jr., *The Black Civil War Soldiers of Illinois: The Story of the Twenty-Ninth U.S. Colored Infantry* (Columbia: University of South Carolina Press, 1998).

59. For more on the role of racial violence in Reconstruction and the "Jim Crow" South, see George C. Rable, *But There Was No Peace: The Role of Violence in the Politics of Reconstruction* (Athens: University of Georgia Press, 1984); Eric Foner, *Reconstruction: America's Unfinished Revolution, 1863–1877* (New York: Harper and Row, 1988); and Nell Irvin Painter, *Exodusters: Black Migration to Kansas after Reconstruction* (1977; reprint, Lawrence: University Press of Kansas, 1986).

Massacre at Plymouth
April 20, 1864

8

WEYMOUTH T. JORDAN JR. AND GERALD W. THOMAS

On the morning of Wednesday, April 20, 1864, the Federal post at Plymouth, North Carolina, commanded by Brig. Gen. Henry W. Wessells, was captured after a four-day siege by a Confederate force under Brig. Gen. Robert F. Hoke. Included among Plymouth's 3,244 defenders (2,834 army and approximately 410 naval personnel) were 80 or so black recruits awaiting assignment to their units, 10 black cooks serving in white regiments, 111 black sailors serving on gunboats, and 166 "Buffaloes" (white North Carolina Unionists) belonging to Companies B and E of the 2d Regiment North Carolina Infantry. In addition, perhaps 1,000 "contrabands" (fugitive slaves) of both sexes and all ages had sought refuge within the town's works.[1] White noncombatants (local citizens and the families of Northern officers and Buffalo soldiers) numbered about 300. Altogether, the military and civilian population of Plymouth was approximately 4,544.

During the days and weeks following the Battle of Plymouth and indeed for the next half century, accounts affirming or denying the murder of captured Buffaloes and blacks proliferated. Some writers alleged a massacre of hundreds of prisoners, others categorically denied atrocity charges, and still others who seemingly had no reason to conceal the truth ignored the subject altogether. Modern historians have similarly disagreed. In *War of Another Kind,* a study of the Civil War in Washington County (of which Plymouth is the seat), Wayne K. Durrill posits the murder of "roughly six hundred U.S. soldiers, most of them black," a figure that would make Plymouth the scene of the largest white-on-black massacre of the war. James M. McPherson also endorses the massacre allegations in his award-winning *Battle Cry of Freedom: The Civil War Era,* quoting the affidavit of a black sergeant named Samuel Johnson who claimed to have seen black prisoners shot, hanged, and bludgeoned. At the opposite extreme, Richard W. Iobst and Louis H. Manarin, in *The Bloody Sixth: The Sixth North Carolina Regiment Confederate States of America,* dismiss Johnson's charge as the "biased opinion of someone with a vivid imagination," and William R. Trotter concludes in a three-page appendix to his *Ironclads and Columbiads: The Civil War in North Carolina, the Coast* that "the preponderance of evidence indicates that this massacre never took place."[2] Surprisingly, three leading authorities on the black experience during the Civil War, Joseph T. Glatthaar, Dudley Taylor Cornish, and Benjamin Quarles (as well as McPherson, in *The Negro's Civil War,* which antedates *Battle Cry of Freedom*), do not mention the subject at all.[3]

The range of opinion and nonopinion among this group of historians may reflect in some cases the secondary importance of the events at Plymouth to the focus of their studies. However, it demonstrates also, particularly with regard to Glatthaar, Cornish, and Quarles, the disputed, contradictory, and inconclusive nature of the evidence. This essay presents and attempts to analyze a larger body of Plymouth massacre evidence than has been brought together previously. That evidence includes military reports, orders, telegrams, and service records, contemporary letters and diaries, regimental records and histories, Federal gunboat logs, prisoner-of-war records, newspaper accounts, reminiscences, and Federal pension applications. The presentation of evidence is preceded by a brief but relatively detailed account of the battle emphasizing the intensity of the fighting, casualties, and surrender negotiations. The authors' focus is upon the following questions: How many of the blacks and Buffaloes at Plymouth, civilians as well as soldiers and sailors, can and cannot be accounted for? Did any escape or attempt to escape before or after Wessells's capitulation? Did any who were captured survive? What was Confederate policy toward black and Southern Unionist prisoners? What was the record of Hoke's command in dealing with such captives? Were there any events during or after the battle that might have provoked a slaughter? Were the circumstances of the Federal surrender or the negotiations that preceded it in any way a factor? How credible and convincing is the evidence that a massacre did or did not take place? And, finally, was there a massacre?

Situated in swampy terrain on the Roanoke River near its Albemarle Sound estuary, Plymouth, with an 1860 population of 409 whites, 401 slaves, and 62 free blacks, was a prewar center for the production of tar, pitch, turpentine, and lumber. The town was occupied in May 1862 by a Federal naval force under Lt. Charles Williamson Flusser and was garrisoned a few weeks later by troops belonging to the command of Maj. Gen. Ambrose E. Burnside. Along with Washington (also known to North Carolinians as "Little Washington"), Beaufort, Morehead City, and Roanoke Island, all of which were captured in the late winter and spring of 1862, Plymouth served as an outpost to the main Federal base at New Bern. Possession of Plymouth enabled the Federals to limit Confederate access to an important breadbasket and naval stores region, close the lower Roanoke, and control the western end of Albemarle Sound. It also established a Federal presence in a region of highly mixed loyalties, providing encouragement and protection to Unionists and a refuge for runaway slaves whose labor was sorely needed by the manpower-short Confederacy.

During the two years following their conquests in eastern North Carolina, the Federals conducted large-scale raids as far west as Goldsboro and Hamilton. Small battles in which the Confederates achieved an occasional success were fought at Kinston, White Hall, Gum Swamp, and elsewhere. However, Confederate attempts to challenge Federal dominance—most notably at Plymouth in December 1862, at New Bern and Washington in March and April 1863, and at New Bern in January and February 1864—ended in failure. In the meantime, irregular units from both sides roamed the country, contributing to the widespread destruction, introducing elements of terror and vendetta and forcing hundreds of civilians to flee their homes.[4] At Plymouth, which had suffered severe damage and partial depopulation, the Federals constructed an impressive network of fortifications, attempted to maintain their combat readiness with infantry drills and artillery practice, and conducted numerous "Chicken & Turkey Raids" into what they facetiously referred to as "almost Loyal N.C."[5] During their off-duty hours, the men devoted themselves to the comforts of garrison life and fraternized with what remained of the local citizenry. Two months before Hoke attacked, Pvt. Warren Lee Goss of the 2d Regiment Massachusetts Heavy Artillery portrayed Plymouth as a fire-scarred

> remnant of what had once been quite a thriving village. . . . [T]he town consisted of a few tumbledown houses that had escaped the flames, two or three brick stores and houses, . . . a medley of negro shanties . . . and a number of rude frame buildings, made for government use. . . .
>
> The place was a general rendezvous for fugitive negroes, who came into our lines by families, while escaping from conscription [impressment] or persecution, and for rebel deserters, who had become lean, hungry, ragged, and dissatisfied with fighting against the Union. Schools had been established for the young and middle-aged colored population. . . . The whole place had a Rip Van Winkle look, as though it had composed itself into a long sleep to awake after the era of revolution and rebellion had passed.[6]

By the spring of 1864, North Carolina, which for two years had been of only sporadic interest to Confederate and Federal officialdom, was in danger of disappearing as a consideration altogether. Gov. Zebulon B. Vance's complaints to the Davis administration of neglect and abuse of authority produced little response, and on the Federal side, a gradual reduction of forces was concluding.[7] The latter process, which was not combined with an attempt to consolidate the Federals' remaining strength, afforded the Confederates an opportunity to gain military superiority at selected points and recover lost ground. Gen. Robert E. Lee, commander of the Army of Northern Virginia, had in fact provided troops for Maj. Gen. George E. Pickett's attack on New Bern in January, but faulty strategy and a subordinate's bungling had negated Pickett's manpower advantage. After easing Pickett out of the picture, Lee decided to give the aggressive young Hoke a chance at the Federals.[8] However, North Carolina operations would be possible only as long as the war's winter hibernation in Virginia continued. With the coming of spring, Lee would have to recall his men.

While Hoke prepared for a new effort in eastern North Carolina, Lt. Gen. Ulysses S. Grant, the recently appointed Federal general-in-chief, made plans for a spring offensive to crush the bloodied but still defiant Confederacy. At the Wilderness, northeast of Richmond, Maj. Gen. George G. Meade's Army of the Potomac would assault and attempt to destroy the Army of Northern Virginia. Southeast of Richmond, on the James River, Maj. Gen. Benjamin F. Butler's Army of the James would land at Bermuda Hundred and cut the Confederate capital's vital railroad communications. In the west, Maj. Gen. William T. Sherman would move south from Chattanooga toward Atlanta. At the same time, Maj. Gen. Franz Sigel would advance up the Shenandoah Valley, and Maj. Gen. Nathaniel P. Banks would attack Mobile. As for North Carolina, Plymouth and Washington, in Grant's opinion, should be abandoned and the troops defending them transferred to Butler. Butler's prospects for success at Bermuda Hundred would be enhanced, and if Butler were victorious, the two North Carolina towns, for whatever they were worth, would fall into Federal hands "naturally."[9] Unfortunately for General Wessells and his men, Grant's recommendation had not been acted upon when Hoke attacked on the morning of April 17.

Although outnumbered by a margin of better than two-to-one, the Plymouth garrison was well supplied, trained, armed, led, and fortified. West of the town, a line of entrenchments, reinforced by two redoubts, stretched southward from a swamp near the river to a point just beyond Plymouth's southwestern limits. There, it made a right angle and extended eastward, before terminating below the town's southeastern corner. In the middle of that east-west segment, guarding the Lee's Mill Road coming up from the south, was Fort Williams, the most formidable of the Federal works. Marshy terrain east of Plymouth seemingly made a Confederate attack from that direction impracticable, except via the Columbia Road, which was defended by Fort Comfort and the Conaby Redoubt. Fort Wessells, situated a short distance west of the southwest corner of the Federal line, covered the Washington Road and, because of its detached position, was vulnerable. Ditches, palisades, and abatis (barricades of felled trees) protected most of the Federal fortifications. About one mile above Plymouth, on the Roanoke, was Fort Gray, whose function was to prevent the passage of Confederate gunboats, particularly an ironclad ram reportedly under construction near Hamilton. As further insurance against the ironclad, which was believed in some Federal circles to be a myth, five unarmored gunboats were on patrol, the river was partially blockaded by pilings, chains, "torpedoes [mines]," and sunken hulks, and a massive 200-pounder Parrott gun was in place at Battery Worth on Plymouth's waterfront. Control of the Roanoke was critical for the Federals: The gunboats were an integral part of their defenses, especially on the weakly fortified eastern side of town, where the forts were open on the river side. The Roanoke was also the only route by which the garrison could receive reinforcements or, if necessary, escape.[10]

For his assault on Plymouth on the morning of April 17, 1864, Hoke marshaled about seven thousand men comprising three infantry brigades, a cavalry regiment, and three artillery battalions. The infantry brigades were commanded by Brig. Gen. Matt W. Ransom (8th, 24th, 25th, 35th, and 56th Regiments North Carolina Troops); Col. John T. Mercer (6th, 21st, and 43d Regiments North Carolina Troops and 21st Regiment Georgia Infantry); and Col. William R. Terry (1st, 3d, 7th, 11th, and 24th Regiments Virginia Infantry). Hoke's cavalry consisted of the 8th Regiment Confederate Cavalry, a mixed unit of North Carolinians and Virginians under Col. James Dearing. Lt. Col. Henry T. Guion and Majs. Edgar Fearn Moseley and John Postell Williamson Read commanded the artillery contingent of approximately thirty-five guns. In addition, Hoke was counting upon the assistance of the ironclad ram *Albemarle*, which, contrary to Federal skeptics, was nearing completion forty miles upriver at Edwards's Ferry.

Wessells's 2,834-man land force consisted, according to a "return of casualties" published in the *Official Records (Army),* of the 16th Regiment Connecticut Infantry (463 men), the 85th Regiment New York Infantry (544), 101st Regiment Pennsylvania Infantry (409), 103d Regiment Pennsylvania Infantry (485), Companies B and E of the 2d Regiment North Carolina Infantry (166), Companies A and F of the 12th Regiment New York Cavalry (121), Companies G and H of the 2d Regiment Massachusetts Heavy Artillery (269), the 24th New York Battery (122), "unattached recruits" (245), and 10 staff officers.[11] The gunboats *Southfield, Miami, Whitehead,* and *Ceres* carried crews of 139, 137, 53, and 45 men, respectively; the crews of the army gunboat *Bombshell* and the steam launch *Dolly* probably numbered about 20 and 16 men each.[12]

Hoke's small army advanced east from Tarboro at ten o'clock on the morning of April 15, passed through Williamston on the sixteenth, and reached Foster's Mill, on Sweetwater Creek about fifteen miles west of Plymouth, later that day. At 5:00 AM on the seventeenth, Hoke's men crossed the creek on a pontoon bridge and moved down the Jamesville Road to within about five miles of Plymouth. There, Terry's brigade, most of Dearing's cavalry, and several batteries were detached to invest Fort Gray, where "very brisk" firing broke out and continued until 10:00 PM.[13] Meantime, Mercer's and Ransom's brigades and some of Dearing's troopers advanced to the junction of the Jamesville and Washington Roads, capturing most of Wessells's pickets. Mercer then deployed his troops astride the Washington Road, with Ransom on his right, and at about 5:00 PM, Confederate artillery opened fire. "[J]ust as our regiment had marched out . . . to the parade ground for dress parade," Pvt. George N. Lamphere of the 16th Connecticut recalled,

> a shot from a field gun . . . struck fairly in our midst. . . . Such a scampering as there was for camp, white gloves and dress coats doffed and fatigue dress donned in a twinkling. A strong skirmish force was at once sent out to reconnoitre. I was in it. We went out in front, across the esplanade to the edge of the timber, and a little beyond . . . [but were soon] compelled . . . to fall back. We held out stubbornly, dodging behind stumps and logs and firing at the enemy. . . . Within a couple of hours all our skirmishers and pickets had been driven in.[14]

Heavy skirmishing broke out in the vicinity of Fort Williams and continued until dawn. According to Commissary Sgt. Nathan Lanpheur of the 85th New York, the night was one of "great comotion." The families of officers and Buffaloes, as well as a few wounded men, were evacuated to Roanoke Island by the steamer *Massasoit,* and the garrison remained on a high state of alert. "[A]ll were on the lookout," Lanpheur recalled, "as it seemed sure now that we were surrounded."[15]

With the coming of daylight on April 18, Federal gunboats and artillery opened fire on suspected Confederate positions and, in the words of Capt.

Ira B. Sampson of the 2d Massachusetts Heavy Artillery, "woke up a Tartar." Hoke replied with a thunderous barrage and an attack on Fort Gray by two companies of the 11th Virginia. After floundering across a "nearly impenetrable" swamp "200 to 300" yards wide and "2 to 4 feet deep," the Virginians stumbled into a "terrible" storm of grapeshot, canister, and small arms fire. "The sad havoc in the ranks was quickly discerned," Pvt. Edward Cook Barnes of the 11th wrote, "and . . . having discovered how formidable the fort [was] and [how] impossible to take by assault . . . our boys were ordered back across that dreaded swamp, wet & shivering with cold . . . having lost severely."[16] During the fighting, the Richmond Fayette Artillery scored several hits on the *Bombshell* and *Dolly,* which was carrying ammunition to Fort Gray. The *Dolly* completed her mission and escaped, but the *Bombshell* staggered back to Plymouth and sank at her dock.[17]

At noon, the Confederates unleashed a concentrated, six-hour bombardment of Fort Wessells, defended by a sixty-nine-man garrison commanded by Capt. Nelson Chapin of the 85th New York. Fort Williams and the town also were subjected to a heavy barrage. Around 6:00 PM, Ransom's men poured out of the woods "in swarms" and made a diversionary "rush" upon Fort Williams, whose covering fire, along with that of Fort Gray and the Federal gunboats, was interfering with Hoke's attempts to subdue Chapin. Shortly thereafter, Mercer's troops, "yelling like so many wild beast[s]" and "nearly hidden in the obscurity of the night," charged Fort Wessells. "[O]ver the works they went," Nathan Lanpheur wrote, "but . . . [our] gallant men repelled . . . every attack with the point of bayonet [and] hand grenades."[18] Unfortunately for Chapin and his troops, the gunboats, unable to determine the range in the increasing darkness, then began firing accidentally into the fort, threatening "every minute" to blow up its magazine.[19] At that point, the course of events becomes uncertain. According to Pvt. Hodijah L. Meade of the 38th Virginia Light Artillery, the defenders of Fort Wessells "cried out that they surrendered, but the noise was so great and the Gun boats still kept up their fire, so it was unheeded and they had to take up arms again in self defence." However, General Wessells and Lt. Lucien A. Butts of the 85th New York (who took command of Fort Wessells after Captain Chapin was mortally wounded) do not mention such an episode in their battle reports dated August 18, 1864, and April 1, 1865, respectively. Wessells stated that the fort surrendered "under a threat of no quarter"; Butts says only that he capitulated in response to Confederate demands when further resistance became hopeless.[20] In any case, it is certain that, at about 11:00 PM, Butts and his men laid down their arms.

Throughout the night of April 18, a "screaming, hissing" "rain of shells"—described by Maj. John W. Graham of the 56th North Carolina as "the heaviest dose of Iron I ever took"—roared through the moonlit skies of Plymouth. "The sight was magnificent," a reporter for the *Daily Richmond Examiner* wrote, "the . . . shell[s] meeting and passing each other through the sulphurous air, appeared as blazing comets with their burning fuses, and would burst with frightful noise, scattering their fragments as thick as hail." Cpl. Samuel J. Gibson of the 103d Pennsylvania, who was huddled in a bombproof and in no position to appreciate the beauty of the occasion, described the experience as "a night of terror."[21]

Meantime, on the evening of the seventeenth, the *Albemarle,* accompanied by the steamer *Cotton Plant,* started down the Roanoke. Engine failure and a broken rudder brought the ungainly vessel to halts of six and four hours on the evening of the seventeenth and the morning of the eighteenth, but at 10:00 PM on the eighteenth, she dropped anchor three miles above Plymouth. There, she was stymied by torpedoes and underwater obstructions until, around 1:00 AM, a boating party sent out to sound the river brought word that the water was high enough to permit her passage.[22] Shortly thereafter, the *Albemarle* steamed in front of the guns of Fort Gray. Alerted to the vessel's approach by a plume of smoke, Capt. Joseph E. Fiske was ready with a flurry of shot and shell. Unfortunately for the Federals, Fiske's best efforts—including a direct hit from a 100-pound shell when the *Albemarle* "was not three hundred feet away"—were totally ineffective.[23] "Down she came," Fiske wrote, "without making a single hostile demonstration, relentless as fate, utterly disregardless of anything we could do, while we in frantic rage fired our muskets and even pistols at her. So near was she that we could hear the orders given to the steersman in a repressed tone. She was the embodiment of fate, the very essence of nightmare."[24] After passing Battery Worth without drawing fire, the *Albemarle* rammed and sank the *Southfield* and drove off the *Miami,* which fled downriver with the *Whitehead* and *Ceres.* Capt. James W. Cooke, the *Albemarle*'s commander, then requested instructions from a jubilant Hoke, who ordered him to open fire on Plymouth.

Under a "galling cross fire" from Hoke's artillery and the *Albemarle,* which "threw sollid shot and shell all over the town," most of the Federals spent April 19 in their bombproofs.[25] "[T]he Rebs are before us, behind us & on each side of us," Corporal Gibson wrote. "[W]e will die 'game' . . . [but] we are 'gone up' unless we get reinforcement."[26] During the afternoon, Ransom's brigade was ordered to move east of the town to the Columbia Road and prepare to attack the next morning. Darkness brought an all-night exchange of fire between the *Albemarle* and one of the Federals' 100-pounders. The Confederate infantrymen lay down in line of battle and, according to Pvt. James Carson Elliott of the 56th North Carolina, "got a good night's sleep."[27]

"At daybreak [on the twentieth]," Major Graham wrote,

> nearly chilled with cold, we [Ransom's brigade] are . . . aroused to make the charge. At first we start in quick time, the gunboat steaming up on our right. Soon it becomes double quick, and "yells" break from the whole line, which are answered by Hoke's [Mercer's] Brigade, on [the] other side. Our Reg't is now charged by a drove of Cattle, but we succeed in flanking them, and soon cross a ditch six feet deep, and a fence on the other side, then into a marsh in some places waist deep, and impassable for our right, which has to be withdrawn, and carried through by a flank.[28]

Emerging from the swamp, "One in a gang and two by themselves," Ransom's men paused briefly to rally and reorganize around their regimental flags. Then, leaving the 8th and 35th and part of the 24th North Carolina to deal with Fort Comfort, the remainder of the brigade charged into Plymouth, precipitating a "most terrific street fight" with Federal infantry firing from windows and doors and from behind barricades. Overpowered, the Federals fled from the "houses, cellars, and bombproofs," in the words of Major Graham, "like a colony of prairie puppies, or ground hogs on the 2d of February."[29] "[N]othing could check our progress," wrote "Lone Star," a pseudonymous member of Ransom's brigade, in a letter to a Raleigh newspaper,

> and in an hour the enemy were all driven into Fort William[s] or the entrenched camp [on Plymouth's western outskirts]. . . . [We then] pushed on for the camp, which the 24th [North Carolina], being on the direct road, soon reached, and opened fire, exposed still to a severe musketry fire from the fort on the flank and the camp in front. In a few minutes the 56th came up on the right by another street, and by their arrival decided the contest, for immediately on the appearance of this additional force, the enemy [in the camp] threw down his arms.[30]

Joined by the 43d North Carolina of Mercer's brigade, Ransom's men turned their attention to Fort Williams, where an unauthorized, headlong charge by the 8th North Carolina into the teeth of Federal cannon was repulsed with severe casualties. Hoke then demanded the fort's surrender, whereupon Wessells emerged for a parley. The formalities of a "hasty introduction" having been observed, Hoke complimented Wessells on his "highly honorable" defense, pointed out the "untenable" nature of the Federal position, and demanded an unconditional surrender.[31] According to Lt. Leonidas L. Polk of the 43d North Carolina, one of several witnesses to the scene, Wessells "protested" that he could not capitulate "with honor" without the approval of his government, which otherwise "would not overlook the fact that he had surrendered a force and strong garrison without damage."[32] Hoke replied "with a tone of sarcasm," Polk wrote, "that, if to be *damaged* was what he desired, he could readily be gratified, but that the dictates of humanity and discretion alike demanded that he should spare further effusion of blood, or loss of life, but intimated to him in plain terms, that if we were compelled to assault the fort, which was now completely surrounded, the responsibility of the terrible consequences must rest on his head." That threat, which Wessells interpreted as an "intimat[ion]" of "indiscriminate slaughter," was noted also by Lt. Col. Henry T. Guion of the North Carolina artillery battalion, who was present during the conversation. According to Guion, Hoke informed Wessells that "he had him invested . . . and if he [Hoke] lost any men in charging the works he would not be responsible for [the] consequences."[33]

At that point in the "interview," according to an unidentified civilian observer, "our boat fired a shot into the fort, when the garrison hauled down their flag. Wessel said it was against his order; that he did not surrender."[34] Hoke then granted Wessells a few minutes to reconsider his decision, pointedly turning as he did so to order Graham's battery to a hillock from which it could fire at point-blank range. Wessells rejoined his men. At about the same time, the *Albemarle* moved into position in "full view" of the fort, and, Polk recalled, "every man . . . clunched his gun with excitement and determination. The long, anxious moments of suspense having expired," the *Albemarle* and "about 20 pieces of field artillery" opened a "furious" cross fire.[35] "This terrible fire had to be endured without reply," General Wessells wrote,

> as no man could live at the guns. The breast-height was struck by solid shot on every side, fragments of shells sought almost every interior angle of the work, the whole extent of the parapet was swept by musketry, and men were killed and wounded even on the banquette slope. . . . This condition of affairs could not be long endured without a reckless sacrifice of life; no relief could be expected, and in compliance with the earnest desire of every officer I consented to hoist a white flag, and at 10 A.M. of April 20 I had the mortification of surrendering my post to the enemy with all it contained.[36]

"[T]he 'Stars and Stripes' began to desend from their defiant position," Lieutenant Polk wrote, and the white flag began rapidly to ascend.... Then one long, wild, prolonged shout, went up from our army, and never was a flag of truce more eagerly and heartily greeted during the war. The door to the fort was thrown open, and the "Rebs" rushed in to see the spoils of their capture.... [The] men and officers [who] were packed in the fort . . . were soon relieved of their arms and accouterments and marched out. Guns, wagons and teams, forage, supplies, ordnance stores, and sutlers' stores, all fell into our hands, and never were the spoils more speedily divided and more earnestly enjoyed.[37]

Wessells's capitulation did not put an immediate end to Federal resistance. Elements of the 16th Connecticut, according to regimental Surgeon Nathan Mayer, lay down their arms some time after Fort Williams was captured. A company of the 85th New York that arrived at Fort Williams as the white flag was raised "attempted to return to its works" to the right of the fort and had to be "cut . . . off" and compelled to surrender. Other Federals to the right of Fort Williams, probably including blacks and Buffaloes (all of whom were stationed on that part of the line), continued to fire from their earthworks and "from houses, trees, and rooftops" until shelled into submission.[38] Fort Gray held out even longer, surrendering several hours later on orders from Wessells.[39]

Casualties in Hoke's command were heavy. No figures were published in the *Official Records,* but service record information from *North Carolina Troops, 1861–1865: A Roster* and the National Archives' Compiled Service Records, together with reports by regimental surgeons and brigade-level officers published in the *Raleigh Daily Confederate,* indicate that Ransom's brigade lost 96 men killed or mortally wounded and 377 wounded. The same sources, supplemented by the *Roster of the Confederate Soldiers of Georgia: 1861–1865* to cover casualties in the 21st Georgia, indicate that Mercer's brigade lost 48 men killed or mortally wounded and 100 wounded.[40] Losses in Terry's brigade were at least 7 men killed and 25 wounded.[41] Hoke's artillery units lost at least 2 men killed and 27 wounded; losses among Dearing's cavalrymen are unknown but probably numbered about 10 killed and 25 wounded.[42] Confederate casualties were thus about 163 men killed and 554 wounded, or roughly 10 percent of Hoke's force.[43]

The number of Federal dead and wounded at the Battle of Plymouth has never been determined; however, Wessells's men were fighting from behind cover or were under the shelter of bombproofs during most of the engagement, and by all accounts, including those of Confederate origin, their casualties were light or moderate. In his official report, Wessells stated that Federal losses "did not exceed 150" men; Surgeon Mayer of the 16th Connecticut put the figure at 125; Lt. George S. Hastings of the 24th New York Battery stated that "Our losses in killed and wounded were over 180"; and Lt. Bernard F. Blakeslee of the 16th Connecticut estimated "fifteen killed and about one hundred wounded."[44] As to the number of Federal prisoners, no official reports are extant, but numerous round-number estimates survive. Surgeon Mayer and Col. John Taylor Wood (President Jefferson Davis's aide-de-camp and personal observer at Plymouth) estimated 2,500; Lt. Leonidas L. Polk of the 43d North Carolina, 2,600; Sgt. John K. Walker of the 6th North Carolina, "over 2200"; Pvt. George W. Love of the 56th North Carolina, 2,400; and two unidentified eyewitnesses whose reports were published in the *Petersburg Daily Express,* 2,300 and 2,500.[45] The most accurate contemporary figures, if specificity is any indication, are 2,257, cited in a letter by Pvt. Josiah Worrell of the 24th Virginia; 2,437, quoted in the *Raleigh Daily Confederate;* 2,480, cited in a letter by Maj. John W. Broadnax, commissary of Ransom's brigade; and 2,390, cited in the diary of Cushing Biggs Hassell, a Baptist minister residing just upriver from Plymouth at Williamston. Hassell came out to see the Federal prisoners when they were marched past his home on April 23 and presumably got his figure from a Confederate officer.[46]

The surrender of Plymouth was followed, as Polk's account suggests, by a looting of the battered town.[47] That "operation" was not exclusively military. After Wessells surrendered, "there was heard one of those indescribable Confederate yells," Cpl. Charles Theodore Loehr of the 1st Virginia Infantry recalled,

> and the regiments were ordered to stack arms, after which the men were informed by General Hoke that they might help themselves to whatever might please their fancy except the horses and wagons. While the men rushed into town, I was left with a detail to guard the main road . . . and prevent . . . outsiders to enter. It only took about ten minutes, and the crowd I held grew in such proportion, I sent word that I was unable with my few men to hold my position, whereupon instruction came calling my guard in, and permitting the crowds that had gathered to rush into the town.

Civilian as well as military property was fair game, and little effort was made to distinguish between that of Confederate and Federal sympathizers.[48] "The men went into the fine residences (from which . . . [the] inmates had departed but two days previous)," Corporal Loehr continued, "cut open the bedding, broke the costly mirrors to get a piece of looking glass, ripped the strings out of the pianos to hang their tin cups on; [and] loaded themselves with female wearing apparel."[49] Three white citizens were reportedly killed while attempting to defend their homes or other possessions.[50] Although Hoke's men clearly were more interested in booty than mayhem, for a time they were not under the control of their officers. That fact, together with the general excitement and confusion, the presence of numerous civilians of uncertain attitudes toward blacks and loyalists, Hoke's intimations of giving no quarter during the surrender negotiations, and the anger that would naturally arise as it became evident that Confederate losses greatly exceeded those of their opponents, suggests that circumstances conducive to the murder of prisoners were extant.

Before examining the fate of the blacks and Buffaloes at Plymouth, it is necessary to discuss briefly the Confederate government's policy toward black prisoners, the white officers who commanded them, and white Southerners captured in Federal uniform. A brief examination will be made also of the treatment accorded to such prisoners by Hoke's units on other battlefields. Clearly, Confederate policies and attitudes, not to mention events that occurred elsewhere, cannot prove or disprove a massacre at Plymouth. Nevertheless, they provide a background and establish patterns of conduct that, in a complex episode characterized by incomplete evidence and vague, contradictory, exaggerated, and sometimes dubious eyewitness testimony, seem essential to arriving at the truth.

Presumably because of the danger of Federal retaliation against Confederate prisoners from border states such as Maryland or rebellious states such as Tennessee that furnished large numbers of men to both sides, no official Confederate policy discriminating against Southern Unionist prisoners was established. "Homemade Yankees" were objects of contempt and hatred and sometimes received short shrift in combat, but they were not officially guilty of treason. Aside from the standard prohibitions against giving aid and comfort to the enemy, treason necessitated desertion from the Confederate military and enlistment in the armed forces of the Union. Because desertion was itself a capital offense, a charge of treason was significant for only two reasons: first, unlike traitors, deserters (including repeat offenders) generally escaped with their necks; and second, deserters, if executed, were put before a firing squad, whereas traitors, to emphasize the heinous nature of their crime, could expect to meet their doom at the end of a rope.[51] Such was the unhappy lot of 22 Confederate deserters who were captured in enemy uniform near New Bern on February 1, 1864: all were court-martialed and hanged at Kinston before the end of the month. The fate of those men was well known to the 166 Buffaloes at Plymouth, at least 35 of whom were themselves deserters and all of whom, like the Kinston victims, were members of the 2d North Carolina Infantry.[52]

Confederate policy regarding black prisoners and the white officers who commanded them was harsh also. On August 21, 1862, after Federal generals David Hunter and John W. Phelps, acting on their own initiative, began raising black units in South Carolina and Louisiana, Confederate Adj. Gen. Samuel Cooper issued General Order No. 60 denouncing Hunter and Phelps as "outlaws." "[I]n the event of the capture of either of them," Cooper stated, "or . . . of any other commissioned officer employed in drilling, organizing, or instructing slaves, with a view to their armed service . . . he shall not be regarded as a prisoner of war, but held in close confinement for execution as a felon at such time and place as the President shall order."[53] On October 13, 1862, the Confederate Congress, anticipating the Lincoln administration's plans to begin large-scale recruitment of black troops, passed legislation mandating that any "slave[s]" captured from the enemy be sent to special depots to be established in each Confederate state. There they would be "employed under proper guard on public works" until reclaimed by their masters.[54] That law remained a dead letter, presumably because relatively few black units had been organized, until March 6, 1863, when Cooper issued General Order No. 25 directing that the authorized depots be established at nineteen localities throughout the Confederacy, including Raleigh. Meantime, President Davis, in a message to Congress on January 12, 1863, announced that, henceforth, white officers captured while commanding blacks would be "deliver[ed] to . . . State authorities" to be "dealt with in accordance with the laws of those States providing for the punishment of criminals engaged in exciting servile insurrection."[55] That procedure, however, was insufficiently rigorous for the iron-fisted Confederate Congress, which on May 1 approved a joint resolution asserting that white officers captured while commanding blacks "ought" to be "put to death or be otherwise punished" by a "military court." On that draconian but prudently advisory and uncodified note, the matter rested.[56]

It is evident that official Confederate policy toward black soldiers and their white officers as prisoners was characterized by a greater degree of animosity and severity toward the whites, who were considered criminals, than the blacks, who possessed a degree of immunity by virtue of their status as property. That preference was decidedly reversed on the battlefield, where Confederate soldiers demonstrated their anathema for uniformed blacks in murderous episodes at Fort Pillow, Tennessee; Fort Wagner, South Carolina; Milliken's Bend, Louisiana; Poison Springs, Arkansas; Saltville, Virginia; Suffolk, Virginia; and the Crater, near Petersburg, Virginia. Each of those incidents transcended the norms of combat to some degree, and all have been categorized, contemporaneously and subsequently, by terms such as "massacre," "atrocity," "butchery," and "slaughter." The Fort Pillow episode, in which Confederate forces under the command of Maj. Gen. Nathan Bedford Forrest denied quarter to several hundred black troops who were endeavoring to surrender, begging for mercy, attempting to hide, playing dead, or fleeing the wrath of the Confederates, did not involve any of Hoke's units. However, it is relevant here because it occurred only eight days before the capture of Plymouth, was a matter of common knowledge in North Carolina, and could have provided a "model" for Confederates of comparable inclinations. It is relevant also because, as the most famous, most spectacular, best documented, and probably the largest white-on-black massacre of the Civil War, it obscured the events at Plymouth both contemporaneously and, it seems likely, for all time.[57]

Suffolk and the Crater are of even greater pertinence than Fort Pillow because the involvement of Ransom's brigade sheds light on that unit's attitude toward uniformed blacks. At Suffolk, on March 9, 1864, Ransom's men captured the camp of a contingent of black cavalrymen belonging to the 2d Regiment U.S. Colored Cavalry. Mayhem ensued. "We did not take any prisoners," an unidentified member of Ransom's brigade wrote:

> Officers and men were perfectly enthusiastic in *killing* the "d——d rascals," as I heard many call them. Supposing that our force was a small one, ten negroes under a white officer, were placed in a house on the further extremity of town for the purpose of picking off our officers. When our line was formed near them to charge the Yanks they fired constantly upon us, killing two, and wounding some. They fought with desperation, seeing the hopelessness of their situation. A few minutes elapsed and the torch was applied to the dwelling. Soon the fire and smoke had its effect— suffocation commenced—one of the infernals leaped from the window to escape the horrible death of burning, a minute more and a dozen bayonets pierced his body; another, and another followed, and shared the same fate. Three stayed and met their doom with manly resolution. They were burned to cinders. After the flames had enveloped the house, and immense clouds of smoke were issuing from . . . within, the crack of a rifle was heard above, and one of the artillery men fell severely wounded in the knee. This was the last fire from the house. Soon it fell and all was ashes. . . .
>
> Ransom's brigade never takes any negro prisoners. Our soldiers would not even bury the Negroes—they were buried by negroes. If any of us should be captured by them, our fate would be hard.[58]

One of Ransom's officers, Maj. John W. Graham of the 56th North Carolina, wrote to his father on March 13, 1864, that the "ladies . . . [of Suffolk] were standing at their doors, some waving handkerchiefs, some crying, some praying, and others calling to us to 'kill the negroes.' (Our Brigade did not need this to make them give 'no quarter,' as it is understood amongst us that we take no negro prisoners.)" Another member of Ransom's brigade, Pvt. Gabriel P. Sherrill of the 49th North Carolina, wrote on March 17 that "wee head a rite prety litel time in suffolk to see the negroes run[.] the negroes wont fite if they have eny chance to run but they will fite if they aire hemed sow that they cant run[.] then they will fite for they know that it is deth eny way if we got hold of them for wee have no quarters for a negroe."[59]

On July 30, 1864, following the explosion of a huge gunpowder mine beneath Confederate lines near Petersburg, black troops belonging to Brig. Gen. Edward Ferrero's division—some of whom advanced with cries of "Remember Fort Pillow" and "No quarter to the rebels"—swarmed into the resulting "crater." There a large number became trapped. Confederate counterattackers, led by a Virginia brigade but including the 25th North Carolina of Ransom's brigade, charged to the brink of the pit and, according to Pvt. William A. Day of the 49th North Carolina,

> fired one volley into the surging mass [of black soldiers], then turned the butts of their guns and jumped in among them. How the negroe's skulls cracked under the blows. Some of them ran over on our side and started for the rear, while others made a dash for their own lines. . . . I, boy like, ran up the line to see them. When I got there they had the ground covered with broken headed negroes, and were searching about among the bomb proofs for more, the officers were trying to stop them but they kept on until they finished up.[60]

According to Day, Mahone's men and the 25th North Carolina "spared the white men as best they could, but negro skulls cracked under the blows like eggshells. They begged pitifully for their lives, but the answer was: 'No quarter this morning, no quarter now.'" "Well had our brave boys taken revenge," Capt. Henry A. Chambers of the 49th North Carolina wrote, "for the unmerciful conduct of the enemy in the morning. Little quarter had in turn been shown those who when flushed with temporary success had cried, 'No quarter to the rebels.'"[61] Ferrero's casualties, the majority of which were sustained during legitimate combat, exceeded 1,300 men out of about 4,300 engaged.

How many black soldiers were in the Plymouth garrison? No black units, it should be emphasized, were present; however, three white officers, Capt. Hiram Leonard Marvin of the 37th Regiment U.S. Colored Troops (3d Regiment North Carolina Colored Troops), Lt. Richard Bascombe of the 38th Regiment U.S. Colored Troops, and Lt. George W. French of the 2d Regiment U.S. Colored Cavalry, were recruiting at Plymouth. There is no evidence that Bascombe, whose appointment in the 38th dated from March 26, 1864, and who could have been at Plymouth for only a few weeks at most, had recruited any blacks by the time of Hoke's attack. However, blacks recruited by Marvin and French made up a portion of Wessells's 245 "unattached recruits," a group subsequently described by Surgeon William M. Smith of the 85th New York as "mostly colored." Marvin's recruiting return for March 1864 shows that on the last day of that month he had 41 recruits at Plymouth. Twenty-six years after the battle, Marvin corroborated that figure when he stated in a pension deposition for Pvt. John Ward, a member of his regiment, that at the time of the battle he had "about 40 [black] recruits" under his command.[62] Lieutenant French's recruiting return for March 1864 has not been located, and French did not survive the war; however, extant muster and descriptive rolls for the 2d Colored Cavalry show that on June 29, 1864, 13 blacks who had enlisted at Plymouth between January 10 and March 10 were mustered into service at Petersburg.[63] In view of the amount of time that elapsed between those men's enlistment and their muster-in dates, it seems likely that most of them were Plymouth escapees. However, their presence during the battle has not been documented.[64]

Several Federal soldiers who participated in the battle later confirmed that fewer than 100 black recruits were present when Hoke attacked. John A. Reed, a private in the 101st Pennsylvania who was serving as a recruiting officer and acting lieutenant in the 2d North Carolina Infantry, estimated that "about eighty colored recruits with a lieutenant in command" were on the right side of the defensive works (the western side of the town). Reed recalled that the recruits had been "armed and equipped" but had not yet joined their regiments. John Donaghy, a captain in the 103d Pennsylvania, stated that during the engagement "a company of colored soldiers"—presumably between about 60 and 90 men—was posted in the breastworks to the right of Fort Williams. Commissary Sgt. Nathan Lanpheur of the 85th New York recalled seeing "a few colored troops that had been enlisted for gen. [Edward A.] Wilds Brigade."[65] All that can be said with certainty is that Marvin had approximately 40 black recruits and that at least 10 black cooks serving in the 103d Pennsylvania, the 85th New York, and the 24th New York Battery were present. Assuming that French, like Marvin, had about 40 recruits, an estimate of 90 uniformed black recruits and cooks at Plymouth seems consistent with the evidence.[66]

If only 90 uniformed blacks were in the Plymouth garrison, how are the rest of the 245 "mostly colored" recruits to be accounted for? The answer is that they and at least a few able-bodied whites were recruited, willingly or otherwise, after the battle began.[67] The combat effectiveness of those black and white "volunteers," who were untrained and presumably not in uniform, seems dubious, but Wessells certainly would have been correct to count them as members of his garrison. The authors' guess is that the 245 "unattached recruits" consisted of approximately 145 blacks who volunteered or were dragooned for the defense of the town, 10 white recruits for the 2d North Carolina Infantry, 10 white civilians who took up arms, and the aforementioned 80 black recruits belonging to the 37th Colored Troops and 2d Colored Cavalry.[68]

One additional group of uniformed blacks may have been at risk during the Battle of Plymouth. The 139-man crew of the gunboat *Southfield* included 40 black seamen, coal heavers, stewards, and other ranks. Of that number, 2 were drowned when the *Southfield* sank, 1 died of wounds after being picked up by the *Albemarle*, 1 was killed ashore by Confederate pickets, 3 were captured, and 27 escaped, were rescued, or survived under uncertain circumstances. The fate of the remaining 6 is unknown.[69]

On the night of April 17, the steamer *Massasoit* departed for Roanoke Island, as stated above, carrying the wounded, the families of officers and Buffaloes, and other white civilians to safety. The next night, the *Massasoit* made a second trip to Roanoke Island with, according to the Rev. Horace James, superintendent of Negro affairs for North Carolina, "many ... [black] women and children."[70] The precise number of black and white evacuees is impossible to determine, but it is likely that on each trip the *Massasoit* carried about 300 women, children, and elderly men, a number that is consistent with the passenger capacity of the vessel.[71] Still another exodus occurred on the night of April 19, when "a considerable number" of Buffaloes "left their companies without authority," appropriated boats and canoes, and set off down the Roanoke. Some were picked up by Federal gunboats; others crossed Albemarle Sound and reached Roanoke Island, where Federal authorities were still trying to round them up weeks later. During the same night, Wessells "suggested" to Oliver R. McNary, acting superintendent of Negro affairs at Plymouth and one of Captain Marvin's recruiting assistants, that "our Negroes" (presumably civilians only) be sent across the river into the swamps. However, according to McNary, "A majority ... refused to leave."[72] Little is known about that small-boat evacuation other than that it occurred; however, based on McNary's statement and the fact that Buffaloes were appropriating boats for their own purposes, it seems unlikely that more than 100 blacks crossed the river. Thus, of the approximately 1,000 black civilians at Plymouth on the afternoon of April 17, a total of perhaps 400 had escaped or been evacuated by the morning of April 20.

How many blacks and Buffaloes were captured at Plymouth? No official figures regarding Buffaloes are extant; however, because those men, unlike the black recruits, had been formally assigned to their unit, the 2d North Carolina Infantry, the fate of nearly all of them can be determined. Suffice it to say at this juncture that, of the 166 Buffaloes present at Plymouth, at least 56 fell into Confederate hands. As to the number of black prisoners, Colonel Wood, President Davis's aide-de-camp, estimated "300 or 400"; 1st Sgt. John William Wynne of the 1st Virginia Infantry and Pvt. George Washington Love of the 56th North Carolina put the figure at 500 (of whom Love believed that "3 hundr[ed] . . . was soldiers"); Pvt. Nicholas Cloer of the 6th North Carolina guessed 600; and Major Graham of the 56th North Carolina and Sgt. Maj. David E. Johnston of the 7th Virginia estimated 700.[73] The *Raleigh Daily Confederate* reported that "about 600 negroes were taken— about 100 men, the balance women and children—not many men who were soldiers." According to another newspaper, 300 blacks—"a portion of . . . [whom were] women and children"—were captured. The *Wadesboro North Carolina Argus,* put the number of black prisoners at 400 but made no distinction between soldiers and civilians; and the *Fayetteville Weekly Intelligencer,* quoting a "gentleman who has just arrived from Plymouth," reported that "Between three and four hundred negro women and children, who had been taken from legal owners, were re-captured. . . . The men were either killed in battle, or made their way to the swamps and forrests. Many of the latter will no doubt be taken."[74] These figures vary so greatly that even approximate estimates are difficult to make; however, it seems safely conservative to suppose that approximately 400 blacks of all descriptions, civilians as well as soldiers, women and children as well as men, were made prisoner. Assuming that the black population of Plymouth on the morning of April 20 was approximately 871 (600 civilians, 90 uniformed recruits and cooks, 145 "volunteers," and 36 sailors) and that approximately 400 blacks were captured by the Confederates, 471 remain to be accounted for.

Reports of a massacre following Wessells's surrender are fairly numerous but are also highly disparate and contradictory. One contends that several hours after the surrender a group of blacks got their hands on weapons and opened fire, precipitating a slaughter by enraged Confederates. Several relate that black soldiers and Buffaloes were shot down as they fled the battlefield before or after the surrender. Others state that blacks were executed by firing squads or were hunted down and killed in the woods and swamps. Denials of massacre reports, some of Federal origin, are extant also. All of those reports are presented in the pages that follow.

One indisputable fact concerning the events at Plymouth on April 20, 1864, is that at some point a desperate rush for the swamps was made by Buffaloes and blacks. Black women and children, as well as recruits and possibly cooks and *Southfield* sailors, took part in the exodus. Those fugitives, according to various accounts, were intercepted by Hoke's men, or pursued into the swamps by them, or both. An unidentified civilian who was at Plymouth during the battle wrote in a letter to the *Raleigh Daily Confederate:* "About 6 o'clock in the morning [four hours before Wessells surrendered] a large body, perhaps six hundred negroes and buffaloes, came out of the Garrett fort [Fort Williams] and made for the nearest point of Peacock swamp. Three companies of cavalry and one of infantry were hunting them there all day, and nearly all were killed. I suppose no prisoners were taken." In a letter to his mother and sisters dated April 24, 1864, Lt. William I. Clopton of the Richmond Fayette Artillery stated that "several hundred negroes & negro officers attempted to escape when the town fell but were pursued & all most the last one of them killed[.] the woods are full of them."[75] "Lone Star," the pseudonymous member of Ransom's brigade quoted above, wrote on April 22: "Not one [member of Wessells's entire command] has escaped, except a few negroes, buffaloes, and deserters, who are scattered in the swamps, and whom our cavalry are hourly shooting or bringing into town. Three or four hundred negro women and children have already given themselves up." Pvt. Charles C. Mosher of the 85th New York recorded in his diary on April 21: "Last evening the Rebs went gunning for the colored troops, who, when the 'jig was up' . . . broke over the works and took to the woods. They were shot down at sight. It was a massacre."[76]

In a postwar account, Pvt. Frank P. O'Brien, an Alabama artillerist, recorded that as Hoke's troops fought their way into Plymouth on the morning of April 20, they encountered a "body of negro soldiers who on the streets and from temporary bastions were fighting with a desperation born only of frenzy and despair." Those men, comprising "two regiments of negro troops," believed that "'The Johnnies' would butcher them in cold blood and would not take one of them alive. This was told to them by the Yankee officers to stimulate them and encourage them to fight to the death." O'Brien wrote that shortly before Wessells's surrender,

> About 800 [blacks] made a break through our lines on the western [eastern] side
> and tried to reach the thickly wooded swampy ground in the direction of Little

Washington. Dearing's cavalry and a detachment of the 25th North Carolina resisted the effort successfully but this was attended with great slaughter as but few reached the swamp alive. Those who were successful in gaining refuge there, were afterward killed or died of starvation. . . . It is a well known fact that for three weeks after the place was captured negor bodies were seen floating out of the swamp into the river. The sight was sickening. Our General [Hoke] and other officers could not be blamed for this. While it is true the rules of civilized warfare did not countenance such terrible retribution let those who might condemn, put themselves in the position of a large body of men who made up that attacking force, and see what they would have done under like circumstances.[77]

Pvt. Warren Lee Goss of the 2d Massachusetts Heavy Artillery wrote in 1867 that "There were about twenty negro soldiers at Plymouth, who fled to the swamps when the capture of the place became certain; these soldiers were hunted down and killed." Lt. Bernard F. Blakeslee of the 16th Connecticut stated in 1875: "During the afternoon [of April 20], the rebel cavalry scoured the woods and shot dead every colored soldier and man that was able to bear arms. The number murdered in this way must have been in the neighborhood of one hundred."[78] Adj. Jacob H. Longenecker of the 101st Pennsylvania recollected in 1870: "During the whole afternoon [after the surrender] . . . we could hear the crack of rebel rifles along the swamps, where they were hunting down the colored troops and loyal North Carolinians. I heard a rebel Colonel say, with an oath, that they intended to shoot every Buffalo . . . and negro they found in our uniform." Lt. Alonzo Cooper of the 12th New York Cavalry recalled in 1888 that while he and other Federal prisoners were under guard at a nearby farm, they heard "the crack, crack, crack of muskets, down in the swamp where the negroes had fled . . . and were being hunted like squirrels or rabbits. . . . [T]he Johnnies themselves laughingly said (when questioned about where they had been after their return), 'They'd been out gunning for niggers.'" Capt. John Donaghy of the 103d Pennsylvania Infantry wrote in 1886: "There was considerable musketry firing heard after the surrender, and we learned that it meant the slaughter of the poor negro soldiers. They were shot down in cold blood after they had laid down their arms; some rushed to the river and tried to escape by swimming across, but few, if any, succeeded."[79]

Blacks who were captured within the fortifications of Plymouth suffered, according to several accounts, a fate similar to those who fled while the battle was in progress. "They showed the Negroes no mercy," 1st Sgt. Oliver W. Gates of the 16th Connecticut recorded in his diary a few weeks after the battle, "but shot some down in cold Blood." Lt. George S. Hastings of the

24th New York Battery wrote in 1870 that "The rebels raised the black flag against the few negroes found in uniform, and mercilessly shot them down." Lieutenant Blakeslee quoted Hastings verbatim in his 1875 history of the 16th Connecticut but increased the number of victims from a "few" to "three or four hundred negroes and two companies of North Carolina troops." According to Blakeslee, "many" Federal soldiers were "eye-witnesses" to those murders, which he categorized as "the Fort Pillow massacre re-enacted." Lieutenant Cooper of the 12th New York Cavalry recollected in 1888 that black soldiers "were drawn up in line at the breastwork, and shot down as they stood." Cooper, who did not provide an estimate of the number of blacks executed, stated that he "plainly saw" the killings while he and other Federal soldiers were held under guard "not over five hundred yards" away. "I watched the whole brutal transaction," Cooper wrote. "When the company of rebs fired, every negro dropped at once, as one man."[80]

Four other Federal soldiers, Warren Lee Goss, John Donaghy, Oliver R. McNary, and George Robbins, also charged that black soldiers were executed in Plymouth after the battle. Goss wrote in 1867 that Negro soldiers "who surrendered in good faith were drawn up in line, and shot down . . . like dogs. Every negro found with United States equipments or uniforms, was (we were told by the rebel guard) shot without mercy." Donaghy, in an 1886 reminiscence, stated that black soldiers "were shot down in cold blood after they had laid down their arms." McNary's account, written in 1900, implies that black civilians as well as soldiers were killed: "Immediately after our men surrendered, the Rebel soldiers commenced firing on the negroes, shooting them down, old and young, wherever they found them; some ran for the timber and were pursued by Dearing's Cavalry and shot as they ran." Robbins, a private in the 16th Connecticut, recalled in 1918 that members of "a Company of negroes [that] had been . . . armed and equipped [presumably, the eighty black recruits] . . . and had not been claimed by their former masters" were "disposed of" three or four days after the battle: "I heard volley firing in the town and asked a nearby guard the reason [and] was told, 'They lined up them d——d niggers you all enlisted and are shooting 'em off'n the dock.'"[81]

In addition to the foregoing stories of flight, pursuit, and mayhem, there is a shocking account related orally to John W. Darden of Plymouth by his father, David Goodman Darden, some years after the war:

> There is a legend in this section which my father stated to me many years ago was true. . . . Even though he was not present and did not take part in the Plymouth campaign his outfit, Company H, 10th N. C. Regiment, was stationed at Rainbow

Banks [near Hamilton]. He was home on sick leave some 15 or 20 days before the battle but by the time of surrender of the town he had sufficiently recovered from his ailment and was about ready to return to his command. Before he did return, however, he visited the battle ground at Plymouth and observed the destruction that had been wrought. He has related to me many times the story of the slaughtering of the negroes on the day of surrender of Ft. William[s] . . . which took place about 11:00 o'clock in the morning. About 3:00 in the afternoon the Confederate soldiers began to assemble on the streets of the town not suspecting any further trouble. There was quartered here in the town as a part of the Federal Army a negro regiment consisting of about 700 men. They fired upon the Confederate soldiers, doing considerable damage. It is not known what caused them to start firing after the surrender. It might have been caused by fright or nervousness, certainly it could not have been orders from the officers of the regiment. After the firing, however, the Confederates charged them with every conceivable weapon in their possession whereupon the negroes ran, taking refuge in Conaby Creek swamp and the flats beyond, scarcely a mile away. They were quickly followed by the infuriated Confederate soldiers and were overtaken in the swamp and flats where they were slaughtered like rats. They must have slain at least 500 of the negro troops. I was told by my father-in-law, B. D. [W.] Latham, a short time before his death that he and other boys of the community, having heard of the great slaughter of negroes, went to the swamp the following Sunday morning and saw hundreds of slain negro troops. He stated to me that he was about 12 years of age at the time and remembered it quite well.[82]

The best known, most detailed, and most spectacular eyewitness account of the Plymouth massacre was provided by an illiterate black soldier named Samuel Johnson. Johnson, who was referred to at the beginning of this chapter, identified himself as orderly sergeant of Company D, 2d Regiment U.S. Colored Cavalry, and claimed that he was assisting Lieutenant French with recruiting for that unit when he (Johnson) was captured at Plymouth. He escaped about eight weeks later and, on July 11, submitted an affidavit to Federal authorities alleging that black troops had been brutally murdered by Hoke's forces. "When I found that the city was being surrendered," Johnson stated,

I pulled off my uniform and found a suit of citizen's clothes, which I put on, and when captured I was supposed and believed by the rebels to be a citizen. After being captured I was kept at Plymouth for some two weeks and was employed in endeavoring to raise the sunken vessels of the Union fleet.

From Plymouth I was taken to Weldon and from thence to Raleigh, N.C., where I was detained for about a month, and was then forwarded to Richmond, where I remained until about the time of the battles near Richmond, when I went with Lieutenant Johnson, of the Sixth North Carolina Regiment, as his servant, to Hanover Junction. I did not remain there over four or five days before I made my escape into the lines of the Union army and was sent to Washington, D.C., and then duly forwarded to my regiment in front of Petersburg.

Upon the capture of Plymouth by the rebel forces all the negroes found in blue uniform, or with any outward marks of a Union soldier upon him, was killed. I saw some taken into the woods and hung. Others I saw stripped of all their clothing and then stood upon the bank of the river with their faces riverward and there they were shot. Still others were killed by having their brains beaten out by the butt end of the muskets in the hands of the rebels. All were not killed the day of the capture. Those that were not were placed in a room with their [white] officers, they (the officers) having previously been dragged through the town with ropes around their necks, where they were kept confined until the following morning, when the remainder of the black soldiers were killed.

The regiments most conspicuous in these murderous transactions were the Eighth North Carolina and, I think, the Sixth North Carolina.[83]

On July 12, the day after Johnson submitted his affidavit, Maj. Gen. Benjamin F. Butler, commander of the Department of Virginia and North Carolina, forwarded it to General Grant. In his covering letter, Butler expressed outrage at the events at Plymouth, stated that Johnson had been "duly cautioned" to tell the "exact truth," and expressed "confidence as to . . . [the] main features and substantial accuracy" of Johnson's statements.[84] As far as can be determined, Grant, who had his hands full at Richmond and Petersburg, did not reply.

Within a few days after the capture of Plymouth, the Northern press reported a massacre of blacks and Buffaloes in the town. The *New York Herald* of April 26, citing an unidentified "informant," disclosed that "all the negroes found after the surrender, were stripped of their clothing and brutally murdered in cold blood." "It must be understood" the *Herald* noted, "that General Wessells had no colored troops at Plymouth, save a few recruits for North Carolina regiments, and the poor unfortunate blacks thus butchered were merely laborers for the government." Under a headline reading "Negro Soldiers Butchered," the *Philadelphia Inquirer* published an article stating that "Two full companies of the Second North Carolina Union (colored) Volunteers were among the captured, the most of whom were led out and shot by the enemy after surrendering. All the negroes who were found in uniform were shot." The *New York Daily Tribune* reported that "All Negroes in Uniform . . . [were] Murdered," and an unidentified Baltimore paper quoted "reports on the streets . . . that the colored union troops at Plymouth . . . were murdered after the surrender."[85] The *North Carolina Times*, of New Bern, reported on April 27: "On the surrender of the place the colored soldiers and 2d loyal North Carolina, stampeded for the swamps. Most of the negroes, we regret to hear . . . have been massacred. The conduct of the rebel soldiery or their officers, or both, are said to have been barbarous in the extreme." On May 7 the same newspaper reported that New Bern was "filled" with "destitute" women and children, many of whom were "doubtless . . . widows and orphans from the recent barbarous butchery of husbands and fathers at Plymouth."[86]

In sharp contrast to the accounts quoted above are several from both Federal and Confederate sources that deny massacre allegations. On or about July 16, 1864, Robert Ould, the Confederate commissioner of prisoner exchanges, received a copy of Sergeant Johnson's affidavit. In an "indorsement," Ould indignantly denounced Johnson's charges as a "villainous lie, and badly told. . . . Samuel Johnson is a bad affidavit man, whatever may be his other excellencies. If the truth is wanted, let inquiry be made of Colonel [Francis] Beach [of the 16th Connecticut], or other captured officers, always excepting the chaplains." (Colonel Beach, it is worth noting, had been exchanged and was available to Federal authorities for questioning.) Surgeon Mayer of the 16th Connecticut wrote six weeks after the battle that although "a thorough plundering was carried on" by Hoke's troops, "cruelties were not perpetrated," and "with the consent of the officers, no negroes were killed." That conclusion, however, was not based on personal observation but on "The fact of their [the Confederates] sending ten wounded negroes into my hospital to be attended to." Two North Carolina cavalry officers also denied that Dearing's troopers slaughtered blacks, Buffaloes, and civilians as they fled toward Peacock Swamp. "[We] were occupying positions to the right," Lt. Col. John Thomas Kennedy and Lt. William Fletcher Parker wrote in 1901,

> and soon it became necessary to change and cross Conaby creek in order to cut off any who might attempt to leave the town in the direction indicated, as many were already passing over in the hope to save themselves from being captured. Many were so badly frightened that when asked to halt and surrender they kept running and were fired upon and killed; but I saw none killed who promptly obeyed the order to halt. . . . [W]hile there were quite a number killed and wounded we were truly glad to see it no worse, and to be convinced that victorious as we were, mercy had not been dethroned.[87]

Confederate newspapers were quick to deny the atrocity charges. The *Wilmington Journal* of May 5 dismissed the *Philadelphia Inquirer* report quoted above as a "ridiculous falsehood," and the *Raleigh Daily Confederate* described the same report as "A Specimen of Yankee Lying."[88] In a decidedly backhanded denial, the *Daily Richmond Examiner* noted with regret: "General Hoke, judging from the large number of his prisoners, does not seem to have made such *thorough work* as that by which Forrest has so *shocked the tender souls,* and *frozen the warm* blood of the Yankees. The resistance he encountered was, probably, not as desperate, and the blood of the victors not so heated."[89]

In January 1909, at a meeting of veterans of the 101st and 103d Pennsylvania, the long-festering massacre allegations of Samuel Johnson, Alonzo Cooper, B. F. Blakeslee, and others were "discussed at some length." The "unanimous" opinion of the veterans was that "the authors . . . were mistaken."[90] Although it was "agreed" that "many negroes and native North Carolina Union soldiers were killed, and perhaps an occasional one brutally murdered, by individual soldiers," charges of a "wholesale slaughter of blacks" were rejected. "Such a holocaust," the veterans stated, "could not have occurred in the hearing" or without the "knowledge" of General Wessells, who "would have instantly taken issue with the Confederates, had he had any suspicion of such atrocities." The veterans felt also that blacks who survived the battle, such as Richard West, a cook in their regiment, would have witnessed or at least heard about the killings, had there been any. According to the veterans, "It would require a stretch of credulity to imagine that such witnesses would have remained silent had they witnessed such brutal atrocity as charged against the Plymouth captors." There could be "no doubt," the veterans concluded, that "there were . . . among [the Confederates] . . . men of brutal proclivities, who took advantage of the excitement and chaos . . . to give vent to their passion and hatred for the unfortunate Negro"; however, "to charge the deeds of a few against all" was "evidence of such bigotry as to condemn the witness."[91]

Shortly after that meeting, one of the veterans, Luther S. Dickey of the 103d Pennsylvania, wrote to General Hoke and Walter Clark, chief justice of the North Carolina Supreme Court and an authority on North Carolina Civil War history, asking them to answer the "charge" regarding the killing of black soldiers. No reply was received from Hoke, who reputedly was in "precarious" health, but Judge Clark's curious and probably evasive response was that "No *armed* [emphasis added] prisoners of any color were killed at Plymouth."[92] Clark referred Dickey's question to John W. Graham, former major of the 56th North Carolina, who by that time was a distinguished attorney, constitutional expert, state legislator, and Democratic political leader.

"I have no hesitation in saying," Graham replied in an equally peculiar denial, "that the reputed killing of any colored troops *the day after* [emphasis added] the capture of Plymouth, N.C., April 20, 1864, is entirely untrue. I heard of nothing of the kind at that time nor have I ever heard of it since until the receipt of your letter."[93] The question essentially at issue, of course, is whether unarmed blacks were murdered on the day of the battle; consequently, neither denial is persuasive. Furthermore, it will be recalled that Graham is the same officer who wrote five weeks before the events at Plymouth that "it is understood amongst us that we take no negro prisoners."

What is known of the fates of individual Buffaloes and blacks whose misfortune it was to find themselves at Plymouth on the day of its capture? In the case of the Buffaloes, the answer is: A great deal. The 166 members of Companies B and E, 2d North Carolina Infantry, who were enumerated on Wessells's casualty report can be accounted for as follows:

Killed in Battle	9
Captured and Executed for Desertion	8
Captured and Died in Prison	35
Captured and Escaped from Prison	5
Captured and Exchanged	6
Captured and Rejoined Confederate Army (deserter)	1
Captured (no further information)	1
Escaped from Plymouth	59
Escaped from Plymouth and Joined Confederate Army	2
Never Reported Missing	9
Reported Missing and Never Accounted for	20
Survived the War (no further information)	7
Unidentified	4

Most of the enlisted Buffaloes captured at Plymouth were sent to the hellhole prison at Andersonville, Georgia; a few were incarcerated in the Plymouth jail or confined at Salisbury, Weldon, or Richmond. Most of their officers were confined initially at Macon, Georgia. Not all of those men arrived at their place of confinement under their own names: When it became evident that Wessells would be compelled to surrender, some 2d North Carolina soldiers who were unable to flee transformed themselves into members of Northern units, assuming false identities or those of men who had been killed during the battle.[94] The number of such transmogrifications is uncertain; however, it is instructive that no burial records exist for any of the thirty-five members of the 2d North Carolina who are known to have died at Andersonville and other Southern prisons. Some may have been buried in unmarked graves, but the rest presumably took their false identities with them to eternity. Among them were at least three who had urgent reasons to conceal their identity: Cpl. Worley Butler and Pvt. William T. Cullipher were deserters from the 59th and 11th North Carolina, respectively, and Pvt. James Hassell, although not a deserter, had been discharged from the 17th North Carolina prior to his enlistment in the Federal army. If identified, Butler and Cullipher, if not Hassell, would certainly have been sent to the gallows.[95]

Those Buffaloes who fled from Plymouth on April 20 either joined the frantic flight into the swamps, swam the Roanoke, or concealed themselves in the river. As was the case with the men who escaped in boats on the night of the nineteenth, some of the fugitives were fished out of the Roanoke or Albemarle Sound by Federal gunboats. For example, Cpl. Nathaniel Miller was picked up in a canoe by the *Ceres* on April 27, and Pvt. James Bird was rescued after having "laid in the swamps . . . three days & nights."[96] Most of the escapees probably headed overland for Washington, where they were evacuated by ship to New Bern or Beaufort. The desperation and determination of those men is apparent in the brief accounts of their flights that have survived. Pvt. John Butler took part in the rush for the swamps shortly before Wessells surrendered and, although wounded in the leg when Dearing's cavalry made a "dash" on his group, crossed the Roanoke, hid for "a day or more," and finally reached his home in Bertie County.[97] First Sgt. James H. Mitchell, a Confederate deserter who would have been hanged if captured and identified, "buried" himself in the muck for "about 10 or 12 hours" before making his way to Washington.[98] Two other deserters, Pvts. William Henry Myers and William W. Byrd, reached Washington with a third soldier, Pvt. James Corbit, after "six day[s] and nights without food . . . in the mud and water."[99] Pvts. Laton Gardner, William Augustus Willoughby, and Doctrin Williams "lay in water in the low grounds two days & one night" and then "waded . . . some ten or more miles" to Federal lines. Such harrowing adventures were probably common; according to Williams, "Nearly all the co[mpany] was . . . trying to escape."[100]

While some members of the 2d North Carolina were fleeing into the swamps, others plunged into the Roanoke and swam for their lives. Nonswimmers hid among the gum and cypress trees or perhaps attempted to float downstream clinging to logs and other flotsam. "[A]ll my company [B] was in that river," Pvt. James W. Skiles wrote with some exaggeration, "we were in that water two nights & one day."[101] Calvin Hoggard, captain of

Company E, "crost the River and waded more than a mile through the Roanoke and Cashie River swamps from shoe deep to wast deep in mud and water and got over in Bettie Co. where he staid in the woods sevrell weeks, the first opportunity he got he went back to his Reg[iment]."[102] Pvts. Worley T. Hoggard, William L. Mitchell, and Henry A. Hobbs, all of whom were Confederate deserters, moved east along the Roanoke. "[We] wade[d] [through the] river pocosin in mud and water one to three feet deep one whole day and night," Hobbs wrote, "and finally made our way to our homes [in Bertie County] and kept concealed about 6 weeks before we could get back to our command."[103]

At least eight Buffaloes who had deserted from Confederate service were executed. Pvt. Benjamin D. Dillon, a deserter from the 17th North Carolina, was court-martialed and executed near Laurel Hill Church, Virginia, October 29, 1864; Lt. James L. Keeter, a deserter from the 11th North Carolina, was executed on an unknown date.[104] It is known also that six Buffaloes were hanged at Hamilton on April 24.[105] Those men and presumably the other Buffalo prisoners were paraded before the 17th North Carolina (a unit raised primarily in the Albemarle Sound region), identified by their former neighbors and Confederate army comrades as deserters, and, after a drumhead court-martial, strung up. None of the six has ever been positively identified; however, according to Federal pension files in the National Archives, Sgt. Joseph H. Fulcher, a deserter from the 17th North Carolina, was "murdered" after being captured at Plymouth. Pvts. Quinton Hobbs and James Hassell, who had served in the 17th, disappeared.[106] Whoever they were, the Hamilton victims, if indeed they were all deserters captured in enemy uniform, were unquestionably subject to execution under the articles of war. Nevertheless, in the absence of any reasonable semblance of due process, the episode seems little more than a lynching. As for members of the 2d who cannot be accounted for, most were probably killed during the fighting of April 17–20 or died under false identities at Andersonville. It is possible also that some were murdered during or after the Federal surrender. In any case, the maximum number of possible massacre victims belonging to the 2d North Carolina, excluding the eight men who were executed later for desertion, is twenty-six: twenty-one missing in action and never accounted for, one who was captured but whose subsequent fate is unknown, and four unidentified.[107]

The fate of the black recruits, sailors, cooks, "volunteers," and civilians captured on April 20 is obscured, in contrast to that of their white counterparts, by an absence of records and by a deliberate effort at concealment by Confederate authorities. Fearful of the Federal reaction if it became known

that captured blacks were being treated as fugitive slaves rather than prisoners of war, Lt. Gen. Braxton Bragg, Confederate chief-of-staff, informed
Governor Vance on April 21, 1864:

> The President directs that the negroes captured by our forces be turned over to you
> for the present, and he requests of you that if upon investigation you ascertain that
> any of them belong to citizens of North Carolina you will cause them to be restored
> to their respective owners. If any are owned in other States you will please commu-
> nicate to me their number and the names and places of residence of their owners,
> and have them retained in strict custody until the President's views in reference to
> such may be conveyed to you. To avoid as far as possible all complications with the
> military authorities of the United States in regard to the disposition which will be
> made of this class of prisoners, the President respectfully requests Your Excellency
> to take the necessary steps to have the matter . . . kept out of the newspapers of the
> State, and in every available way to shun its obtaining any publicity.[108]

Davis's request regarding publicity was apparently honored by Vance,
for it seems that no newspapers survive containing references to the disposition of the Plymouth blacks. Nevertheless, it is known that some captives
were remanded to slavery. Titus Hardy, a contraband from Tyrrell County
who was serving as a cook with the 103d Pennsylvania, was reclaimed by
his master and remained in bondage until the end of the war. Richard
West, another cook from the 103d, was sent to Rainbow Banks, on the
Roanoke River near Hamilton, to work on the fortifications at Fort Branch.
Charles White, a *Southfield* sailor, was forced to become a servant to the
officers of the *Albemarle*.[109] Most of the prisoners were put to work initially
as manual laborers: Lieutenant Colonel Guion recorded in his journal on
April 21 that "all the captured slaves" were busy demolishing Fort Wessells "even with the ground."[110] Those prisoners who were not remanded
to their masters within the next two weeks may have been sent to Wilmington to construct fortifications at Fort Fisher.[111] As far as can be determined,
the only black confined in a Confederate prison was John Rolack, a cook in
the 85th New York. Rolack, a light-complexioned, hazel-eyed mulatto who
presumably either passed himself off as a white or was mistaken for one,
was sent to Andersonville. He died there on September 23, 1864, of scurvy
and dysentery.[112]

Hardy, White, West, and Rolack are by no means the only black military
personnel who survived the alleged massacre at Plymouth. The survival of
7 cooks and 30 *Southfield* sailors can be conclusively documented. Also,
there were at least 20 to 35 survivors among the black recruits: the *North*

Carolina Times reported that 20 recruits reached New Bern on April 24, and Captain Marvin stated in an 1890 pension deposition that about 15 of his men escaped.[113] In short, the number of men who cannot be accounted for (that is, the number of *possible* atrocity victims among the 80 recruits, 10 cooks, and 40 sailors) is between 54 and 69: 45 to 60 recruits, 3 cooks, and 6 *Southfield* crewmen (as stated previously, 4 *Southfield* blacks were killed in action). A number of the missing men probably died in legitimate combat, or were remanded to slavery, or, like some of their white comrades, returned to their homes and never rejoined their units.[114] A few may have been among the 10 wounded "negroes" (presumably, including civilians as well as military personnel) who were sent to the hospital of Surgeon Mayer. All things considered, it seems reasonable to suppose that a maximum of about 40 black recruits, cooks, and sailors could have been victims of a massacre.

As was the case with the white North Carolina Unionists, the blacks who escaped from Plymouth had harrowing adventures. John Ward, a recruit of the 37th Colored Troops, sustained a head wound and rib injury as he fled the battlefield. He avoided possible execution by "laying on the ground until night" and then crept away and walked to Little Washington. Ward stated that "all of the company [the black recruits of the 37th Colored Troops] were taken prisoners, Capt. Marvin with them."[115] Jackson Miller, another recruit, was picked up on the banks of Albemarle Sound by the *Miami* after three days in the swamps, and Alexander Lewis, a fireman on the *Southfield*, "swam into the swamp" and spent thirteen days in "water up to my wast." Swollen up "in a Bloat" and afflicted with rheumatism that plagued him the rest of his life, Lewis was finally rescued by a gunboat. William R. Cradle, a "third class boy" on the *Southfield*, was thrown into the water when his ship was rammed by the *Albemarle* but was picked up by a dinghy from the *Miami*. "Many of the men were drowned and some were shot while in the water," Cradle later recalled. "I barely escaped from drowning." "Henry," a contraband belonging to William S. Pettigrew of Washington County, was "forced to shoulder his musket in the defence of the place [Plymouth]" but escaped across the Roanoke in a small boat on the night of the nineteenth. After subsisting in the swamps for sixteen days on "frogs & a few crackers," he returned to Plymouth, "nearly exhausted from famine & exposure," and was remanded to his master.[116] One additional black, the only black soldier known to have been taken in uniform, probably survived if he remained in the hands of the Virginians who captured him. According to Sgt. Maj. David E. Johnston of the 7th Virginia, on the morning of April 20, just prior to the surrender of Fort Williams,

Information came that the enemy was escaping by the Washington road and we were ordered to move at a double quick by the right flank. . . . A rapid double quick soon found us across the . . . road in line of battle. A few stragglers were captured as they attempted to pass us—among them a large, burly negro in the full uniform of a United States soldier. He, being the first negro soldier we had seen, was quite a sight for us. He was very badly scared for he thought we would eat him blood raw, but we had no idea of doing him hurt. In a few minutes thereafter the enemy in Fort Williams lowered his flag and we marched into the town.[117]

There is one other piece of evidence suggesting that uniformed blacks were captured. In a telegram to Vance on April 23, Gen. P. G. T. Beauregard stated that "I will have delivered to you [at Raleigh] the negro prisoners captured at Plymouth & with your consent send the slaves captured to Wilmington." The distinction that Beauregard makes between "negro prisoners" and "slaves" suggests that the former were uniformed blacks who, Beauregard believed, were still alive three days after the battle. What became of those men is unknown. Some were undoubtedly reclaimed at Plymouth or Raleigh by their masters.[118] Others may have been sent, as was Richard West, the cook from the 103d Pennsylvania, to Rainbow Banks to construct fortifications. Others may have been executed by a firing squad on the Plymouth docks on April 23 or 24, presumably to eliminate them as witnesses to a new massacre on the heels of Fort Pillow. The latter possibility, however, seems doubtful. Private Robbins, the source of the execution report, did not actually see any killings, his reminiscence was produced fifty-four years after the fact, and his charges are not corroborated by other witnesses. Furthermore, unless West was captured in civilian clothes and not identified as a soldier, there is no obvious reason why he should have been spared when others were not. In short, there is little convincing evidence that uniformed black prisoners who survived the immediate aftermath of the Battle of Plymouth were treated as anything other than runaway slaves.

Because the number of uniformed black recruits, cooks, and sailors massacred at Plymouth probably could not have exceeded 69, it is clear that if a massacre of as many as 600 blacks occurred, it included not only some of the approximately 145 "volunteers" but also other black civilians, possibly including women and children. Shortly after the battle, a report began circulating among North Carolina slave owners that runaway slaves had been killed. Catherine Ann Edmondston, wife of an affluent Halifax County planter, recorded in her diary on April 22 that "Amongs the killed & prisoners were numbers of negroes who had run off from their masters living here in this community. Some of the young men which brother [John Devereux Jr.] lost last winter were among the number. Many of Mr. Ed Hill's were killed."[119] At first glance, it would seem that Edmondston's information, recorded only two days after the battle, could be based only on hearsay; however, the steamer *Cotton Plant,* loaded with Confederate dead and wounded, passed upriver on April 19, and it is possible that she was receiving firsthand reports before the battle was over. Even so, it seems impossible that an accurate reckoning of the number, let alone the names, of blacks who had been killed could have been made two days after the battle. The likelihood is that Edmondston's comment was based on the rumors of heavy black casualties and a supposition by Ed Hill that all contrabands who were not captured had been killed.[120]

Before attempting to determine a probable scenario of events at Plymouth, a critical look must be taken at the evidence. Several qualitative considerations will guide that procedure. First, contemporary accounts will be considered more reliable than those written postbellum, which are more subject to memory failure and, in the authors' opinion, embellishment. Second, massacre affirmations by Confederate witnesses, who presumably had every reason to deny the truth, and massacre denials by Federal witnesses, who presumably had every reason to affirm the truth, will be considered more credible than massacre denials by Confederate witnesses or massacre affirmations by Federal witnesses. Third, detailed accounts will be given more weight than those lacking specificity. Finally, the *absence* of massacre reports in the contemporary writings of persons who were at Plymouth on April 20, 1864, will be considered significant: A few executions might have taken place unobserved or been ignored as of minor consequence, but between 300 and 600 murders would require dozens of perpetrators, would be seen by scores of witnesses, and would create a body-disposal problem of which hundreds of other persons would be aware (and that would far exceed anything described in the writings that have survived). In short, if the events at Fort Pillow eight days earlier are any indication, the slaughter of 300 to 600 soldiers and civilians would have produced—if not immediately, at least after the surviving Federal prisoners were released—a substantial amount of detailed, eyewitness testimony. The number of victims at Fort Pillow, it might be noted, did not exceed 204.[121]

In the opinion of the authors, claims such as the following are grossly exaggerated: B. F. Blakeslee's, that "three or four hundred negroes and two companies of North Carolina troops" were shot in "cold blood"; Frank P. O'Brien's, that "About 800" black soldiers ran for the swamps but "few" reached them alive; the *Raleigh Daily Confederate*'s, that "perhaps six hundred negroes and buffaloes" were hunted down and killed in Peacock Swamp; David G. Darden's, that "at least 500 . . . negro troops" were slain in the swamp along Conaby Creek [Peacock Swamp]; and B. D. W. Latham's, that he saw "hundreds" of bodies in the swamps.[122] All of those reports, except the *Daily Confederate*'s, are postwar, none possesses the specificity one would expect from an eyewitness to such a horrific event or scene, and each contains errors, inconsistencies, or other elements that raise serious doubts about its reliability. As has been demonstrated, Blakeslee errs egregiously in claiming that two companies of Buffaloes were massacred, and his figure regarding the number of blacks killed was superimposed on a much lower estimate by another author. O'Brien seemingly posits almost as many killings as there were blacks in Plymouth on the day of its capture (in fact, hundreds survived). And the *Daily Confederate* erroneously assumes that *every* black who made it to the swamps was killed. (The *Daily Confederate* reported also that the entire 139-man crew of the *Southfield* was drowned, whereas it is known that there were at least 124 survivors).[123] The David G. Darden account, which his son, John W. Darden, presents as a "legend," is the younger Darden's recollection of the oral recollection of someone who did not witness the events that he describes. B. D. W. Latham's memory of having seen dead blacks in the swamps, also quoted by John W. Darden, is probably accurate; however, Latham was eleven years old at the time and recounted the story orally shortly before his death in 1928 (approximately sixty years after the event). At best, Latham's recollection of "hundreds" of bodies is, like many of the postwar stories, meager evidence from which to adduce a massacre of the staggering dimensions it depicts.[124]

On a more general level, it is simply impossible to believe that so many Confederates and Federals who were present on the day that Plymouth fell could have failed not only to see but also to take any note whatever in their contemporary writings of the slaughter of between 300 and 600 persons. Eyewitnesses whose letters, diaries, journals, and reports fail to note any killings include 1st Sgt. John W. Wynne and Pvts. Edwin Baker Loving and Charles A. Wills of the 1st Virginia; Pvt. Josiah Worrell of the 24th Virginia; Lt. Leonidas L. Polk and Pvt. William Beavans of the 43d North Carolina; Pvt. James C. Elliott of the 56th North Carolina; Lt. Col. Henry T. Guion of the 10th North Carolina Artillery; Pvt. Hodijah L. Meade of the 38th Virginia Artillery; Capts. Ira B. Sampson and Joseph E. Fiske of the 2d Massachusetts Heavy Artillery; Sgt. Maj. Robert H. Kellogg, Sgt. Samuel E. Grosvenor, and Cpls. Charles G. Lee and William H. Jackson of the 16th Connecticut; Lt. Lucien A. Butts, Cpl. Albert H. Bancroft, and Pvt. Asa W.

Root of the 85th New York; Confederate Brig. Gen. James G. Martin; and General Wessells himself.[125] At least one Federal officer, Surgeon Mayer of the 16th Connecticut, specifically dismissed the charge, and in 1909, veterans of the 101st and 103d Pennsylvania, in reaching a "unanimous" opinion that a massacre did not take place, affirmed that not one man present at the meeting had witnessed such an event. Even the Federal authorities, it seems, were unconvinced by the atrocity reports: Congress investigated Fort Pillow, the Crater, and the Kinston hangings, but presumably, because of the same paucity of hard evidence that has confounded historians, no official investigation of the Plymouth massacre was undertaken after the battle, after the Federal captives who survived imprisonment were released, or post-bellum. Indeed, it is not clear that the subject was even raised by the various congressional committees on the conduct of the war. President Lincoln is known to have taken a personal interest in the Fort Pillow massacre, threatening retribution if the charges were proved, but according to Attorney General Edward Bates, when Plymouth was discussed by Lincoln's cabinet at a meeting of April 26, "the horrid story [was] . . . not believed."[126]

The accuracy, not to say the veracity, of the most important and specific piece of massacre evidence, the report of Orderly Sgt. Samuel Johnson, is dubious also. At the time of the Battle of Plymouth, the orderly sergeant of Company D, 2d Colored Cavalry, was a black named Henry Williams.[127] No soldier named Samuel Johnson served at any time in the 2d Colored Cavalry, and no "Lieutenant Johnson," the officer to whom Sergeant Johnson claimed he was remanded as a servant, was serving in the 6th North Carolina in April and May 1864.[128] The very fact that Sergeant Johnson survived a massacre that would have focused on strong, healthy young black men such as he presumably was suggests that his accusations are either lies or exaggerations. One wonders also how Johnson managed to see, and why he was permitted to see, so many and such a variety of violent episodes when so many other eyewitnesses writing contemporaneously apparently saw none. The suspicion arises that Butler, whose abolitionist principles were among the most impassioned of any Federal general, concocted the story to support the widespread massacre rumors that were in circulation but which could not be confirmed because most of the Plymouth garrison was in Confederate hands. In short, the initial atrocity rumors may have produced a piece of bogus evidence that has been cited ever since as positive proof of a massacre.

Three other stories of Confederate brutality, all of postwar origin, are also suspect. According to Captain Donaghy, the 85th New York prisoners included a white hospital steward named Appleton who had been a druggist in New Orleans before the war and had deserted from a Confederate regiment. "Surrender meant death to him," Donaghy wrote, "and when our flag went down, he, in his desperation, swallowed a dose of morphine to end his life, but was saved by the surgeon and others, who . . . prevented him from sleeping." After several days of "continual dread of being recognized and shot as a deserter," he was identified: "A rebel noncommissioned officer with a squad of men came along our rank and asked me if I knew Appleton. I said, 'No,' but he was recognized and pointed out by one of the rebels. Appleton had a look of despair on his face. . . . It was very sad to see him led away. I never heard of him again."[129] That story, which implies that Appleton was executed, is dubious because no soldier by that name served in the 85th New York or any other Federal unit that was present at Plymouth. A private by the name of Silas Appleby served in the 85th; however, he was a native and resident of Allegany County, New York, and was a farmer by profession, and there is no evidence that he was ever in Louisiana. Also, he died of disease at Andersonville on August 27, 1864. Presumably, "Appleton" could be Appleby only if Donaghy got Appleby's name, profession, and personal history wrong, if Appleby was executed at Plymouth for reasons other than those specified by Donaghy, and if an unidentified Buffalo who assumed Appleby's name died at Andersonville.[130]

The other two incidents relate to deaths that allegedly occurred on the battlefield. According to Surgeon Smith, George Higley, a white private belonging to the 85th New York and a renowned deer hunter and sharpshooter, refused to hand over his double-barreled hunting rifle after the surrender and was "mercilessly shot to death." Higley's service records, his widow's pension application, and death records of Andersonville prison all indicate that he died at Andersonville in July 1864. Unlike the "Appleton" case, in which it is conceivable that "Appleton's" identity was assumed by a Buffalo, there is no doubt that it was Higley who died at Andersonville: His death was confirmed by two comrades from the 85th who saw his remains.[131]

Finally, there is the case of "Alec" Johnson, a black cook in the 85th New York, who, again according to Surgeon Smith, literally fought to the death. "At Plymouth," Smith wrote, "'Alec' refused to surrender, and fell fighting on his own account, pierced with bullets." That episode seems more believable than those involving "Appleton" and Higley; however, the records of the 85th do not indicate that a black cook named Alec Johnson served in that unit.[132]

If one divides the Plymouth massacre evidence into two categories labeled "swamp fugitives atrocity reports" and "battlefield atrocity reports," the former are, in the opinion of the authors, indisputably more convincing than the latter. There is an ample number of contemporary, corroboratory accounts by both Confederates and Federals that a flight to the swamp took place and that the fugitives were pursued and hunted down. However, most reports of "battlefield" atrocities are of postwar origin, or are not the testimony of eyewitnesses, or are unsubstantiated by other reports, or are of dubious accuracy. Assuming that reports in the "battlefield" category are honest accounts of what the writer saw, or remembered having seen, or at least believed to be the truth, the conflicting and unconvincing nature of those reports can be at least partially explained by two factors: the confused and sequential nature of the Federal garrison's surrender, and the fact that some of the Federals, apprehending lethal violence, either attempted to escape or, in a few cases, fought to the death.[133] As was outlined previously, the surrender process included a "no quarter" conference between Hoke and Wessells on the morning of the twentieth as well as unsuccessful attempts by Fort Wessells and Fort Williams to capitulate and continued resistance after General Wessells surrendered. In addition, Confederate surrender demands were issued on April 17, shortly after Hoke reached Plymouth, on the evening of April 18, prior to and after the surrender of Fort Wessells, on the morning and evening of April 19, and on the morning of April 20, prior to the Hoke-Wessells parley. Little or nothing is known concerning most of those episodes, but at least one of them included, according to a letter that Wessells wrote in 1885, a threat of no quarter by Colonel Dearing.[134] According to Charles C. Mosher, the recipient of the letter, Wessells stated that Colonel Dearing "came in under a flag of truce, and demanded the surrender of the town, or there would be no quarter shown. 'His request was not granted, and you know the results. It is not a pleasant thing to think about.'"[135] "No quarter" rumors that spread in both armies as a result of the surrender conferences undoubtedly exacerbated the fears of blacks and Buffaloes, inducing the flight of some and the last-ditch resistance of others. In addition, the complex surrender process created a nebulous situation in which neither side could be quite certain who had surrendered or had been surrendered and who had not. Thus, it seems possible that some Confederates, unaware of the status of a particular enemy soldier or group of soldiers, mistakenly fired on men who had surrendered. Conversely, it is possible that some Federal witnesses mistook for murder the killing of blacks and Buffaloes who had not yet surrendered or been surrendered or who refused to surrender. The alleged killing of "Alec" Johnson is perhaps a case in point. Assuming that the story is true, Surgeon Smith would have had to be in close proximity to Johnson to have understood the circumstances of his death; however, another observer, more distant from the scene and knowing only that Wessells had surrendered, might well have concluded that he was witnessing an atrocity.

The dubious nature of some of the evidence notwithstanding, it is clear that blacks and Buffaloes were killed at Plymouth under circumstances that merit the appellation "massacre." The authors estimate that there were 80 black recruits, 145 black "volunteers," 10 black regimental cooks, 36 black sailors, and a maximum of 600 black laborers and other black civilians in Plymouth on the morning of April 20. In the authors' judgment, the fate that befell those 871 unfortunates and the 26 Buffaloes who cannot be accounted for was approximately as follows: At some point prior to Wessells's capitulation, a great flight to the swamps and woods by perhaps 500 blacks and about 50 Buffaloes took place. The fugitives, particularly the Buffaloes and uniformed blacks, were very much in fear for their lives, and a few carried weapons. Confederate infantry units in the vicinity opened fire, and Dearing's cavalry charged the group, shooting and sabering down some of its members who refused to halt or were too terrified to do so. Blacks and Buffaloes who reached the swamps and woods were pursued by at least one company of the 25th North Carolina, by Dearing's cavalry, and probably by the 1st Virginia.[136] Most of the Buffaloes and black noncombatants were taken alive, but some blacks captured in uniform were summarily executed. In the excitement of the "hunt," a few women and children were also killed or wounded, accidentally or otherwise. Because of the difficult nature of the terrain and the concealment provided by the thick tangle of trees and other vegetation, most of the adult male fugitives escaped. Meanwhile, in Plymouth, the Confederate activity of preference for several hours following Wessells's surrender was without any doubt whatever a general sacking of the town.[137] Nevertheless, some blacks captured in uniform were shot out of hand. Those captured by Terry's Virginians survived for the moment, but some were dispatched later—perhaps on the Plymouth dock on April 23 or 24. Some black male civilians were murdered also. Most of the killings were carried out by individual Confederates, but it is possible that there were one or two incidents in which small numbers of blacks were shot by ad hoc firing squads. The number of blacks, uniformed and otherwise, who were murdered in Plymouth on April 20 was probably no more than 10. Fifteen more may have been executed on April 23 or 24, presumably on orders sent down from Richmond. Forty were killed as they fled the battlefield, 40 were hunted down and dispatched in the swamps, and 10 died under circumstances that qualify as legitimate combat. Approximately 350 escaped, and approximately 400, including a few uniformed soldiers and many women and children, were taken prisoner and survived. Of the 26 missing Buffaloes, some escaped and never rejoined their command, some died in combat, some died under false names at Andersonville, and 5 or so were murdered in the swamps or in the town. There is no evidence that General Hoke ordered or encouraged a massacre and very little that Terry's brigade was involved. With the possible exception of the 8th North Carolina, Mercer's brigade may have been innocent also. Ransom's brigade and Dearing's cavalrymen, it appears, were the probable culprits.

As indicated above, the answer to the question, Was there a massacre at Plymouth? is, in the authors' opinion, yes. Even the Pennsylvania veterans, in dismissing accounts of a "holocaust," concluded that "many" blacks were killed, and contemporary testimony alone substantiates a verdict of at least limited mayhem. However, the parameters of the massacre are more difficult to define. Some of the dead were uniformed and possibly armed black recruits and Buffaloes who were fleeing while the battle was in progress. Firing on such individuals was clearly permissible under the usages of military law; but given the fact that most of the fugitives were running not to escape captivity but because they expected to be murdered if taken alive, the moral justification is less evident. The presence of women and children in the group further complicates matters. Undoubtedly, some Confederate officers hesitated to command their men to open fire; however, because the fugitives were preponderantly military-age males, some officers issued such a command, and many individual soldiers probably fired without instructions. An effort apparently was made to avoiding hitting anyone who obeyed orders to halt, but some women and children were probably shot accidentally. Under circumstances of such moral, legal, and practical complexity and ambiguity, it would seem that some who died in the rush for the swamps were massacre victims and some were not. In any case, it is evident that massacre charges were inevitable.

Those considerations notwithstanding, it should be said plainly that there can be no justification for the killing of blacks and Buffaloes, uniformed or otherwise, after the battle. The definition of a "massacre" is open to debate, but the authors define one, in a battlefield context, as the deliberate killing of unarmed and unresisting soldiers or civilians who have been surrendered by someone in authority, who are endeavoring to surrender as a group or individually, or who are asking for quarter or mercy. Even by that narrow definition, there were probably at least 50 "massacre" victims at Plymouth.

On April 25, Hoke advanced against Little Washington, which was evacuated without a fight on April 30. Five days later, as Hoke massed his forces to attack New Bern, Grant struck at the Wilderness. Hoke and most of his command were immediately recalled by Lee, putting an end to the Confederates' promising attempt to evict the Unionists from eastern North Carolina. Amid the bloody battles that took place in Virginia that spring and summer, charges of a massacre at Plymouth were seemingly forgotten. Plymouth, garrisoned by several companies of the 50th Regiment North Carolina Troops, once again fell into obscurity. The town was recaptured by the Federals on October 31, and Wessells's men began returning home from Confederate prisons the following January. However, in the absence of atrocity charges by Wessells and other Federal officers, the massacre question was dropped. Although some facts concerning the events at Plymouth are ascertainable and, as has been demonstrated in the foregoing pages, many qualified deductions, informed speculations, and conditional conclusions are possible, the episode remains in many respects an enigma. Time may reveal a mass grave containing hundreds of broken skulls and other irrefutable evidence of calculated or random butchery. More likely, a perpetrator's "smoking gun" letter will come to light describing how naked, terrified, piteously pleading blacks and Buffaloes were bayoneted and bludgeoned in the mire. Until then, the Roanoke River swamps will retain their secrets.

Notes

This essay was originally published in *North Carolina Historical Review* 73 (Apr. 1995): 125–93. Reprinted with permission of the *North Carolina Historical Review*. The essay appears here in an abridged form, without the appendixes and ancillary matter originally in its footnotes.

The authors express their appreciation to Henry L. Mintz of Hallsboro, who traveled extensively to locate manuscripts for their essay. Mary C. Dowden of East Hartford, Connecticut, located a number of valuable manuscripts at the Connecticut State Library and the Connecticut Historical Society. Mallie H. Dalton allowed us to photocopy the letters of her Civil War ancestor, Josiah Worrell. Gerry S. Caughman and David W. Gaddy each contributed manuscript material. Patricia Monte and Jimmy Hardison of the Port o' Plymouth–Roanoke River Museum provided several useful manuscripts, critiqued the article, and conducted one of the authors on a tour of the battlefield. The essay was critiqued also by William Lang Baradell, Jan M. Poff, Matthew M. Brown, and Trudy M. Rayfeld of the Historical Publications Section of the North Carolina Division of Archives and History. Michael T. Meier and DeAnne Blanton of the National Archives, Richard J. Sommers of the U.S. Army Military History Institute, Ervin L. Jordan Jr. of the Alderman Library of the University of Virginia, and Guy R. Swanson of the Museum of the Confederacy went well beyond the call of duty in providing research assistance.

1. Rev. Horace James, *Annual Report of the Superintendent of Negro Affairs in North Carolina, 1864* (Boston: W. F. Brown, 1865), 34; logbook entries of USS *Whitehead,* Jan. 6, Jan. 31, and Mar. 1, 1864, Records of the Bureau of Naval Personnel, RG 24, National Archives, Washington, D.C. (hereafter cited as Naval Logbooks); Nelson Chapin (85th Regiment New York Infantry) to his son, Nov. 1, 1863 (typescript), *Civil War Times Illustrated* Collection, U.S. Army Military History Institute, Carlisle Barracks, Pa.

2. Wayne K. Durrill, *War of Another Kind: A Southern Community in the Great Rebellion* (New York: Oxford University Press, 1990), 207; James M. McPherson, *Battle Cry of Freedom: The Civil War Era* (New York: Oxford University Press, 1988), 793; Richard W. Iobst and Louis H. Manarin, *The Bloody Sixth: The Sixth North Carolina Regiment Confederate States of America* (1965; reprint, Gaithersburg, Md.: Butternut Press, 1987), 199; William R. Trotter, *Ironclads and Columbiads: The Civil War in North Carolina: The Coast* (Winston-Salem, N.C.: John F. Blair, 1989), 417–19. See also John G. Barrett, *The Civil War in North Carolina* (Chapel Hill: University of North Carolina Press, 1963), 220.

3. See Joseph T. Glatthaar, *Forged in Battle: The Civil War Alliance of Black Soldiers and White Officers* (New York: Free Press, 1990); Dudley Taylor Cornish, *The Sable Arm: Black Troops in the Union Army, 1861–1865* (1956; reprint, Lawrence: University Press of Kansas, 1987); Benjamin Quarles, *The Negro in the Civil War* (Boston: Little, Brown, 1953); and James M. McPherson, ed., *The Negro's Civil War: How American Negroes Felt and Acted During the War for the Union* (New York: Random House, 1965). Most nineteenth-century Civil War historians were silent on the alleged massacre at Plymouth. See Horace Greeley, *The American Conflict: A History of the Great Rebellion in the United States of America, 1860–'65, Its Causes, Incidents, and Results: Intended to Exhibit Especially Its Moral and Political Phases, with the Drift and Progress of American Opinion Respecting Human Slavery from 1776 to the Close of the War for the Union,* vol. 2 (Hartford, Conn.: O. D. Case, 1867), 533–34, 619–20; George W. Williams, *A History of the Negro Troops in the War of the Rebellion, 1861–1865, Preceded by a Review of the Military Services of Negroes in Ancient and Modern Times* (New York: Harper and Brothers, 1888), 257–72; and Joseph Thomas Wilson, *The Black Phalanx: A History of the Negro Soldiers of the United States in the Wars of 1775–1812, 1861–1865* (Hartford, Conn.: American Publishing, 1888), 315–60. See also John William Draper, *History of the American Civil War,* vol. 3 (New York: Harper and Brothers, 1870), 190–91.

4. William E. Dunn to his sister, Dec. 13, 1863 (typescript), *Civil War Times Illustrated* Collection.

5. O. Leland Barlow (16th Regiment Connecticut Infantry) to Jane E. Barlow, Feb. 28 and Jan. 31, 1864, Barlow Papers, Salmon Brook Historical Society, Granby, Conn.

6. Warren Lee Goss, *The Soldier's Story of His Captivity at Andersonville, Belle Isle, and Other Rebel Prisons* (Boston: Lee and Shepard, 1867), 55. See also O. L. Barlow to J. E. Barlow, Jan. 31, 1864, Barlow Papers; and Richard H. Lee to "Cousin Ada," Mar. 2, 1864 (typescript), Lee Papers, Salmon Brook Historical Society.

7. *The War of the Rebellion: A Compilation of the Official Records of the Union and Confederate Armies,* 128 vols. (Washington, D.C.: Government Printing Office, 1880–1901), ser. 1, 33:482, 282 (hereafter cited as *OR*).

8. *OR,* ser. 1, 51 (pt. 2): 857. See also ibid., 872; and *OR,* ser. 1, 33:1292.

9. Ulysses S. Grant, *Personal Memoirs of U. S. Grant,* vol. 2 (New York: Charles L. Webster, 1886), 138; *OR,* ser. 1, 33:283, 916, 981.

10. John Donaghy, *Army Experience of Capt. John Donaghy* (Deland, Fla.: E. O. Painter, 1926), 144; John William Wynne to his father, Apr. 24, 1864, Wynne Family Papers (typescripts), Virginia Historical Society, Richmond; *Daily Richmond Examiner,* May 3, 1864; Zephaniah W. Gooding to Richard Gooding, Mar. 28, 1864, Zephaniah W. Gooding Papers, Special Collections Department, Duke University Library, Durham, N.C. See also Nathan Lanpheur, "Fall of Plymouth," 4, 7, Nate Lanpheur Papers, Duke Special Collections; George Nathan Lamphere, "Experiences and Observations of a Private Soldier in the Civil War" (typescript), 7–8, Civil War Roster Project doc. no. 1003, North Carolina State Archives, Division of Archives and History, Raleigh; *OR,* ser. 1, 33:482; miscellaneous records relating to the *Miami, Whitehead,* and *Ceres,* entry 464, boxes 233, 245, 232, Naval Records Collection of the Office of Naval Records and Library, RG 45, National Archives; and Paul H. Silverstone, *Warships of the Civil War Navies* (Annapolis, Md.: Naval Institute Press, 1989), 102.

11. *OR,* ser. 1, 33:297, 301; Frederick Henry Dyer, *A Compendium of the War of the Rebellion, Comp. and Arranged from Official Records of the Federal and Confederate Armies, Reports of the Adjutant Generals of the Several States, the Army Registers, and Other Reliable Documents and Sources* (Des Moines, Iowa: Dyer Publishing, 1908), 1725; 10th Regiment U.S. Colored Troops, Records of Movements and Activities of Volunteer Union Organizations, M594, reel 206 (microfilm), Compiled Records Showing Service of Military Units in Volunteer Union Organizations, Records of the Adjutant General's Office, 1780s–1917, RG 94, National Archives.

12. See muster rolls dated Mar. 31, 1864, for USS *Miami, Southfield,* and *Ceres,* and muster roll dated Dec. 31, 1863, for USS *Whitehead,* Records of the Bureau of Naval Personnel, RG 24, National Archives (hereafter cited as Navy Muster Rolls). No muster rolls are available for the *Bombshell* or *Dolly.*

13. Joseph Emery Fiske to his father and mother, Dec. 1, 1864, in *War Letters of Capt. Joseph E. Fiske (Harvard, '61): Written to His Parents During the War of the Rebellion from Andover Theological Seminary and Encampments in North Carolina and from Southern Prisons* (Wellesley, Mass.: Maugus Press, n.d.), 57.

14. Lamphere, "Experiences and Observations," 8; William M. Smith, "The Siege and Capture of Plymouth," in *Personal Recollections of the War of the Rebellion: Addresses Delivered Before the New York Commandery of the* [Military Order of the] *Loyal Legion of the United States, 1883–1891,* vol. 1 (New York: New York Commandery of the Military Order of the Loyal Legion of the United States, 1891), 328. For other accounts, see Joseph M. Whitehill (103d Pennsylvania) to Robert F. Hoke, Apr. 17, 1894, Robert F. Hoke Papers, Private Collections, North Carolina State Archives; John A. Reed, *History of the 101st Regiment Pennsylvania Veteran Volunteer Infantry, 1861–1865* (Chicago: L. S. Dickey, 1910), 127; Alonzo Cooper, *In and Out of Rebel Prisons* (Oswego, N.Y.: R. J. Oliphant, 1888), 13–14; Robert Hale Kellogg, *Life and Death in Rebel Prisons: Giving a Complete History of the Inhuman and Barbarous Treatment of Our Brave Soldiers by Rebel Authorities, Inflicting Terrible Suffering and Frightful Mortality, Principally at Andersonville, Ga., and Florence, S.C., Describing Plans for Escape, Arrival of Prisoners, with Numerous and Varied Incidents and Anecdotes of Prison Life* (Hartford, Conn.: L. Stebbins, 1865), 25–26; and Oliver W. Gates (16th Connecticut) diary, [May 1864], Connecticut Historical Society, Hartford.

15. Lanpheur, "Fall of Plymouth," 8. See also Julian Whedon Merrill, comp., *Records of the 24th Independent Battery, N.Y. Light Artillery, U.S.V.* (New York: Ladies Cemetery Association of Perry, N.Y., 1870), 213.

16. Ira B. Sampson diary, Apr. 18, 1864, Ira B. Sampson Papers, Southern Historical Collection, University of North Carolina Library, Chapel Hill (first quotation only); Edward Cook Barnes to "Dear Charlie," Apr. 30, 1864, Barnes Family Papers, Manuscripts Department, University of Virginia Library, Charlottesville. See also Joseph E. Fiske, "An Involuntary Journey Through the Confederacy," in *Civil War Papers Read Before the Commandery of the State of Massachusetts, Military Order of the Loyal Legion of the United States,* vol. 2 (Boston: F. H. Gilson, 1900), 514; Barnes to "Dear Charlie," Barnes Family Papers; Wynne to his father, Wynne Family Papers; and "Civil War Reminiscences of Captain Edward Payson Reeve [1st Regiment Virginia Infantry]," unpaginated, Edward Payson Reeve Papers, Southern Historical Collection.

17. "Record of Events," abstract of Mar.–Apr. 1864 muster roll for Company D, 38th Battalion Virginia Light Artillery, Compiled Service Records of Confederate Soldiers Who Served in Organizations from the State of Virginia, M324, reel 254 (microfilm), Records of Confederate Soldiers Who Served During the Civil War, RG 109, National Archives. See also Hodijah Lincoln Meade (38th Virginia Light Artillery) to "Lottie [his sister]," Apr. 29, 1864, Meade Family Papers, Virginia Historical Society; Wynne to his father, Wynne Family Papers; John W. Darden, "Story of Washington County," 2, North Carolina Collection, University of North Carolina Library, Chapel Hill; and David E. Johnston, *Four Years a Soldier* (Princeton, W.Va.: privately printed, 1887), 297.

18. Robert Hale Kellogg (16th Connecticut) diary, Apr. 18, 1864 (first and second quotations), Connecticut Historical Society; Benjamin H. Jones (21st Georgia) to his brother, Apr. 21, 1864, quoted in *Historical Society of Washington County Newsletter,* fall 1991; *OR,* ser. 1, 33:302; Lanpheur, "Fall of Plymouth," 14–15. See also Charles D. Camp and Benjamin F. Jones, "History of the Twenty-first Georgia Regiment," in *History of the Doles-Cook Brigade, Army of Northern Virginia, C.S.A., Containing Muster Rolls of Each Company of the Fourth, Twelfth, Twenty-first, and Forty-fourth Georgia Regiments, with a Short Sketch of the Services of Each Member, and a Complete History of Each Regiment, by One of Its Own Members, and Other Matters of Interest,* ed. Henry W. Thomas (Atlanta: Franklin, 1903), 360.

19. Lanpheur, "Fall of Plymouth," 15; Darden, "Story of Washington County," 4–5; Edwin Baker Loving journal, 47, Virginia State Archives, Richmond.

20. Meade to "Lottie," Meade Family Papers; *OR,* ser. 1, 33:298 (see also ibid., 302–3); Darden, "Story of Washington County," 5.

21. *Daily Richmond Examiner,* May 3, 1864 (first and fourth quotations); John Washington Graham to William Alexander Graham, Apr. 24, 1864, in Max R. Williams, ed., *The Papers of William Alexander Graham,* vol. 6 (Raleigh: Division of Archives and History, 1976), 74 (second and third quotations). See also Samuel J. Gibson diary, Apr. 19, 1864, S. J. Gibson Papers, Library of Congress, Washington, D.C.; and Cooper, *In and Out of Rebel Prisons,* 16.

22. See *Official Records of the Union and Confederate Navies in the War of the Rebellion,* 30 vols. (Washington, D.C.: Government Printing Office, 1894–1922), ser. 1, 9:656–58 (hereafter cited as *ORN;* all citations are to series 1, volume 9).

23. Fiske, "Involuntary Journey," 514.

24. Ibid. See also Gilbert Elliott, "The Career of the Confederate Ram 'Albemarle,'" *Century Illustrated* 36 (May–Oct. 1888): 423.

25. Gibson diary, Apr. 19, 1864, Gibson Papers; Paul C. Helmreich, "The Diary of Charles G. Lee [16th Connecticut Infantry] in the Andersonville and Florence Prison Camps, 1864," *Connecticut Historical Society Bulletin* 41 (Jan. 1976): 14 (Apr. 19, 1864); Wynne to his father, Wynne Family Papers; diary entry for Apr. 19, 1864, William Beavans (43d North Carolina Regiment) Books, Southern Historical Collection.

26. Gibson diary, Apr. 19, 1864, Gibson Papers. The situation, in Gibson's estimation, was "*Right Smart Blue.*"

27. James Carson Elliott, *The Southern Soldier Boy: A Thousand Shots for the Confederacy* (1907; reprint, Wendell, N.C.: Avera Press, 1979), 14.

28. J. W. Graham to W. A. Graham, Apr. 24, 1864, in Max Williams, *Papers of Graham,* 6:75–76. See also Samuel E. Grosvenor diary, Apr. 20, 1864, and Kellogg diary, Apr. 20, 1864, Connecticut Historical Society.

29. Pinckney Rayburn Young, "A Partial Record of the Experiences of P. R. Young [25th North Carolina] as a Confederate Soldier in the War Between the States," 3, Daniel Augustus Tompkins Papers, Duke Special Collections; Gibson diary, Apr. 20, 1864, Gibson Papers; Robert Davidson Graham, "Fifty-Sixth North Carolina," in Walter Clark, ed., *Histories of the Several Regiments and Battalions from North Carolina in the Great War, 1861–'65,* 5 vols. (Raleigh: State of North Carolina, 1901), 3:343 (third and fourth quotations). See also Charles C. Mosher diary, Apr. 20, 1864, Seneca Falls Historical Society, Seneca Falls, N.Y.; *Hartford Evening Post,* Sept. 18, 1874; Lanpheur, "Fall of Plymouth," 22; William Hyslop Sumner Burgwyn, "Ransom's Brigade," in Clark, *Histories of Several Regiments,* 4:574; and Bernard F. Blakeslee, *History of the Sixteenth Connecticut Volunteers* (Hartford, Conn.: Case, Lockwood, and Brainard, 1875), 58–59.

30. *Raleigh Daily Confederate,* Apr. 30, 1864.

31. *Polkton (N.C.) Ansonian,* July 12 and 19, 1876; *OR,* ser. 1, 33:299 (second and third quotations).

32. *Polkton Ansonian,* July 19, 1876. See also Henry T. Guion journal, Apr. 20, 1864, William Alexander Hoke Papers, Southern Historical Collection.

33. *Polkton Ansonian,* July 19, 1876; *OR,* ser. 1, 33:299; Guion journal, Apr. 20, 1864, Hoke Papers.

34. Quoted in *Raleigh Daily Confederate,* May 3, 1864.

35. Guion journal, Apr. 20, 1864, Hoke Papers; *Polkton Ansonian,* July 19, 1876; Wynne to his father (third and fourth quotations), Wynne Family Papers. See also Merrill, *Records of 24th N.Y. Battery,* 217.

36. *OR,* ser. 1, 33:299. See also George Winfield recollections, Grinnan Family Papers, Virginia Historical Society; Gibson diary, Apr. 20, 1864, Gibson Papers; and Beavans diary, Apr. 20, 1864.

37. *Polkton Ansonian,* July 19, 1876. See also Wynne to his father, Wynne Family Papers.

38. Robert H. Moore II, *The Richmond Fayette, Hampden, Thomas, and Blount's Lynchburg Artillery* (Lynchburg, Va.: H. E. Howard, 1991), 103. See also *New Bern North Carolina Times,* June 1, 1864; and Smith, "Capture of Plymouth," 341.

39. Fiske to his father and mother, 58; William Henry Morgan, *Personal Reminiscences of the War of 1861-5: In Camp on Bivouac—on the March—on Picket—on the Skirmish Line—on the Battlefield—and in Prison* (Lynchburg: J. P. Bell, 1911), 186. See also Wynne to his father, Wynne Family Papers.

40. See Louis H. Manarin and Weymouth T. Jordan Jr., comps., *North Carolina Troops, 1861-1865: A Roster,* 13 vols. to date (Raleigh, N.C.: Division of Archives and History, 1966-), 4:267-393, 521-625, 6:538-648, 7:251-349, 355-454, 9:358-461, 10:293-392, 13:592-704; *Raleigh Daily Confederate,* Apr. 30, May 2, and May 5, 1864; and Lillian Henderson, comp., *Roster of the Confederate Soldiers of Georgia, 1861-1865,* vol. 2 (Hapeville, Ga.: Longino and Porter, n.d.), 838-934.

41. *Richmond Daily Dispatch,* Apr. 27, 1864; undated clipping of an item reprinted in an unidentified North Carolina newspaper from *Lynchburg Daily Republican,* North Carolina Adjutant General's Roll of Honor Scrapbook, Adjutant General's Papers, North Carolina State Archives; Lee A. Wallace Jr., *1st Virginia Infantry,* 3d ed. (Lynchburg, Va.: H. E. Howard, 1985), 48; Lee A. Wallace Jr., *3d Virginia Infantry,* 2d ed. (Lynchburg, Va.: H. E. Howard, 1986), 46; David F. Riggs, *7th Virginia Infantry,* 2d ed. (Lynchburg, Va.: H. E. Howard, 1982), 48; Robert T. Bell, *11th Virginia Infantry* (Lynchburg, Va.: H. E. Howard, 1985), 61; Ralph White Gunn, *24th Virginia Infantry* (Lynchburg, Va.: H. E. Howard, 1987), 52.

42. *Raleigh Daily Confederate,* May 5, 1864; Peter E. Hines to William A. Holt, Apr. 27, 1864, William A. Holt Papers, Southern Historical Collection.

43. "Report of Killed and Wounded of Hoke's Division at the Battle of Plymouth, North Carolina, April 18th, 19th, and 20th, 1864," Eleanor S. Brockenbrough Library, Museum of the Confederacy, Richmond, Va.

44. *OR,* ser. 1, 33:300; "Little Mare" [Surgeon Nathan Mayer], "The Sixteenth Regiment at Plymouth," *Connecticut War Record* 2 (June 1864): 216; quoted in Merrill, *Records of 24th N.Y. Battery,* 217; Blakeslee, *Sixteenth Connecticut Volunteers,* 61; *Raleigh Daily Confederate,* Apr. 27, 1864. See Dyer, *Compendium,* 823; Frederick Phisterer, *Statistical Record of the Armies of the United States* (New York: Charles Scribner's Sons, 1883), 216; and Frank Moore, ed., *The Rebellion Record: A Diary of American Events, with Documents, Narratives, Illustrative Incidents, Poetry, etc.,* vol. 8 (New York: G. P. Putnam and D. Van Nostrand, 1867), 69. See also Donaghy, *Army Experience,* 158.

45. [Mayer], "Sixteenth Regiment at Plymouth," 216; *OR,* ser. 1, 51 (pt. 2): 870; diary entry for Apr. 20, 1864, Leonidas Lafayette Polk Papers, Southern Historical Collection; John K. Walker to his father, Apr. 21, 1864, John K. Walker Papers, Duke Special Collections; George W. Love to his sister, Apr. 24, 1864, Matthew N. Love Papers, Duke Special Collections; *Petersburg (Va.) Daily Express* dispatch dated Apr. 21, 1864, quoted in *Charlotte (N.C.) Western Democrat,* May 3, 1864.

46. Josiah Worrell to his wife, Apr. 24, 1864, Josiah Worrell Letters (photocopies), Civil War Roster Project doc. no. 1002, North Carolina State Archives; *Raleigh Daily Confederate,* May 3, 1864; John W. Broadnax to Thomas Ruffin, Apr. 22, 1864, in J. G. de Roulhac Hamilton, ed., *The Papers of Thomas Ruffin,* vol. 3 (Raleigh: North Carolina Historical Commission, 1920), 384; Cushing Biggs Hassell diary, Apr. 23, 1864, Cushing Biggs Hassell Papers, Southern Historical Collection.

47. *Petersburg Daily Express* dispatch dated Apr. 21, 1864, quoted in *Charlotte Western Democrat*, May 3, 1864; *Wilmington (N.C.) Journal*, May 19, 1864; James, *Annual Report of Negro Affairs*, 34. See also James Carson Elliott (56th North Carolina) to ———, Apr. 23, 1864, Elliott letter (photocopy), Civil War Roster Project doc. no. 1008, North Carolina State Archives.

48. Darden, "Story of Washington County," 6. See also Goss, *Soldier's Story*, 61.

49. Darden, "Story of Washington County," 7. See also Robert Moore, *Richmond Fayette Artillery*, 103; and *Petersburg Daily Express*, Apr. 25, 1864.

50. Oliver R. McNary, "What I Saw and Did Inside and Outside of Rebel Prisons," in *War Talks in Kansas: A Series of Papers Read before the Kansas Commandery of the Military Order of the Loyal Legion of the United States* (1906; reprint, Wilmington, N.C.: Broadfoot, 1992), 26; Blakeslee, *Sixteenth Connecticut Volunteers*, 60. See also Robert Vern Jackson, ed., *North Carolina: 1860 Census Index*, vol. 2 (North Salt Lake City: Accelerated Indexing Systems International, 1987), 1448–49.

51. William Gilham, *Manual of Instruction for the Volunteers and Militia of the Confederate States* (Richmond: West and Johnston, 1861), 546, 552.

52. Roland Dixon to John A. Judson, Apr. 13, 1864, and George W. Jones to Walter S. Poor, Apr. 15, 1864, Roland Dixon and George W. Jones service record files, 2d Regiment North Carolina Infantry, Compiled Service Records of Volunteer Union Soldiers, M401, reels 11 and 12 (microfilm), Records of Volunteer Union Soldiers Who Served During the Civil War, RG 94, National Archives; *OR*, ser. 1, 33:948–49.

53. *OR*, ser. 1, 14:599.

54. *OR*, ser. 2, 5:844.

55. Ibid., 808. See also ibid., 844–45.

56. Ibid., 940.

57. See U.S. Congress, Joint Committee on the Conduct of the War, *Fort Pillow Massacre*, 38th Cong., 1st sess., 1864, H. Rept. 65; *OR*, ser. 1, 32 (pt. 1): 502–623; John L. Jordan, "Was There a Massacre at Fort Pillow?" *Tennessee Historical Quarterly* 6 (June 1947): 99–133; Albert Castel, "The Fort Pillow Massacre: A Fresh Examination of the Evidence," *Civil War History* 4 (Mar. 1958): 37–50; John Cimprich and Robert C. Mainfort Jr., "Fort Pillow Revisited: New Evidence about an Old Controversy," *Civil War History* 28 (Dec. 1982): 293–306, "Dr. Fitch's Report on the Fort Pillow Massacre," *Tennessee Historical Quarterly* 44 (spring 1985): 27–39, and "The Fort Pillow Massacre: A Statistical Note," *Journal of American History* 76 (Dec. 1989): 830–37; and Lonnie E. Maness, "The Fort Pillow Massacre: Fact or Fiction," *Tennessee Historical Quarterly* 45 (winter 1986): 287–315. For a careful analysis and evenhanded appraisal of General Forrest's role at Fort Pillow, see Brian Steel Wills, *A Battle from the Start: The Life of Nathan Bedford Forrest* (New York: Harper Collins, 1992), 179–96.

58. Quoted in *Charlotte Daily Bulletin*, Mar. 18, 1864.

59. J. W. Graham to W. A. Graham, Mar. 13, 1864, in Max Williams, *Papers of Graham*, 6:43; Gabriel Powell Sherrill to George Monroe Wilkinson, Mar. 17, 1864, George Monroe Wilkinson Letters, Catawba Historical Museum Archives, Newton, N.C. See also G. P. Sherrill to "My Dear Friend," Mar. 24, 1864, Wilkinson Letters.

60. William Alburtus Day, *A True History of Company I, 49th Regiment, North Carolina Troops, in the Great Civil War, Between the North and the South* (Newton, N.C.: Enterprise Job Office, 1893), 84.

61. William Alburtus Day, "The Breastworks at Petersburg," *Confederate Veteran* 29 (May 1921): 175; T. H. Pearce and Selby A. Daniels, eds., *Diary of Captain Henry A. Chambers* (Wendell, N.C.: Broadfoot's Bookmark, 1983), 210 (July 30, 1864).

62. Smith, "Capture of Plymouth," 324; Hiram L. Marvin deposition dated Sept. 6, 1890, in John Ward pension application file, Federal Pension Applications Files, Records of the Veterans Administration, RG 15, National Archives (hereafter cited as Federal Pension Application Records). See also Plymouth Recruiting Return of the 37th U.S. Colored Troops for Mar. 1864

(dated Apr. 16, 1864), Records of Movements and Activities of Volunteer Union Organizations, RG 94.

63. See Muster and Descriptive Roll dated June 29, 1864, for the 2d Regiment U.S. Colored Cavalry, Records of Movements and Activities of Volunteer Union Organizations, RG 94.

64. Edmund C. Blount to Charles H. Foster, Feb. 9, 1864, Edmund C. Blount service record file, 2d Regiment North Carolina Infantry, Compiled Service Records of Volunteer Union Soldiers, M401, reel 10, RG 94; Stephen T. Andrews to [Maggie], Feb. 23, 1864, Stephen T. Andrews Letters (photocopies), Civil War Roster Project doc. no. 1005, North Carolina State Archives. See also Goss, *Soldier's Story,* 54.

65. Reed, *101st Pennsylvania Infantry,* 54; Donaghy, *Army Experience,* 150; Lanpheur, "Fall of Plymouth," 7. See also George Robbins, "Some Recollections of a Private in the War of the Rebellion, 1861–1865," 31, Connecticut Historical Society, Hartford.

66. For information on the identified "colored cooks," see the service record files in the records of the 24th New York Battery, 85th Regiment New York Infantry, and 103d Regiment Pennsylvania Infantry, Compiled Service Records of Volunteer Union Soldiers, RG 94. See also Smith, "Capture of Plymouth," 343.

67. John A. Hedrick to Benjamin Sherwood Hedrick, May 8, 1864, Benjamin Sherwood Hedrick Papers, Duke Special Collections.

68. Smith, "Capture of Plymouth," 333, 329; Donaghy, *Army Experience,* 150.

69. See miscellaneous records relating to USS *Southfield,* box 573, Office of Naval Records and Library, RG 45; muster roll for USS *Southfield,* Mar. 31, 1864, and muster roll for USS *Miami,* June 30, 1864, Navy Muster Rolls; *Annual Report of the Secretary of the Navy,* in *Message of the President of the United States and Accompanying Documents to the Two Houses of Congress,* 38th Cong., 2d sess., Dec. 5, 1864–Mar. 3, 1865; Henry Gray, Burrill Sharp (alias Burrill Watson), Peter Skinner, and Charles White pension application files, Federal Pension Application Records; "Casualties in the U.S. Navy, April 1861–July 1865," entry no. 36, Records of the Bureau of Medicine and Surgery, Department of the Navy, RG 52, National Archives; and *ORN,* 642, 645–46, 657.

70. James, *Annual Report of Negro Affairs,* 35. See also Goss, *Soldier's Story,* 57.

71. *ORN,* 424, 641; John A. Reed to C. H. Foster, Jan. 30, 1864, John A. Reed service record file, 101st Regiment Pennsylvania Infantry, Compiled Service Records of Volunteer Union Soldiers, RG 94; Frank Moore, *Rebellion Record,* 68; H. L. Meade to "Lottie," Meade Family Papers.

72. *OR,* ser. 1, 33:299; McNary, "Inside and Outside of Rebel Prisons," 4.

73. *OR,* ser. 1, 51 (pt. 2): 870; Wynne to his father, Wynne Family Papers; G. W. Love to his sister, Apr. 24, 1864, Love Papers; Nicholas Cloer to his father and mother, May 14, 1864, Lewis Leigh Jr. Collection, U.S. Army Military History Institute; J. W. Graham to W. A. Graham, Apr. 24, 1864, in Max Williams, *Papers of Graham,* 6:69; Johnston, *Four Years a Soldier,* 301. See also Charles Theodore Loehr, *War History of the Old First Virginia Infantry Regiment, Army of Northern Virginia* (Richmond: William Ellis Jones, 1884), 44; and John W. Broadnax to Thomas Ruffin, Apr. 22, 1864, in Hamilton, *Papers of Ruffin,* 384.

74. *Raleigh Daily Confederate,* May 3, 1864; undated clipping from an unidentified newspaper, Adjutant General's Roll of Honor Scrapbook, North Carolina State Archives; *Wadesboro North Carolina Argus,* Apr. 28, 1864; *Fayetteville (N.C.) Weekly Intelligencer,* May 10, 1864. See also *Richmond Daily Dispatch,* Apr. 22, 1864.

75. Quoted in *Raleigh Daily Confederate,* May 3, 1864; William I. Clopton to his mother and sisters, Apr. 24, 1864, John Clopton Papers, Duke Special Collections.

76. *Raleigh Daily Confederate,* Apr. 30, 1864; Mosher diary, Apr. 21, 1864, Seneca Falls Historical Society. See also Morgan, *Personal Reminiscences,* 189.

77. Bossie O'Brien Handley Baer, "With the Passing Years," undated typescript incorporating the reminiscences of Frank P. O'Brien, 27–28, Civil War Roster Project doc. no. 1004, North Carolina State Archives. See also Eli Peal to Lauvesta Peal, May 1, 1864, Eli Peal Paper, Private

Collections, North Carolina State Archives; and William A. Biggs to his sister, May 3, 1864, Asa Biggs Papers, Duke Special Collections.

78. Goss, *Soldier's Story,* 61; Blakeslee, *Sixteenth Connecticut Volunteers,* 73. See also Samuel P. Bates, "One Hundred and First Regiment," in *History of the Pennsylvania Volunteers, 1861–5,* vol. 3 (Harrisburg, Pa.: H. Singerly, 1870), 606.

79. Bates, "One Hundred and First Regiment," 606–7; Cooper, *In and Out of Rebel Prisons,* 33; Donaghy, *Army Experience,* 155. See also John Washington Graham, "The Capture of Plymouth, 20 April, 1864," in Clark, *Histories of Several Regiments,* 5:190; *Wilmington Journal,* Apr. 28, 1864; William Judson Abernethy diary, Apr. 21–22, 1864, U.S. Army Military History Institute; Luther M. Baldwin to ——, Apr. 23, 1864, Nettleton-Baldwin Family Papers, Duke Special Collections; and J. A. Hedrick to B. S. Hedrick, Apr. 25, 1864, Hedrick Papers.

80. Gates diary, [May 1864], Connecticut Historical Society; quoted in Merrill, *Records of 24th N.Y. Battery,* 217; Blakeslee, *Sixteenth Connecticut Volunteers,* 60; Cooper, *In and Out of Rebel Prisons,* 34. See also Darden, "Story of Washington County," 5–6.

81. Goss, *Soldier's Story,* 61; Donaghy, *Army Experience,* 155; McNary, "Inside and Outside of Rebel Prisons," 4; Robbins, "Recollections of a Private," 31. See also James, *Annual Report of Negro Affairs,* 35; and Frank Moore, *Rebellion Record,* 69.

82. Darden, "Story of Washington County," 8–9. Latham was born on Mar. 29, 1853, and was therefore eleven years old at the time of the Battle of Plymouth.

83. *OR,* ser. 2, 7:459–60.

84. Ibid., 459.

85. *New York Herald,* Apr. 26, 1864; *Philadelphia Inquirer,* Apr. 30, 1864; *New York Daily Tribune* item reprinted in *Daily Richmond Examiner,* Apr. 26, 1864; item from an unidentified Baltimore newspaper reprinted in *Salem (N.C.) People's Press,* May 5, 1864. See also photocopy of an undated clipping from the *New York Daily Tribune,* Civil War Roster Project doc. no. 1007, North Carolina State Archives.

86. *North Carolina Times,* Apr. 27 and May 7, 1864.

87. *OR,* ser. 2, 7:468; [Mayer], "Sixteenth Regiment at Plymouth," 216; John Thomas Kennedy and William Fletcher Parker, "Seventy-Fifth Regiment (Seventh Cavalry)," in Clark, *Histories of Several Regiments,* 4:83.

88. *Wilmington Journal,* May 5, 1864; *Raleigh Daily Confederate,* May 2, 1864.

89. *Daily Richmond Examiner* item of Apr. 29, 1864, reprinted in the *North Carolina Times,* May 7, 1864.

90. Luther S. Dickey, *History of the 103d Regiment Pennsylvania Veteran Volunteer Infantry, 1861–1865* (Chicago: L. S. Dickey, 1910), 269, 310–11.

91. Ibid., 269–70.

92. Quoted in ibid., 270.

93. Quoted in ibid.

94. Mosher diary, Apr. 20, 1864, Seneca Falls Historical Society; Ezra T. Burgess to George Q. Whitney, Mar. 29, 1909, Correspondence, Papers, etc., of 16th Connecticut Volunteer Association Affairs, Connecticut State Library, Hartford. See also Robert A. Hawley (Holley) service record file, 16th Regiment Connecticut Infantry, Compiled Service Records of Volunteer Union Soldiers, RG 94; Donaghy, *Army Experience,* 155; and Reed, *101st Pennsylvania Infantry,* 135.

95. John D. Biggs deposition dated Dec. 19, 1902, in Benjamin Gibson pension application file, Federal Pension Application Records; Eighth Census of the United States, 1860: Martin County, N.C., Population Schedule, 753, National Archives (microfilm, North Carolina State Archives). See also Benjamin Gibson service record file, 2d Regiment North Carolina Infantry, Compiled Service Records of Volunteer Union Soldiers, M401, reel 11, RG 94; and Benjamin Gibson service record file, 61st Regiment North Carolina Troops, Compiled Service Records of Confederate Soldiers, M270, reel 545.

96. Marcus Bird affidavit dated June 7, 1890, in James Bird pension application file, Federal Pension Application Records. See also logbook of USS *Ceres,* Apr. 27, 1864, Naval Logbooks; and *ORN,* 641.

97. John Butler affidavit dated July 9, 1889, in John Butler pension application file, Federal Pension Application Records.

98. William Henry Myers and William W. Byrd joint affidavit dated Mar. 19, 1888, in James H. Mitchell pension application file, Federal Pension Application Records.

99. James Corbit and W. W. Byrd joint affidavit dated Jan. 2, 1892, in William H. Myers pension application file, Federal Pension Application Records.

100. Doctrin Williams deposition dated Mar. 15, 1890, in Laton Gardner pension application file, Federal Pension Application Records.

101. James W. Skiles deposition dated Mar. 17, 1890, in Laton Gardner pension application file, Federal Pension Application Records.

102. Timothy Hoggard deposition dated Sept. 8, 1890, in Calvin Hoggard pension application file, Federal Pension Application Records; Logbook of USS *Whitehead,* May 31, 1864, Naval Logbooks.

103. Henry A. Hobbs affidavit dated Dec. 9, 1889, in Worley T. Hoggard pension application file, Federal Pension Application Records.

104. James L. Keeter service record file, 2d Regiment North Carolina Infantry, Compiled Service Records of Volunteer Union Soldiers, M401, reel 12, RG 94; Thomas Carver service record file, 35th Regiment North Carolina Troops, Compiled Service Records of Confederate Soldiers, M270, reel 393.

105. Gibson diary, Apr. 24, 1864, Gibson Papers. See Donaghy, *Army Experience,* 156; *Wilmington Journal,* May 5, 1864; and *Richmond Daily Dispatch,* Apr. 23, 1864.

106. See George Morris affidavit dated Dec. 9, 1892, in Kenneth Butler pension application file, Federal Pension Application Records; and "List of Prisoners Confined in Jail at Plymouth Sept 9th 1864," James Merritt Pittman Collection, Private Collections, North Carolina State Archives.

107. Helmreich, "Diary of Charles G. Lee," 15 (Apr. 21, 1864); Goss, *Soldier's Story,* 62; Gibson diary, Apr. 23, 1864, Gibson Papers; Asa W. Root (85th New York) diary (typescript), 9 (Apr. 22, 1864), Historical Museum of the D. R. Barker Library, Fredonia, N.Y. See also Mosher diary, Apr. 20, 1864, Seneca Falls Historical Society; Francis M. Shaw (101st Pennsylvania) diary, May 1, 1864, Civil War Miscellaneous Collection, U.S. Army Military History Institute; Henry E. Savage (16th Connecticut) diary, Apr. 20, 1864, Connecticut State Library; and Kellogg, *Life and Death in Rebel Prisons,* 38.

108. *OR,* ser. 2, 7:78.

109. See Titus Hardy affidavit dated Aug. 1, 1891, in Titus Hardy (alias Thus McRae) pension application file, Federal Pension Application Records; Richard West deposition dated Mar. 11, 1902, in Richard West pension application file, Federal Pension Application Records; and Charles White deposition dated Nov. 4, 1902, and Charles White declaration dated Aug. 7, 1890, in Charles White pension application file, Federal Pension Application Records.

110. Guion journal, Apr. 21, 1864, Hoke Papers.

111. *OR,* ser. 1, 51 (pt. 2): 872; W. H. C. Whiting to P. G. T. Beauregard, Apr. 29 and May 2, 1864 (telegrams), Pierre Gustave Toutant Beauregard Papers, Private Collections, North Carolina State Archives; J. A. Bracey to William Bracey, May 4, 1864, William Sheppard Lyman Collection, Private Collections, North Carolina State Archives. See also P. G. T. Beauregard to Z. B. Vance, Apr. 23, 1864 (telegram), Zebulon B. Vance, Governors Papers, North Carolina State Archives.

112. See John Rolack service record file, 85th New York Infantry, Compiled Service Records of Volunteer Union Soldiers, RG 94; Joseph Sharp and John S. W. Eagles depositions dated Feb. 14, 1891, in George Burdin pension application file, Federal Pension Application Records. See also James Harris and Kindred Garris depositions dated Feb. 14, 1891, in same file.

113. See Hiram L. Marvin deposition dated Sept. 6, 1890, in John Ward pension application file, Federal Pension Application Records; and *North Carolina Times,* Apr. 27, 1864. See also service record files for John Berden, Jordan Edwards, Abram Jones, George Jones, Jackson Miller, David Smithwick, William Smithwick, Moses Turner, and John Ward, 37th Regiment U.S. Colored Troops, Compiled Service Records of Volunteer Union Soldiers, RG 94.

114. See Anderson Reddick and Peter Ruffin pension application files, Federal Pension Application Records.

115. John Ward deposition dated May 13, 1890, in John Ward pension application file, Federal Pension Application Records. See also Hiram Marvin deposition dated Sept. 6, 1890, John Berden and Abram Jones joint deposition dated Nov. 20, 1877, and John Berden deposition dated July 18, 1890, in John Ward pension application file, Federal Pension Application Records.

116. Logbook of USS *Miami,* Apr. 23, 1864, Naval Logbooks; James B. Farrand affidavit dated June 18, 1889, and Alexander Lewis declarations dated July 9, 1890, and Sept. 6, 1888, in Alexander Lewis pension application file, Federal Pension Application Records; William R. Cradle deposition dated July 8, 1911, in William R. Cradle pension application file, Federal Pension Application Records; William S. Pettigrew to James C. Johnston, Aug. 9, 1864, Hayes Collection, Southern Historical Collection. See also John Berden deposition dated July 18, 1890, in John Ward pension application file, Federal Pension Application Records.

117. Johnston, *Four Years a Soldier,* 300–301; Loving journal, 48, Virginia State Archives. See also David Emmons Johnston, *The Story of a Confederate Boy in the Civil War* (Portland, Ore.: Glass and Prudhomme, 1914), 242.

118. P. G. T. Beauregard to Z. B. Vance (telegram), Apr. 23, 1864, Vance Papers. See also Robbins, "Recollections of a Private," 31.

119. Beth Gilbert Crabtree and James W. Patton, eds., *"Journal of a Secesh Lady": The Diary of Catherine Ann Devereux Edmondston, 1860–1866* (Raleigh: Division of Archives and History, 1979), 551 (Apr. 22, 1864).

120. Eighth Census of the United States, 1860: Halifax County, N.C., Slave Schedule, 49 (microfilm, North Carolina State Archives).

121. John Jordan, "Was There a Massacre?" 99. See also Joint Committee on the Conduct of the War, *Fort Pillow Massacre;* and *OR,* ser. 1, 32 (pt. 1): 502–623.

122. Blakeslee, *Sixteenth Connecticut Volunteers,* 60; Baer, "With the Passing Years," 27–28; *Raleigh Daily Confederate,* May 3, 1864; Darden, "Story of Washington County," 8–9.

123. See USS *Southfield* casualty list, Records of the Bureau of Medicine and Surgery, RG 52; pension application files for *Southfield* crewmen (as identified in the foregoing casualty list), Federal Pension Application Records; and *ORN,* 645, 708.

124. Durrill, *War of Another Kind,* 207; Kellogg, *Life and Death in Rebel Prisons,* 35.

125. Charles A. Wills to Mary J. Wills, Apr. 22, 1864 (two letters of same date), Charles A. Wills Papers, Manuscripts and Rare Books Department, College of William and Mary Library, Williamsburg, Va. See also James G. Martin to his wife, Apr. 27, 28, 29, and May 1, 2, 5, and 7, 1864, Starke, Marchant, and Martin Family Papers, Southern Historical Collection; William H. Jackson diary, Connecticut State Library; Albert H. Bancroft diary, in *Fifth Annual Report of the Chief of the Bureau of Military Statistics* [1867–68] (Albany, N.Y.: N.p., n.d.), 610–12 (Apr. 17–May 6, 1864); Leonidas L. Polk to Sallie Polk, Apr. 20 and 24, 1864, Polk Papers; *Richmond Whig,* May 5, 1864; and *Daily Richmond Examiner,* May 3, 1864.

126. Howard K. Beale, ed., *The Diary of Edward Bates, 1859–1866* (originally published in *Annual Report of the American Historical Association for the Year 1930;* reprint, New York: Da Capo, 1971), 361. See also Roy P. Basler, ed., *The Collected Works of Abraham Lincoln,* vol. 7 (New Brunswick, N.J.: Rutgers University Press, 1953), 302–3, 328–29, 345–46; Joint Committee on the Conduct of the War, *Fort Pillow Massacre;* and *Daily Richmond Examiner,* Apr. 30, 1864.

127. Henry Williams service record file, 2d Regiment U.S. Colored Cavalry, Compiled Service Records of Volunteer Union Soldiers, RG 94.

128. Samuel Johnson pension application file, Federal Pension Application Records.

129. Donaghy, *Army Experience,* 161–62.

130. Andrew B. Booth, comp., *Records of Louisiana Confederate Soldiers and Louisiana Confederate Commands,* 3 vols. (1920; reprint, Spartanburg, S.C.: Reprint Co., 1984); Consolidated Index to Compiled Service Records of Confederate Soldiers, RG 109; Donaghy, *Army Experience,* 155–56.

131. Smith, "Capture of Plymouth," 343. See also George W. Kelley affidavit dated Oct. 18, 1870, and George W. Kelley and Henry F. Clapp joint affidavit (undated) in George W. Higley pension application file, Federal Pension Application Records; and Dorance Atwater, *A List of Union Soldiers Buried at Andersonville* (New York: Tribune Association, 1866), 35.

132. Smith, "Capture of Plymouth," 343.

133. Ibid., 341–42.

134. *Daily Richmond Examiner,* Apr. 25, 1864; Helmreich, "Diary of Charles G. Lee," 14 (Apr. 20, 1864).

135. Mosher diary, "Events of 1864" (entry dated Sept. 10, 1894), Seneca Falls Historical Society; Johnston, *Four Years a Soldier,* 298–99.

136. James Dearing to his wife, Apr. 20, 1864, Dearing Family Papers, Virginia Historical Society.

137. Wynne to his father, Wynne Family Papers; Beavans diary, Apr. 20, 1864; James B. Jones diary, Apr. 29, 1864, Jones Family Papers, Southern Historical Collection; William A. Biggs to his sister, May 3, 1864, Biggs Papers. See also *Wadesboro North Carolina Argus,* May 5, 1864; and James Elliott, *Southern Soldier Boy,* 15.

The Battle of the Crater
The Civil War's Worst Massacre

9

BRYCE A. SUDEROW

After fighting his way south from the Rapidan to the gates of Richmond during May and June 1864, Lt. Gen. Ulysses S. Grant found himself stalemated in front of the formidable trenches protecting Petersburg, the rail junction that supplied the Confederate capital.

During June and July 1864, soldiers of Maj. Gen. Ambrose E. Burnside's 9th Corps tunneled under the Confederate lines outside Petersburg and filled two galleries with eight thousand pounds of gunpowder. The goal was to explode the gunpowder to create a breach in the Confederate lines and to rush troops through the gap to seize Cemetery Hill. It was supposed that once this commanding position was taken, the Confederates would be forced to abandon Petersburg and Richmond, Gen Robert E. Lee's Army of Northern Virginia would be beaten into submission, and the war would end.

At 4:45 AM on July 30, 1864, the Federals detonated the explosives beneath a salient held by Brig. Gen. Stephen Elliott Jr. and his South Carolina brigade, destroying one battery and a regiment and a half of infantry. In their place was a huge smoldering hole in the ground measuring 150–200 feet long, 60 feet wide, and 30 feet deep. Shortly after the explosion, three white divisions were sent, one after the other, to exploit the break, but they were so badly led that they were easily driven back into the "Crater," as the place quickly became known. At 8:00 AM, Brig. Gen. Edward Ferrero's 4th Division (U.S. Colored Troops), numbering 4,200 officers and men, was ordered forward, its two brigades led by Cols. Joshua K. Siegfried and Henry Goddard Thomas. Siegfried's brigade consisted of the 27th, 30th, 39th, and 43d U.S. Colored Infantry Regiments. Thomas's brigade was composed of the 19th, 23d, 28th, 29th, and 31st U.S. Colored Infantry.[1]

Despite heavy opposition from Brig. Gen. Matt W. Ransom's North Carolina brigade and portions of Elliott's South Carolinians, the 30th and 43d U.S. Colored Troops (USCT) of Siegfried's brigade seized the last Confederate trench that stood between them and Cemetery Hill, capturing 150 prisoners. Thomas's brigade assaulted simultaneously on Siegfried's left but was repulsed with heavy losses in his lead regiment, the 31st USCT. He reformed and advanced a second time at 9:00 AM, this time with the 29th USCT in the lead. Both brigades were met by a furious counterattack by Brig. Gen. David A. Weisiger's Virginia brigade and Brig. Gen. Ambrose R. Wright's Georgia brigade from Brig. Gen. William Mahone's division. After fierce fighting, most of Siegfried's and Thomas's soldiers were driven back into Union lines or into the Crater, where they joined white troops already seeking shelter there.

At least four Confederate assaults were launched at the Crater between 9:30 AM and 1:00 PM. It finally fell to Brig. Gen. John C. C. Sanders's Alabama brigade of Mahone's division at one o'clock. The Federals took over four thousand casualties in what Grant himself called "the saddest affair I have ever witnessed in the war."[2] Careful examination of eyewitness accounts, including contemporary letters, demonstrates that several massacres occurred during and after the Battle of the Crater. The first took place when Weisiger's Virginians and Wright's Georgians killed black soldiers who had been wounded and others who were trying to surrender as the Rebels charged and cleared the trench of Siegfried's brigade. They also killed black soldiers who had been sent to the rear as prisoners.

George Bernard of the 12th Virginia, Weisiger's brigade, said his comrades littered the trench with murdered blacks:

> A minute later I witnessed another deed which made my blood run cold. Just about the outer end of the ditch by which I had entered stood a negro soldier, a noncommissioned officer (I noticed distinctly his chevrons) begging for his life of two Confederate soldiers who stood by him, one of them striking the poor wretch with a steel ramrod, the other holding a gun in his hand, with which he seemed to be trying to get a shot at the negro. The man with the gun fired at the negro, but did not seem to seriously injure him, as he only clapped his hand to his hip, when he appeared to have been shot, and continued to beg for his life. The man with the ramrod continued to strike the negro therewith, whilst the fellow with the gun deliberately reloaded it, and, placing its muzzle close against the stomach of the poor negro, fired, at which the latter fell limp and lifeless at the feet of the two Confederates. It was a brutal, horrible act, and those of us who witnessed it from our position in the trench a few feet away could but claim: That is too bad! It is shocking!
>
> Yet this, I have no doubt from what I saw and afterwards heard, was but a sample of many other bloody tragedies during the first 10 minutes after our men got into the trench, many of whom seemed infuriated at the idea of having to fight negroes.
>
> Within 10 minutes the whole floor of the trench was strewn with the dead bodies of negroes, in some places in such numbers that it was difficult to make one's way along the trench without stepping upon them.[3]

Lt. Freeman Bowley of the 30th USCT wrote:

> We were the last to reach the Crater by way of the traverse, and the rifles of the Union
> soldiers were flashing in our faces when we jumped down in there. As I landed in-
> side, I turned for a second to look back, and caught a glimpse of the Confederates
> bayoneting the wounded men who had just been shot down.[4]

In a letter to his sweetheart dated August 5, 1864, Pvt. Henry Van Lewvenigh Bird of the 12th Virginia wrote:

> Saturday's fight was a bitter struggle. No furlough wounds given *there* and no *quarter*
> either. Prayers for mercy and the groans of the wounded were alike hushed in death.
> There was no volley and cheers to excite the men to the work of death. The knowl-
> edge of dishonor to the loved ones behind if we failed and victory before us if we
> succeeded earned everything before it resistlessly. The negro's charging cry of "No
> quarter" was met with the stern cry of "amen" and without firing a single shot we
> closed with them. They fought like bulldogs and died like soldiers. Southern bayo-
> nets dripped with blood and after a brief but bitter struggle the works were ours.
> The only sounds which now broke the stillness was some poor wounded wretch
> begging for water and quieted by a bayonet thrust which said unmistakenly "Bois
> ton sang. Tu n'aurais plus de soif." [Drink your blood. You will have no more thirst].[5]

Dorsey Binion of the 48th Georgia, Wright's brigade, wrote:

> When we got to the works it was filled with negroes and they were crying out "no
> quarter" when a hand to hand conflict ensued with the breach of our guns and bayo-
> nets and you may depend on it we did not show much quarter but slayed them. Some
> few negroes went to the rear as we could not kill them as fast as they passed us.[6]

After driving Ferrero's division into the Crater, Mahone's division hunted
down blacks who were hiding in bombproofs and slaughtered them from
about 10:00 AM until noon in a second massacre. The ones they spared were
sent to the rear, but many of these prisoners were killed in a third massacre
as they ran rearward. Artillerist William Pegram provided evidence that the
Confederates killed blacks as they went to the rear and that they also hunted
down and murdered others who hid in Confederate bombproofs. In a letter dated August 1, 1864, Colonel Pegram wrote:

> I think over two hundred negroes got into our lines, by surrendering and running
> in, along with the whites, while the fighting was going on. I don't believe that much
> over half of these ever reached the rear. You could see them lying dead all along the
> route to the rear. There were hardly less than six hundred dead—four hundred of
> whom were negroes. As soon as we got upon them, they threw down their arms in

surrender, but were not allowed to do so. Every bomb proof I saw, had one or two dead negroes in it, who had skulked out the fight & been found & killed by our men. This was perfectly right, as a matter of policy.[7]

The fourth massacre occurred after the Federals in the Crater surrendered. Michael L. Kerrick of Mahone's division wrote:

The Negros hollared No Quarter, Remember Fort Pillow and when our boys charged they took them at their word. At least some did. They killed them with the butts of their muskets. They piled them up three or four deep in the ditches.[8]

Lieutenant Bowley wrote:

As the Confederates came rushing into the Crater, calling to their comrades in their rear, "The Yankees have surrendered!" some of the foremost ones plunged their bayonets into the colored wounded.[9]

After the war, Mahone tried to evade responsibility for the butchery, but he was found to have incited his men to murder the blacks. According to a member of Sanders's Alabama brigade:

General Mahone walked in front of the lines and told us that the negroes in the Crater had holloed "Remember Fort Pillow! No Quarter!" He said it was a life and death struggle, and for us not to take any of them, but to load our guns, fix bayonets, and go stooped as far as we could without being seen; and then to rise and go in among them, and give them h——; and we tried to obey orders. Just before the job was completed General Mahone sent orders to us not to kill quite all of them.[10]

William A. Day of the 49th North Carolina in Ransom's brigade, Maj. Gen. Bushrod R. Johnson's division, described the massacre in the Crater and the murder of fugitive blacks who were hiding in the bombproofs:

They rushed up to the works which were working alive with Yankees both white and black. They halted on the brink and fired one volley into the surging mass, then turned the butts of their guns and jumped in among them. How the negroe's skulls cracked under the blows. Some of them ran over on our side and started for the rear, while others made a dash for their own lines, and a great many of them made their escape. I, boy like, ran up the line to see them. When I got there they had the ground covered with broken headed negroes, and were searching about among the bomb proofs for more, the officers were trying to stop them but they kept on until they finished up.[11]

It is clear that a massacre occurred. How large was the massacre? An examination of the nominal lists of casualties for each of the nine black regiments engaged, as well as the 1st and 2d Brigade and 4th Division casualty lists, reveals that 219 officers and soldiers belonging to the 4th Division were killed, 681 wounded, and 410 missing, a total loss of 1,310 (see table 9.1).[12]

TABLE 9.1. NOMINAL LIST OF CASUALTIES, 4TH DIVISION (COLORED), 9TH CORPS, AT THE CRATER, JULY 30, 1864

	KIA	WIA	POW	TOTAL
1st Brig.				
27th USCT	11	45	18	74
30th USCT	18	99	78	195
39th USCT	15	92	47	154
43d USCT	13	81	23	117
Subtotal	57	317	166	540
2d Brig.				
19th USCT	24	87	3	114
23d USCT	75	116	119	310
28th USCT	13	65	11	89
29th USCT	21	55	47	123
31st USCT	29	41	64	134
Subtotal	162	364	244	770
Total	219	681	410	1,310

Note: KIA indicates killed in action; *POW*, prisoner of war; and *WIA*, wounded in action.

The figure of 219 seems impossibly low for two reasons. The Confederates claimed they buried 750 Yankees after the battle; yet, according to the nominal lists of casualties for the Crater, only 504 Federals were killed, 219 of them black soldiers. In other words, the Confederates claimed they had buried 246 more bodies than are listed by the Federal casualty table. Also, although the nominal lists give the number of missing blacks at 410, the Confederates state they captured only 200 black soldiers. One newspaper said that "Amongst the eleven hundred prisoners taken by our forces last Saturday, at Petersburg, two hundred were negroes."[13] A study of a list of the 410 black soldiers who were missing and an examination of the service records and pension records of all 410 of these soldiers produces shocking results:[14]

    205 killed
     13 mortally wounded
     62 wounded in action

3   mortally wounded and captured
13   wounded in action and captured
72   captured
Total: 368 (of 410; the other 42 were not casualties)

The breakdown by regiment is shown in table 9.2. According to these adjusted figures, the black 4th Division lost 423 killed, 13 mortally wounded, 744 wounded, 3 mortally wounded and captured, 13 wounded and captured, and 73 captured—a total of 1,269 men.

TABLE 9.2. ADJUSTED LIST OF CASUALTIES, 4TH DIVISION (COLORED), 9TH CORPS, AT THE CRATER, JULY 30, 1864

	KIA	MW	WIA	MWIA & POW	WIA & POW	POW	TOTAL
1st Brig.							
27th USCT	24	1	47	0	0	0	72
30th USCT	62	2	118	1	3	5	191
39th USCT	32	1	106	0	0	6	145
43d USCT	26	1	87	0	0	3	117
Subtotal	144	5	358	1	3	14	525
2d Brig.							
19th USCT	27	0	87	0	0	0	114
23d USCT	118	4	131	0	2	37	292
28th USCT	19	1	66	0	0	1	87
29th USCT	48	0	56	1	6	11	122
31st USCT	67	3	46	1	2	10	129
Subtotal	279	8	386	2	10	59	744
Total	423	13	744	3	13	73	1,269

Note: KIA indicates killed in action; *MW*, mortally wounded; *MWIA*, mortally wounded in action; *POW*, prisoner of war; and *WIA*, wounded in action.

One startling fact is that although 410 blacks were missing after the battle, the Confederates captured only 85 prisoners and killed 423 blacks, counting the missing who were slain. At the Crater, the ratio of blacks killed to wounded was 423 to 757, about 1 to 1.8. In the Civil War, the average ratio of killed to wounded was 1 to 4.8. These statistics make it clear that the massacre at the Crater was the worst massacre of blacks during the Civil War. Only two other massacres rival its carnage. At Fort Pillow, blacks belonging to the 1st Battalion, 6th U.S. Heavy Artillery (Colored), and to Company D, 2d U.S. Light Artillery (Colored), lost 185 killed, 40 wounded, and 51 captured, a total loss of 276.[15] At Poison Springs, Arkansas, the 1st Kansas (Colored) lost 117 killed and 65 wounded.[16]

Perhaps it is time to reexamine more closely other Civil War battles to see whether massacres of black soldiers occurred there as well. Possible candidates include Milliken's Bend, Louisiana; Mound Fort, Louisiana; Olustee, Florida; Saltville, Virginia; and New Market Heights, Virginia.

Notes

This essay was originally published in *Civil War History* 43 (Sept. 1997): 219–24. Reprinted with permission of the Kent State University Press.

1. According to Bvt. Maj. Gen. Henry G. Thomas, Siegfried's brigade numbered 2,000 and Thomas's 2,300. Henry Goddard Thomas, "The Colored Troops at Petersburg," in Robert Underwood Johnson and Clarence Clough Buel, eds., *Battles and Leaders of the Civil War,* 4 vols. (1887–88; reprint, New York: Thomas Yoseloff, 1956), 4:563.

2. *The War of the Rebellion: A Compilation of the Official Records of the Union and Confederate Armies,* 128 vols. (Washington, D.C.: Government Printing Office, 1880–1901), ser. 1, 40 (pt. 1): 17 (hereafter cited as *OR*).

3. George Bernard, *War Talks of Confederate Veterans* (Petersburg, Va.: Fenn and Owen, 1892), 169.

4. Freeman Bowley, "A Boy Lieutenant in a Colored Regiment," *National Tribune,* June 29, 1899.

5. Henry Van Lewvenigh Bird to Margaret Randolph, Aug. 5, 1864, Bird Family Papers, Virginia Historical Society, Richmond.

6. Letter, Dorsey M. Binion, Aug. 1, 1864, Michael Musick Collection, U.S. Army Military History Institute, Carlisle Barracks, Penn.

7. Quoted in James I. Robertson Jr., ed., "The Boy Artillerist," *Virginia Magazine of History and Biography* 98 (Apr. 1990): 243.

8. Letter, Michael L. Kerrick, Aug. [July?] 30, 1864, folder 8, doc. 110, Petersburg National Park, Library, Petersburg, Va.

9. Bowley, "Boy Lieutenant."

10. B. F. Phillips, "Wilcox's Alabamians in Virginia," *Confederate Veteran* 15 (Nov. 1907): 490.

11. William Alburtus Day, *A True History of Company I, 49th Regiment, North Carolina Troops* (Newton, N.C.: Enterprise Job Office, 1893), 84.

12. These lists were obtained from two sources: entry 652, box 33, and entry 653, box 16, RG 94, National Archives. Entry 652 consists of casualty lists for each Union regiment serving in the war, and box 33 contains lists for black regiments. Entry 653 consists of casualty lists for the various Union armies and is arranged by corps within those armies; box 16 contains casualties for the 4th Division, 9th Corps, throughout its entire existence as a unit.

13. *Richmond Examiner,* Aug. 4, 1864.

14. Civil War (Union) Compiled Military Service Records, 19th, 23d, 27th, 28th, 29th, 30th, 31st, 39th, and 43d U.S. Colored Infantry, Military Service Branch, RG 94, Records of the Adjutant General's Office, 1780s–1917, National Archives, Washington, D.C. See also the pension files for those regiments, also in RG 94.

15. See John Cimprich and Robert C. Mainfort Jr., "The Fort Pillow Massacre: A Statistical Note," *Journal of American History* 76 (Dec. 1989): 836.

16. *OR,* ser. 1, 34 (pt. 1): 754.

Symbols of Freedom and Defeat

African American Soldiers, White Southerners, and the Christmas Insurrection Scare of 1865

10

CHAD L. WILLIAMS

On October 22, 1865, E. G. Baker, a white planter from Panola, Mississippi, wrote to three of his state legislators with regard to the trouble African American soldiers were creating among the freed people in the state and the horrors he believed they would inevitably bring to fruition. "I am no alarmist," said Baker, "but I tell you most seriously that the whole south is resting upon a volcano." He warned that if black troops "are not removed from our mids pretty Soon . . . our negroes will refuse to hire will grow more & more insolent." Worse, the troops "will stimulate the negroes to insurrection & will then lend them a helping hand." The only solution, Baker concluded, was to "get the negro troops removed from the State. Cannot it be done?" Like many of his fellow agriculturists, Baker suspected African American troops of leading ex-slaves in preparations for a massive Christmas uprising, in which white planters throughout the South would be slaughtered and their lands taken.[1]

The Christmas Insurrection Scare of 1865 occupies a unique location in the history of the postwar American South. Viewed within the context of the military defeat of the Confederacy, emancipation, and the economic and political reorganization of the South as a region, the rumors of insurrection that gripped the countryside demonstrated not only the fear and uncertainty of the white planter class but the hope and promise for the future of the newly liberated African American population. What makes this event even more significant is the fact that it did not take place. Despite apprehensions that led white Southerners to prepare actively for an armed confrontation with black soldiers and rebellious freedmen, the South remained free of incident. Examining the Christmas Insurrection Scare of 1865, this essay discusses the symbolic power of African American troops and their role in fueling the fear of white Southerners during the closing months of the year.

210

Historians have given limited attention to the significance of African American soldiers in their respective analyses of the Christmas Insurrection Scare. The response of white Southern planters to the presence of African American soldiers represents a significant aspect of this event as well as the larger history of the postwar South. Reactionary behavior due to white racial ideology was clearly an important force in shaping the panic. Historians, however, must view the Christmas Insurrection Scare as more than a product of white hysteria fueled by the trauma of defeat at the hands of the North. With the South in a state of political, social, and economic flux, the actions taken by white Southern planters in response to the presumed threat of an impending uprising represented a strong form of political protest and resistance towards the federal government and the changes brought about by the Civil War.[2]

By virtue of their symbolism, African American soldiers played a significant role in shaping this phenomenon. For both freed people and the white planter class, they embodied the full ramifications of emancipation and defeat with the conclusion of the war. Whereas the sight of African Americans in uniform inspired freed people to relish their newly gained freedom, this symbolic value, in the eyes and minds of Southern planters, translated into fear and uncertainty. Although the actual threat of organized violent retaliation on the part of African American soldiers and conspiratorial ex-slaves was nonexistent, the psychological endangerment they posed for white planters and former slaveholders was nevertheless real. As an accessible target of white hostility, black soldiers represented a perceived social, economic, and physical threat to Southern society in the wake of emancipation and the defeat of the Confederacy. While rumors of government land distribution to the freed people served as a foundation and a strong force in sustaining the panic, the symbolism of African American troops stimulated preconceived racial prejudices that white Southerners had of black people and their behavior. As rumors often do, the threatened insurrection took on a life of its own and soon became accepted as fact. In the end, the Christmas Insurrection Scare was as much a product of a dangerous combination of white racism, the ramifications of defeat, and resistance to a new South as it was of any actual physical danger that African American soldiers and freed people posed to the safety and stability of the region.[3]

President Abraham Lincoln issued the Emancipation Proclamation on January 1, 1863, thereby altering the course of the Civil War and undermining the stability of the Southern racial order. The proclamation, in letter only, freed more than three million slaves from bondage and sanctioned the enlistment of African American men into the Union army. Finally accepting the important role they would need to play in the war effort, Lincoln's decision to utilize ex-slaves in the Union forces changed both the tide and meaning of the increasingly bloody conflict. Well aware of the effect that Lincoln's action would have on its slave population, the South reacted with outrage. Confederate president Jefferson Davis, in his message to the Confederate Congress on January 12, 1863, declared that Union officers captured in command of black regiments would be turned over to state governments for punishment as "criminals engaged in inciting servile insurrection." Despite this response from the Confederacy, the establishment of the Colored Troops Division of the Adjutant General's Office on May 22, 1863, which coordinated the organization and operation of black regiments, institutionalized the use of African American men in the United States Army. By the war's end, 178,975 had enlisted in the army, comprising approximately 8 percent of the Union ground forces.[4]

With the end of the war, the defeated Confederate South grudgingly accepted the presence of U.S. troops as an occupying force. More so than during the war itself, African American soldiers constituted a significant portion of the postwar forces. Of the 226,611 men serving in September of 1865, 83,079, or 36.7 percent, were black. Because African American soldiers entered the army later than most white soldiers, their three-year mandatory term of service expired later than that of their white contemporaries. By November 1865, the United States Army had mustered only 33,234 black soldiers out of its forces. As increasing numbers of white regiments were taken out of service and removed from the South, the proportion of African American troops increased, as did white hostility and tension towards them.[5]

The presence of African American soldiers held powerful and conflicting symbolic values for African American and white Southerners alike. Ex-slaves marveled at the sight of black troops, only recently held in bondage, demanding obedience from their former masters. For freed men and women, the African American soldier represented the end of generations of suffering under the oppression of slavery, as well as hope for future prosperity. A soldier in the famed 54th Massachusetts Infantry, during his march through Charleston, South Carolina, recalled: "I saw an old colored women with a crutch—for she could not walk without one, having served all her life in bondage—who, on seeing us, got so happy that she threw down her crutch and shouted that the year of jubilee had come." Furthermore, freed people perceptively recognized the effect African American soldiers had on white behavior. In a letter to the United States Secretary of War Edwin M. Stanton regarding the conduct of local white people, an African American minister from Georgia wrote, "when colored Soldiers are about they are afraid to kick colored women, and abuse colored people on the Streets, as they usually do." Throughout the South, freed people expressed similar sentiments, as African American soldiers frequently obstructed acts of hostility and violence from defeated Confederate soldiers and disgruntled ex-slaveholders. Freed people embraced the troops as heroes, protectors, and liberators.[6]

In stark contrast, most white Southerners viewed African American soldiers with abhorrence. The antebellum Southern way of life received a crushing blow with Union victory. Southern whites not only had to come to grips with the physical and economic implications of defeat but with the social, political, and cultural consequences as well. While white Southerners, by and large, strongly opposed the presence of Federal troops in their midst, they held unrelenting disdain for African American soldiers, in particular, as the embodiment of the subversion of slavery, the destruction of the Confederacy, and the arrival of a new social order that promised to differ profoundly from the old. Moreover, African American troops personified the triumph of the Union and magnified the humiliation of the Southern people. A general sense of shame and dishonor overcame the defeated Confederates. They saw African American soldiers forced upon them as the worst imaginable form of punishment. From their perspective, the actions of the federal government in stationing black regiments in the South were cruel and vindictive, with the sole intent to disgrace and insult white Southern manhood and womanhood. A sergeant in the 39th United States Colored Infantry observed that the presence of his regiment in a small town in Kinston, North Carolina, was "perfectly exasperating to the citizens." Despite the pleas of white residents for divine intervention to "deliver them from the hands of the *smoked Yankees*," the sergeant reported, "their prayers in this case were like all others offered by rebel hearts; and the next thing they saw was the *smoked Yankees* marching some of their fellow citizens to jail at the point of a bayonet." The sight of former slaves, now in the authoritative role of armed guards, epitomized just how dramatically the South had been transformed. This symbolism shaped and dictated the relationship between white Southerners and African American troops.[7]

Rooted in proslavery racial ideology, long-held insecurities regarding black behavior were brought into the open by the presence of African American soldiers. Fear of insurrection had existed throughout the period of slavery. Constant tension, both underlying and overt, characterized the peculiar institution and subsequently defined the interaction between slaves and their masters. Although white slave owners held firm to the belief that they knew their blacks, the possibility of slaves striking out in violent fashion against their masters remained frighteningly real. Events such as the Haitian Revolution, the Gabriel Conspiracy, and the Nat Turner Rebellion, in particular, heightened the anxiety of white slaveholders and led to tighter methods of control. The white planter class took extreme precautions to ensure that revolts would not occur by placing limitations on the freedom of movement for both slaves and free black people, prohibiting black people from owning weapons, and restricting slaves from congregating in large groups without white supervision. These attitudes continued after emancipation in the form of intense acrimony between white planters and African American soldiers.[8]

Throughout the antebellum era, dread of armed African Americans occupied a dominant place in the psyche of white slaveholders. They generally viewed armed black people as potential insurrectionists and threats to their physical safety and financial security. Against such a historical backdrop, the presence of African American soldiers represented white Southerners' worst fears. While slavery might have been abolished with the defeat of the Confederacy, white Southerners maintained a strong psychological connection to the institution. Openly brandishing their weapons, African American troops brought new life to the fears first entrenched in the minds of white people during slavery and ushered in a movement throughout the South to disarm the black population, using both legal and extralegal means. Because of their access to weapons, African American troops were accused of supplying freed people with guns to be used in the alleged massive insurrection, during which white planters would be murdered in unprecedented numbers.[9] The fact that soldiers constantly fraternized with freed people only served to heighten white apprehensions and reaffirm their potentially calamitous influence.

During slavery, white slaveholders had circulated the myth of a happy, docile, and content slave population. As bedrock in the legitimization of the institution, this construction served the purpose of reinforcing the paternalistic relationship that existed between slave and master. However, as African American regiments occupied the South and interacted with the freed people, former slaveholders saw a potential threat to the delicate bond they so desperately guarded. In the eyes of the majority of white Southerners, African American soldiers encouraged the growing assertiveness of freed people with the end of slavery. Slavery required the enforcement and constant regulation of certain customs of behavior of black people, such as submission to authority and acquiescence when in the presence of whites. With emancipation and the enlistment of African American soldiers, white supremacy and the principles behind slavery became increasingly difficult to maintain. Freed black men and women, sometimes with the encouragement of the soldiers themselves, often intentionally rebuked traditional Southern customs. Frustration among the white planter class over their inability to control their former slaves and predict their actions led to the scapegoating of African American soldiers and sowed the seeds of the approaching insurrection scare.[10]

While slavery and white racial ideology shaped the social terrain of the postbellum South, the economic ramifications of the war—including the confiscation of some nine hundred thousand acres of Confederate plantation lands—set the insurrection panic into motion. White planters feared that their former slaves would soon control the region's plantations. Although seemingly farfetched, this idea, so prevalent among the white Southern aristocracy, was not completely unfounded. The question of Union-controlled lands and distribution to the freed people became an explosive political issue well before hostilities ceased. During Maj. Gen. William T. Sherman's climactic march from Atlanta to the sea, thousands of contraband slaves attached themselves to his forces. In response to rumors of their mistreatment, Secretary of War Edwin M. Stanton traveled to Savannah to meet with Sherman and representatives of the Georgia freed people. When informed that the freed people sought land of their own to cultivate and eventually to possess, Stanton and Sherman drafted the most radical field order of the war, Special Field Order No. 15. Issued on January 16, 1865, it "reserved and set apart for the settlement of the negroes now made free by the acts of war and the proclamation of the President of the United States" lands encompassing "The islands from Charleston south, the abandoned rice-fields along the rivers for thirty miles back from the sea, and the country bordering the Saint John's River, Fla." The military wasted little time in carrying out the order, as Brig. Gen. Rufus Saxton supervised the settlement of some forty thousand freed people on the lands of ex-slaveholders by the middle of 1865. This action not only enraged white planters but also imbued ex-slaves with hopes that they would indeed have control of the land they had toiled on for years and felt a natural entitlement to.[11]

Suspicions regarding the government's intentions and rumors of a large-scale distribution among the freed people increased as the war came to an end. As Congress debated the future of the South, the issue of what to do with confiscated plantations received immediate attention. Although President Andrew Johnson, in his Amnesty Proclamation of May 29, 1865, stated that the restoration of most property to its former owners would occur, the apprehensions of white Southern planters were not at all eased by the likes of Rep. Thaddeus Stevens of Pennsylvania and other anti-Confederate Radical Republicans. Bent on punishing the "traitorous confederation" of the South, Stevens argued that "the property of the chief rebels should be seized and appropriated to the payment of the National debt, caused by the unjust and wicked war which they instigated." More significantly, he proposed the allotment of forty acres of Rebel land to each freed adult male, totaling an estimated forty million acres. While this did not take place and the majority of confiscated lands were indeed restored to white planters, the previous uncertainty planted seeds of doubt in fertile ground, and the roots of the insurrection panic took hold of Southern imaginations. Rumors circulated that the freed people would receive land at the end of the year and would subsequently refuse to contract with their former masters. Combined with uneasiness about the success of a new contract labor system, rumors of black people who "boldly avow their intention to take the lands that have been promised them by Christmas," as a member of the Louisiana legislature wrote in November 1865, weighed heavily on the minds of white people throughout the South.[12]

African American troops were instrumental in creating and sustaining these fears. White planters viewed them as a disruptive force in labor relations, as well as the source of the perceived increasing insolence of freed people. Furthermore, planters insisted that African American soldiers encouraged ex-slaves to view themselves as the rightful owners of the lands of their former masters and, if necessary, to reclaim it by force. The opinion that African American regiments stationed in the former Confederate states actively undermined labor discipline, thus creating the necessary conditions among the freed people for an insurrection to take place, was extensive. Mississippi provisional governor William L. Sharkey exclaimed: "It is hoped the black troops will be speedily removed from the county. If this should be done we may be able to manage the negroes in the country." The lack of a secure labor force exacerbated the suspicion of white planters towards their former slaves as well as tensions with African American troops. With the end of the year approaching, white planters faced the tenuous situation of negotiating contracts with, in many cases, the same individuals they once held in perpetual servitude. Unable to comprehend black people in any capacity other than as plantation laborers, many planter class whites feared African American soldiers were advising freed people not to make contracts for the upcoming year. In his letter to the three Mississippi state legislators, E. G. Baker informed them: "The Negro Soldiery here are constantly telling our negroes, that for the next year, The Government will give them lands, provisions, Stock & all things necessary to carry on business for themselves,— & are constantly advising them not to make contracts with white persons, for the next year.—Strange to say the negroes believe such stories in spite of facts to the contrary told them by their ~~masters~~ employers." The South's anxiety regarding the consequences of the abolition of slavery, combined with the need for white planters to procure a labor force, culminated in a profusion of complaints about the behavior of African American troops.[13]

The only action worse than freed people receiving land from the government at the end of the year, propertied whites feared, was what would occur when their former slaves learned the government had no intention whatsoever of giving them land. Whites believed that when the New Year arrived and freed people realized that the promise of land distribution was false, an extensive massacre of white people would take place, with the liberated slaves, aided by black troops, claiming the property for themselves. In October 1865, Governor Sharkey of Mississippi wrote to Freedmen's Bureau Commissioner O. O. Howard of the impending insurrection expected to take place during the winter months, resulting from the freed population's not receiving a division of property. He went on to detail that African American troops "are relied on to carry out this massacre. That of the negroes in the country have arms, procured from soldiers or officers, which it is supposed they are providing for carrying out their diabolical scheme. . . . I therefore suggest . . . some agent or agents to travel through the South to instruct the negroes that they must depend on their labor, and not think of a distribution of property."[14] Apprehensions about the future of the Southern plantation economy under a system of free labor and the presence of African American soldiers made for a potentially explosive combination.

White planters lodged a multitude of grievances against African American troops with the Freedmen's Bureau and the Colored Troops Division. Prominent among the complaints were stories of African American soldiers encouraging ex-slaves to seek revenge against their former masters. E. G. Baker wrote that rumors were circulating among freed people that when the soldiers were withdrawn, "the whites will endeavor to enslave them again." Thus, "they are urged to begin at an early day, perhaps about Christmas, a massacre of the whites" so that "if the whites are got out [of] the way here, that then they will have no further apprehension—& that this Country will then be given to them by the northern people forever as an inheritance."[15]

These claims speak to the insecurity white planters felt concerning not only the safety of their property but their lives as well.

As with most rumors, it is difficult to locate exactly when and where the Christmas Insurrection Scare began. Historians have used the reports of alarmed white Southerners and federal officers to trace word of general property division and black-inspired violence to the North and South Carolina coasts during the early summer of 1865. Likewise, evidence exists of alarm surfacing in July of 1865, not only in North Carolina but also in south and central Georgia as well. Ella Gertrude Clanton Thomas, a wealthy Georgia plantation mistress, chillingly wrote in her journal on July 30, 1865: "It is very much to be hoped we are at the worst of this transition state of the Negroes. If not God have mercy upon us. Sis Anne said the other day that she thought things would go on so until Christmas and then there would be some sort of this—with a very significant gesture across the throat—." Taking into consideration that Sherman's Field Order No. 15, both directly and indirectly, affected these very same areas, it is possible to trace the origins of the Insurrection Scare to this general locale.[16]

Accounts of an anticipated insurrection, however, were not regionally isolated. Occurring principally in rural areas, the panic spread throughout the entire South in a relatively short period of time in the late summer and early autumn months of 1865. Like wildfire, news of the impending massacre at the hands of freed people led by African American troops traveled from county to county and from state to state. The *Washington Daily National Intelligencer* reported that white people believed "a conspiracy had been organized among the blacks, extending from the Mississippi river to South Carolina, and that an insurrection was contemplated about Christmas." By November, rumors of the insurrection had spread to more than sixty counties and half a dozen parishes throughout all eleven states of the former Confederacy. Editors of sensational Southern newspapers, with outlandish stories about discoveries of caches of guns found among freed people and about groups of armed black men drilling in the woods, reaffirmed what easily excitable white planters already feared with the end of slavery. No area of the South escaped the insurrection scare.[17]

That white planters associated the insurrection rumors with the Christmas holidays of 1865 was not coincidental. In a December letter to the Union commander of his state, South Carolina provisional governor James Lawrence Orr observed that during "Christmas week, which has always been a holiday for the negroes, they will congregate in large numbers at the villages and towns where they will get liquor and while under its influence I fear that collisions will occur between them and the whites." During slavery, all holidays, particularly Christmas and New Year's, generated significant apprehension among white people for fear of slave insurrections. In South Carolina, ironically, it became almost traditional for white people to anticipate these occasions with anxiety rather than pleasure. Ella Gertrude Clanton Thomas of Georgia reflected on Christmas day of 1858, "I sometimes think that we are like inhabitants at the foot of Vesuvius, remaining perfectly contented among so many dangers." Slaveholders, albeit briefly, relaxed traditional discipline and allowed enslaved black men and women to spend time with their families and friends. This window of semi-freedom allowed slaves to engage in activities and behavior that otherwise would be cause for castigation at the hands of their masters. The grim reality that African Americans were now free and had greater access to weapons and alcohol distinguished the Christmas season of 1865 from those of previous years, making the holidays cause for little celebration for many whites throughout the South.[18]

With the end of the year quickly approaching, propertied whites placed greater credence in the rumors of an impending insurrection. In late November, a white planter from South Carolina, when asked by a correspondent from the *Nation* about a rumored uprising, responded: "I look for it, sir, in January. I regard it as almost certain to occur." He added that "the negroes have made up their minds that land is to be given them at New Year's, and of course it will be a great disappointment to them when they find that time has gone by and nothing has been done for them." Resigned to the impending violence, the planter concluded, "some families will be murdered and some property destroyed. . . . It will begin the work of extermination."[19]

Although white Southerners were not monolithic in their behaviors and actions, they nevertheless took the threat of a disturbance led by African American soldiers with great seriousness and mounting urgency. The gravity of the insurrection panic motivated some white families to relocate to areas where they felt more secure. In Mississippi, the severity of the rumors and the fear of violence during the Christmas season were strong enough to compel residents in southwest Madison County and in adjoining Yazoo County to flee their plantations and seek protection in nearby towns. Although not the most common course of action taken by white Southerners in reaction to the circulating insurrection rumors, this response demonstrates how genuinely unnerved many individuals and families became.[20]

Many others took alternative steps to ensure their safety and to prepare for the seemingly growing possibility of violent conflict. With the same spirit, language, and action with which threats of insurrection were responded to during slavery, large segments of the white population readied themselves for the continuation of the war, this time to be waged against the freed people. From local groups to government officials in all areas of the South, cries went out for the creation of militias of armed white men to patrol certain areas and stop the insurrection before it began. In Alabama, for example, delegates to the state's constitutional convention in September of 1865 prioritized a petition to the provisional governor for authority to organize militia companies to protect the white population from racial upheaval. Similar events took place in Texas, where Gov. Andrew J. Hamilton organized the creation of civilian militias in response to insurrection rumors. Militia units often consisted of ex-Confederate soldiers, undoubtedly anxious to avenge their defeat at the hands of Union forces. Reporters from the *New Orleans Tribune,* upon observing bills in the parish of St. Helena, Louisiana, calling the state militia to arms, wrote that the organization of the militia was "nothing short of a reorganization of the rebel army in disguise." In response to growing apprehension, the white citizens of Wilmington, North Carolina, quickly organized fifteen to eighteen home guard companies. Of this event, the *Washington Daily National Intelligencer* reported, "the people here are sensitive about the negroes as the holidays approach" and "should anything occur there will be sufficient force for the emergency."[21]

The actions of Mississippi governor Benjamin G. Humphreys demonstrated the depth of the panic and the intense dislike Southern governments had for African American soldiers. Acting more as a national broker of the planters' interests than as a government representative, Humphreys went to great lengths to ensure the physical and economic security of propertied whites and the removal of African American units from his state. On November 4, 1865, the governor issued a proclamation urging the immediate organization of volunteer militia companies. He followed this action with a letter to the Adjutant General's Office, requesting weapons for the purpose of arming a state volunteer militia made up of ex-Confederate soldiers. As reported by Maj. Gen. A. Joseph Osterhaus, the need for an armed militia stemmed from the fact that the governor "and the Southern people generally were apprehensive of a negro insurrection." According to Osterhaus, Humphreys believed, "When the Colored troops were mustered out they would be a large dangerous element in the Community of men who had been taught the use of arms and had some crude knowledge of fortifications." The governor intensified his resolve in a telegram to President Andrew Johnson, in which he detailed alleged atrocities committed by African American troops that justified their immediate removal. Apparently, his plea was not warmly received, as Johnson replied that the troops would be withdrawn when "peace and order can be maintained without them." Despite the lack of support from the federal government, Humphreys directed militia companies into tense counties of Mississippi, where the fears of white planters ran highest, with orders to disarm the freed people. This action, however, served only to increase hostilities.[22]

The organization of white local and state militias led to the most common response by the white population to the fear of insurrection: violence against freed people, in general, and against African American soldiers, in particular. Because African American soldiers represented the defeat of the South, the end of slavery, and the destruction of the old social and racial order, outrages against them took on an extremely symbolic nature. Acts of ritualized brutality against African American troops, frequently expressed in the form of assaults and murders, symbolized resistance to change and the desire to maintain a strict system of racial domination.[23]

White militia groups were responsible for much of the violence perpetrated upon African American soldiers. The militias or other vigilantes acting in the name of the government, organized for the specific purpose of preventing an insurrection, committed the majority of outrages recorded against freed people. In reality, the difference between militia units and white vigilante groups was virtually indiscernible. Often without government consent, groups of armed white citizens convened to secure white supremacy and the safety of the South. Ranging in size and force, they patrolled the countryside, closely monitoring the behavior of the freed people and African American troops stationed in the area. This frequently translated into harassment and acts of violence. In a letter to O. O. Howard, Pvt. Calvin Holly, a black soldier in Vicksburg, Mississippi, wrote of the white population in the area: "They have been accusing the colered peple of an insorection which is a lie, in order that they might get arms to carry out their wicked designs. . . . For to my own knowledge I have seen them buying arms and munitions ever since the lins have been opened and carring them to the country." Bands of white men, such as those whom Private Holly described, falsely claimed to be government officials and violently forced black soldiers to relinquish, against their will, weapons acquired during the war. Likewise, miltias and vigilante groups targeted and sought to disarm freedmen, many of whom had specifically armed themselves for protection against disorderly whites.[24]

Inconsistent is the best way to describe the responses by the Freedmen's Bureau and the United States Army to the claims by planter class whites regarding the behavior of African American troops and the fear of an insurrection. Government officials recognized and dismissed as false most of the complaints registered against African American troops for inciting an insurrection among the freed people. A Mississippi Freedmen's Bureau official noted that the claim of an approaching insurrection "has been used for some time by the people in order to get rid of negro troops and the Bureau." Lt. Col. A. J. Willard, the commander of a military subdistrict in South Carolina, insisted to his superiors that there was "no indication of any insurrectionary effort or feeling" among the freed people. He acknowledged that "blacks have larger expectations than it will be possible to gratify," but their response to inevitable disappointment would be political rather than violent: "They look to memorializing and influencing the government as a means of securing their desires." Maj. Gen. George Meade reached similar conclusions in a letter to Secretary of War Stanton. The commander of the Military Division of the Atlantic recognized that "the people of the South are very much prejudiced against these troops, that they really believe they are actively employed disorganizing the laboring population, and not to be relied on in the event of being called on to suppress a negro insurrection, the chronic terror of the South." However, General Meade said he "could get no evidence to justify these fears and prejudices."[25]

The Freedmen's Bureau took steps to defuse the insurrection panic by assuring propertied whites that the rumors were indeed false and by informing freed people not to expect a division of land at the end of the year. On November 19, Freedmen's Bureau commissioner Howard issued a general circular to the freed people, stating in part that "it is said that land will be taken from the present holders and be divided among them [freedmen] on next Christmas or New Year's. This impression, wherever it exists, is wrong." Howard concluded by expressing his hope for "kind feeling and mutual confidence between the blacks and the whites."[26] While the impact of his announcement on quelling the fears of white planters is difficult to ascertain, Howard's efforts demonstrate the bureau's incredulous attitude toward rumors of an insurrection.

Government officials did recognize, however, that the presence of African American troops in the South was indeed a problem with potentially disastrous consequences. The bureau, as a whole, was sympathetic and responsive to the complaints of white planters concerning the removal of African American units. Often backed by local Union army commanders and Freedmen's Bureau agents that offered support, white people flooded federal offices with requests for the removal of African American soldiers from the South. Some military personnel, such as Maj. Gen. Quincy A. Gillmore, head of the Department of South Carolina, were hesitant to remove and discharge African American regiments for fear that once released from military discipline they would cause even greater trouble in communities throughout the South. Nevertheless, government officials acknowledged that something had to be done to resolve the problem of African American troops and their contentious relationship with white Southerners.[27]

The actions and policies of Lt. Gen. Ulysses S. Grant demonstrate how the position adopted by the United States government concerning African American soldiers and their future in the South evolved over time. Grant realized that the removal of African American units, although an important step toward reconciliation with the South, was not a simple decision. To remove them, in his opinion, would be akin to bowing to racism and conceding the futility of securing black civil equality in the region. He therefore did not immediately approve of taking African Americans out of service as soon as possible. Grant advocated reconciliation with the South, but not at the price of risking the safety of the freed people and the integrity of the federal government.[28]

In spite of his beliefs regarding African American civil rights in the South, Grant ultimately capitulated to the pressure of the white planter class. In August of 1865, with complaints mounting, Grant requested that the War Department muster out all African American regiments raised in the North. In a letter of December 18 to President Johnson, Grant advocated the removal of African American troops from the interior sections of the South, to be replaced by white troops. He stated that "the presence of black troops, lately slaves, demoralizes labor both by their advice and furnishing in their camps a resort for the freedmen for long distances around." Grant went on to add that many freed people believed that their masters' property, by right, belonged to them and therefore should not be protected by sympathetic African American soldiers. Recognizing the volatile nature of the situation, Grant assumed the "danger of collisions" if the removal of black troops from the South did not occur. With this decision, Grant chose the reconciliation of the South with the North over the security of the civil and political rights of African Americans.[29]

Between October of 1865 and October of 1866, the United States Army mustered 72,039 African Americans out of service, leaving 12,985 on active duty. By October 1867, none continued to serve in the South. Local white planters reacted to the removal of African American regiments from overtly hostile areas of the South with great relief. After the withdrawal of African

American troops from the St. Landry Parish in Louisiana, a local newspaper editor rejoiced in a December article, "Now reader, don't you really think that we all breathe more freely since the black troops left our atmosphere?"[30] Though anxieties may have eased, the removal of African American regiments left freed people in many areas of the South without their primary means of protection from the recriminations of the white population. In the end, freed people paid the price, often with their lives, for reconciliation between the North and the South.

Despite the fears of white people throughout the South, the end of the year passed without an incident of black-instigated violence. There is no evidence that any semblance of an insurrection took place on or around the Christmas holidays of 1865. On December 28, the *Washington Daily National Intelligencer* published accounts from three different Southern cities—Petersburg, Virginia; Norfolk, Virginia; and Raleigh, North Carolina—that no serious disturbances occurred among freed people. With the headline "The Anticipated Insurrection," the report went on to proclaim: "There have been no disturbances caused by the negroes, who have behaved themselves very well in this city and the adjacent country. They have been quiet and orderly for the season, and never before were so few seen on the streets during the Christmas holidays."[31]

The fact that no organized acts of violence by African American troops or freed people against Southern whites took place, despite the widespread belief this would occur, speaks volumes to the level of panic that overcame the region at the end of the war. John T. Trowbridge, a respected Northern journalist who toured eight states of the former Confederacy after the war, wrote of hearing about the rumors of the Christmas Insurrection, only to witness an incident where a group of ex-Confederate soldiers robbed and murdered an African American man. The fear among white planters that African Americans would not make contracts for the upcoming year likewise proved false. Despite hopes for land ownership, the vast majority of freed people realized their only hope for income rested in the fields of their former masters.[32]

With the South quiet, the paranoia of many white Southerners became glaring. Never missing an opportunity to demonstrate the senselessness of the former Confederates, the *New Orleans Tribune* ridiculed the absurdity of the "black conspiracy." In an irony-filled editorial, the radical African American newspaper noted the fact that for two months "the whole country had been startled" and that the South "had been warned, time and again, that a terrific revolution would occur." Along with black laborers, armed with spades, pitchforks, and scythes, "the colored regiments were announced as ready to march to Washington, in spite to the entreatments and exertions of their officers, to drive away Gen. Grant, and proclaim another Petion [person?] President of the United States." These claims were confounded by threats of "the burning of the cities, the confiscation and division of lands, the assassination of the whites, the rape of women—all that the imagination of our enemies could devise was predicted." But, as the paper mockingly reported, "Christmas has come and is over," with nothing of the sort taking place. Instead, African American soldiers "were sent back without protection among the hords of armed men they had conquered on the battle-field. The patriotic soldier was disgraced, and in many cases his life jeopardized, to please the caprices of rebel planters, and quiet the hypocritical fears of nervous secesh women." The editor concluded by posing the question, "Shall our brethren be permitted to return to their homes without means of defense—and shall the colored patriot be deprived of his arms and delivered up without means of protection into the hands of the rebel militia?"[33]

In the case of many African American soldiers and their families, the answer to this question was yes. Although the widely believed insurrection did not take place, the South was by no means devoid of violence during the Christmas holidays. Accounts exist that detail acts of violence inflicted upon African American soldiers and freed people during this time. With tensions high, black soldiers and former slaves became the easy targets of racist and hostile whites. An officer of the United States Colored Infantry reported an incident on December 24 in which an ex-Confederate colonel "Shot at Soldiers belonging to the 42nd USCI and made threats that he could start the war again in Morgan County, Ala, and the streets of Decatur would yet run with Yankee blood." Proclaiming that "no g——d d——d Yankee could stay in his country—meaning the South," the colonel swore that "as soon as Yankee Bayonets are gone the negroes will be . . . or made slaves as of old." Although no accounts specifically refer to the threat of insurrection as a motivating force behind the perpetration of violence against African American soldiers and freed men and women, it is not unreasonable to think that it was a factor.[34]

In retrospect, preventing the Christmas Insurrection Scare of 1865 fell far beyond the control of government officials, regardless of their feeling toward white Southerners or African American soldiers. The reality remained that once news had begun to spread, white people did not need the actions of supposedly murderous freed people and unruly black troops to confirm their beliefs. Firmly convinced that the freed people expected the Yankees to give them confiscated lands, white planter class Southerners prepared to take up arms once again, this time against their former slaves. Even as Freedmen's Bureau officials attempted to defuse tensions associated with the panic, white planters could not and would not be convinced otherwise. The fervor with which white planters believed and acted upon the rumors demonstrated not only the depth of their racism but also the lengths they would go to in order to resist political and social change in the South.

Given the upheaval surrounding the end of the Civil War, as well as the historical fears held by white Southerners, it is not surprising that the rumors of an approaching insurrection led by African American soldiers were widely believed. African American soldiers represented an extremely powerful psychic and symbolic fear that struck at the core of white trepidation about the behavior of black people, their financial security, and the future of a war-ravaged Southern society. However, the tales of insurrection so strongly believed by the white Southern planter class resulted from their inability to accept the existence of a new South, where black people were not merely chattel, as it did with any realistic threat that African American soldiers posed. As a discursive mechanism, the rumored insurrection hastened the disarmament and ultimate removal of African American troops from the South and set the tone for the social and political acrimony of Reconstruction. Upon final assessment, the resistance, hostility, and insecurity of Southern whites themselves combined with the symbolic presence and actions of African American soldiers to fuel the Christmas Insurrection Scare that consumed the South in the closing months of 1865.

Notes

This essay was originally published in *Southern Historian: A Journal of Southern History* 21 (spring 2000): 40–55. Reprinted with permission of the *Southern Historian: A Journal of Southern History*.

The author owes a special debt of gratitude to James McPherson and Nell Irvin Painter, who provided him with advice and intellectual support throughout the various stages of his essay. Finally, he extends a thank you to his friends and colleagues at Princeton University, in particular Malinda Lindquist, Madeleine López, George Sarabia, and Jennifer Weber, for their criticism and helpful suggestions.

1. E. G. Baker to three Mississippi state legislators, Oct. 22, 1865, in Ira Berlin, Joseph P. Reidy, and Leslie S. Rowland, eds., *The Black Military Experience*, ser. 2, vol. 1 of *Freedom: A Documentary History of Emancipation, 1861–1867* (Cambridge: Cambridge University Press, 1982), 748.

2. Although the Christmas Insurrection Scare has not gone unrecognized in the historiography of the Civil War and Reconstruction, there have been few historical works devoted specifically to the scare itself. The two most extensive discussions are Steven Hahn, "'Extravagant Expectations' of Freedom: Rumour, Political Struggle, and the Christmas Insurrection Scare of 1865 in the American South," *Past and Present* 157 (Nov. 1997): 122–58; and Dan T. Carter, "The

Anatomy of Fear: The Christmas Day Insurrection Scare of 1865," *Journal of Southern History,* 42 (Aug. 1976): 345–64. Both essays devote relatively little attention to the impact of African American soldiers in shaping the scare.

3. In "'Extravagant Expectations' of Freedom," Hahn provides an excellent analysis of the role rumor played in fueling the panic and its function as a discursive and political tool.

4. The first steps towards the full enlistment of African American men in the Union army occurred with the Militia Act of July 17, 1862, which authorized Lincoln to enroll African Americans into any war efforts for which they were deemed competent. This included service as soldiers, a step that the administration was not yet prepared to take. Although African American men were not sanctioned to enlist in the army until 1863, the Union had allowed African Americans to join the navy as early as August 1861. An estimated 18,000 African American men, as well as several dozen African American women, served in the Union navy throughout the duration of the war. James M. McPherson, *Battle Cry of Freedom: The Civil War Era* (New York: Ballantine, 1988), 500, 563, 566; Ira Berlin, Joseph P. Reidy, and Leslie S. Rowland, *Freedom's Soldiers: The Black Military Experience in the Civil War* (New York: Cambridge University Press, 1998), 20 n; extract from the Annual Report of the Secretary of War, Honorable Edwin M. Stanton, Nov. 22, 1865, *The Negro in Military Service,* RG 94, National Archives, Washington, D.C. For general discussions of the presence and significance of African American soldiers in the Civil War, see Berlin, Reidy, and Rowland, *Freedom's Soldiers;* Noah Andre Trudeau, *Like Men of War: Black Troops in the Civil War, 1862–1865* (Boston: Little, Brown, 1998); James M. McPherson, ed., *The Negro's Civil War: How American Negroes Felt and Acted During the War for the Union* (New York: Pantheon Books, 1965); Benjamin Quarles, *The Negro in the Civil War* (Boston: Little, Brown, 1953); and Dudley Taylor Cornish, *The Sable Arm: Black Troops in the Union Army, 1861–1865.* New York: Longmans, Green, 1956.

5. Extract from the Annual Report, RG 94; James E. Sefton, *The United States Army and Reconstruction, 1865–1877* (Baton Rouge: Louisiana State University Press, 1967), 50.

6. J. H. W. N. Collins [Sergeant,] Co. H, 54th Massachusetts Infantry, Savannah, Ga., to *Christian Recorder,* Mar. 19, 1865, in Edwin S. Redkey, ed., *A Grand Army of Black Men: Letters from African-American Soldiers in the Union Army, 1861–1865* (New York: Cambridge University Press, 1992), 78–79; H. M. Turner to Edwin M. Stanton, Feb. 14, 1866, in Berlin, Reidy, and Rowland, *Black Military Experience,* 757.

7. Berlin, Reidy, and Rowland, *Black Military Experience,* 735; Leon F. Litwack, *Been in the Storm So Long: The Aftermath of Slavery* (New York: Vintage Books, 1979), 268; N. B. Sterrett [Commissary Sergeant], 39th USCI, Kinston, N.C., to *Christian Recorder,* July 2, 1865, in Redkey, *Grand Army of Black Men,* 172–73; Brooks D. Simpson, *Let Us Have Peace: Ulysses S. Grant and the Politics of War and Reconstruction, 1861–1868* (Chapel Hill: University of North Carolina Press, 1991), 103.

8. Joel Williamson, *The Crucible of Race: Black-White Relations in the American South since Emancipation* (New York: Oxford University Press, 1984), 17, 19.

9. Dan T. Carter, *When the War Was Over: The Failure of Self-Reconstruction in the South, 1865–1867* (Baton Rouge: Louisiana State University Press, 1985), 192–202.

10. Eric Foner, *Reconstruction: America's Unfinished Revolution, 1865–1877* (New York: Harper and Row, 1988), 80; Litwack, *Been in the Storm,* 269.

11. The meeting between Stanton, Sherman, and a group of twenty black ministers and church officers took place on Jan. 12, 1865. The spokesman for the group, Garrison Frazier, upon being asked how the freedmen could best take care of themselves and assist the government in maintaining their freedom, responded, "The way we can best take care of ourselves is to have land, and turn in and till it by our labor—that is, by the labor of the women, and children, and old men—and we can soon maintain ourselves and have something to spare." *The War of the Rebellion: A Compilation of the Official Records of the Union and Confederate Armies,* 128 vols. (Washington, D.C.: Government Printing Office, 1880–1901), ser. 1, 47 (pt. 2):39, 60 (hereafter cited as *OR*);

McPherson, 841–42. For more information on land dispersal to freedmen in the South, Sherman's order, and Saxton's response, see Willie Lee Rose, *Rehearsal For Reconstruction: The Port Royal Experiment* (London: Oxford University Press, 1964); and Hahn, "'Extravagant Expectations' of Freedom," 140.

12. "Reconstruction," speech delivered in Lancaster, Pa., Sept. 6, 1865, reprinted in Beverly Wilson Palmer and Holly Byers Ochoa, eds., *The Selected Papers of Thaddeus Stevens*, vol. 2, *April 1865–August 1868* (Pittsburgh: University of Pittsburgh Press, 1998), 13, 19. Thaddeus Stevens was arguably the most influential and outspoken member of Congress during the Civil War and Reconstruction before his death in 1868. Because of his uncompromising commitment to the Union, Hans Trefousse writes, "To Northerners he seemed the incarnation of radicalism and to Southerners the embodiment of aggression and vindictiveness" (*Thaddeus Stevens: Nineteenth-Century Egalitarian* [Chapel Hill: University of North Carolina Press, 1997], xii). Excerpt from the *Washington Daily National Intelligencer,* sent by C. G. Dallgreen, member of Louisiana Legislature, to Maj. Gen. O. O. Howard, Nov. 30, 1865, Letters Received, Freedmen's Bureau Records, RG 105, National Archives. Nancy Cohen-Lack provides an excellent discussion of Texas and the role that rumors of land distribution played in stimulating fears of an insurrection among white planters and government officials in the state in "A Struggle for Sovereignty: National Consolidation, Emancipation, and Free Labor in Texas, 1865," *Journal of Southern History* 58 (Feb. 1992): 89–94.

13. Berlin, Reidy, and Rowland, *Black Military Experience,* 736; William L. Sharkey to Maj. Gen. O. O. Howard, Jackson, Miss., Oct. 10, 1865, Letters Received, RG 105; Baker to three state legislators, 747. Note that Baker initially wrote "masters" before recognizing his error and replacing it with the word "employers." The fact that he had to correct himself is indicative of the difficulty for many white planters to view blacks as anything but slaves.

14. William L. Sharkey to O. O. Howard, Oct. 10, 1865, Letters Received, RG 105.

15. Baker to three state legislators, 748.

16. Hahn, "'Extravagant Expectations' of Freedom," 126; Carter, "Anatomy of Fear," 346–47; Virginia Ingraham Burr, ed., *The Secret Eye: The Journal of Ella Gertrude Clanton Thomas, 1848–1889* (Chapel Hill: University of North Carolina Press, 1990), 276 (entry dated July 30, 1865).

17. Hahn, "'Extravagant Expectations' of Freedom," 143; excerpt from *Washington Daily National Intelligencer,* Nov. 29, 1865, Letters Received, RG 105; Carter, *When the War Was Over,* 194; Litwack, *Been in the Storm,* 426.

18. James L. Orr to Maj. Gen. Daniel Sickles, Dec. 13, 1865, in Carter, *When the War Was Over,* 201; Joel Williamson, *After Slavery: The Negro in South Carolina During Reconstruction, 1861–1877* (Chapel Hill: University of North Carolina Press, 1965), 250; Burr, *Secret Eye,* 166 (entry dated Dec. 25, 1858); Carter, *When the War Was Over,* 201.

19. Quoted in *Nation,* Nov. 23, 1865.

20. William C. Harris, *Presidential Reconstruction in Mississippi* (Baton Rouge: Louisiana State University Press, 1967), 90.

21. Williamson, *After Slavery,* 251; Carter, "Anatomy of Fear," 349; Cohen-Lack, "Struggle for Sovereignty," 69, 92–94; *New Orleans Tribune,* Dec. 23, 1865; *Washington Daily National Intelligencer,* Dec. 23, 1865. It is significant that the *Tribune* was one of the largest and most politically conscious black newspapers in the South during Reconstruction. Operated by free persons of color and read by black people throughout the state, the *Tribune* strongly advocated full equality and was an important vehicle for expressing the political aims of black people and Republicans in the state of Louisiana (in fact, the subtitle of the *Tribune* read "Official Organ of the Republican Party of Louisiana"). The editorials of the paper were strongly biased against the former Confederacy and the Democratic Party but offer valuable insight into the thoughts and aspirations of freedmen in the wake of emancipation and the end of the Civil War.

22. Hahn, "'Extravagant Expectations' of Freedom," 148; Report on Requests to Arm Militia, A. Jos. Osterhaus, Nov. 16, 1865, Colored Troops Division, Adjutant General's Office, RG

94, National Archives; *Daily National Intelligencer,* Nov. 24, 1865; Harris, *Presidential Recon-struction,* 91.

23. Acts of violence against freedmen in the wake of emancipation were extremely common. In many respects, violence in the postbellum South replaced the institutional repression inflicted upon black people during slavery. Evidence suggests, however, that violence against black troops held an added meaning. Black troops as symbols of change in the South made the atrocities perpetrated against them by white assailants distinct from those committed against other black people. For example, a soldier of the 1st U.S. Colored Infantry regiment reported that when he returned to his former master's house in Tennessee to leave some money for his wife, he was assaulted with an axe and robbed of all his possessions, including his money, a pistol, a rifle, and his boots, which the offending white mob forced his wife to remove. Testimony of a soldier of the 1st USCI, Knoxville, Tenn., Oct. 4, 1865, Colored Troops Division, RG 94. In conjunction with this point, the *New Orleans Tribune,* Nov. 21, 1865, observed that black men who left certain counties in Louisiana to enlist in military service "cannot now return to see their families and friends except at the risk of being shot down." The fact that black soldiers were abused, however, cannot be immediately associated with the Insurrection Scare. Well after the fall and winter months of 1865, discharged black soldiers were victims of individual as well as organized violence, as evidenced by the Memphis Riot of 1866. See Altina L. Waller, "Community, Class and Race in the Memphis Riot of 1866," *Journal of Social History* 18 (winter 1984): 233–46. Further research is needed to connect individual or isolated acts of violence against black soldiers directly to the insurrection panic. A starting point would be to examine whether reported instances of violence against black troops increased as the end of the year approached. The symbolic nature of violence against black troops, however, must be recognized in order to fully understand the significance of their presence among white Southerners.

24. Harris, *Presidential Reconstruction,* 91; Pvt. Calvin Holly to Maj. Gen. O. O. Howard, Dec. 16, 1865, in Berlin, Reidy, and Rowland, *Black Military Experience,* 755. See Discharged North Carolina Black Soldiers to the North Carolina Freedmen's Bureau Assistant Commissioner, Jan. 1866, in ibid., 801–2; and Harris, *Presidential Reconstruction,* 90.

25. Col., Assistant Commissioner Sam Thomas to O. O. Howard, Vicksburg, Miss., Nov. 13, 1865, Letters Received, RG 105; Lt. Col. A. J. Willard to Capt. Geo. W. Hooker, Nov. 19, 1865, in Berlin, Reidy, and Rowland, *Black Military Experience,* 753; excerpt from Maj. Gen. George G. Meade to Honorable E. M. Stanton, Sept. 20, 1865, in ibid., 747.

26. "General Circular To Freedmen" issued by O. O. Howard, Major General Commissioner, Bureau Refugees, Freedmen, and Abandoned Lands, in *New Orleans Tribune,* Nov. 19, 1865.

27. Sefton, *United States Army,* 52; Litwack, *Been in the Storm,* 271.

28. Simpson, *Let Us Have Peace,* 103.

29. Ibid., 113; Ulysses S. Grant to President Andrew Johnson, Dec. 18, 1865, in *Negro in Military Service,* RG 94.

30. *OR,* ser. 3, 5:1029, 1047; excerpt from the *Opelousas Courier,* reprinted in *New Orleans Tribune,* Dec. 19, 1865.

31. *Washington Daily National Intelligencer,* Dec. 28, 1865.

32. In his 1866 published account of life after the Civil War, Trowbridge wrote:

> I had heard much about the anticipated negro insurrections at Christmas time. But the only act of violence that came to my knowledge, committed on that day, was a little affair that occurred at Skipworth's Landing, on the Mississippi shore, a few miles below the Arkansas and Louisiana line. Four mounted guerillas, wearing the Confederate uniform, and carrying Spencer rifles, rode into the place, robbed a store kept by a Northern man, robbed and murdered a negro, and rode off again, unmolested. Very little was said of this trifling operation. If such a deed, however, had been perpetrated by freedmen, the whole South would have rung with it, and the cry of "Kill the niggers!" would have been heard from the Rio Grande to the Atlantic.

J. T. Trowbridge, *The South: A Tour of its Battle-Fields and Ruined Cities* (Hartford, Conn.: L. Stebbins, 1866), 355.

33. *New Orleans Tribune,* Dec. 27, 1865.

34. Extract from letter of 1st Lt. J. W. Sidwell, 40th USCI, to Bvt. Maj. Gen. B. H. Grierson, Decatur, Ala., Dec. 31, 1865, Colored Troops Division, RG 94.

"A Very Long Shadow"   11
Race, Atrocity, and the American Civil War

MARK GRIMSLEY

Following the battle of the Crater in July 1864, Confederate artillerist William R. J. Pegram penned a well-satisfied letter to his younger sister Jennie. The Army of Northern Virginia, he wrote, had at last come face-to-face with a full division of African American troops. He had been hoping for such an encounter, believing it would prove good for morale. He was not disappointed. The Confederates had repelled their black attackers with a fury born of pure racial hatred. They had taken few prisoners. Instead, they killed as many blacks as possible—including many who attempted to surrender. Wounds received at the hands of blacks seemed only to provoke them. With evident relish, Pegram told of one Confederate infantryman who received a bayonet in the cheek. Rather than "throw down his musket & run to the rear, as men usually do when they are wounded," the enraged infantryman had fought on until he had killed "the negro." All in all, the encounter with the African American division had produced "a splendid effect on our men."[1]

Episodes like these are not the sort that Americans like to recall when they consider their Civil War. Indeed, for decades they were almost part of a hidden history—not forgotten, exactly, but ignored because they did not fit the agreed-upon interpretation of the conflict. In the years following the Civil War, as David W. Blight has shown, three interpretations of the conflict collided: one version based on sectional reconciliation, another based on white supremacy, and a third, "emancipationist vision, embodied in . . . conceptions of the war as the reinvention of the republic and the liberation of blacks to citizenship and Constitutional equality."[2] The third vision, however, proved unusable in a republic that remained dominated by white voices and white power. It quickly became submerged beneath an interpretation of the war that emphasized the moral grandeur of the Union and Confederate *white* combatants. The essays in this collection represent what might be called the first generation of scholarship regarding Confederate atrocities against African American troops. That it comes only on the eve of the Civil War's sesquicentennial should not be wholly surprising, for the subject directly and powerfully undermines the reconciliationist vision.

It is, of course, impossible to find moral grandeur in the massacres at Olustee, Plymouth, Poison Spring, Fort Pillow, the Crater, and the other places discussed in this volume. Small wonder these events have been so long shrouded in obfuscation or drowned in silence. Small wonder that a common response to their discussion is resentment, for the reconciliationist vision remains strong. If white Americans have in recent years shown a willingness to celebrate the achievement of the 179,000 black soldiers who fought for the Union, that willingness has not generally extended to a dispassionate appraisal of the racism those same blacks confronted—from Northern and Southern whites alike—in the years before, during, and after the Civil War. One does not have to look far for an explanation.[3] The issue of racism is not something remote in time and place. It is, on the contrary, part of the living present and therefore very much contested terrain. Emphasize racism in American history, and you make, however reluctantly, a very strong statement about the society that history has created.

Emphasize racism in America's wars, and if anything, you have done something even less palatable. White Americans are particularly reluctant to consider the racist underpinnings of their republic in the context of its wars, which are generally viewed as moments in which the nation's highest values have been defended and exalted. Numerous military historians exhibit a similar reluctance that takes two main forms. The first admits a connection between racist attitudes and racially motivated atrocities but questions whether racism has animated official policy, strategy and tactics.[4] The second tends to see the racist explanation for atrocities as superfluous, pointing instead to the inherent brutality of war, the cultural distance between antagonists, and tit-for-tat reciprocity.[5]

Such skepticism is not altogether misplaced, for questions of motivation are among the most difficult for historians to resolve. Nevertheless, the policy of the Confederate government and the conduct of Confederate soldiers toward African Americans were so blatantly racist that together they offer one of the best case studies of the interplay between racism and atrocity in the American experience. The articles in this collection have amply described both the policy and the conduct. Even so, it is fair to ask: What do we know, once we know that the Confederate South harbored sufficient fear and loathing toward African Americans to enslave prisoners of color as a matter of policy and frequently to slay them as a matter of practice? The answer should be a deeper, more nuanced understanding of the nature of white racism as it operated in Civil War America.

White racism is a subject that has already received a great deal of study, mostly with three emphases: racism as an *ideological/cultural construct,* racism as a system of *economic exploitation,* and racism as a *psychological phenomenon.*[6] Historians have largely concentrated on the first two, partly because ideas and economic structures generate the kind of evidence preferred by historians, and partly because historians—with certain conspicuous exceptions—tend to shy from social psychological explanations. The effect of this concentration has been to focus attention primarily on elites, who have been, at once, the most articulate voices concerning race and also the dominant political and economic actors. Yet, the strength of racism has always lain principally in the strength of its acceptance by ordinary whites. They might know little about scientific racism and less about racism as a tool of class oppression, but they understood a great deal about what W. E. B. Du Bois termed the "psychological wage" of an ascribed racial superiority.[7]

No definition of *racism* commands universal assent, but anthropologist Audrey Smedley neatly encapsulates the predominant viewpoint. Race, she explains, is not a scientific reality but a sociocultural invention. It is "a *set of beliefs and attitudes about human differences, not the differences themselves*" (emphasis in original).[8] These beliefs and attitudes have not existed since time immemorial. They are not a "natural" way of viewing human beings— though the greatest strength of racism is its ability to sustain the illusion that race is a natural category. Rather, as scholars have repeatedly demonstrated, race, as a way of dividing up humanity, first emerged during the era of European discovery. Ivan Hannaford, who has written perhaps the most exhaustive study of race in Western thought, concluded that "it was not until the late seventeenth century that the pre-idea [of race] began to have a specific connotation different from that of *gens* (Latin, clan) and to be used in conjunction with a new term—'ethnic group'"—and later still that racism emerged as a systematic, coherent worldview.[9]

In the paragraph above, *race* and *racism* are used almost interchangeably. The conflation is intentional, for without racism the classification of human beings into races would be pointless. Racism involves, first, the division of people into dominant and inferior groups on the basis of physical appearance, and then, the ascription of desirable traits to the dominant group and undesirable traits to the inferior group. This division and ascription varies from one society to another, according to the needs and purposes of the dominant group. The racist ideologies of Nazi Germany, Hirohito's Japan, Victorian England, and Jacksonian America had different roots, assuaged different cultural anxieties, manifested themselves in different ways, and therefore should be understood within their own unique context.

Because racism is frequently vicious and ugly, it is too easily conflated with racial hatred. In fact, however, the essence of white racism is the *preservation of white privilege;* that is, the dominant position of white power and values.[10] That privilege can take a variety of forms, many of them so obvious that, paradoxically, whites overlook them completely. Here, a present-day illustration may be helpful. In 1988, a feminist scholar at Wellesley College compiled a list of forty-six ways in which her whiteness operated, on an everyday basis, to make her life less burdensome. A sample:

> I can if I wish to arrange to be in the company of people of my race most of the time. . . . I can go shopping alone most of the time, pretty well assured that I will not be followed or harassed. . . . I can turn on the television or open to the front page of the paper and see people of my race widely represented. . . . I can be pretty sure that if I ask to talk to "the person in charge," I will be facing a person of my race. . . . My culture gives me little fear about ignoring the perspectives and powers of people of other races. . . . I can be sure that if I need legal or medical help, my race will not work against me.[11]

It might be supposed that whites have always enjoyed a privileged status in American life, but during the earliest period of English colonization, this was not the case. Their New World society faithfully reflected the social distinctions of the mother country. Family of origin mattered. Religion mattered. Wealth mattered. A white skin did not. Numerous English settlers were servants, indentured for a period of years—usually five to seven—under conditions not far removed from outright slavery.[12]

Until late in the seventeenth century, the lot of English indentured servants and black slaves was strikingly similar. Servants were often badly treated by their masters. Many perished of disease or overwork before their term of service expired. But many others, English and African alike, survived and acquired their freedom. A few blacks even held bondsmen of their own, most famously in the case of Anthony Johnson, a planter on Virginia's Eastern Shore.[13] Moreover, the social distance between indentured servants, poor freemen, and African Americans (slave or free) was not very great. They frequently labored together, drank together, worshipped together, slept together—literally and metaphorically—and intermarried. They had far more in common with each other than with the gentry who monopolized wealth and power, particularly in Virginia.[14]

Around 1670, the Virginia governing elite began a more or less conscious program of discrimination between English indentured servants and African American slaves. Tentative at first, the program accelerated dramatically after

Nathaniel Bacon's failed rebellion in 1676.[15] The phenomenon of aggrieved Englishmen, free blacks, and slaves making common cause against the gentry suggested that, in defeating Bacon's rebellion, Virginia's governing elite had dodged a bullet. Next time, they might not be so lucky. As Edmund S. Morgan observes, "If freemen with disappointed hopes should make common cause with slaves of desperate hope, the results would be worse than anything Bacon had done." The gentry's answer to the problem, "obvious if unspoken and only gradually recognized, was racism, to separate dangerous free whites from dangerous blacks by a screen of racial contempt."[16]

Over the next three decades, the Virginia House of Burgesses passed a number of laws that benefited even the poorest English person and marginalized even the most prosperous African American. During the same period, steps were taken to make enslavement the normative status for African Americans. While exact figures are unavailable, it is clear that free non-whites—African Americans, mulattoes, and Indians—continued to live in colonial Virginia even after the creation of the color bar. But by the turn of the eighteenth century, the laws of Virginia emphasized that their free status was anomalous. They could neither serve in the militia, hold public office, nor testify in court proceedings; and nonwhite women, unlike their English counterparts, were subject to taxation. Finally, in 1723, the House of Burgesses codified into law what was already becoming common practice, namely that "no free negro, mulatto, or indian whatsoever, shall have any vote at all at the election of burgesses, or any other election whatsoever."[17] As with other colonial legislation, this one underwent routine review by the British Lords of Trade and Plantation, whose attorney-general looked askance at the idea of arbitrarily stripping "all free persons, of a black complexion (some of whom may, perhaps, be of considerable substance), from those rights, which are so justly valuable to every freeman."[18] The Lords of Trade and Plantation duly asked Gov. William Gooch to explain the rationale for the legislation. Gooch replied that the Virginia Assembly had decided upon the curtailment of the franchise in order "to fix a perpetual Brand upon Free Negros and Mulattos."[19]

But if the gentry did all it could to "fix a perpetual Brand" on blacks and thereby generate Edmund S. Morgan's "screen of racial contempt," it is not at all clear that whites observed it. A few—too impoverished and too bitter with the gentry to have any truck with slavery—actually encouraged blacks to revolt.[20] More commonly, blacks and poor whites worked together, socialized together, and worshipped together, a pattern that continued for most of the eighteenth century.[21] And while white prejudice toward Africans and

African Americans was present, as Philip D. Morgan astutely points out, an antagonistic attitude toward blacks could be attributed more to *cultural distance* than racial animosity. It tended to be greatest during times when many unacculturated Africans—ignorant of white language and customs—entered the colonies. It weakened during periods in which most African Americans understood English customs and language. In any case, Morgan found many indications that whites and blacks continued to interact closely throughout much of the eighteenth century. Plainly, English settlers availed themselves of the privileges that the gentry extended to them and denied nonwhites. But they did not possess the reflexive racial hostility that would become characteristic of the nineteenth and twentieth centuries.[22]

Military service provides a telling indicator of interracial attitudes during the colonial and revolutionary periods. It is clear that the governing authorities were reluctant to place African Americans under arms, but they sometimes did. Blacks defended South Carolina during the Yamasee War of 1715–16.[23] Blacks living in Georgia were armed to ward off encroachments by the Spanish in Florida.[24] A few blacks helped track down the perpetrators of the Stono Slave Rebellion in 1739.[25] And over five thousand African Americans served in the revolutionary armies during the War for Independence.[26]

With regard to the latter struggle, the debate over whether to enlist African Americans is instructive. Gen. George Washington and his staff initially opposed their service, fearing that it would destabilize the institution of slavery. But faced with the pressing need for manpower, coupled with the need to counter British attempts to enlist slaves by promising to free them, Washington, the Continental Congress, and most states quickly reversed themselves. Those who continued to oppose the expedient were mainly planters, "who figured to themselves terrible consequences."[27] In 1782, Washington attributed the failure to arm slaves in South Carolina to the "selfish Passions" of that state's gentry.[28] Two arguments against the employment of African American troops that would become fundamental in the Civil War were conspicuously minor during the Revolution. Few believed that blacks would make poor soldiers. And few worried that white soldiers would feel degraded if asked to serve alongside them.[29]

The sea change in white attitudes toward blacks occurred in the decades following the Revolution. By 1830, the mere sense of white privilege had given way to the racial hatred we observe at Poison Spring and Fort Pillow. Three principal developments defined and delineated this explosive shift.

First—and ironically—was the Revolution's political emphasis on liberty, which logically required either the abandonment of slavery or a justification that did not contradict the dictum that all men were created equal. With a limited dependence on the institution, Northern states adopted the former course, but the South, far more implicated with slavery, went no further than an expanded program of manumission coupled with considerable hand-wringing about slavery as a regrettable but necessary evil—necessary, white Southerners argued, because blacks were racially inferior in intelligence, moral rectitude, and ability to compete economically with whites.[30] Emancipation would therefore be a disaster. In the words of a 1782 petition in Virginia, it would cause "Want, Poverty, Distress and Ruin to the Free Citizens, Neglect, Famine, and Death to the helpless black infants and superannuated Parents; Horrors of all the Rapes, Murders, and Outrages, which a vast Multitude of unprincipled, unpropertied, vindictive, and remorseless Banditti are capable of perpetrating . . . and lastly Ruin to this now free and flourishing Country."[31]

The fears of "Rapes, Murders, and Outrages" intensified in the wake of the apocalyptic 1791 slave uprising in Saint Domingue. Said one commentator, it illustrated all too well "the madness which a sudden freedom from restraint begets—the overpowering burst of a long buried passion, the wild frenzy of revenge, and the savage lust for blood, all unite to give the warfare of liberated slaves, traits of cruelty and crime which nothing earthly can equal."[32]

Second, the alleged inferiority of African Americans offered a way to calm the social anxieties of whites buffeted by an increasingly competitive market society. However humble their status, they could rest assured that they were part of the in-group. The humbler one's own status, the more tenaciously one clung to the status bestowed by owning a white skin. A British visitor wrote in 1807 of the indignant response he received when he called upon a New England acquaintance and inquired of the maid who answered the door, "Is your master home?" Her reply was curt: "I am Mr. ——'s *help.* I'd have you know, *man,* that I am no *sarvant;* none but *negers* are *sarvants.*"[33] "African slavery," noted the *Edgefield (S.C.) Advertiser* in 1850, "makes every white man in some sense a lord. . . . Here the division is between white free men and black slaves, and every white is, and feels that he is a MAN." Whiteness gave them access to legal protection, political participation, and economic opportunity. By contrast, nowhere in the slaveholding South could African Americans vote, and the situation elsewhere was not much better. In the nonslaveholding states, blacks were barred, legally or by custom, from the ballot box in all but five New England states and everywhere were consigned to the lowest rungs of economic life. Several states made it a crime for African Americans even to enter the state.[34]

Finally, white Americans north and south feared "amalgamation": the genetic mixing of white and black that they assumed would follow any loosening of the social barriers between the two races. As early as 1630, a Virginia settler was publicly whipped for "abusing himself to the dishonor of God and the shame of Christians, by defiling his body by lying with a negro."[35] Nearly every colony—and subsequently almost every state—enacted laws against interracial marriages. During the 1830s, charges that abolitionists favored "amalgamation" sparked two major urban riots in the antebellum North; the same accusation was eventually hurled at the nascent Republican Party.[36]

As these examples make clear, white Americans shared a common antipathy toward African Americans. The key difference was that in the nonslaveholding states it took the form of "aversive racism," a desire to live apart from African Americans—ideally, to see them disappear from American life; whereas in the slaveholding South, it took the form of "dominative racism," a conviction that African Americans formed a necessary component of Southern society, provided they remained under stringent white control.[37] During the 1850s, these two types of racism confronted one another over the question of slavery in the territories. Southern whites stridently insisted that they had a perfect right to take their slave property anywhere in the Union. Northern whites increasingly wanted these vast regions kept clear of African Americans, slave or otherwise. Southern politicians, however, found it useful to equate this desire to restrict slavery with a desire to ban it outright.

As a result, the election of Abraham Lincoln to the presidency in 1860 convinced many Southern whites that their dominative racism was in jeopardy; still worse, that the "Black Republicans" recklessly, if not intentionally, courted the destruction of the South. To make the point, they harped on the now-classic features of white racism. First, they insisted that "our fathers made this a government for the white man, rejecting the negro, as an ignorant, inferior, barbarian race, incapable of self-government, and not, therefore, entitled to be associated with the white man upon terms of civil, political, or social equality." The incoming Lincoln administration, by contrast, was determined "to overcome and strike down this great feature of our Union ... and to substitute in its stead their new theory of the universal equality of the black and white races."[38]

Second, Southern whites argued, this Republican blatting about equality was likely to provoke a race war. It was all too reminiscent of the French republican rhetoric in the 1790s, which had allegedly precipitated the slave revolt in Saint Domingue. "[T]he negro heard all the ill-omened words, and he, born in Africa, the slave, whose head was always in danger, perhaps to repair some skull-built wall of a kinky-headed chief, who, hunted down, captured, famished in his native land, could easily view his change as a blessed one—he, too, rose, with all the fury of the beast, and scenes were then enacted over a comparatively few planters, that the white fiends [of the North] would delight to see re-enacted now with us."[39] Finally, the ultimate result would be an amalgamation of the races. What Southerner "can without indignation and horror contemplate the triumph of negro equality, and see his own sons and daughters in the not distant future associating with free negroes upon terms of political and social equality?" The two races would be "continually pressing together." Under such circumstances, "amalgamation or the extermination of the one or the other would be inevitable."[40]

In fact, the secessionist picture of a Republican Party in favor of black equality was grossly overdrawn. As is well known, the Lincoln administration began the conflict with a commitment to curb the rebellion without touching slavery, and it moved toward emancipation with notable reluctance. The reluctance stemmed partly from a desire to avoid antagonizing Southern Unionists in the Confederate and border states but also from an understanding that many Northern whites objected to emancipation as well. "I think that the best way to settle the question of what to do with the darkies would be to shoot them," wrote one New York soldier in 1861.[41] As for the idea of placing African Americans in uniform, a Pennsylvania soldier believed it would cause a rebellion within the Union army "that all the abolisionist this Side of hell Could not Stop." The Southern people might be rebels, he continued, "but they are White and God never intended a nigger to put white people down."[42]

Even after emancipation, the Union government's policy toward African Americans remained decidedly racist. For months, black soldiers were paid less than their white counterparts—an expedient that Lincoln considered necessary to make the use of African American military manpower palatable at all. Black refugees were forced into squalid contraband camps that were constructed and abandoned at the whim of Union officials. Others were forced into contract labor arrangements with their erstwhile masters, on terms little removed from slavery. Many were impressed into service with Union construction gangs; a common tactic was to surround a black church on Sunday mornings, when its congregation was at worship, and then grab the able-bodied men as they emerged.[43]

Moreover, a substantial number of African Americans were humiliated, tortured, and even killed by Union soldiers. A soldier stationed in coastal

South Carolina recounted how ten New Yorkers had seized and raped "a Negro girl about 7–9 years old."[44] In Virginia, Northern soldiers grabbed two "niger wenches . . . turned them upon their heads, & put tobacco, chips, sticks, lighted cigars & sand into their behinds."[45] Halted by an African American sentry with orders to prevent unauthorized horsemen from riding through the streets of Alexandria, Virginia, an enraged Michigan cavalryman ran him through with a saber.[46]

As these examples suggest, the Confederates were far from having a monopoly on lethally racist sentiments. In carrying out massacres of African Americans at Olustee, Poison Spring, and elsewhere, they were not tapping into a unique Southern inheritance but rather a broader white American inheritance. One can find corroboration of this in the widespread pillaging and gratuitous murders that volunteer soldiers from all parts of the United States committed against Mexican civilians during the war of 1846–48, to say nothing of the Bear River and Sand Creek massacres against the Northern Shoshone, Cheyenne, and Arapaho Indians in January 1863 and November 1864, respectively.[47]

The principal difference between Northern and Southern conduct toward African Americans may be found less in the moral superiority of one side or the other than in utilitarian considerations. Racism has never existed as an independent phenomenon. Just as during the post–Revolutionary period it arose to serve a political and social-cultural agenda, so, too, it undergoes modification whenever the achievement of that agenda appears to require it. Thus, Union soldiers who began the war with a deep antipathy toward African Americans could find themselves able to accommodate African American comrades in arms when such a step seemed necessary to ensure victory over the Confederacy. The Confederate government belatedly reached its own decision to accept African Americans into the ranks of its military. Predictably, some of the Confederate rank-and-file objected, but most agreed with members of the Army of Northern Virginia's Texas Brigade: "[T]he great peril of the country, and the extreme emergency, should prompt all friends of the cause to lay aside all prejudice."[48] Even the young artillerist William R. J. Pegram, who described the slaughter of blacks at the Crater with such relish, came to embrace the idea of black soldiers in gray uniforms. Near the end of the war, he congratulated a kinsman on his success in "raising your negro regiment," adding that the recruitment of slaves met "with general approbation" within the army.[49]

Both the Union and the Confederacy's recruitment of African American soldiers, however, came about in the course of pursuing the political and social agendas of whites. A few weeks before the firing on Fort Sumter, a Michigan newspaper declared, "This government was made for the benefit of the white race ... and not [for] negroes."[50] Any one of hundreds of newspapers, North or South, could have made the same claim, and neither the Civil War nor Reconstruction altered that basic belief. That is why the North so quickly forgot about the contribution of its 179,000 black soldiers, why the South preferred to forget its belated experiment with black troops, and why both sides rapidly buried the truth of the massacres at Olustee, Poison Spring, Fort Pillow, and the Crater. To do otherwise would raise questions about the inner nature of the Civil War that each would rather not address. It would require white Americans to examine aspects of themselves they would rather not examine.

For ultimately, anyone who ventures into a topic of this sort goes spelunking down black cataracts of human imagination and action. Psychologist Elisabeth Young-Bruehl asserts that the central dynamic of racism is the projection of one's darkest impulses onto others.[51] The savagery, degradation, the lack of self-restraint that whites perceived in African Americans was shown by events to be part of their own character. Carl Jung famously termed this phenomenon "the shadow," areas of the self so hideous that an individual cannot, without great effort, take ownership of them. They manifest themselves in the form of emotion, "and the cause of the emotion appears to lie, beyond all possibility of doubt, in the *other person*. No matter how obvious it may be that it is a matter of projections, there is little doubt that the subject will perceive this himself. He must be convinced that he throws a very long shadow before he is willing to withdraw his emotionally-toned projections from their object."[52]

As with individuals, so with whole societies. The United States has cradled some of humanity's highest ideals. But it has also cast a very long shadow. And until the shadow is accepted and understood, its power to harm everyone—the nation included—is vast.

Notes

1. Quoted in Peter S. Carmichael, *Lee's Young Artillerist: William R. J. Pegram* (Charlottesville: University of Virginia Press, 1995), 130.

2. David W. Blight, *Race and Reunion: The Civil War in American Memory* (Cambridge: Harvard University Press, 2001), 2.

3. Ira Berlin, Barbara J. Fields, Steven F. Miller, Joseph P. Reidy, and Leslie S. Rowland, eds., *Slaves No More: Three Essays on Emancipation and the Civil War* (New York: Cambridge University Press, 1992), 203.

4. For example, the distinguished historian of U.S. government policy toward American Indians, Francis Paul Prucha, refuses to characterize that policy as racist. Instead, he contrasts the

cries for extermination from frontiersmen and "exasperated frontier commanders" with an "honorable" policy pursued with surprising continuity by the federal government. The best word for the guiding ideology, in his view, is "paternalism": "a determination to do what is best for the Indians according to white norms." Francis Paul Prucha, *The Great Father: The United States Government and the American Indians,* abr. ed. (Lincoln: University of Nebraska Press, 1986), x, 3. Brian McAllister Linn takes a similar view of U.S. military policy and conduct toward the Filipino *insurrectos* and civilian population. See his *The Philippine War, 1899–1902* (Lawrence: University Press of Kansas, 2000), esp. 322–28. In *Battle: A History of Combat and Culture* (Boulder, Colo.: Westview, 2003), John A. Lynn acknowledges racially motivated atrocities on both sides of the 1941–45 Pacific War but sees little connection between the virulently racist propaganda concerning the Japanese and the U.S. government's prosecution of the war, especially its strategic bombing campaign against Japanese cities, first with incendiaries and ultimately with nuclear weapons.

5. This is implicitly the view taken by Gerald F. Linderman in *The World Within War: America's Combat Experience in World War II* (New York: Free Press, 1997), which finds numerous cases of virtually identical behavior on the part of U.S. troops toward both German and Japanese adversaries. Dave Grossman considers racial and ethnic antagonism as a subset of cultural distance. See his *On Killing: The Psychological Cost of Learning to Kill in War and Society* (Boston: Little, Brown, 1995), 190–94. Joanna Burke emphasizes the difficulty of assigning explanatory power to any single factor underlying a given atrocity. See her *An Intimate History of Killing: Face to Face Killing in 20th Century Warfare* (New York: Basic Books, 1999), 194.

6. For a slightly different taxonomy, see Thomas C. Holt, "Explaining Racism in American History," in *Imagined Histories: American Historians Interpret the Past,* ed. Anthony Molho and Gordon S. Wood (Princeton: Princeton University Press, 1998), 107–19.

7. W. E. B. Du Bois, *Black Reconstruction in America, 1860–1880* (1935; reprint, New York: Russell and Russell, 1962), 700.

8. Audrey Smedley, *Race in North America: Origin and Evolution of a Worldview,* 2d ed. (Boulder, Colo.: Westview, 1999), xi.

9. Ivan Hannaford, *Race: The History of an Idea in the West* (Baltimore: Johns Hopkins University Press, 1996), 5–6. This sentence summarizes an argument that consumes the first 187 pages of the book.

10. See, e.g., Michael Omi and Howard Winant, *Racial Formation in the United States from the 1960s to the 1990s,* 2nd ed. (New York: Routledge, 1994).

11. Peggy McIntosh, "White Privilege and Male Privilege: A Personal Account of Coming to See Correspondences Through Work in Women's Studies," in *Critical White Studies: Looking Behind the Mirror,* ed. Richard Delgado and Jean Stefancic (Philadelphia: Temple University Press, 1997), 293–94.

12. Sharon V. Salinger, *"To Serve Well and Faithfully": Labor and Indentured Servants in Pennsylvania, 1682–1800* (Cambridge: Cambridge University Press, 1987); Stephen Innes, *Work and Labor in Early America* (Chapel Hill: University of North Carolina Press, 1988).

13. Anthony Johnson's life and significance are ably analyzed in T. H. Breen and Stephen Innes, *"Myne Own Ground": Race and Freedom on Virginia's Eastern Shore, 1640–1676* (New York: Oxford University Press, 1980).

14. Philip D. Morgan, *Slave Counterpoint: Black Culture in the Eighteenth-Century Chesapeake and Lowcountry* (Chapel Hill: University of North Carolina Press, 1998), 8–10.

15. The first discriminatory law, passed in 1667, decreed that Christian baptism did not alter the status of slaves. A 1670 statute forbade even baptized Indians and African Americans from owning "Christian" servants, though they were not "debarred from purchasing any of their own color." A. Leon Higginbotham Jr., *Shades of Freedom: Racial Politics and Presumptions of the American Legal Process* (New York: Oxford University Press, 1996), 47–48.

16. Edmund S. Morgan, *American Slavery, American Freedom: The Ordeal of Colonial Virginia* (New York: Norton, 1975), 328.

17. Quoted in Theodore W. Allen, *Invention of the White Race*, vol. 2, *The Origin of Racial Oppression in Anglo-America* (New York: Verso, 1997), 241.

18. Quoted in ibid.

19. Quoted in ibid., 2:242.

20. Merton L. Dillon, *Slavery Attacked: Southern Slaves and Their Allies, 1619–1865* (Baton Rouge: Louisiana State University Press, 1990), 8.

21. Mechal Sobel, *The World They Made Together: Black and White Values in Eighteenth-Century Virginia* (Princeton: Princeton University Press, 1987), esp. 44–53, 204–13.

22. Philip Morgan, *Slave Counterpoint*, 8–13, 301–9. See also Dillon, *Slavery Attacked*, 7–11.

23. Gary B. Nash, *Red, White, and Black: The Peoples of Early North America*, 4th. ed. (Upper Saddle River, N.J.: Prentice-Hall, 2000), 127–28.

24. Allen, *Invention of the White Race*, 2:252.

25. Peter H. Wood, *Black Majority: Negroes in Colonial South Carolina from 1670 Through the Steno Rebellion* (New York: Alfred A. Knopf, 1974), 319.

26. Charles Patrick Neimeyer, *America Goes to War: A Social History of the Continental Army* (New York: New York University Press, 1996), 82–83.

27. Christopher Gadsden quoted in ibid., 77.

28. Quoted in ibid., 80.

29. This conclusion is implicit in the discussions of the American debate on the use of African American soldiers in Neimeyer, *America Goes to War*, 72–85; and Peter Maslowski, "National Policy Towards the Use of Black Troops in the Revolution," *South Carolina Historical Magazine* 73 (Jan. 1972): 1–17.

30. Duncan J. MacLeod, "Toward Caste," in *Slavery and Freedom in the Age of the American Revolution*, ed. Ira Berlin and Ronald Hoffman (Charlottesville: University of Virginia Press, 1983), 217–36.

31. Quoted in Ira Berlin, *Slaves Without Masters: The Free Negro in the Antebellum South* (New York: Pantheon Books, 1974), 88–89. Not all defenders of slavery were Southerners. Indeed, Larry E. Tise has argued that the systematic defense of slavery actually began in New England. See his *Proslavery: A History of the Defense of Slavery in America, 1701–1840* (Athens: University of Georgia Press, 1987).

32. Quoted in George M. Fredrickson, *The Black Image in the White Mind: The Debate on Afro-American Character and Destiny, 1817–1914* (1971; reprint, Middletown, Conn.: Wesleyan University Press, 1987), 54.

33. Quoted in David R. Roediger, *The Wages of Whiteness: Race and the Making of the American Working Class* (New York: Verso, 1991), 47.

34. Quoted in Orville Vernon Burton, *In My Father's House Are Many Mansions: Family and Community in Edgefield, South Carolina* (Chapel Hill: University of North Carolina Press, 1985), 146; Eric Foner, *The Story of American Freedom* (New York: W. W. Norton, 1998), 74–75.

35. George M. Fredrickson, *White Supremacy: A Comparative Study in American and South African History* (New York: Oxford University Press, 1979), 100.

36. Ibid., 153; Ronald T. Takaki, *Iron Cages: Race and Culture in 19th-Century America* (New York: Oxford University Press, 1979), 114.

37. See Joel Kovel, *White Racism: A Psychohistory* (New York: Pantheon, 1970).

38. Quoted in Charles B. Dew, *Apostles of Secession: Southern Secession Commissioners and the Causes of the Civil War* (Charlottesville: University Press of Virginia, 2001), 29.

39. Quoted in ibid., 40–41.

40. Quoted in ibid., 54.

41. Quoted in Bell Irvin Wiley, *The Life of Billy Yank: The Common Soldier of the Union* (Indianapolis: Bobbs-Merrill, 1952), 109.

42. Quoted in ibid., 120. See also James M. McPherson, *What They Fought for, 1861–1865* (Baton Rouge: Louisiana State University, 1994), 60–64.

43. See, e.g., Dudley Taylor Cornish, *The Sable Arm: Black Troops in the Union Army, 1861–1865* (1956; reprint, Lawrence: University Press of Kansas, 1987), 184–95; Joseph T. Glatthaar, *Forged in Battle: The Civil War Alliance of Black Soldiers and White Officers* (New York: Free Press, 1990), 169–76; and Berlin et al., *Slaves No More*, 77–186.

44. Quoted in Wiley, *Life of Billy Yank*, 114.

45. Quoted in ibid.

46. H. P. Moyer, *History of the 17th Pennsylvania Cavalry* (Lebanon, Penn.: Sowers, 1911), 257.

47. On depredations during the Mexican-American War, see especially Paul Foos, *A Short, Offhand, Killing Affair: Soldiers and Social Conflict During the Mexican-American War* (Chapel Hill: University of North Carolina Press, 2002). On massacres in the Far West, see Alvin M. Josephy Jr., *The Civil War in the American West* (New York: Random House, 1991).

48. Quoted in J. Tracy Power, *Lee's Miserables: Life in the Army of Northern Virginia from the Wilderness to Appomattox* (Chapel Hill: University of North Carolina Press, 1998), 251.

49. Quoted in Carmichael, *Lee's Young Artillerist*, 158.

50. Quoted in Eugene H. Berwanger, *The Frontier Against Slavery: Western Anti-Negro Prejudice and the Slavery Extension Controversy* (Urbana: University of Illinois Press, 1967), 3.

51. Elisabeth Young-Bruehl, *The Anatomy of Prejudices* (Cambridge: Harvard University Press, 1995).

52. Carl Jung, "Aion: Phenomenology of the Self," in *The Portable Jung*, ed. Joseph Campbell, trans. R. F. C. Hull (New York: Penguin, 1971), 146.

Select Bibliography

The following are some suggested readings. For citations to the works cited in each chapter, see the chapter endnotes.

Books

Aptheker, Herbert. *Negro Slave Revolts in the United States, 1526–1860*. New York: International Publishers, 1939.

Bailey, Anne J., and Daniel E. Sutherland, eds. *Civil War Arkansas: Beyond Battles and Leaders*. Fayetteville: University of Arkansas Press, 2000.

Bearss, Edwin C. *Steele's Retreat from Camden and the Battle of Jenkins' Ferry*. Little Rock: Arkansas Civil War Centennial Commission, 1967.

Berlin, Ira, Barbara J. Fields, Steven F. Miller, Joseph P. Reidy, and Leslie S. Rowland, eds. *Slaves No More: Three Essays on Emancipation and the Civil War*. New York: Cambridge University Press, 1992.

Blight, David W. *Beyond the Battlefield: Race, Memory, and the American Civil War*. Amherst: University of Massachusetts Press, 2002.

———. *Frederick Douglass' Civil War: Keeping Faith in Jubilee*. Baton Rouge: Louisiana State University Press, 1989.

———. *Race and Reunion: The Civil War in American Memory*. Cambridge: Harvard University Press, 2001.

Cavanaugh, Michael A., and William Marvel. *The Battle of the Crater: "The Horrid Pit," June 25–August 6, 1864*. Lynchburg, Va.: H. E. Howard, 1989.

Christ, Mark K., ed. *Rugged and Sublime: The Civil War in Arkansas*. Fayetteville: University of Arkansas Press, 1994.

Cimprich, John. *Slavery's End in Tennessee, 1861–1865*. University: University of Alabama Press, 1985.

Clinton, Catherine, and Nina Silber, eds. *Divided Houses: Gender and the Civil War*. New York: Oxford University Press, 1992.

Cornish, Dudley Taylor. *The Sable Arm: Black Troops in the Union Army, 1861–1865*. New York: Longmans, Green, 1956. Reprint, Lawrence: University Press of Kansas, 1987.

Durden, Robert F. *The Gray and the Black: The Confederate Debate on Emancipation*. Baton Rouge: Louisiana State University Press, 1965.

Fellman, Michael. *Inside War: The Guerrilla Conflict in Missouri During the American Civil War*. New York: Oxford University Press, 1989.

Foner, Jack D. *Blacks and the Military in American History*. New York: Praeger Publishers, 1974.

Freehling, William W. *The South Versus the South: How Anti-Confederate South-erners Shaped the Course of the Civil War*. New York: Oxford University Press, 2001.

Fuchs, Richard L. *An Unerring Fire: The Massacre at Fort Pillow*. Rutherford, N.J.: Fairleigh Dickinson University Press, 1994.

Glatthaar, Joseph T. *Forged in Battle: The Civil War Alliance of Black Soldiers and White Officers*. New York: Free Press, 1990.

Hollandsworth, James G. *The Louisiana Native Guards: The Black Military Experience During the Civil War*. Baton Rouge: Louisiana State University Press, 1995.

Hurst, Jack. *Nathan Bedford Forrest: A Biography*. New York: Alfred A. Knopf, 1993.

Jenkins, Wilbert L. *Climbing Up to Glory: A Short History of African Americans During the Civil War and Reconstruction*. Wilmington, Del.: SR Books, 2002.

Jordan, Ervin L., Jr. *Black Confederates and Afro-Yankees in Civil War Virginia*. Charlottesville: University Press of Virginia, 1995.

Kelly, Orr, and Mary Davies Kelly. *Dream's End: Two Iowa Brothers in the Civil War*. New York: Kodansha International, 1998.

Kerby, Robert L. *Kirby Smith's Confederacy*. New York: Columbia University Press, 1972.

Lanning, Michael Lee. *The African-American Soldier: From Crispus Attucks to Colin Powell*. Secaucus, N.J.: Carol Publishing Group, 1997.

Malacluso, Gregory J. *The Fort Pillow Massacre: The Reason Why*. New York: Vantage Press, 1989.

Marvel, William. *The Battle for Saltville: Southwest Virginia in the Civil War*. Lynchburg, Va.: H. E. Howard, 1992.

McPherson, James M., ed. *The Negro's Civil War: How American Negroes Felt and Acted During the War for the Union*. New York: Vintage Books, 1965.

Miller, Edward J., Jr. *The Black Civil War Soldiers of Illinois: The Story of the Twenty-Ninth U.S. Colored Infantry*. Columbia: University of South Carolina Press, 1998.

Nalty, Bernard, C. *Strength for the Fight: A History of Black Americans in the Military*. New York: Free Press, 1986.

Quarles, Benjamin. *The Negro in the Civil War*. Boston: Little, Brown, 1953.

Ramold, Steven J. *Slaves, Sailors, Citizens: African Americans in the Union Navy*. DeKalb: Northern Illinois University Press, 2002.

Rea, Ralph R. *Sterling Price: The Lee of the West*. Little Rock: Pioneer Press, 1959.

Smith, John David, ed. *Black Soldiers in Blue: African American Soldiers in the Civil War Era*. Chapel Hill: University of North Carolina Press, 2002.

Sommers, Richard J. *Richmond Redeemed: The Siege at Petersburg*. New York: Doubleday, 1981.

Trudeau, Noah Andre. *Like Men of War: Black Troops in the Civil War, 1862–1865*. Boston: Little, Brown, 1998.

Westwood, Howard C. *Black Troops, White Commanders, and Freedmen During the Civil War*. Carbondale: Southern Illinois University Press, 1992.

Wills, Brian Steel. *A Battle from the Start: The Life of Nathan Bedford Forrest*. New York: Harper Collins, 1992.

Articles

Aptheker, Herbert. "Negro Casualties in the Civil War." *Journal of Negro History* 32 (January 1947): 10–80.

Bailey, Anne J. "Was There a Massacre at Poison Spring?" *Military History of the Southwest* 20 (fall 1990): 157–68.

Ballard, Michael. "Plymouth North Carolina: A Good Time to Pray." *Civil War Times Illustrated,* April 1986, 16–25, 47.

Castel, Albert. "Fort Pillow: Victory or Massacre?" *American History Illustrated,* April 1974, 4–11.

Churchill, Edward M. "Betrayal at Ebenezer Creek." *Civil War Times Illustrated,* October 1998, 52–59.

Cimprich, John, and Robert C. Mainfort Jr. "The Fort Pillow Massacre: A Statistical Note." *Journal of American History* 76 (December 1989): 830–37.

———. "Fort Pillow Revisited: New Evidence about an Old Controversy." *Civil War History* 28 (December 1982): 293–306.

Cornish, Dudley Taylor. "Kansas Negro Regiments in the Civil War." *Kansas Historical Quarterly* 20 (May 1953): 417–29.

Davis, William C. "The Massacre at Saltville." *Civil War Times Illustrated,* February 1971, 4–11, 43–48.

Dyer, Brainerd. "The Treatment of Colored Union Troops by the Confederates, 1861–1865." *Journal of Negro History* 20 (July 1935): 273–86.

Fisher, Mike. "The First Kansas Colored—Massacre at Poison Spring." *Kansas History* 2 (summer 1979): 121–28.

———. "Remember Poison Spring." *Missouri Historical Review* 74 (April 1980): 323–42.

Freehling, William W. "Why Civil War Military History Must Be Less than 85 Percent Military." *North and South* 5 (February 2002): 14–24.

Gallagher, Gary W. "How Should Americans Understand the Civil War?" *North and South* 2 (November 1998): 8–18.

Grimsley, Mark. "Race in the Civil War." *North and South* 4 (March 2001): 36–46, 52–55.

Huch, Ronald. "Fort Pillow Massacre: The Aftermath of Paducah." *Illinois State Historical Society Journal* 66 (spring 1973): 62–70.

Lockett, James D. "The Lynching Massacre of Black and White Soldiers at Fort Pillow, Tennessee, April 12, 1864." *Western Journal of Black Studies* 22 (summer 1998): 84–93.

Lovett, Bobby L. "The Negro's Civil War in Tennessee, 1861–1865." *Journal of Negro History* 41 (January 1976): 36–50.

———. "The West Tennessee Colored Troops in Civil War Combat." *West Tennessee Society Papers* 34 (October 1980): 53–70.

Maness, Lonnie E. "The Fort Pillow Massacre: Fact or Fiction?" *Tennessee Historical Quarterly* 45 (winter 1986): 287–315.

Marvel, William. "The Battle of Saltville: Massacre or Myth?" *Blue and Gray Magazine* 8 (August 1991): 10–19, 46–60.

Pohanka, Brian C. "Carnival of Death." *America's Civil War,* September 1991, 30–36.

Preisser, Thomas M. "The Virginia Decision to Use Negro Soldiers in the Civil War, 1864–1865." *Virginia Magazine of History and Biography* 83 (January 1975): 98–113.

Reid, William G. "Confederate Opponents of Arming the Slaves." *Journal of Mississippi History* 22 (October 1960): 249–70.

Richards, Ira D. "The Battle of Jenkins' Ferry." *Arkansas Historical Quarterly* 20 (spring 1961): 3–16.

———. "The Battle of Poison Spring." *Arkansas Historical Quarterly* 18 (winter 1959): 338–49.

———. "The Engagement at Marks' Mills." *Arkansas Historical Quarterly* 19 (spring 1960): 51–60.

Ryan, James G. "The Memphis Riots of 1866: Terror in a Black Community During Reconstruction." *Journal of Negro History* 62 (July 1977): 243–57.

Scott, Donald. "Camp Penn William Penn's Black Soldiers in Blue." *America's Civil War,* November 1999, 44–49, 82.

Sommers, Richard J. "The Dutch Gap Affair: Military Atrocities and the Rights of Negro Soldiers." *Civil War History* 21 (March 1975): 51–64.

Stanchak, John E. "A Legacy of Controversy: Fort Pillow Still Stands." *Civil War Times Illustrated,* September/October 1993, 18, 25, 75–78.

Tap, Bruce. "'These Devils Are Not Fit to Live on God's Earth': War Crimes and the Committee on the Conduct of the War, 1864–1865." *Civil War History* 42, (1996): 116–32.

Trudeau, Noah Andre. "Kill the Last Damn One of Them." *MHQ: The Quarterly Journal of Military History* 8 (1996): 86–93.

Urwin, Gregory J. W. "'Cut to Pieces and Gone to Hell': The Poison Spring Massacre." *North and South* 3 (August 2000): 45–57.

———. "'A Very Disastrous Defeat': The Battle of Helena." *North and South* 6 (December 2002): 26–39.

Williams, T. Harry. "Benjamin F. Wade and the Atrocity Propaganda of the Civil War." *Ohio State Archeological and Historical Quarterly* 48 (January 1939): 33–43.

Williams, Walter. "Again in Chains: Black Soldiers Suffering in Captivity." *Civil War Times Illustrated,* May 1981, 36–43.

Contributors

Anne J. Bailey is a professor of history at Georgia College & State University. She is the author of numerous book chapters, more than one hundred forty articles and book reviews, and six books on the American Civil War, including *War and Ruin: William T. Sherman and the Savannah Campaign* and *The Chessboard of War: Sherman and Hood in the Autumn Campaigns of 1864,* which received the Richard Barksdale Harwell Award from the Civil War Round Table of Atlanta. She is coeditor of the Great Campaigns of the Civil War series at the University of Nebraska Press and editor of the *Georgia Historical Quarterly* and the *SCWH Newsletter* (the quarterly publication of the Society of Civil War Historians).

Albert Castel taught for thirty-one years at Western Michigan University before retiring in 1991. Among the books he has published are *Sterling Price and the Civil War in the West; The Presidency of Andrew Johnson;* and *Decision in the West: The Atlanta Campaign of 1864.* Among the awards he has received are the Albert J. Beveridge Prize (Honorable Mention) from the American Historical Association, the Lincoln Prize from the Lincoln and Soldiers Institute at Gettysburg College, the Harold L. Peterson Award from the Eastern National Park and Monument Association, the Truman Award from the Civil War Round Table of Kansas City, and the Harwell Award from the Atlanta Civil War Round Table.

David J. Coles is an assistant professor of history at Longwood University in Virginia. He is an associate compiler of the six-volume *Biographical Rosters of Florida's Confederate and Union Soldiers, 1861–1865* and an associate editor of the five-volume *Encyclopedia of the American Civil War.*

Derek W. Frisby earned his doctorate from the University of Alabama with a dissertation chronicling West Tennessee Unionists during the Civil War. He has published several articles on the Civil War and was formerly an editor of the *Southern Historian,* published by the University of Alabama.

Mark Grimsley, an associate professor in the Department of History at Ohio State University, is the author of *And Keep Moving On: The Virginia Campaign, May–June 1864* and *The Hard Hand of War: Union Military Policy Toward Southern Civilians, 1861–1865,* which won the Lincoln Prize. He is the coauthor of *Gettysburg: A Battlefield Guide.*

James G. Hollandsworth Jr. is the dean of the graduate school, a professor of psychology, and a lecturer in history at the University of Southern Mississippi. He is the author of *An Absolute Massacre: The New Orleans Race Riot of July 30, 1866,* which looks at the Reconstruction era, as well as two books on the Civil War, *The Louisiana Native Guards: The Black Military Experience During the Civil War* and *Pretense of Glory: The Life of General Nathaniel P. Banks.*

Weymouth T. Jordan Jr. is the head of the Civil War Roster Project in the Office of Archives and History of the North Carolina Department of Cultural Resources. He is the coauthor of *Soldier of Misfortune: Alexander Welch Reynolds of the United States, Confederate, and Egyptian Armies,* the editor of the multivolume *North Carolina Troops, 1861–1865: A Roster,* and the author or coauthor of several articles in the *North Carolina Historical Review* and the *New Mexico Historical Review.*

Bryce A. Suderow is a professional researcher and writer who lives in Washington, D.C. He is the author of *Thunder in Arcadia Valley: Price's Defeat, September 27, 1864,* as well as several articles in *North and South, Civil War History, Civil War Times Illustrated, Kansas History,* and *Kepi.* He is currently writing a book on a portion of the Siege of Petersburg.

Gerald W. Thomas, a graduate of East Carolina University at Greenville, is an audit manager with the U.S. General Accounting Office in Washington, D.C.

Gregory J. W. Urwin is a professor of history at Temple University and an associate director of the Center for the Study of Force and Diplomacy. He is the author or editor of seven books, including *Facing Fearful Odds: The Siege of Wake Island; Custer Victorious: The Civil War Battles of General George Armstrong Custer;* and an annotated reprinting of A. F. Sperry's *History of the 33d Iowa Infantry Volunteer Regiment, 1863–6* (coedited with Cathy Kunzinger Urwin). His publications have been awarded the General Wallace M. Greene Jr. Award from the Marine Corps Heritage Foundation and the Harold L. Peterson Award from the Eastern National Park and Monument Association. He serves as the general editor of the Campaigns and Commanders series at the University of Oklahoma Press.

Howard C. Westwood worked with the law firm of Covington and Burling in Washington, D.C., before his death in 1994. He received the 1992 Servant of Justice Award from the Legal Aid Society of the District of Columbia and is the author of *Black Troops, White Commanders, and Freedmen During the Civil War* as well as several articles on Civil War history.

Chad L. Williams is a graduate student in the Department of History at Princeton University, where he specializes in late-nineteenth- and early-twentieth-century United States and African American history. He is currently completing his dissertation on African American soldiers in World War I.

Index

Ackerstrom, John C., 114, 128–29, 50

Alamo, 120

Albemarle (ironclad ram), 157, 160–61, 162, 170, 182, 183

Aldrich, A. P., 50n31

Alexandria, Louisiana, 20

Alexandria, Virginia, 240

Alfred (black servant/soldier), 143

Allegany County, New York, 188

Allen, Albert, 60

al Qaeda, 12

Anderson, Charles T., 135

Anderson, Charles W., 92, 93, 94–95, 96, 97, 99

Anderson, Ransom, 99

Andersonville, Georgia, 48, 78–79, 80–81, 121, 179, 180, 181, 182, 188, 191

Andrew, John A., 49n27

Annapolis, Maryland, 117

Antietam, Maryland, 1

Appleby, Silas, 188

Appleton, John, 67, 72, 80, 88n80

Arapaho Indians, 240

Arkadelphia, Arkansas, 135

Arkansas Department of Parks and Tourism, 3, 132

Army of Northern Virginia (Confederate), 156, 203, 240

Army of Tennessee (Confederate), 59

Army of the James, 9, 156

Army of the Potomac, 126n4, 156

Army of the Tennessee, 130n66

Ash, John, 78

Atlanta, Georgia, 10, 156, 215

Atlanta Appeal, 98–99

Atlanta Daily Intelligencer, 74, 75–76

atrocities: against American Indians, 8, 240; against Confederate soldiers, 9, 11, 14, 17n23, 74, 120, 144–45; against Filipino insurgents, 8; against fugitive slaves, 7, 11, 13–14, 19–20, 25, 30, 100, 142–43, 146, 153–54, 171–74, 183, 184–85, 188–91, 239–40; against U.S. Colored Troops, 6–8, 10, 11, 12–14, 24, 29, 30, 39, 55, 61, 65, 73–77, 82, 83–84, 86n32, 89, 93, 94, 95–101, 104, 107, 111–14, 118, 121, 122, 123, 124, 132, 134–37, 139, 141–42, 143, 145–46, 153–54, 166–68, 171–77, 178, 183, 184, 185, 187, 188–91, 204–8, 221, 229n23, 231, 232, 236, 240, 241; against USCT officers, 12–13, 24, 52–62, 62n2, 80–82, 136, 172; in Vietnam War, 8; against white Union soldiers, 7, 79, 106, 114, 117, 118, 121, 149n21, 165–66, 173, 176–77, 178, 181, 187; in World War II, 8, 242n4–5

Bacon, Nathaniel, 235

Bacon's Rebellion, 235

Baker, E. G., 210, 217, 228n13

Baldwin, Florida, 67, 68

Ball's Bluff, Virginia, 125

Baltimore, Maryland, 112, 117

Bancroft, Albert H., 186

Banks, Nathaniel P., 20, 54, 60, 133, 156

Barber's Plantation, Florida, 68, 72

Barber's Station, Florida, 68, 70

Barnes, Edward Cook, 159

Barteau, C. R., 92, 93, 95, 97

Barton, William, 69, 71, 72

Bascombe, Richard, 169

Bassett, Alman, 54, 56

Bataan Death March, 8

Bates, Edward, 187

Bates, James C., 5, 6

Baton Rouge, Louisiana, 57

Bauskett, William T., 84

Bayou Macon, Louisiana, 22

Beach, Francis, 177

Bear River, Idaho: atrocities, 240

Beaufort, North Carolina, 154, 180

Beaufort, South Carolina, 36, 48n7

Beauregard, Pierre G. T., 35–38, 68, 184

Beavans, William, 186

Beecher, James, 70, 82

Colored Troops Division, Adjutant General's
  Office, 212
Colquitt, Alfred H., 70–71
Columbia, South Carolina, 60
Columbia, Tennessee, 53, 54, 55
Comstock, F., 54, 56
Confederate army: raising of black troops by,
  240
Confederate Congress, 38, 43, 46, 48, 48n4, 52,
  166, 212
Confederate Veteran, 3
Conn, George L., 53, 54, 57–58
Continental Congress, 236
Cooke, David G., 53, 54, 59
Cooke, James W., 160
Cooper, Alonzo, 173, 174, 178
Cooper, Samuel, 166
Corbit, James, 180
Corinth, Mississippi, 107
Cormal, Thomas, 57
Cornish, Dudley Taylor, 52, 69, 154
Cotton Plant (steamer), 160, 185
Counsel, George, 51n57
Cradle, William R., 183
Crater. *See* Petersburg Crater, Virginia
Crawford, Samuel J., 143–44, 145
Crawford, William A., 134
Crews, J. M., 127n22
Crouch (atrocity witness), 55–56, 63n6
Cullipher, William T., 180

Dahlgren, John A., 67
Daily Richmond Examiner, 160, 178
Dallas Herald, 22
Dalton, Georgia, 59
Dana, Charles, 21
Darden, David Goodman, 174, 186
Darden, John W., 174–75, 186
Darien, Georgia, 69
Davis, Henry Winter, 106
Davis, Jefferson, 35, 36, 39, 42–43, 48, 48n4,
  50n47, 122, 156, 164, 166, 171, 182, 212
Davis, Jefferson C., 10–11
Dawson, James McCall, 136, 145
Day, William A., 168, 206
Dearing, James, 157, 158, 163, 173, 174, 177, 180,
  189, 190, 191
Decatur, Alabama, 225
Democratic Party, 104, 106, 123–24, 126n4, 228n21
DeMorse, Charles, 137, 150n40

Department of Alabama, Mississippi, and East
  Louisiana (Confederate), 129
Department of Arkansas, 132
Department of South Carolina, 223
Department of South Carolina, Georgia, and
  Florida (Confederate), 35
Department of the South, 66, 69
Department of the Trans-Mississippi (Confeder-
  ate), 20, 30, 41, 57, 58, 63n10, 135, 141
Department of Virginia and North Carolina, 176
De Soto Mound, Louisiana. *See* Plantation Mound,
  Louisiana
Devereux, John, Jr., 184–85
Dewitt, Elisha, 54, 56, 59
Dickey, Luther S., 178
Dillon, Benjamin D., 181
Direct Tax Law, 65
District of Cairo, 113
District of East Florida (Confederate), 70
District of Florida, 68, 82, 83
District of Louisiana (Confederate), 20
District of Memphis, 107
District of Middle Florida (Confederate), 81
District of Texas (Confederate), 20
District of Vicksburg, 130n66
Division of the Atlantic, 222
Dolly (steam launch), 158, 159
Donaghy, John, 169, 173, 174, 187–88
Douglass, Frederick, 122, 123
Drake, Francis, 142
DuBois, W. E. B., 233
Duckworth, W. L., 108, 127n22
Dunlap, Clara, 138
Du Pont, Samuel F., 49n7
Durrill, Wayne K., 153

Eakin, John R., 139–40
East, John, 58, 60, 63n10
Ebenezer Creek, Georgia, 10–11
Edgefield (S.C.) Advertiser, 237
Edmondston, Catherine Ann, 184–85
Edwards, John N., 142
Edwards's Ferry, North Carolina, 157
18th Iowa Volunteer Infantry Regiment, 133, 149n21
18th Texas Volunteer Infantry Regiment, 145
8th Confederate Cavalry Regiment, 157
8th Regiment North Carolina Troops, 157, 160,
  176, 191
8th U.S. Colored Infantry Regiment, 65, 69, 71,
  73, 76